THE CANON OF ANCONA

THE CANON OF ANCONA

RAFFAELE MARTELLI,
MISSIONARY IN WESTERN AUSTRALIA

JOHN J KINDER

First published in 2026 by
UWA Publishing
Crawley, Western Australia 6009
www.uwap.uwa.edu.au

UWAP is an imprint of UWA Publishing
a division of The University of Western Australia

This book is copyright. Apart from any fair dealing for the purpose of private study, research, criticism or review, as permitted under the *Copyright Act 1968*, no part may be reproduced by any process without written permission. Enquiries should be made to the publisher.

The authors have made every effort to contact copyright holders for material used in this book. Any person or organisation that may have been overlooked should contact the authors.

Copyright © John Kinder 2025

The moral right of the author has been asserted.

ISBN: 978-1-76080-321-6

 A catalogue record for this book is available from the National Library of Australia

Cover design by Elizabeth Gourlay
Cover image: Edmund Henderson, Toodyay, Greenmount,
courtesy of the National Gallery of Australia, Canberra, Wordsworth Collection
Typeset in 12 point Bembo Book
Printed by Lightning Source

 uwapublishing

For
Silvia

Contents

List of Illustrations   ix

Preface   xi

CHAPTER ONE
Ancona   *1811–1835*   1

CHAPTER TWO
Your Probity and Virtue   *1835–1836*   9

CHAPTER THREE
Food of the Mind   *1836–1843*   13

CHAPTER FOUR
To Be Pope, the Pope Must Be King   *1843–1846*   21

CHAPTER FIVE
The Lively Leader of the New Things   *1846–1850*   33

CHAPTER SIX
A Holy Crusade: God Wills It!   *1848–1850*   49

CHAPTER SEVEN
To Consecrate the Rest of My Life to the Exercise of the Priestly Ministry   *1851*   61

CHAPTER EIGHT
A Benedictine at Heart Though He Does not Wear the Habit *1851–1853*   69

CHAPTER NINE
Amid the Immense Solitude of the Ocean   *April–August 1853*   81

CHAPTER TEN
A Bare and Melancholic Shore   *1853–1855*   93

CHAPTER ELEVEN
The Lord is Walking through Your Town   *1854–1855*   107

CHAPTER TWELVE
Over the Hills   *1856–1857*   121

CHAPTER THIRTEEN
The Prison Affects My Spirit as the Haemorrhoids Affect
    My Body   *1858–1862*   135

CHAPTER FOURTEEN
Informed on All Matters Happening in Rome   *1859–1862*   151

CHAPTER FIFTEEN
This Idle Paper Talk   161

CHAPTER SIXTEEN
Labouring in a More Fertile Field   *1862–1868*   175

CHAPTER SEVENTEEN
My Ten Years Are Up   *1862–1868*   191

CHAPTER EIGHTEEN
To Convert and Civilise   205

CHAPTER NINETEEN
My Earthly Paradise   *1868–1870*   217

CHAPTER TWENTY
Et Nihil Coepimus   *June–August 1870*   227

CHAPTER TWENTY-ONE
Insignificant Service   *1871–1872*   239

CHAPTER TWENTY-TWO
Ripening for Glory   *1872–1878*   251

CHAPTER TWENTY-THREE
Always on the Move   *1878–1880*   263

CHAPTER TWENTY-FOUR
To Lay My Bones in New Norcia Ground   *1880*   273

CHAPTER TWENTY-FIVE
Conclusion   285

Notes   293

Bibliography   327

Acknowledgements   343

Index   345

List of Illustrations

Barnaba Mariotti (attr.), 'View of Ancona and its port', c. 1861 (Ancona, Pinacoteca Civica Francesco Podesti)	3
Augusto Bedetti, the inauguration of the new Arsenal in Ancona, 12 March 1843 (Ancona, Pinacoteca Civica Francesco Podesti)	28
Ercole Morelli, 'The Amnesty granted by His Holiness Pius IX', 1846 (Milan, Civica Raccolta Stampe Achille Bertarelli AS g 7–32)	34
The painting of the Madonna who 'turned her eyes' in 1796 (Ancona, Duomo)	34
Evaristo Masi (attr.), Illustration of festivities in Piazza Grande on 21 August 1846 (Ancona, Pinacoteca Civica Francesco Podesti)	37
Portrait of Pope Pius IX by Martelli's friend Francesco Podesti (Biblioteca Apostolica Vaticana, *Vat. Lat.* 13949)	39
Ercole Morelli, 'Great God, Bless Italy. To Pius IX' (10 Feb 1848) (Milan, Museo del Risorgimento)	47
Francesco Podesti, 'The Oath of the Anconitans', 1850 (Ancona, Pinacoteca Civica Francesco Podesti)	57
Edmund Henderson, 'Toodyay, Green Mount West Australia', 1854 (National Gallery of Australia, Wordsworth Collection)	119
School of Bartolmeon Estaban Murillo, The Archangel Raphael (NNA 1875.701)	193
Canon Raffaele Martelli, c. 1875 (NNA W6-B4-4-383)	256
Canon Raffaele Martelli, c. 1875 (NNA W10.1.7)	256
Canon Raffaele Martelli and unidentified youth, perhaps Frederick Mead Caranet, c. 1875 (NNA W6-B4-4-321)	257
New Norcia Cemetery. At the foot of the monumental tomb of Abbot Torres we can read the gravestones of Venancio Garrido (left) and Raffaele Martelli (right) (The author)	281

Preface

When the sou'-wester dropped, the lighters ferried the passengers ashore. Six at a time they set foot on Australian soil at Bathers Beach, huddled together against the cold. It was 17 August 1853.

The forty-four missionaries made an impressive group. Dressed in clerical black, they fell to their knees intoning the *Te Deum*, in thanks for deliverance from trial. 'We praise thee, O God: we acknowledge thee as the Lord; O Lord, in thee have I trusted: let me never be confounded.'

They had sailed halfway around the globe to work in a mission to Aboriginal Australians. All but four were Benedictine monks from Spain. The others were three Irishmen, two lay teachers and a young priest, and then one missionary who was at first indistinguishable from the Spaniards. A closer look would have revealed that his differently styled black robes and clean-shaven look marked him as different. He was an Italian priest, and aged 42, he was one of the oldest of the group. His name was Raffaele Martelli.

He is remembered in two simple plaques on opposite sides of the world. In his hometown of Ancona, on Italy's Adriatic coast, a large square in the city's historic centre is named *Piazzale Raffaele Martelli*. A plaque gives his dates – 1811–1880 – and the reason why he is honoured, summed up in a single word, *Letterato*, 'man of letters'. The second plaque is in the small monastic town of New Norcia, 130 km north of Perth, Western Australia. On a tombstone at the centre of the graveyard, we can read this inscription, in Latin:

> Here lies Rev. Dom. Canon Raphael Martelli, Italian, a learned and apostolic man. He died in this mission of New Norcia, Western Australia, on the third day of August 1880, in his seventieth year.[1]

This book tells the life that lies between these two humble stone memorials. After a rich and varied but ill-fated life as a priest in Italy,

Martelli lived the last 27 years of his life in Western Australia in the service of the Catholic church and the people of this place.

The events that led him to board a ship of missionaries bound for the southern hemisphere shaped every aspect of his time in Australia. He came to 'convert and civilise' Aboriginal Australians, but for most of his Australian years he was required to minister to the growing European population of the young colony. He avoided all public positions, even when offered.

His choice to live in the obscurity of humble service creates difficulties for the biographer. He appears in very few official records. If he kept a diary or memoirs, nothing has survived. Most of what can be known of his Australian years is found in his correspondence with other priests, who travelled to Australia with him. Like all who made the perilous journey to the south seas, Martelli maintained a special bond with his former shipmates.

The richest source of our knowledge is the correspondence Martelli kept up with Bishop Rosendo Salvado, abbot of New Norcia. It was the friendship with Salvado that brought Martelli to Australia, and the archives of the Benedictine community of New Norcia contain nearly four hundred letters from Martelli to Salvado and to a few other monks. However, not a single letter that Martelli received from his Benedictine friends has survived. Searches have been carried out in all the places where he lived, without a trace. Reading through Martelli's letters to the missionaries at New Norcia is, therefore, a little like listening to a person talking on the telephone. You can hear that person speaking, but without the voice on the other end of the line, you only have the dialogue, in fact less than half because much of what you do hear is difficult to interpret without the other voice.

The story told in this book is therefore based in very large part on Martelli's own words, some published essays and speeches from his Italian years and letters he wrote in Western Australia. Without the 'other half' of his epistolary conversations, these words can give at best a limited understanding of the man, 'in his own words' so to speak. To build a more complete picture, we would need to know what his friends said to him and about him. In preparing this book I have gathered every possible scrap of information and insight recorded by those who knew him. I hope it is enough to capture the essence of the man.

He lived during the tumultuous years that led to the end of the thousand-year-old Papal States and to the unification of modern Italy. He came to a British colony struggling to survive on the western edge of the Australian continent. The only constant seemed to be change.

This book has been written, as all Australian history must be written, against the background of the unresolved trauma afflicting Aboriginal Australians. Martelli came to this land expressly to work with Aboriginal people. Although circumstances prevented him from doing this, he was forced to confront first-hand the ambiguities of missionary work at the colonial frontier. He approached these questions with the world view of an educated European of the mid-nineteenth century. Like Salvado and the Benedictine monks, he became part of the colonial system and, at the same time, an outsider with respect to the British colony.

Martelli's letters to Salvado from 1853 to 1864 were written in Italian. Translations are quoted from a volume published by Abbey Press. All other translations from Italian and from other languages are mine, except where otherwise indicated. From 1864, Martelli switched to English in his correspondence with Salvado. He wrote English with great facility – despite his protestations to the contrary – and to great effect, but not always correctly. In quoting Martelli, I have reproduced his English exactly as he wrote it, keeping his spelling and grammar even where they deviate from the norm.[2]

CHAPTER ONE

Ancona

1811–1835

Raffaele Martelli was born half a world away from the fledgling British colony in which he lived out the second half of his life. Ancona is a medium-sized city on Italy's Adriatic coast. Halfway up the peninsula, it is the only port between Brindisi in the south and Venice in the north and is the capital of Le Marche, one of Italy's most beautiful regions.

The best way to approach Ancona is by sea. If you catch one of the huge car ferries that arrive from Croatia, Greece or Turkey, you sail up Italy's Adriatic coast as far as the towering mass of Mount Conero, rising 600 metres white and sheer out of the sea. The promontory ends at the hill known as the Guasco.

> Upright, atop the Guasco,
> the city's cathedral
> all white, fixed
> on a sea cliff of eternity.

So sings modern dialect poet Franco Scataglini. The Cathedral, in gleaming pink and white stone mined from the Conero, is one of the finest examples of Italian Romanesque. Dedicated to San Ciriaco, the patron saint of Ancona, it stands like a sentry watching over the city and is the first thing of Ancona you see. Thomas Trollope, older brother of Anthony, thought it 'the most finely situated church in Europe'.[1]

At the Guasco hill, the coast turns back in on itself and forms a marvellous natural harbour before completing almost a full circle and sweeping northwards again. The inhabitants proudly claim that Ancona is the only city in Italy where you can see the sun rise and set over water.

Ancona is built on this crooked promontory, which to the Greeks looked like a bent arm so they called their earliest settlement *ankòn*, meaning 'elbow'. They came in 387 BC, Doric Greeks from Sicily. The Cathedral stands on the Guasco like the temples of Siracusa and other Sicilian cities. Still today, Ancona calls itself 'the Doric city', *la città dorica*.

Our ferry passes beneath the Guasco hill and rounds the North Mole. We pass the majestic Arch of Trajan. Elegant and tall, built around AD 100, it honours the Roman Emperor who developed the port to provide safer *accessum Italie*, entry to central Italy from the eastern Mediterranean. At the Arch, we turn and face the city for the first time.

The city nestles along the south side of the harbour, between the two hills that are its natural definition. At the beginning of the nineteenth century, the city was entirely contained between them: the Guasco with the Cathedral to the east, and to the west the Astagno, on which stands the Cittadella, the military fortress built in the Renaissance to help re-establish papal power in central Italy. Between these two monuments of ecclesiastical and military power, the land drops to a valley on which the city was built in a shallow swathe of narrow streets as far back as the medieval walls. These did not extend much beyond the church of San Domenico, at the top of Piazza del Plebiscito, encircling the city from hill to hill. In

Barnaba Mariotti (attr.), View of Ancona and its port (c. 1861)

Raffaele Martelli's time, the cramped space, less than a kilometre and a half from hill to hill and barely 300 metres from the water's edge to the old walls, housed seventeen thousand souls. Another twelve thousand eked a living in hamlets outside the walls in the Piana degli Orti, the 'plain of the vegetable gardens'.[2]

The cramped conditions of Raffaele Martelli's Ancona are difficult to imagine now, apart from the small historical centre below the Cathedral. In the decades following Italy's Unification in 1861, the old walls were mostly demolished, large squares opened up (Piazza Roma and Piazza Cavour) and grand tree-lined avenues pushed inland, linking outlying suburbs and villages in a shapeless urban sprawl. To make it even more difficult to imagine how Ancona looked in 1811, the city suffered catastrophic Allied bombing during the Second World War, and a massive earthquake in 1972 destroyed more buildings in the historic centre.

Since medieval times, Ancona had been part of the Papal States, the territory that cut the Italian peninsula in two from coast to coast. But Raffaele Martelli was born into revolutionary times. In 1811, the city was in the hands of the French Emperor, Napoleon Bonaparte. He had declared himself King of Italy and was attempting to reshape Italian politics and culture in the image of the secular French republic.

In Ancona, the new ideas were well received by an influential minority, drawn from the middle class, a few leaders of the upper class, the clergy and the city's large Jewish population. The top and bottom of Ancona's population – the nobility and the peasantry – and most of the clergy rejected the revolutionary movement. In Italy, tensions between the social classes were not as exacerbated as they had been in pre-revolutionary France, and the peasantry saw the invader less as a liberation from servitude and more as an attack on deeply held religious beliefs and practices and the world view that informed them.

The middle class supported the French regime it stood to gain most as Napoleon overhauled the city administration and revitalised the port. This is the class into which Raffaele Martelli was born.

Angelo Martelli was a Customs Officer and in the 1812 census he was classified as a *possidente*, a 'landowner'. This was a clearly defined position in the social hierarchy of the time, halfway between the nobility on the one hand, and the poor and *miserabili* on the other. His wife, Costanza Diadrini, brought wealth and connections to the marriage, as over three or four generations the Diadrini had married strategically into land-owning families like the Garganelli and the Albertini. They made their home in the wealthy parish of Santa Maria della Piazza, near the port, occupying the fifth floor at number 8, Contrada dei Quattro Cavalli – the famous fountain with the four seahorses is now in Piazza Roma. While an enthusiastic adherent to the new things Napoleon brought, Angelo was also a devout *confratello* of the Compagnia del Santissimo Sacramento, which owned the building they inhabited.[3]

Raffaele was the youngest of his parents' eight children. But he was one of only three children in the home. Three of the eight children had died in infancy. The eldest, Marianna, Raffaele's godmother, was already married. And the eldest son was away fighting for Napoleon.

Young Raffaele was marked from birth by the family's political sympathies. On the day he entered the world, 13 March 1811, his eldest brother, Francesco, was wounded while fighting for the Italian Navy alongside the French in the Battle of Lissa, an island in the mid-Adriatic. He lost an eye, earning him the nickname l'Orbo, the blind man, and was captured by the English, who sent him to exile on Malta for two years.[4]

Two days later, the infant was taken by his father to be registered. The city office recorded his given names as Napoleone Mariano Melchiorre. Napoleon was a popular name among supporters of the new regime, though this had nothing to do with the dubious Saint Napoleon whose feast was fixed on the emperor's birthday, 15 August, to deflect popular devotion from the ancient feast of the Assumption. When the child was baptised the following day, however, in the church of San Nicola, the baptismal certificate contains a fourth given name, in Latin: Napoleon Raphael Marianus Melchior. He was always known by the name added for the sacrament, that of the archangel – Raffaele in Italian, but Raphael in Latin and in English.[5]

By the time Raffaele started school, Napoleon Bonaparte was dead, and the Congress of Vienna had tried to turn the clock back, restoring all the old absolute rulers up and down the peninsula – Austrian Hapsburgs in the north and Spanish Bourbons in the south, separated by the Papal States, under the temporal rule of the pope.

The youngest of the Martelli children attended primary school and middle school in the new San Martino site, on the other side of the city, and then high school in the seminary near the Cathedral. These thirteen years of schooling followed a coherent curriculum that integrated faith, ideas and history in a unified model.[6]

At the heart of the curriculum was Christian Doctrine. Primary school gave a grounding in Italian grammar (most Italians at this time spoke a dialect as their first language), history, geography and arithmetic. In the final two years, pupils were introduced to

Latin language and literature. The three years of middle school, the *ginnasio*, added Classical Mythology, Logic and Metaphysics, and Geometry as the foundation of classical architecture.

Language and literature – the subjects in which Raffaele excelled early – were not just for effective communication but were the key to truth. The curriculum ranged over two millennia, from the Latin of Cicero, Caesar, Virgil, Livy, Horace and Tacitus, to texts in Italian ranging from the thirteenth century to the present. The unifying principle was how the moral foundations of the ancient philosophers were perfected by the glories of Italy's Christian history. The history of language and literature was of a piece with the history of Italy itself.

There is almost no record of Raffaele's school years, except for the ceremony from the end of his final year of the *ginnasio*. On 6 September 1827, guests were treated to poetry and music on the grand theme of the Golden (sixteenth) Century of Pope Leo X and its 'Revival (*risorgimento*) of arts and letters in Italy'. Raffaele must have topped the graduating class, as he was the first student to speak. He and a companion read their own composition, a Dialogue between the shades of Dante and Petrarch, in the Elysian fields, about the election of Leo X. The poem was in *terza rima*, the forbidding rhyme scheme invented by Dante, consisting of lines of eleven syllables that rhyme *aba bcb cdc* and so on. After a musical interlude, the second half featured students reading sonnets they had written on the great artists and writers of the golden century: Ariosto, Michelangelo, Bramante, Raphael, Titian, Leonardo and Martelli's personal favourite, Torquato Tasso, 'prince of the modern epic and poet of the universe'.[7]

The comprehensive and integrated cultural formation Raffaele acquired from these school years remained with him all his life, giving him a religious foundation, an intellectual frame of reference and a set of moral principles that he never abandoned.

Aged sixteen, Raffaele moved out of home into the seminary for the seven years of preparation of priesthood. Though it was a short walk from the family home, students did not visit their families during term. Perhaps the separation did not weigh so much on Raffaele, as circumstances in the family home had changed dramatically. Following the death of his mother, his father Angelo remarried in 1824.

Teresa Morelli was the daughter of a new colleague at the Customs House. Francesco Morelli and his wife Anna Maria Ludovisi were Roman and moved to Ancona in 1820. Teresa was in her mid-twenties when she was given in marriage to Angelo Martelli, who was 54. The couple had a daughter in 1826, named Cleofina after Angelo's recently deceased daughter from his first marriage, and a second daughter, Aldemira, was born around 1832. Raffaele remembered Teresa fondly when, in Australia, he heard of her death in 1865: 'She was only a stepmother to me but had none of the odious qualities usually associated with that title. A more good-natured lady I have seldom seen. She was an angel in our home.'[8]

Separation from 'those who lived in the world' defined the ideal of the priesthood and shaped life in the seminary. The elegant uniform Martelli now donned underlined the separation: following the Roman model, a deep purple soutane or cassock, with a sky-blue collar and ribbon, and over that a soprana of the same colour, a cloak closed at the neck but otherwise open and without sleeves. For the coloured trim, Ancona chose scarlet for the buttons and cuffs of the soutane, the facings of the soprana and the two long ribbons that hung down its back from shoulders to floor. The head was always covered, with a biretta inside the seminary and a broad hat outdoors.[9]

The students learned discipline and conformism in an institution that moulded every aspect of their personality. Daily devotions gave shape to the clerical life: Meditation and Mass in the morning, two examinations of conscience in the afternoon and evening, the Rosary or the Office of the Blessed Virgin in the afternoon, a short spiritual reading and a visit to the Blessed Sacrament before the early evening walk. Meditation aimed at asceticism, not mysticism. The Eucharist was a priestly privilege but held little interest theologically or liturgically and was used to build up 'extra-liturgical piety'. Seminarians were advised to attend Mass with a booklet of private prayers compiled by the archbishop, because 'with nothing in front of their eyes, they will be free to wander and be distracted from even the most interesting rite'. In later life, Martelli would often ask priest friends to 'remember him in the Holy Sacrifice': celebration of the Mass was a unique bond among the ordained clergy, but it emphasised the distance between priest and faithful rather than bringing them together in a common liturgical gesture.[10]

The educational institutions of the city were being reformed from top to bottom by the archbishops of the time. During the seven years, Raffaele was taught by erudite, accomplished and authoritative scholars. After three years of philosophy, the four years of theological study also included Liturgy, Gregorian Chant, and Church History. In so far as they contemplated politics and the workings of the world, Professor Mariano Bedetti taught the 'duties of subjects and the rights of governors'.[11]

In 1834, aged just twenty-three, Raffaele Martelli was ordained a priest, on Saturday 20 September, and celebrated his first Mass the following day. He was immediately appointed as professor of language and literature in the seminary.[12]

CHAPTER TWO

Your Probity and Virtue

1835–1836

Martelli was clearly destined for great things. He soon came to public notice through his dedication to works of practical charity. In the summer of 1836, Ancona was struck by an outbreak of cholera. Each day for three months, the dead were transported to a field on top of the Astagno hill and cremated, until a violent storm at the end of October washed the contagion from the city. The victims numbered 716 among the 25,000 inhabitants. Raffaele Martelli was one of a group of sixteen priests who visited the sick in the Fatebenefratelli Hospital, working around the clock in six-hour shifts at serious risk to their own health and requiring long periods of quarantine. The afflicted included French soldiers stationed in the city, and French king Louis Philippe awarded a gold medal recognising the group's 'generous dedication' to their leader, Benedictine monk Pietro Casaretto.[1]

Casaretto was one year older than Martelli. After going through primary school and two years of minor seminary together, Pietro left to pursue a monastic vocation. He returned to Ancona for health reasons and was Spiritual Director in the seminary at the time of the cholera outbreak. Martelli's friendship with Pietro Casaretto would later play a crucial role in his decision to travel to Australia.[2]

The selfless display of public service and personal courage during the plague must have contributed, the following year, to the election of the youthful professor Martelli to the rank of 'Canon'. This ecclesiastical honour was conferred, Archbishop Nembrini told him, because of 'your honourable life and customs, your probity and virtue'.

The role of Canon is an ancient institution in the Christian church, though not exported to some countries in the New World, including Australia. In origin it is connected to the daily recitation of the Liturgy of the Hours. St Benedict's reform of monastic practice in the sixth century gave primary importance to public worship, which he called *officium*, the 'Work of God'. The Divine Office consisted of reciting all 150 psalms each week, together with other prayers, hymns and scripture readings. During the Middle Ages, monks gathered at seven canonical hours around the clock to chant the Office but, as the number of churches grew, priests were allowed to pray the psalms privately. To continue public prayer in cathedrals, bishops would select a group of priests whose special responsibility it was to pray the Office together in the cathedral, as the monks did in their monasteries. These priests were called Canons (Greek for 'rule') and formed a 'Chapter', since their regular meetings included reading aloud a chapter from the rule that governed their common life.[3]

In Martelli's time, Ancona had two Chapters: one at the Cathedral and the second – to which Martelli was elected – in the Illustrious Collegiate Church of Santa Maria della Piazza and San Rocco. The church of Santa Maria della Piazza is one of Ancona's most precious jewels. A well-preserved Romanesque church, with a marvellously decorated facade, it was erected in the eleventh and twelfth centuries over the ruins of Ancona's first Christian basilica, dedicated in the fourth century to St Stephen. St Augustine relates that a sailor who witnessed the first martyrdom collected a stone that struck the saint on the elbow (Greek *ankòn*) and brought it to Ancona. To this day the stone is displayed in a crypt of the Duomo. The piazza in front of the church, close to the harbour's edge, was originally the city's marketplace and was the centre for all important civic events in the city until the construction of Piazza Grande.[4]

Martelli's investiture took place in January 1837, in an ancient and arcane ritual. After reciting, on his knees, a solemn profession of faith and swearing on the Gospels to be faithful to the Church and to the present and future bishops of Ancona, he took *veram, realem, actualem, et corporalem possessionem* of his Canonicate. The other Canons clothed him in the sacred regalia and led him by the hand around the church. He knelt in prayer before the Blessed Sacrament exposed, rose to his feet, kissed the altar, touched all the altar cloths and candleholders, and opened the tabernacle door where the Blessed Sacrament was kept and touched the Holy Pyx. He then proceeded around the church, touching all the sacred vessels and opening and closing all the doors one by one, taking corporal possession of it all. Finally, he entered the choir, ringing the bell as he did so. He was 'installed' in his own stall and given everything necessary to carry out his canonical duties. The ceremony was sealed by the kiss of peace offered him by the other Canons present.[5]

The elevation was significant and visible. Canons wore a rochet and, over it, a deep purple mozzetta of silk or, during the winter months, of wool. In public celebrations, they processed next to the bishop. The prebend he received would prove an invaluable source of private income for Martelli when he fell on straitened times.

The primary obligation of the Canons was to 'gather in choir, at the appointed times, to chant the Divine Office aloud, with the modesty and devotion appropriate to Ministers of God destined to emulate in the earthly Jerusalem the songs of the angelic choirs in the heavenly Jerusalem'. This Martelli did on Sundays and important feast days. Making a deep bow before the Cross and a medium bow to both sides of the choir, he entered his stall. For two hours the Canons recited the psalms, canticles, antiphons and prayers of the day using the ancient melodies of Gregorian chant, their voice 'uniform, clear, sonorous, without haste and respecting a pause at the asterisk in the middle of each line'. Egregious mistakes in the chanting, and misdemeanours like absence from choir or waving to others in the church, were punished through a system of points, *puntature*, which converted to monetary fines.

The experience of regular, collective choral prayer would be an important element in Martelli's later attraction to life in a Benedictine community. To the end of his life in Australia, the recitation of the Divine Office gave shape and meaning to Martelli's days. An obituary included this vignette from his last years in Newcastle (modern Toodyay):

> Often have I met him at friends' houses at a distance from Newcastle, and, as either of the canonical hours approached, would he ask to be let alone, and withdrawing himself to the end of the verandah, or a corner of the room, he would draw forth his Breviary and quietly recite his appointed office.[6]

The prestigious title too was one he treasured, even in Australia where Canons did not exist, though the title was familiar to Anglicans. The only attempt to establish a cathedral chapter in Australia was made by Archbishop Polding in Sydney but was rejected by Rome. In Western Australia, he was always 'Canon Martelli'.[7]

Still just twenty-six years of age, Raffaele Martelli was already recognised as a professor at the seminary and honoured as a Canon. His recent predecessors in the seminary Chair of Rhetoric and Eloquence went on to distinguished ecclesiastical careers. Mariano Bedetti wrote church history and Luigi Pauri was rector of the seminary while Martelli was a student. Gaetano Baluffi and Lorenzo Barili were both prefect of the city's *ginnasio* and both became Cardinals. Martelli was entering a genealogy of distinction and a career of promise.

CHAPTER THREE

Food of the Mind

1836–1843

Martelli taught in the minor seminary, the three years that marked the end of 'high school'. After this, students would leave school to enter the workforce or proceed to the major seminary to prepare for the priesthood. He taught *Retorica* (Latin and Italian grammar), *Eloquenza* (Latin and Italian literature) and *Storia* (the history of Italy, focusing on the time following the fall of the Roman Empire).

Retorica laid the foundations of correct usage and effective communication, and *Eloquenza* taught the literary masterpieces of the tradition. In Christian eloquence, purity of language and form became the vehicle for the communication of divinely inspired truth. Martelli once wrote that, like the truth itself, Christian Eloquence is 'strong only in its divine weapons and beautiful only in its own native light'. Beauty, said St Thomas Aquinas, is the splendour of the truth.[1]

Martelli's choice of texts for his teaching of Italian history reveal the liberal political convictions he had imbibed from his family. Historian Alberto Banti has identified a body of writings that during the first half of the nineteenth century taught a generation to despise foreign occupation and oppression and inspired patriots with the ideals of the Risorgimento movement. The texts of this 'Risorgimento canon' were inspired by the Romantic movement that swept into Italy with the French invasion. For two centuries, Classicism had prized order and balance. The Enlightenment insistence on the use of reason gave way to the sensibility of free individuals who forged their own relationships with love, nature, history and death. As Romantics explored the power of emotion, history and religiosity, they rediscovered Italy's medieval past, which inspired literature, art, music and architecture ('neo-Gothic').[2]

Memoirs of Raffaele Martelli's students tell us that he introduced the works of the Risorgimento canon into his courses on Italian history and literature. Napoleone Ascoli was, as his surname suggests, Jewish: up to a third of modern Jewish Italian surnames are derived from place names. Ascoli venerated his high-school teacher all his life and wrote the only surviving account of Martelli after his death. Martelli offered 'an example of true religious tolerance', Ascoli remembered, demonstrating how 'absurd and cruel it was to deny the food of the mind to youths who had the right to be educated since nature had gifted them with intelligence equal to those of his own religion'.[3]

Students of differing religious allegiance, and of none, were enthralled by Martelli's rich humanity and his love of Italy. In 1843, fourteen-year-old Gaspare Finali arrived at the seminary from nearby Cesena. In his *Memoirs*, he remembers Martelli with lines from the *Divine Comedy*:

For I remember well and now lament
the cherished, kind, paternal image of You.[4]

These are the poignant lines with which Dante recalls his own teacher, Brunetto Latini. However, Dante goes on to praise Latini because 'there in the world, from time to time, you taught me how man makes himself immortal', while Finali wryly remarks that Martelli did not bother trying to teach him how man makes himself immortal – because 'he would have been wasting his time'.

What Finali remembered most fondly of his school years was the way Martelli made his heart beat at the name 'Italy' as he spoke of the fatherland and civilisation. He vividly recalled their first meeting:

> Martelli sent for me and questioned me about my previous studies. He asked to see some sample of my writings and to be certain about my ability he set me to compose some poetry on topics he suggested. I came away from that first interview with *The Betrothed* and the poetic works of Alessandro Manzoni. I had to confess to him that, although I was well familiar with Italian and Latin classics, I had never heard of Manzoni. That was the style of teaching of the time.

Martelli took particular care in developing the talents of his bright new student, even obtaining special permission to give him access to books that were off limits for students:

> He lived in two small rooms, one of which served as his personal library. To allow me to use the library, even when he was absent, he gave me a key with permission to take any book I chose to my own room. Because he respected the laws of the Church, and in any case wished to avoid any trouble because I was reading books on the Index of Prohibited Books, he took the precaution of obtaining special permission for me.

The book Martelli gave the young Finali at their meeting was Alessandro Manzoni's *The Betrothed* (*I Promessi Sposi*). Published only three years earlier, Italy's bestselling novel of the century became a touchstone for Catholics of all stripes. Good triumphed over evil, the poor and the devout were vindicated as their godless oppressors were confounded by events or yielded to the grace of conversion, and all human affairs were inexorably governed by all-seeing and all-powerful Providence. Manzoni's faith in Providence had little to say to revolutionary patriots, however, and the novel is conspicuously absent from Banti's Risorgimento canon.[5]

The other texts Ascoli and Finali recall from their history lessons with Martelli were nineteenth-century poets who celebrated the greatness of Italy's past, lamented its current state of division and backwardness and urged Italians to recover their faith and courage. He would recite the odes of Giovanni Berchet, who cursed those 'who gazed on this land of sorrow without weeping'; Leopardi's *All'Italia*, that cries to Italy, 'Who has reduced you to this?'; and Foscolo's *Dei Sepolcri* with its long list of the giants of Italy's cultural past. The students thrilled to Giusti's biting satires on the state of contemporary Italy, the nationalist odes of Vincenzo Monti and Gabriele Rossetti and Italian history retold by Benedictine monk Luigi Tosti. They read of medieval bravery and self-sacrifice in Guerrazzi's *L'Assedio di Firenze* and D'Azeglio's *Nicolò de' Lapi*.

Martelli brought other European languages and literatures into the classroom. From France, he taught the novels and plays of Victor Hugo, the histories of Guizot and Thiers. He gave young Finali an English grammar to study, since he judged England the home of 'the first among modern literatures'. Italian liberals, like their peers all over Europe, admired the English passion for liberty, the peaceful alternation of political power within English parliamentary democracy and the balance of power between Church and State.[6]

From Italy's long literary tradition, Martelli taught writers not favoured by Restoration authorities: the dispassionate, 'scientific' histories of Guicciardini and Machiavelli and then fourteenth-century Petrarch, not his lyrical and tormented love poetry but patriotic works like *Italia mia*, which was famously quoted by Machiavelli:

Manhood will take up arms
against mere rage: that fight will not be long,
if in Italian hearts
the old Italian valour is still strong.[7]

Martelli held two literary masterpieces in special veneration. Catholic epics both, they offered a religious vision of earthly struggle in the perspective of cosmic destiny. Both explore the breadth of human experience, horizontally so to speak, in light of the vertical spiritual reality of the human person. Both authors were idiosyncratic in their linguistic choices, exploiting the expressive resources of Italian and its dialects to create bold new poetic language.

Torquato Tasso (1544–1595) was hugely popular in the nineteenth century for his masterpiece *Gerusalemme Liberata* [*Jerusalem Delivered*]. Published in the embattled climate of the Counter-Reformation and the recent battle of Lepanto (1571), it tells of the First Crusade of 1099, when the armies of Christendom fought to recapture Jerusalem. Tasso's sprawling epic spoke to Catholic audiences in Risorgimento Italy. It celebrated the triumph of Christianity through force of arms. It told of a chaotic world brought to order through reason and obedience to the will of God as communicated through church authority.

Towering over the entire Italian tradition stood the paternal figure of Dante Alighieri (1265–1321). Liberals thrilled to the encyclopaedic range of subject matter and language, from the sublime to the scurrilous and everything in between, the fearless criticism of corruption within church structures, the passionate love of Italy. For exactly the same reasons, the masterpiece was suspect to the church hierarchy. In the seminary in nearby Osimo, Dante and Petrarch were absent from the syllabus. In Perugia, as late as 1846, seminary students hid their copies of the *Comedy* under their mattresses.[8]

Martelli's first published essay was on Dante and his passion for Italy. It first appeared in episodes in *Il Tiberino*, an important

Roman journal, and was republished as a slim volume in 1844, with an official imprimatur from the Episcopal Censor. Its innocuous title was *A little autumn trip to Mount Catria in October 1842.*[9]

In the long autumn school holidays, Martelli and an unnamed friend hiked to the monastery of Fonte Avellana, situated on Mount Catria in the Appennine mountains. The essay opens with the lines of the *Paradiso* in which Dante identifies the monastery and its secluded location. The visit to the ancient monastery where, according to tradition, Dante wrote a section of the *Divine Comedy*, was the pretext for a song of praise to Italy's physical beauty and cultural riches, together with a cry of indignation at the country's present wretched condition.[10]

The monastery is one of Italy's oldest, founded around 980. Martelli is careful to celebrate some of its most illustrious monks. St Peter Damian, a cardinal, and since 1828, a Doctor of the Church, was a fearless reformer of church practice: Dante places him among the contemplative spirits in his *Paradiso* but has him deliver excoriating criticism of corrupt clergy. Guido of Arezzo, who invented the modern musical stave, added 'so much sweetness and majesty to Catholic liturgy'.

When Martelli was taken to the room where Dante was believed to have stayed, words failed him utterly. All he could do was recite from memory two of the most dramatic and best loved moments from the *Inferno*: the hymn to love in Dante's meeting with Francesca da Rimini, and the terrible encounter, in the very pit of Hell, with Count Ugolino and other 'traitors to the fatherland'.

The next morning, at three hours past midnight, as bells summoned the monks to chapel to chant their psalms, Martelli and his companion set out in the company of an expert guide. The four-hour climb to the summit was physically demanding: 'perhaps the divine poet had no harder time than we did, when he followed his guide up the mountain where the human spirit purges the dark stain of the world'.

Martelli describes the landscape with images from the Romantic literature of the time. As they followed a pale lantern, the still night air was, like Foscolo's abandoned cemeteries, pierced only by the 'lugubrious cry of the hoopoe'. The silent horror of the forests, the roaring of mountain torrents, the plunging precipices and menacing formations of towering rock, the wild and fearful forces of nature alternating with playful shows of coloured flowers, herbs and berries, all created an experience of the sublime that opened Martelli's heart to the beauty that lay at his feet once at the summit.

Then, standing 1700 metres above sea level, his body lighter in the thin air, Martelli enjoys a 'sublime illusion that makes one feel closer to the starry abodes, so that the scornful thought of all that is beautiful and great on earth, on the wings of sweet delirium, is enheavened'. This last verb Martelli takes straight from *Paradiso* (III, 97), a word – *inciela* – that Dante created and used only once. The view at his feet translates into an artistic landscape of Italy's cultural heritage. He could make out Urbino to the north and Perugia to the south, birthplaces of Raphael and his teacher Perugino. Martelli could see only the tragedy of Italy's subjugation to foreign arms. Petrarch's great ode, *All'Italia*, came piercingly to his mind: 'If our own hands have done this, who can rescue us now?'

For all that he inspired his students with patriotic literature from across the centuries, Martelli's own favourite reading was none of these. Love of the fatherland could only grow from personal moral renewal. Gaspare Finali recalled that Martelli treasured above all the *Imitation of Christ* by Thomas à Kempis, the fifteenth-century masterpiece of Christian asceticism. The most widely translated book in history after the Bible, this spiritual classic promises solace and peace, but only to those prepared to undergo an unrelenting examination of conscience, attitudes and behaviour. Thomas wrote for people in religious life and also for those 'living in the world and following a secular vocation'. Its one hundred short chapters made it ideal for daily meditation.[11]

Finali remembered Martelli 'almost always had his copy of the *Imitation*, a small edition, with him'. He was fond of walking in the countryside, and on Sundays would accompany groups of students to the country house owned by the Seminary at the southern end of Ancona. This was two miles from the city centre, in the Posatora district on the Astagno hill, and from its elevated position gave splendid views back to the city and harbour. As they rested, Martelli would pull the *Imitation* from the pocket of his voluminous cassock and read excerpts to the students. Many years later, on hearing of Martelli's death, Finali would ask to have Martelli's copy as a keepsake of his revered teacher.[12]

CHAPTER FOUR

To Be Pope, the Pope Must Be King

1843–1846

The term 'liberal' covered a range of meanings in early nineteenth-century Italy. Some liberals were monarchists, others republicans, some were Catholic, others anti-clerical. What united them was belief in liberty and the right of citizens to express their freedom through constitutional government.

The fires of liberal hopes lit by Napoleon were snuffed out by the Restoration that followed 1815. All constitutional rule was abolished and the absolute rulers of the ancient regime returned to the different Italian States. In the Papal States, frustration with the inefficient and inequitable papal government was widespread. Fifteen years of efficient French administration had left their mark. It would be easier, some said, to transform the goddesses that Napoleon had painted in the papal palaces into madonnas than to change the minds of the young, who had known only the French regime. Reformers went underground. They banded together in illegal secret societies, like Freemasonry or the Carbonari.[1]

When Francesco Martelli, Raffaele's eldest brother, returned from his two years exile on Malta, he joined the Carbonari. He quickly acquired a reputation as a revolutionary hothead. To celebrate Napoleon's birthday, he copied out a sonnet from a friend and read it aloud to an admiring audience in a tavern in nearby Fabriano. The poem is testimony to popular resentment against the papal administration. Here is the text with a prose translation to bring out the inflammatory content.

Governo senza forma di governo,	A government without the form of government,
Despoti senza leggi, Delegati	Despots without laws, Priestly Delegates growing
Preti arricchiti, popoli affamati,	rich, while the people grow hungry,
Nessun sistema, provvisorio eterno.	No system, everything eternally provisional.
Libero imbarco, monopolio interno,	Free entry to foreign goods, internal monopoly,
Ludibrio e scherno a tutti i Potentati,	Mockery and scorn to all Potentates,
Discordia fra Consalvi e i Porporati,	Discord between Consalvi and the Cardinals,
E mal sicuri da nemico esterno.	No security against foreign enemies.
Gl'istessi dazi, la prediale istessa.	The same old taxes on goods and property,
Demanio in mani svergognate e ladre,	Public land in shameless, thieving hands,
Il vizio inulto e la virtù depressa.	Vice unpunished and virtue downtrodden,
Le spiaggie esposte a le nemiche squadre	The coastline exposed to enemy forces
.... Ed ogni classe oppressa	And every social class oppressed
Ecco il ben che recocci il Santo Padre.	– this is the good we have got from the Holy Father.

Unfortunately, Francesco left the text in the pocket of trousers he forgot in the house where he spent the night. The owners of the house reported it to the police. In the first political trial in the Marche after the Restoration, possession of this little ditty earned Francesco two more years in a papal jail.[2]

He and the other Martelli brother, Antonio, acquired further notoriety during the 1831 revolts. On the election of the new pope, Gregory XVI, city after city rose in revolt and declared the end of the Pope's temporal authority. The sheltered world of the seminary was not immune. Some students staged a demonstration, crying *Viva l'Italia* and *Viva la libertà*. A number, including future patriots Giovanni Ornani and Domenico Buglioni, were expelled.[3]

Antonio Martelli joined a march into Piazza del Papa during the 1831 uprising to demand the resignation of the Apostolic Delegate. When papal soldiers retaliated, three of Antonio's companions were killed, while he was among the wounded. The next day a stand-off between the papal garrison and rebel forces was famously broken by Francesco. He galloped along the city walls to plant a tricolour flag on Porta Pia, the great gate guarding the southern entry to the city. As the uprising gathered momentum, Francesco joined rebels heading for Rome, supported by French troops under Prince Louis Napoleon. Outside, Perugia Francesco found himself alongside the prince during a skirmish with papal mercenaries. A soldier, lying on the ground, picked up a musket and took a shot at the prince. He missed and Louis drew his pistol, only to spare him: 'There, I grant you your life'. As he turned to ride on, the ungrateful assassin took aim for a second attempt. Francesco Martelli set upon him with his sabre so that the second shot also missed its target. He had saved the life of the future Emperor Napoleon III.[4]

In the seminary, Raffaele must have felt the eyes of the authorities were on him.

The failure of the 1831 uprisings inspired Giuseppe Mazzini to establish a new national movement, *Giovine Italia* (Young Italy), with a clear objective: 'one, free, independent, republican Italy'. Ancona became the headquarters for the entire Marche region and police reports warned that the city was becoming a breeding ground for revolution.[5]

Anti-clerical republicans now seized the initiative in the Risorgimento. This does not mean that religion disappeared from the national debate. Religion was at its heart. The Italian Risorgimento was not, initially, about removing religion from the life of the State. It was rather about different understandings of what 'religion' meant and what kind of State could be founded on correct religious principles. As one historian puts it, 'no political community could be rethought or refounded outside some sort of religious framework'. At the very least, religion was deemed to represent a 'vital prerequisite for the survival of any society'.[6]

Religious sentiment inspired all early patriots. Silvio Pellico suffered ten years hard labour in an Austrian prison for his membership of the Carbonari, and on his release in 1830, wrote *Le mie prigioni*, 'My Prisons'. Raffaele Martelli wept as he read how Pellico rediscovered his faith during the ordeal and forgave his prison guards. Count Metternich said the book did more harm to Austria than a battle lost. Mazzini's Giovine Italia movement was certainly anti-clerical, preaching a civil religion without pope, priests or any intermediaries between the soul and the Creator. But its programme was soaked in religious language and images. A new age was dawning, Mazzini preached, of the universal religion of Humanity. Under the motto 'God and People', Giovine Italia was an 'Apostolate of the People', its key ideals 'faith', 'sacrifice', 'martyrdom' and 'mission'.[7]

As Mazzini's republicans dictated the terms of the national debate, Catholic liberals like Raffaele Martelli found themselves on the margins. All over Europe, Catholics of liberal persuasion struggled to reconcile faith and reason, freedom and obedience, nationalism and devotion to a transnational church. This was especially difficult in Italy. The stumbling block was the 'Roman question'. At the centre of the peninsula stood the seat of the universal Church and its political territories. Any discussion of national unity in Italy immediately ran into the temporal power of the Papacy: for Mazzini's republicans, the major obstacle to national redemption; for loyal Catholics, a guarantee of the pope's ability to give spiritual leadership without fear of political interference. It was inconceivable that the pope should be a political subject of any secular power. As Martelli put it, years later in Australia, 'The temporal power is essential for the free exercise of the spiritual power' or, more succinctly, 'In order to be pope, the pope must be king'.[8]

A breakthrough came in 1843. A bold new programme for Catholic liberals was set out in *On the Moral and Civil Primacy of the Italians* by Vincenzo Gioberti, a priest from Piedmont. It became the bestselling book of the Risorgimento.

Gioberti's solution to the 'Roman question' was brilliant. He made the temporal power the centre of national renewal. Italians had lived so closely with Catholicism for so long – eighteen centuries – that 'while others may be Catholic without being Italian, one cannot be perfectly Italian without being Catholic'. Gioberti's programme grew organically out of Italy's religious and political past. Italy should become an independent federal state. The various political systems up and down the peninsula, based on differences of climate, terrain, language and culture, would be safeguarded and their princes would remain in place, under the moral authority of the Roman Pontiff.

It is easy to see why Gioberti's vision appealed to Martelli. First, its inspiration was religious. Civilisation developed out of religious belief. On the political level, the project respected tradition; it rejected internal revolution and outside interference; it left political structures intact though calling for more dialogue between princes and peoples and more openness to representative and, eventually, constitutional government. And Gioberti's programme meshed with Martelli's Romantic love of the Middle Ages.

The incompatibility between Mazzini's republicanism and Gioberti's moderate liberalism was most telling in their view of the origins of Italian identity. Mazzini accepted the view the Renaissance had constructed of itself, minimising the distance between the modern world and the ancient world, interpreted as secular, and maximising the distance between modern Europe and the Middle Ages, interpreted as a time of superstition and clerical self-interest. Republicans claimed liberalism arose in the fifteenth century when the Renaissance rediscovered classical Greek and Roman thought, which led to the Enlightenment and the advances of the eighteenth century.

Gioberti showed how it was Christianity that placed the individual front and centre as the fundamental unit of political life. The idea that lay at the heart of liberalism was the moral equality of individuals. This idea was born in the Christian experience and had developed, slowly and imperfectly, under the medieval Papacy.

Gioberti's programme was known as 'neo-guelphism', a reference to the medieval factions of Guelphs who supported the Papacy versus Ghibellines who fought for the Emperor.

Martelli captured this difference of perspective years later, in Australia. He preached a sermon in Fremantle on the good that Christianity had done around the world. His argument comes straight from a popular and widely translated book by his own teacher of rhetoric, Gaetano Baluffi, *The Charity of the Church, a Proof of her Divinity*. The truth of the Christian faith is not demonstrated by comparing Christian countries with non-Christian ones. The real difference emerges between life in Europe before and after the advent of Christianity. The 'ancient world' was far from the secular society of civic virtue and democratic cooperation depicted by modern-day republicans. The religion of pagan Rome defined a world based on natural inequality, where rights were assigned to persons according to predetermined categories, such as class, gender, race and so on. Charity, the expression of a new way of relating to others, came into the world through the Christian event. This is how Martelli put it to a Fremantle congregation in 1862:

> Only a glance at the old world is sufficient to learn how much we owe to Christ, even in a human point of view, on account of the law of charity he has promulgated to his followers. What is the spectacle exhibited to our eyes? The altars of the pagan gods often streaming with the blood of man; the chief of the family a tyrant, authorized to sell or even to do away with his offspring; children who came to the world with imperfect limbs, doomed to perish; woman looked upon as an inferior being, a beast of burden to be thrown away according to the whims of its owner; prisoners of war either put to death or destined to perpetual slavery; the slave not reckoned as a human being, but an article of property which it was lawful to destroy and cast to fatten the inmates of a fishpond, as was the case with a Roman consul [Vedius Pollio]; the bloody struggle and the agonizing

pangs of the expiring gladiator, made the sports which delighted the grave senator and the delicate maiden.[9]

The year 1843 was not only the year when Raffaele Martelli embraced a new political programme of Catholic liberalism. It was also the beginning of his public role as official orator of Ancona. Traditionally, the priest who held the Chair of Rhetoric and Eloquence in the city's seminary would deliver speeches and compose prayers and hymns for important public occasions. Such public pronouncements were highly stylised, and Martelli showed he was master of rhetorical form and poetic expression, yet, from his earliest forays into public life, he struck a note that was new. Alongside the conventional praise of the pope and other rulers, Martelli sang the praises of Italians and Italy's glorious past, deplored the occupation by foreign powers and called for social justice, particularly education, for the downtrodden.

Two years earlier, Pope Gregory had toured his northern territories. In Ancona, the pope promised 80,000 scudi for a major expansion of the shipyards and a new Customs House to be named 'Gregoriana'. Two years later, Cardinal Tosti, Pro-Treasurer of State, laid the foundation stone on the feast of St Gregory, 12 March 1843. In two days of festivities, Martelli gave voice to the city's gratitude in epigraphs, in Italian and Latin, that were displayed all over the city, and a hymn that was set to music by maestro Gioachino Malucci, from the Bologna Philharmonic Academy. The hymn opened an evening concert of popular melodies from the operas of Donizetti and Bellini.

For all the faults of the antiquated papal administration, devotion to the institution of the papacy and the person of the pope was at an all-time high in the mid-nineteenth century. In Italy, public attitudes towards Catholicism were contradictory. Those personally responsible for corruption and injustice were condemned by public opinion; however, the institution of the Papacy itself was believed capable of reforming and renewing itself. Jesuit historian Giacomo Martina describes this mood as one of

Augusto Bedetti, The inauguration of the new Arsenal in Ancona, 12 March 1843

'mistrust in persons and trust in the institution'. These tensions are on full view in Martelli's first public oratory.[10]

The text of Martelli's hymn is lofty in language and tone as it heaps praise on the generosity of 'the supreme Prince' and on the proverbial industry of Ancona's craftsmen who would build new ships from the mighty oaks of the Appennines. Two stanzas must have raised eyebrows. Though Austrian and French troops had been absent from the Papal States for five years now, Martelli openly urges vigilance.

> Let no foreign axe ring out again
> in Italic forests: they are ours, they are gifts
> that Nature bestowed on our land.
>
> Ah! Silence to the ill-advised, crazed
> suggestion that we ourselves should arm the hand
> that has already opened so many wounds in our breast.[11]

Such an open expression of nationalism was unusual in a cleric performing so important a public gesture. The church was a transnational reality and the pope was divinely appointed as universal pastor. The theological and ideological position in favour of papal supremacy was known as ultramontanism. The term originally referred to Catholics in France and Germany who looked for leadership and authority over the mountains, *ultramontane*, to Rome rather than to the leaders of their national church. Martelli's apparent belief in national destiny sat uneasily with faith in a transnational church. Yet, here was this belief in a hymn for a cardinal.

Italy, rather than the universal church, appeared again as Martelli's frame of reference in August. Archbishop Cadolini had recently been 'raised to the sacred purple'. For his first visit to the seminary as a cardinal, Martelli lauds Cadolini for his fame that spreads not in Ancona or the Eternal City or in the universal Church, but through all Italy. 'The fame of his name resounds in every town of Italy: the Sebeto, the Olona and the great king of Italic rivers speak of him'. The three rivers flowed through Naples, Milan and Rome and thus Martelli elegantly covers south, north and central Italy. One can imagine the mild-mannered cardinal wondering, with a moment's discomfort, at this unorthodox expression of homage from his exuberant young Professor of Eloquence.[12]

Something else happened in Ancona in 1843. In November, police accused a group of persons of plotting a military coup in Ancona for the following Easter. At their trial in June 1844 before a Political-Military Commission with full powers, Captain Muzzarelli of the Light Artillery (*Cacciatori a Cavallo*) provided a list of 49 civilians and military personnel who, he was reliably informed, were 'among the most ardent and insolent enemies of the government'. Martelli is absent from the list and is not mentioned anywhere in the voluminous trial documentation. A short *Relazione* or Summary of the deposition was later printed in Rome, where 'the Martelli brothers' are mentioned twice in witness statements: someone asked a friend in a letter to pass on greetings to a number of people including the two brothers, and a letter written by another person claimed that the two brothers were 'members of the sect'. Nothing more is said of them.[13]

Nevertheless, half a century later, Ancona's City Librarian and historian Palermo Giangiacomi published a short article about the 1844 trial in the local newspaper, entitled 'Patriots from Ancona in the Risorgimento'. The article cites Captain Muzzarelli's damning phrase and lists 100 names: the 49 from the trial and then a second list of 51 persons. These include: 'Martelli Antonio, a clerk in the Customs Office, and his brother Professor Raffaele, a priest'. Giangiacomi does not cite his source and the origin of the list of 51 remains a mystery. In any case, the description of Raffaele Martelli as an 'ardent and insolent enemy of the government' was picked up by local historians Gualtiero Santini and Mario Natalucci. It was cited by the Comune of Ancona when it named a city square in honour of Martelli in 1960.[14]

A reputation has survived of a liberal priest plotting – ardently and insolently – against the papal regime. There is, however, no evidence that Martelli engaged in any direct political action, least of all violent insurrection. His liberal convictions took shape in his educational work.

There were two sides to the Italian Risorgimento, 'one political and revolutionary, the other literary and scientific'. Martelli avoided the former – with one egregious exception – and dedicated himself to education. That was the proper arena for his priestly contribution to the nationalist cause.[15]

When a young student died that same year, Martelli, in his eulogy, singled out four virtues for special praise. The young Antonio was 'faithful to devout exercises, respectful and grateful towards his superiors, easy-going and courteous to his peers, daily more loving of study'. This is not, as a modern eye might see it, a descending order of importance, as it were from heaven-bound piety down to the tedium of the dusty classroom. Rather, each of these virtues is the foundation of the one that follows, in a movement upwards and outwards from inner relationship with God, to obedience to superiors – religious and domestic – to charity towards peers, to the desire to know and understand the world of self and others. Four years later, when Europe was on the brink of revolutions, Martelli stressed the power of education: 'if the time has come for our people to lift their eyes to their own honour, I believe that the people must look first to public education'.[16]

Meanwhile, the change was in the air. Pope Gregory died on the first day of June 1846. As Cardinal Cadolini set off for the conclave in Rome, the Municipal Council and a 'group of clergy' appealed to him to elect a new pope who would care for the needs of his subjects and implement overdue reforms. The letter is lost, but it must have been something like the one presented to the Cardinal of nearby Osimo, begging him to elect a Pontiff 'who, with wisdom and clemency, will heal the serious ills and needs of the city by identifying and eliminating their causes, rather than through the harsh and ineffective use of coercion'. Martelli was surely a signatory.[17]

One of the shortest conclaves in modern history elected the longest-serving pope in Christian history. He took the name Pius IX. Martelli shared in the universal rejoicing. For one thing, Giovanni Maria Mastai Ferretti was a local, born and educated in nearby Senigallia, just 30 kilometres from Ancona. Martelli knew members of the Mastai and Ferretti families. What is more, Pius was widely believed to be a liberal.

Austrian Chancellor Metternich said he had expected 'anything but a liberal Pope'. Cardinal Lambruschini, who had gone into the conclave as the intransigent favourite, sneered that in the Mastai household 'even the cats are liberal'. Liberals remembered the 1831 rebellions, when the pope's cousins Gabriele and Pietro Ferretti took up arms. Pius, then bishop of Spoleto, defused a tense standoff by persuading the rebels – including Francesco Martelli – to lay down their arms in return for safe passage abroad. Before his election, Pius was a popular bishop, organising relief and charity after an earthquake, visiting prisoners in jail and promoting programmes for street children. It was rumoured the new pope read Gioberti and had brought a copy to Rome to present to the new pope.[18]

Pius enjoyed a honeymoon period of extraordinary universal support. Mazzini himself wrote an open letter of support to Pius, while maintaining his aversion to the church Pius headed. For Raffaele Martelli, Pius was the very incarnation of Gioberti's neo-guelph dream for Italy, the reconciliation between the Catholic religion and the Italian nation. The myth of the 'liberal Pope' united the disparate elements that before 1846 held progressive opinions. Catholics who embraced the modern ideas, the patriotic clergy, and opponents of the Church institutions were all temporarily united in a common hope. It would not last long.[19]

CHAPTER FIVE

The Lively Leader of the New Things

1846–1850

'Viva Pio Nono! Long live Pius IX!'

A month after his election, Pius announced an amnesty for a thousand political prisoners, including those exiled on Corfù since the 1831 revolts. There was nothing new about a papal amnesty, but liberal enthusiasm for Pius gave this gesture a whole new meaning. It was the springboard for Raffaele Martelli's public patriotism.[1]

The Papal States erupted in jubilation. The text of the amnesty was displayed everywhere, and people wrote poems, painted portraits, and published allegorical prints. One of the best-known lithographs was by Ercole Morelli. He was the youngest brother of Raffaele Martelli's stepmother Teresa. He was ten years younger than Raffaele, who called him a 'cousin'. Morelli produced a lithograph to celebrate the amnesty, inspired by Raphael's *Liberation of St Peter* in the Vatican.[2]

Morelli not only celebrates Pius; he compares the enlightened papacy of Pius to the dark days of his predecessor, Gregory XVI.

Ercole Morelli, *The Amnesty granted by His Holiness Pius IX* (1846)

The painting of the Madonna who 'turned her eyes' in 1796

On the right, a prisoner sleeps in a moonlit cell. On the wall he has carved '1831', the year of the uprisings and his exile, and the election of Gregory. An angel wakes the prisoner, casting off his chains, and points to the scene on the other side of the image. There a new day dawns over Ancona, framed by the Arch of Trajan and the Duomo atop the Guasco hill. On a grassy meadow, the prisoner is welcomed home by his wife, children and pet dog, while another male clasps his hands skywards in a prayer of thanks. Seated on billowing clouds, Christ blesses the sleeping prisoner, attended by two angels: one plays a consoling harp while the other, bearing a sword of justice, gazes with satisfaction on the joyous reunion, backlit by a rainbow bearing the name PIO IX. In the top corners of the print, capital letters announce: 'He whom God has sent to us, speaks words of God, and men will bless him because he heard the groans of those who were languishing'.

Ancona proclaimed a week of festivities. Raffaele Martelli led the city in the first three days of religious celebration. On 17 August, he stood in the Duomo before the painting of Mary Queen of All Saints. A painting, its origins lost in the mists of time, shows Mary pale and serene, her eyes downcast in an attitude of modesty and prayerful resignation. It was one of the city's most venerated objects.

In 1796, as Napoleon Bonaparte approached Ancona, a huge crowd of the faithful had witnessed the eyes in the painting open and Mary's lips part in a smile as she gazed out from the painting with maternal protection. When Napoleon entered the city, he ordered the miraculous painting be brought to him. As he took hold of a sash studded with precious stones that crowned the image, the bystanders saw the colour drain from his face as he stopped and returned the sash to its place. He told no one what he saw but abandoned the plan to confiscate the painting and ordered simply that it be kept in the Cathedral, though covered by a cloth.[3]

Now, half a century later, Raffaele Martelli stood before the miraculous image as the voice of Ancona. It was only right to give thanks to Mary, since 'no grace comes down to us from heaven without your mediation'. His prayer was not in the high-flown poetry usual for such occasions, but in straightforward prose, formal and elegant, accessible to all. Like his cousin Morelli, Martelli drew comparisons: Pius's amnesty has drawn a 'veil over the past' and will 'put an end to vendettas, hatred and anger'.[4]

Not everyone was impressed. The Canons of the Cathedral protested that the lofty task had not been entrusted to one of them. Martelli's friends got his prayer printed quickly to forestall rivals and the archbishop let it slide, but Martelli was already ruffling feathers.[5]

After a day of pause for the annual fair, the civic celebrations turned the city into a spectacle of light and colour. Everywhere were flowers, wreaths of laurel and olive, brightly coloured ribbons, flags bearing the new pope's coat of arms, and banners bearing the portrait of Pius and the text of the amnesty. Pius was the first pope of the mass-media age: his smiling face was reproduced in books and newspapers and on objects of every kind: coins, medals, scarves, brooches, even cigar-holders and drink coasters. By night, the city came alive with lanterns everywhere. In the Jewish ghetto, candles of different colours strung from house to house formed 'a multi-coloured pavilion magically suspended over the heads of those who passed below'. There were horse races, boat races, brass bands, orchestras, fireworks.[6]

The main event took place in Piazza del Papa. The piazza is a spectacular open-air auditorium, a long thin rectangle like a hull of a beached ship, its open bow facing the harbour and the stern rising to the church of San Domenico. A statue of Pope Clement stands at the top end of the square with ramps of stairs on both sides.[7]

On a hot summer's evening, the packed square was decorated with flags and lanterns, columns and statues. A stage was erected in front of the pope's statue. A huge frame, topped by statues representing Faith, Hope, Charity and Religion, supported a white cloth that hid some surprise to come. The evening's entertainment was Giuseppe Verdi's *Ernani*, arranged for the civic orchestra.

Evaristo Masi (attr.), Illustration of festivities in Piazza Grande on 21 August 1846

Opera was a powerful way for spreading the ideas and images of Romanticism that were so important for the Risorgimento movement. Every Italian city had its own opera house, where all social classes experienced the evolving ideas of the day. Martelli regularly attended the new Teatro delle Muse (Theatre of the Muses).

Verdi's *Ernani* was a smash hit: in two years it had been performed in eighty Italian cities. The title role was the ideal Romantic hero, a rebel who defies tyrannical authority and sacrifices his life rather than break a vow. Young men sported 'Ernani hats', *cappelli alla Ernani*, the type worn by the rebel-lover in Francesco Hayez's painting of 'The Kiss'.[8]

To celebrate the papal amnesty, a two-hundred-strong orchestra performed the third act of the opera, in which Charles V celebrates his election as Holy Roman Emperor by granting his own amnesty. When the trombones blared out the notes of the emperor's aria 'Forgiveness for all', *Perdono a tutti*, the white cloth on the stage fell away revealing the text of Pius's amnesty in letters of gold, and a yellow-and-white papal flag was unfurled with the words 'To Immortal Pius IX, Ancona in gratitude'. Out of the flag flew a white dove with an olive branch in its beak. Two hundred children bearing torches ran from the top of the piazza down either side of the stage – like two streams of lava from a volcano, the newspapers said – reuniting on the lower level of the square. Bells rang out, answered by cannons from ships in the harbour; fireworks rained down copies of poems in praise of the pope.[9]

Martelli not only composed the city's prayer of thanks for the election of Pius, but also composed epigraphs. The longest of these was printed on posters half a metre high and displayed around Piazza del Papa. It was reprinted several times in other cities and opened a published collection of texts in praise of the new pope.[10]

'Acclaim, Christians, acclaim, THE IMMORTAL PIUS IX, chosen by God to govern the Church', the epigraph opens triumphantly. In short sharp sentences, Martelli praises fourteen attributes of the new pope, some based on past experience, others on future hope. Comparisons with the previous pontificate are allusive but undisguised.

Pius will revive business, trade and science, and restore Italy's status as 'queen of the seas', resist foreign influence and end the bitter rivalries between Italian States and between Italians of different political persuasion. He will show Christian charity to the poor. And the topic closest to Martelli's heart: he begged Pius to promote education and put an end to ignorance, 'the most harmful enemy of religion'.

Martelli wrote another short epigraph in praise of Pius, on behalf of Ancona's large Jewish community, two thousand strong with two synagogues. The dark streets of Ancona's ghetto were so narrow that two people could not walk abreast. Little now remains, but the present-day Via Lata, between Corso Mazzini and Corso

Portrait of Pope Pius IX by Martelli's friend Francesco Podesti

Garibaldi, is a claustrophobic reminder. Within the Italian Church, a 'pro-Jewish' school of thought gained currency following the French Revolution. Against the mainstream view that held Jews forever guilty of the death of Jesus, Martelli subscribed to the alternative view, writing in 1846 that 'Christ taught in his gospel to have charity for our neighbours, whatever faith they profess'.[11]

As Martelli became bolder in his support of the new papacy, his position in the city was coming under serious scrutiny. Even before the August celebrations, the archbishop had written to his Episcopal Chancellor about Martelli: 'I hear rumours about the seminary that are full of complaints and a source of great bitterness for me. Finali and Paolinelli etc etc are being ruined by bad books, which the sect [Giovine Italia?] is spreading within the holy institution.'

Martelli would later recall, with masterly understatement, 'I had the misfortune of not being in good harmony (*non essere in buona armonia*) with the archbishop'.[12]

The truth was that Pius was no liberal. He never had been. As a young bishop in 1833, he wrote, 'I hate and detest the thoughts and actions of liberals to the marrow of my bones, though I do not care much for the fanaticism of the so-called *papalini* [fanatical papal agitators] either. What I would love to find with the Lord's help is the middle path – the Christian middle path and not the diabolical one in vogue today – but will it be possible?' In November 1846, his first encyclical *Qui pluribus* condemned the ills 'of these deplorable times' – liberalism, rationalism, pantheism, socialism and communism. He worked to alleviate the condition of his subjects, but he wanted to strengthen, not weaken, his position as spiritual *and* temporal ruler. He could not accept constitutional compromise and certainly had no time for the neo-guelph utopia of a federal Italy with himself as president. Liberals like Raffaele Martelli, however, were swept up in what historians now call the 'myth of Pius'. They interpreted the pope's reforms in ways Pius never intended.[13]

With his public statements during the August celebrations, Martelli was overreaching his grasp. The following month he was in Rome. He met with senior clerics including Monsignor Capalti, Secretary of the Congregazione degli Studi, the second most powerful person in the papal education system. Martelli found him to be 'pious and cultured'.[14]

On 1 October, Martelli was back in Ancona and informed Capalti of his decisions. This letter has not survived, but a copy of Capalti's reply sums up the issues. The Secretary opens with a mellifluous rebuke. He reminded the young professor, still just thirty-five years of age, of the need to be circumspect and tender towards his young, impressionable pupils:

> I am pleased to read, in your welcome letter of the first day of this month, that you are thinking seriously of continuing to

give assistance to your relatives in need and of using your far from common literary talents for the benefit of the young. I am certain that your time in this exemplary Capital City and the conversation with men mature in probity and prudence have led you to making a lasting resolve to adopt greater circumspection and religious tenderness towards the inexpert minds of your pupils.[15]

It would seem Martelli had been thinking of leaving his teaching position at the seminary. Had he made himself so unpopular? What would he do if he left the seminary? And who were the men 'mature in probity and prudence' that Martelli met in Rome? Probably senior educators, but was he already sounding out a future in the missions?

The financial difficulties of Martelli's 'relatives in need' are also unknown, but it is clear that the family was now in straitened circumstances. With his professorial salary and Canon's stipend, Martelli was taking on the role of benefactor towards his own family. Capalti went on to promise support for Martelli's appointment as permanent Professor of Rhetoric in the *ginnasio*, presumably if he should leave the seminary. He would ask friends in Ancona to make a house available that Martelli could sublet for a modest income. So Martelli continued to teach and draw a salary, but with financial assistance from a powerful backer.

The beginning of a new academic year the next month was the perfect opportunity for Martelli to revise his behaviour, in light of Capalti's advice. This he was unable, or unwilling, to do.

He began to work outside official structures. With a former student, Carlo Faiani, Martelli established night schools for the children of the poor. Martelli knew his young friend was the leader of the Ancona cell of Mazzini's Giovine Italia. Perhaps he chose not to know too much, or perhaps he would work towards a shared goal with anyone, whatever their ideological formation. Patriotic histories of Ancona link Faiani and Martelli as the two leading agitators for social reform in the city, Faiani working among the lowest classes (*populo minuto*), Martelli 'from his professor's chair'.[16]

In private homes, the most prominent liberal youths of the city – Filippo Barattani, Antonio Giannelli, Cesare Bruni, Vincenzo Lesti, and many others – taught literacy and numeracy, free of charge, to groups of eight to ten children from poor backgrounds. The need was real: the first census after Italian unification in 1861 estimated national *illiteracy* at 75%, with Ancona slightly better at 70 per cent.[17]

By 1846, the evening classes reached a total of six hundred students, in addition to the daytime 460. Archbishop Cadolini supported education for the poor but was suspicious of these new night schools because he knew who was teaching in them. He cautioned the prominent liberal members of his clergy, especially his Vicar General Lorenzo Barili, who was related to Faiani by marriage, 'You wish to give too much light to the young'.[18]

Faiani died of illness, aged just twenty-eight years, on 13 June 1846, assisted in his final moments by Martelli. At a memorial Mass a year later, Martelli delivered the eulogy. The text has not survived but it has been claimed that it was an anonymous publication entitled *Elogio di Carlo Fajani*, 'Eulogy of Carlo Faiani'.[19]

The published *Elogio* is an incendiary document. The real villains who made Faiani's work so difficult were not anti-liberals but the rich and powerful of Ancona who failed to act out of timidity and the fear of choosing sides. They are no better than the pusillanimous in Dante's *Inferno* (III, 63): 'displeasing to God and to his enemies'. The text rounded on the political establishment with terrible force:

> If you, the rich and powerful of the earth, are miserly in giving any succour to the misery of others, if you take no interest in the moral welfare of the lower classes, if you seek not to be brothers to the people but to suppress them with hunger and with chains, you will have only yourselves to blame if, when the people's chains do get broken, they tear you to pieces like beasts.[20]

It is most unlikely this published eulogy was the work of Martelli, but the mere association with such a violent contestation of the constituted order placed him seriously at odds with his bishop. Archbishop Cadolini recorded in his memoirs, 'Canon Raffaele Martelli, the lively leader of the new things [*novarum rerum alacer dux*] praised the deceased with a funeral oration; he lifted him up to the stars; he promised to greet him soon with a kiss of profound friendship; he provided a monument and inscription for the tomb'. He summoned his exuberant Canon and 'with strong encouragement recommended prudence'.[21]

For the second time in less than a year, an ecclesiastical superior had reminded Martelli of the virtue of prudence. It was a serious reprimand. Thomas Aquinas, following Aristotle, defined prudence as 'right reason in action'. The Tridentine Catechism cited prudence as one of the virtues most necessary in a priest: ordination 'is to be conferred only on those who by their holiness of life, their learning, faith and prudence, are able to bear it'.[22]

The lively leader of the new things, however, was by now totally swept up in liberal enthusiasm for Pius, whom he dubbed 'the reformer pope'. Martelli's public appearances became bolder in their calls for ongoing reform.[23]

At first Martelli introduced a new periodical publication to Ancona. Harmless enough, *L'Artigianello* was a Roman weekly, designed as its name suggests – 'the little artisan' – for young people being educated for a trade. It was distributed free of charge to pupils of night schools and otherwise sold by monthly subscription at the very limited price of five baiocchi. Within a year, it was selling 5000 copies a week, thanks to a network of distributors throughout the Papal States. Founding editor Ottavio Gigli honoured Martelli with a symbolic 'silver medal' for his energetic promotion of these new educational materials.[24]

In its four short years of life, the paper was a barometer of the development of moderate liberalism. In 1845, under Gregory XVI, the original subtitle read 'Moral, religious and educational reading: at the service of night schools of religion and of families' and the masthead showed a group of children gathered round a priest in cassock and biretta. The second year dropped the reference to religion and the image showed a family listening to the father of the household reading from the *Artigianello*. In 1847, the subtitle borrowed from Mazzini's political vocabulary to add the phrase 'for the education of the people'.[25]

Martelli wrote four short pieces for the paper over a three-year period, conventional tales of moral edification. The moral lessons are not just for the individual but have a sting of social criticism in their tail. In the tale of a young patrician who takes in a youth being mistreated by his father, the closing line is a provocative appeal: 'Pray, dear readers, that many among the rich may feel in their hearts the desire to imitate him'.[26]

Martelli's name began to appear also in a very different kind of broadsheet. *Il Piceno* was a new weekly paper in Ancona, founded by patriots – *carbonari* and *mazziniani* – who had spent time in exile after 1831.[27]

Early in 1848, Martelli used *Il Piceno* to publicise a speech in favour of the education of the underprivileged. On 30 January, he was guest speaker at the opening of the 'Institute of free education for the children of the poor' in Rimini, 100 kilometres up the coast.[28]

At the grand ceremony, Martelli spoke for an hour. He could speak as an Italian, to an audience of Italians, since Pius 'has begun to restore the dignity stolen from this Italy, once reduced to nothing more than a geographical expression'. The local paper reported the speech was much appreciated by 'those who admire the new art of oratory'. It was quickly published as a monograph.[29]

Martelli's central argument was that ignorance – and the vice it produces – is the greatest obstacle to human progress. Education should develop the use of reason, God's 'noble gift', a guide for each person to seek the true and the good. He applauds the distinction between mere *istruzione* – training for employment – and *educazione* – education of the whole person. He commends the school for assigning to each child a tutor who, with great prudence, will guide the tender youth, just like the 'visible angel' who accompanied the young Tobias on his journey to adulthood. This was his own namesake, the archangel Raphael.

The new educational initiatives – considered subversive by many – were the continuation of a glorious tradition of Catholic education. Martelli quotes theorists Gioberti, Aporti and Tommaseo, and boldly places the founders of the Rimini Institute alongside the saints who established religious orders dedicated to the education of the poor: Italian St Jerome Emiliani, founder of the Somascans, Spaniard St Joseph Calasanz, founder of the Piarists, and St Jean-Baptiste de la Salle, the French founder of the De La Salle Brothers.

The very next day, still in Rimini, Martelli sent a report on the event direct to *Il Piceno*. This was unorthodox enough, but even more galling to church authorities was the fact that Martelli's summary was not an article for publication but a chatty letter to the editor, Carissimo Fogacci, signed 'Your affectionate friend'.[30]

Martelli's report would have been controversial if written by a lay person. Coming from one of the leading clerics in the city, it must have caused consternation. When he compliments the bishop of Rimini for encouraging his priests to support the Institute, the implicit comparison with the lukewarm establishment of Ancona is unmissable.

It is difficult to imagine that Martelli had not discussed his ideas on these subjects with the archbishop. Perhaps Martelli simply – and not for the last time – could not contain his impatience. The cautious and tolerant archbishop must have been shocked to see one of his most trusted clerics air such matters in the columns of the secular press. Had the brilliant young Canon taken it on himself to give his archbishop advice through a public forum, as the editors were fond of doing? Or was he turning his back on the ecclesiastical establishment and throwing in his lot with his intrepid and likeminded lay friends?

In Rome, Pius IX was losing control of events. The problem was not this or that policy move, but the Pope's indecision. He would introduce reforms, then modify or withdraw them, always in the hope of maintaining his bond with the people. Metternich, in Vienna, was worried. The greatest threat to the status quo was not liberalism but instability. Austria acted.

On 17 July 1847, as Italian cities celebrated the first anniversary of Pius's amnesty, eight hundred Austrian troops crossed the pope's northern border and occupied the garrison in the city of Ferrara. Technically this was justified under the Congress of Vienna, but to do so without consultating the Pope was an insult. Metternich's move backfired. Pius became the lightning conductor for nationalist outrage. When the Austrians withdrew in December, the mood in the Papal States was at fever pitch.

Pius could not control a situation he had unwittingly created. As governments around Europe and in the other Italian States made concessions to their restless subjects, he issued a proclamation on 10 February 1848 to remind his spiritual children that the welfare of the Papal States came not from force of arms but from the gift of faith. He concluded with a most extraordinary statement:

> Great God, bless Italy and keep safe for her this most precious of gifts, the faith. Bless her with the blessing that your Vicar, with his face to the ground, humbly begs of you.

The effect was electric. The crowds heard what they wanted to hear. While Metternich dismissed 'Italy' as a 'geographical expression', here was the Supreme Pontiff prostrating himself before the Almighty to beg divine blessing on the nation searching for its own political identity. Pius unwittingly gave patriots a new battle cry: 'Great God, bless Italy'.

This was the title of another successful lithograph by Martelli's cousin Ercole Morelli. Pius mounts a throne where the Gospel sheds beams of light. As Italy kneels before him, Pius looks to heaven holding a banner with a cross and the words, 'In this sign you shall conquer', the words Emperor Constantine saw in the sky in AD 312. Now it became the battle cry for a new crusade against the 'Germans'. Victory is foreshadowed in the bottom right where the angel of Morelli's 1846 lithograph now drives a devil into Hell. The quotation in the top right reads, 'The demon departed, clenching his terrible claws on nothing', from the Dantesque *Basvilliana* by Vincenzo Monti, one of Martelli's favourite writers. The lines in the top left are from Dante himself: 'he is in search of liberty, which is so dear, as he well knows who gives his life for it'.[31]

The words and actions of Pius IX were a match that lit fires of nationalist rebellion in Paris, Vienna and Budapest. The time was ripe. Bad harvests in 1845 and 1846 produced an economic crisis, growing industrialisation in England and France disturbed the ancient class system, and calls for constitutional government and self-determination grew louder among the middle class in France, the German States, Prussia and the Hapsburg Empire. Europe was on the brink of revolution. Italian liberals knew their time had come.

Ercole Morelli, *Great God, Bless Italy! To Pius IX* (10 Feb 1848)

CHAPTER SIX

A Holy Crusade: God Wills It!

1848–1850

On 8 March 1848, Raffaele Martelli walked the short distance down Via Pizzecolli from San Carlo seminary to the church of San Francesco alle Scale. It was Ash Wednesday and the huge church was packed to hear the first of the Lenten sermons. The guest preacher this year was the controversial friar Ugo Bassi.

Bassi, a native of the rebellious Romagna to the north of Ancona, was the most famous of the itinerant preachers of his day. He would preach for two to three hours at a time, now reducing his audience to tears, now whipping them into a frenzy of religious or patriotic fervour. Men wept at his words, women cut off their hair to sell and in Bologna in 1848 they donated one earring to the cause of national independence. The *moda alla Bassi* – to wear only one earring – became fashionable throughout Italy.

Martelli shared Bassi's nationalism and his message of moral reform. The collective political mission could only be achieved through personal and collective moral renewal. Both priests railed against blasphemy as a sign of moral decay. 'The noble tongue gifted to us by Providence as further proof of our privileged place among the nations', Martelli wrote, 'will we so abuse it when we remember that the first utterances in our national language were a tribute to religion?' The *Canticle of the Creatures*, which St Francis of Assisi wrote in his native dialect, was always the first poem in anthologies of Italian literature.[1]

As Bassi mounted the pulpit in Ancona, Europe was rising in revolution. From Paris to Vienna, liberals ousted absolute monarchs. In northern Italy, Venice and Milan rose, and in Turin, King Carlo Alberto declared war on Austria.[2]

The papal administration was afraid Austria might again cross into the Papal States, to block any patriots joining Piedmont's war. Two armies set out from Rome to defend the border, one of regular forces, and the 'Roman Legion', which included volunteer units. One of these was the Roman University Battalion, *Battaglione universitario romano*. On 25 March, in Piazza del Popolo, Martelli's former student Gaspare Finali, together with Augusto Silvagni and Luigi Alibrandi, handed the Battalion its official flag. The unity of Italian nationalism and Catholic faith was woven into the cloth. Onto the red, white and green stripes were sewn a red velvet cross to recall the glories of the Crusades, and two sashes in the papal colours of silver and gold. The young volunteers called themselves *crociati*, Crusaders, and adopted the war cry of their medieval forebears, *Iddio lo vuole*, 'God wills it'.

Martelli watched the volunteers march into Ancona on the afternoon of 8 April. He greeted old friends: in the First Roman Legion he found his artist 'cousin', Major Ercole Morelli, and his dear friend Pietro Regnoli.

The next day, at an open-air Mass in Piazza del Papa, Raffaele Martelli followed Ugo Bassi in signing up as a military chaplain. He was assigned to the University Battalion, with the officer's rank of *sotto Maggiore*, 'sub-major', a rank invented by the volunteers for their chaplains, lower than a major but higher than a captain.[3]

This was surely a holy crusade. Archbishop Cadolini blessed the young volunteers and the pope's representative, Apostolic Delegate Monsignor Achille Maria Ricci, told them they marched with the blessing of the pope himself. He would pray for them from the altar of Mary Queen of All Saints:

> Italy and the Papacy, Independence and Rome are in full concord. For Pius, a fatherland is no longer an idea, a desire, a prayer. It has been granted to you; you shall keep it free, as free as your souls, given to you by God. [...] Soldiers of the city, I will follow you with my prayers. Farewell. From the summit of St Ciriaco, at the foot of the altar, I will pray to Our Virgin that the Blessing of Heaven may come down upon you. LONG LIVE RELIGION, LONG LIVE PIUS IX, LONG LIVE THE ITALIAN NATION![4]

They marched out of the city on 12 April, amid wild scenes of cheering and celebration. In Imola, Martelli and the other officers stayed in the palace of the archbishop, Gaetano Baluffi, Martelli's former teacher. He too promised prayers.[5]

By the time the volunteers reached the border at the Po River, Pius IX had realised his well-meaning gestures had unleashed forces that were out of his control. On 29 April, he issued an Allocution. War against Austria was out of the question. The Vicar of Christ was the father of all humanity and he could not set one part of his flock against another.

The incredulous volunteers invented all sorts of explanations for what they considered at best a change of heart and, at worst, a betrayal: Bassi believed the Pope had become the prisoner of scheming cardinals, others suspected more sinister forces. Whatever rationalisations were bandied about, the fact was that, when he crossed the Po with the University Battalion on 2 May, Raffaele Martelli was defying the wishes of the pope.

For six weeks the students saw action in the battles of Cornuda and Treviso and then in Vicenza. Marshall Radetzky (of the Strauss waltz) was magnanimous towards the vanquished. Martelli's friend Pietro Regnoli sought solace in the thought that 'the unexpected and vigorous resistance, which showed how much strength we still had in us, improved the terms of surrender'. The pontifical troops marched out of Vicenza with full military honours.[6]

The University Battalion split in two. The majority, including some chaplains, continued on to Venice where they joined the ill-fated defence of the Venetian Republic. Martelli was one of seven officers and 120 soldiers who turned immediately for home, a decision he was later relieved to have taken: 'my conduct, thank Heavens, was such that it deserved none of the criticism received by many others who wore the same uniform'.[7]

The young students had lost two of their number with over thirty wounded. They would now learn, as Captain Filippo Zamboni wrote, that 'war takes more victims off the battlefield than on it'. As they trudged across the low-lying, mosquito-infested lands of the Po Valley, six more perished in the hot, humid summer.[8]

Martelli's eulogies for the six young victims were published individually in Bologna. Once back in Ancona, Martelli gathered them into a single volume entitled *Eulogies of certain young Crusaders, soldiers of the Roman University Battalion, in the war for Italian independence fought in the year 1848, read at their funerals by the chaplain Professor Raffaele Martelli*.[9]

They are the nearest we have to a statement of Martelli's political belief. He does not identify with any of the factions in the struggles of the time but, like Gioberti, he develops a unitary vision of Italy's destiny, built on its religious heritage and the cultural tradition that grew out of it. National unification is the fulfilment of a destiny whose roots are two millennia deep.

The fallen students are 'martyrs' for the fatherland, or the cause of the nation. They died, like the Christian martyrs of early times, at the hands of 'barbarians'. 'This Italy of ours' (*questa Italia nostra*) for which the young men offered their lives under the banner of the tricolour bearing the cross, will be 'free, independent, glorious'.

The yearning for liberty is identified not with a political programme but with the universal 'religious sentiment'. This is 'the most noble instinct in which humanity finds solace and its greatest boast'. Religion has long been made out to be the enemy of freedom, but it is the glory of the nineteenth century to have recovered the true sense of these priceless gifts:

> Religion and freedom have long been portrayed as enemies, by those with interests in keeping them apart. Now they embrace as sisters and recognise they share the same celestial origin. This event is, in my opinion, the greatest glory of this century and the greatest achievement of progressive Christian civilisation.

Catholicism and liberalism (here we see him use the word for the first time) grow together from the same source. Martelli's liberalism is an expression of his religious faith:

> It has become clear that one can be devout and at the same time liberal, and that one can be liberal without ceasing to be devout; in fact one cannot be an enlightened Christian without becoming a wise liberal, since liberalism proclaims nothing but the Gospel, applied not only to the lowly but also to the great, not only to domestic life but also to political and social relations.

He adapted John 15:13 to his vision: 'Greater love has no man than this, that he lay down his life for his brothers *and his native land*'. Of one student, he says that the fatherland, *patria*, came second only to God in his thoughts. Of another, love of religion and love of the fatherland were 'entwined'.

The contribution of women to the political struggle receives special homage. They not only gave precious assistance to the wounded, but also showed the same stoical self-sacrifice as men. Martelli praised one mother who urged her son to sacrifice private sentiments to those of the nation.

Martelli wrote an introduction to the collected eulogies and dated it 4 November 1848. He had been back in Ancona for three months and might have taken this opportunity to mend bridges and dampen the divisions in the city. Whether it was lingering grief or unshakeable conviction, Martelli did nothing to soften the impact of the text. This use of the evangelical 'putting the sword back in its place' (Matthew 26:52) sounds most unconciliatory:

> Let earthly forms, the lives of our dear ones, our own blood, let them all depart, but let the sword not be returned to its scabbard until the demons of the North be driven out of the Italian paradise.

To those who did not share his grief at the loss of young lives and his belief in the cause for which they died, he shows contempt:

> Let them fall silent, these worthless souls! Let them not sadden the generous hearts of the young with their wailing! Let them be silent, if the voice of the glory of the fatherland is dumb in them, if the words 'national dignity', 'social rights', 'self-determination of peoples' mean nothing to them!

To gauge the effect these collected orations must have had in Ancona, we need look no further than a public statement from his fellow priests. Back in April, just a fortnight after Martelli marched to war with the volunteers, *Il Piceno* published a 'Protest by the Vicars Forane (country clergy) and Parish Priests of the Diocese of Ancona', presumably with tacit approval of the hierarchy. We are accused, they began, of being 'retrograde, sworn enemies of Pius IX, in cahoots with the enemies of freedom and with foreigners'. They speak now only to ensure their silence is not interpreted as an admission of guilt. Hot-headed liberals had no monopoly on patriotic feeling:

> We protest that we have nothing to do with the enemies of Italy and their followers: that we venerate and love Pius IX not only

as the successor of Peter but also as our excellent Prince; that we too love Italy and we desire and hope for its independence.

The writers could claim, at least, to have prudence on their side:

> These are our sentiments and the sentiments of our clergy. If there were ever any exceptions (and which social group is without exception?), let them be ascribed to an excess of timid prudence, an error not a fault; let them be ascribed to the very newness of the events which are happening with incredible speed leaving far behind them those who wish to examine every step so as to move with caution and certainty.[10]

In Rome, the situation spiralled into chaos. The pope's prime minister was assassinated and Pius fled to Gaeta on the south coast. On 9 February 1849, Mazzini declared the end of the pope's temporal power and the establishment of a Roman Republic that would rule 'in the name of God and the People'. Garibaldi led an army into the city, with Ugo Bassi as his personal chaplain.

Moderate liberals could no longer claim to be taken seriously by either side of the conflict. For intransigents, their disobedience to the pope had contributed to the unfolding disaster. To republicans, they were discredited by their misplaced trust in the papacy.

Ancona was overrun by opposing mobs of disaffected youth. Political ideals degenerated into violence on both sides. The old papal-supported Centurions sprang back into life, and young liberals formed gangs like Infernal Company (*Compagnia Infernale*) or Society of Killers (*Società degli Ammazzarelli*). They spread terror throughout the city, with knife-attacks on high-profile conservatives and simple priests, sometimes in broad daylight.[11]

Pius appealed to Austria and France to drive the republicans out of Rome. Louis Napoleon bombed the Eternal City with papal authorisation. Austria could not allow France to establish influence over Rome and moved south, occupying Bologna in May. Only Ancona blocked their march to Rome.

As the city prepared for the inevitable, sieges of the past were recalled. The 1173 attack by Emperor Frederick Barbarossa, in the thirteenth-century account by Boncompagno da Signa, was foundational to the city: 'just as Italy identified its founding father in Dante Alighieri, so Ancona found its own heroism in the tale of Boncompagno'. In 1844, the City Council commissioned a painting from Francesco Podesti, who fought alongside Martelli in the University Battalion.[12]

'The Oath of the Anconitans' captures the moment when the populace swore to defend their city to the death. Against the background of the Arch of Trajan and the Cathedral, the elderly and blind senator Bonifacio Faziolo stands on the steps of the Palazzo degli Anziani, clutching the city's flag, inspiring his fellow citizens. Opposite him, resplendent in red, Barbarossa's emissary Archbishop Christian of Mainz stares, incredulous, as German ambassadors are bundled away. Two humble heroes stand out. To the left is a young widow named Stamira, her left hand on her sword and her right hand raised to heaven. She crept out of the city walls and set fire to the enemy's war machines. Standing behind the elderly senator, a young priest named Giovanni di Chio raises his hands in prayer. He swam across the harbour in a storm and with an axe cut the anchor rope of the admiral's ship, which caused the sinking of several enemy vessels. The painting remains to this day a potent symbol of the city's proud past.

Ancona's defiance rang out in the Teatro delle Muse. Verdi's *La battaglia di Legnano* narrates the crushing defeat of Frederick Barbarossa at the hands of proud, independent Italian city-states. Act IV is entitled *Morire per la patria*, 'To Die for the Fatherland'.

The siege opened on 25 May 1849, with attacks from land and sea. After twenty-five days, the superior forces of the aggressor and the lack of food and water brought the city to its knees, in unconditional surrender, on 19 June: 316 bombs had fallen on the city, the number of dead was estimated between 500 and 1000 with twice as many wounded, and many buildings were destroyed or damaged. Martelli is cited in local histories for his work during the

Francesco Podesti, *The Oath of the Anconitans* (1850)

siege, assisting poor families and caring for the dead and wounded at considerable danger to his own safety. He worked on the city's Damage Assessment and Assistance Commission.[13]

This catastrophe was the ultimate humiliation for Martelli and other liberal clergy. Twelve months ago they had marched for the glory of Italy and Christendom. Now Martelli wept as the Pope returned to Rome under the protection of a despised and perfidious foreign power, and in Ancona the flag of his beloved Pius IX flew again through the brutality and arrogance of a hated former foe.[14]

Austria occupied Ancona for a decade. Martial law was brutal. A dozen men were immediately executed by firing squad. Floggings were designed to create maximum terror: victims were strapped face down on a bench in a cavernous courtyard of the law courts so that their cries echoed out into the narrow streets. Aristide Tuzi was engaged to Martelli's stepsister Aldemira. During a search of the house where he lived with his widowed mother, Austrian police found blankets, cartridge cases and berets he had kept from his days in the Republican army. Aristide received thirty strokes of the hazelwood cane, while his mother got away with a fine of fifty *scudi*.[15]

Martelli left his position at the seminary – Ascoli says he resigned before he could be dismissed. But he could count himself lucky, as he heard of the punishments meted out to other priests who had followed liberalism to its disastrous end. Ugo Bassi was executed by Austrian soldiers: his last words were 'Long live Jesus! Long live Mary! Long live Italy!' Gioberti's books were placed on the Index of Forbidden Books.[16]

We know little of how Raffaele Martelli lived under martial law. All night schools in Ancona were closed, and he was surviving on the high school position Capalti had secured for him, a private school he was allowed to operate under supervision and his Canon's stipend. By the end of 1849, he faced financial uncertainty.

Details are scanty but his family's fortunes were unravelling. His elderly father Angelo seems to have sold off most of his land holdings shortly before he died in 1850. His younger stepsister, Aldemira, found herself without a dowry. To marry Aristide Tuzi, she was forced to appeal to the *Monte dei Poveri della Comunità di Ancona*, 'Mount (of Piety) for the Poor', a charitable organisation that provided dowries to girls in need. Her application describes the family in unflattering terms: 'an elderly mother, another unmarried sister and two brothers in financial hardship'. Her request was turned down, so it was Raffaele who provided the dowry and trousseau when the marriage took place in October 1850.[17]

These problems could have been resolved eventually. Priests elsewhere found ways to deal with the same challenges. In Modena near Bologna, Fr Gaetano Chierici, who would later be in contact with Martelli in Australia, lost his position in the city's seminary after he gave a pistol to students marching to war. Chierici considered leaving Modena but stayed, ultimately regaining his teaching position.

Martelli's sense of disillusionment, however, was overpowering. Liberal ideals had been hijacked by the sacrilegious republicans, while bishops denounced every expression of patriotic sentiment as an attack on the pope, the Church and legitimate authority. But it seems too that he was unwilling or unable to compromise. The opposition of the Ancona establishment was intense, but the rigidity was as much on Martelli's side. His personality would not allow him to deny the principles on which he had wagered so much. He seemed incapable of biding his time to wait for things to improve. If he could not stay in Ancona, he would not be welcome anywhere else in Italy. Just a few years past Dante's 'mid-point in the journey of our life', Martelli decided his personal salvation had to be worked out beyond Italy's shores.[18]

The nineteenth century was a 'springtime' of missionary activity, without parallel in the history of the Church. Napoleon's attacks on the Church were followed by a universal religious revival that found one of its most potent symbols in the foreign missions. By the end of the century, more than two hundred missionary support societies were active in Europe, encouraged by the European 'discovery' of the New World and the new technologies of transport and communication.[19]

In Ancona, Martelli saw plenty of inspiration to the missionary life. The Marche region boasted a proud history: Franciscans had travelled to Asia and Africa; Macerata was famous for Matteo Ricci, the first European to enter the Forbidden City and who died in Beijing after thirty years in China. In the seminary's Church of the Gesù, Martelli would see, in a side chapel on the left of the nave, the large painting by Sebastiano Conca that shows St Francis Xavier arriving in Japan. Former professors and students from his seminary days had worked overseas and would now play a role in his next momentous step.

Missionaries were in the news in Ancona. In early 1850, Martelli read, in *Il Piceno*, an enthusiastic report on the success of Catholic missions in Australia. The Benedictine mission led by Archbishop Polding had built one monastery for monks and one for nuns as well as a seminary and a Cathedral; a number of 'Australians', that is Aborigines, had taken the habit and missionaries everywhere were making 'innumerable' conversions and 'educating the savages in agriculture and civilisation'. However, most reports on overseas missions in *Il Piceno* were about North America. Martelli confided secret thoughts to Pietro Regnoli, but could not bring himself to put his dreams into words, even to his closest friend:

> If I could settle certain domestic responsibilities, I would think of going more than a thousand miles from these parts. 'Oh, so you too want to go digging for gold in California?', I imagine you asking me. On the contrary: riches have never had any appeal for me. 'So where do you want to go?' I want to become…, but no, I do not want to say it for fear that you will laugh in my face. Enough, who knows.[20]

How to proceed? In the *Imitation of Christ*, the chapter on prudence advised him: 'Listen to wise and sensible advice and be guided by someone who is better than you, rather than following your own opinions'.[21]

CHAPTER SEVEN

To Consecrate the Rest of My Life to the Exercise of the Priestly Ministry

1851

The friendships Martelli had up to this point grew out of shared political ideals: social justice, education for the disadvantaged, a united Italy. His crisis now was not about social causes, or broken relationships with church authorities and political allies. The problem was interior, his own: how to make sense of his life's calling, how he and his contingent vocational choices stood in relation to his life's journey. He seems to have reached the awareness that without the horizon of his own ultimate destiny, those friendships, while socially useful, had become insufficient and lacking in what he held most dear. During 1850, he called on a few trusted friends who would understand the depth of his dilemma and had the means to help.

His 'old master and friend and benefactor', Lorenzo Barili suggested he contact the Benedictines. Tommaso Gallucci had been two years behind him in the seminary and was now in Imola, as Vicar General to Cardinal Baluffi, the former professor of rhetoric at the seminary. Gallucci and Baluffi had spent five years in South America. Both men offered to provide references for Martelli to Cardinal Barnabò, Secretary of Propaganda Fide.[1]

The Sacred Congregation for the Propagation of the Faith, to give its full title (*propaganda fide* is simply the Latin for 'the Propagation of the Faith'), is known today as the Congregation for the Evangelisation of Peoples. It was created in 1622 in an attempt to limit political control of missions, especially by Spain and Portugal, by bringing all Catholic missionaries under centralised ecclesiastical authority in Rome.

The only other person in Ancona Martelli says he discussed the matter with was the French Consul. Monsieur Léonce Mazuyer wrote on his behalf to the Congrégation pour la Propagation de la Foi, 'Society for the Propagation of the Faith'. This was a private association, with offices in Paris and Lyons, founded in 1822 by laywoman Pauline Jaricot. It was highly successful in providing financial support to missionary activity around the world.

Martelli had prudent advisers, but no clear path forward. He needed to tread carefully. Relations with Archbishop Cadolini had deteriorated to breaking point: he feared his archbishop 'might be not too disposed to speak in my favour'. Without permission from his superior, Martelli would not be accepted anywhere in the Catholic world.[2]

On Boxing Day 1850, the winter season at the Teatro delle Muse opened with Verdi's *Nabucco*. In its stirring chorus *Va', pensiero*, the exiled Hebrew slaves weep for their beloved homeland now in the hands of foreign oppressors. Martelli had attended the triumphal premiere season in 1844. How bitter and melancholy it was now to hear those lofty patriotic sentiments again, in a city languishing under martial law. Martelli acted.

On the second day of the new year, Martelli followed advice from Tommaso Gallucci. He wrote to their mutual friend, Pietro Casaretto.

Casaretto had become an important figure in the Benedictine revival of the nineteenth century. In 1850, Pius IX appointed him

Abbot of the monastery of Santa Scolastica, in Subiaco near Rome. While all countries had suffered under Napoleon's plundering of monasteries – all but two per cent of the Benedictine houses in Europe were closed – Italy was particularly badly affected. By mid-century, monastic life in the country was at a low ebb. Even where structures and institutions continued, the inner life of monastic communities had disintegrated into individualism and worldliness. Santa Scolastica was in a depressed state.³

Casaretto's task was to restore authentic monastic life at Subiaco. His solution was to return to a strict interpretation of the Benedictine Rule, the so-called 'primitive observance', and to train monks for the foreign missions. He gained the nickname of 'missionary monk'.⁴

'Very Reverend Don Pietro', Martelli wrote to his old friend, with a mix of first-name familiarity and deference to his new abbatial status,

> on the advice of my friend, Mgr Gallucci, Vicar General in Imola, I am taking the liberty of disturbing you in order to reveal to you a decision I have reached, which you will probably be able to help me carry out. Having decided to consecrate the rest of my life exclusively to the exercise of the priestly ministry and having discussed this with certain pious and prudent persons here, I have decided to place myself at the disposal of Propaganda, so that I might be sent to the Foreign Missions, counting on my knowledge of the French language and of English which I am already beginning to speak and write.⁵

What did he mean by 'consecrate the rest of my life exclusively to the exercise of the priestly ministry [*ministero sacerdotale*]'? Does the priestly ministry not include the education of the young, the promotion of Christian values among youth and the broader society? If this was not the priestly ministry, what was?

During the 1840s, Martelli wrote that the best way for priests to regain respect among the people was to work to reconcile 'religion and civilisation, science and faith, the papacy and Italy'. Two years on, the model of the politicised priesthood lay in ruins. Martelli retreated to the Tridentine vision of the priest he had learned in San Carlo seminary. A priest was the ideal 'salt of the earth and light of the world', but he retained, above all, his sacred nature as a man set apart.[6]

Martelli came clean about his rift with Archbishop Cadolini and the clerical establishment in Ancona. 'The errors that could be held against me', he conceded,

> are, I believe, principally these two: I applauded with some enthusiasm the reforms Pius IX introduced at the beginning of his reign, and I followed the Pontifical armed forces into the Veneto region in 1848, as Chaplain of the University Battalion.

These 'errors' were in part the result of devoting more time to intellectual and cultural formation at the expense of spiritual development. He shares with Casaretto the fruits of a long self-examination:

> I have spent my life so far studying profane texts far more than ecclesiastical ones and I need to spend some time in one of the Seminaries that prepare those who are dedicating themselves to that ministry.[7]

Knowing Casaretto had connections to the English Benedictines, Martelli confessed his preference for an English-speaking destination: North America, or even Oceania because he knew 'the English were doing good work there'.

Casaretto's immediate response was to discourage Martelli from approaching Propaganda Fide. Though his missionary monks were at the service of Propaganda, Casaretto kept them under his authority as their monastic superior.[8]

Casaretto offered two alternatives. First, he pointed Martelli towards the Society for the Propagation of the Faith in France.

But the French Consul had no reply from his letter to the Society. Besides, Martelli confessed to a fear of 'finding myself isolated' and was looking for the 'assistance, direction and protection that are not lacking to those persons who are members of a family'.[9] He knew his limitations:

> I am afraid that, since I am no longer young (40 years of age) and have an old habit of living free of every obligation of cloistered life, this might make me unsuitable to bending to a rule (that may be a little strict) and to a uniform tenor of life.

The financial pressures showed. He confessed to the need to find 'the certainty of finding, at the end of my career, a shelter for my old age'.

For these reasons, Martelli was happy to consider Casaretto's second suggestion: to come directly to Subiaco and take up a teaching position there as he prepared himself for missionary work. This plan seemed to satisfy Martelli's conditions: a religious 'family', spiritual formation, financial security, training for missionary work. He was happy to accept, but not ready to commit:

> The project you offer me makes me happy in this respect, because I would stay there as long as I thought necessary in order to test myself and to acquire the skills for the ministry, all the time remaining free of every bond.[10]

The first condition for his work as a missionary priest was, he realised, his own inner conversion. To recover the meaning of his priestly ministry, he needed to go to its source. The *Imitation of Christ* spoke clearly: 'by seeking to love You alone, I have found both You and myself' (III, 8).

He could not do it alone. Martelli seems already aware that Christian obedience, especially in the monastic tradition, is an expression of friendship. Subiaco offered him the authoritative guide of Christian friendship. He hoped to encounter there some person who could sustain him in his future life abroad, someone who shared his projects and hopes but, crucially, lived these out within the same ultimate horizon:

> And then if in the end I were ready to take the great step, could I not take flight for the first time in the company of some expert Benedictine missionary?[11]

The fearless preacher and military chaplain had suffered such a loss of self-confidence that he was in need of a new beginning:

> Since I am aware of my limited aptitude for the serious and holy ministries, I would accept no role except one that depended on a person capable of guiding me through virtue and experience. No task would be too humble for me, and knowing how to carry out the relevant duties would be sufficient for me.[12]

In April, Casaretto invited Martelli to come as soon as possible. Martelli estimated it would take four or five months of private lessons to reach financial independence.

Lorenzo Barili acted as intermediary. He knew how compromised Martelli was in Ancona, so he suggested that, once Martelli had completed his time in Subiaco, Casaretto should recommend him to missionary organisations as his religious superior. This would obviate the need for permission from Archbishop Cadolini, who might be reluctant to release his volatile but gifted priest.

By mid-July, all was in order. Martelli just had to finalise his financial situation in Ancona. He would accept whatever salary Casaretto offered him.[13]

For the duration of this protracted correspondence, Martelli was obsessed with secrecy. He begged Casaretto to use the information in his first letter 'with prudence' – this virtue will never abandon him now. Till the last minute, he could not avoid a vague unease that all might come to nought: 'until I am out of Ancona I do not feel I can be free of the fear that some unexpected obstacle may get in my way'.[14]

It is not clear what he was so afraid of. Certainly, he could not be sure of the support of the archbishop. Did Martelli fear that Cadolini would refuse to him the letter of release, the *exeat*? Cadolini was not known for a vindictive streak, and in 1850 he was approaching eighty and in poor health. Perhaps there were powerful members of Cadolini's curia who might not hesitate to frustrate the ambitions, even missionary ones, of a wayward liberal clergyman.

In any case, Martelli succeeded, from January to August, in planning a clean getaway from his home city, in complete secrecy.

Archbishop Cadolini died on 1 August 1850 and his successor, Antonio Benedetto Antonucci, was not installed until the following month. During the interregnum, on 26 August, Raffaele Martelli caught the coach bound for Rome. He would never see Ancona again.[15]

CHAPTER EIGHT

A Benedictine at Heart Though He Does not Wear the Habit

1851–1853

The Abbey of Santa Scolastica in Subiaco, like most Benedictine houses, keeps a daily Chronicle. It lists comings and goings and significant events. The Italian name *Libro di Memorie* captures its purpose: to insert the life of a single community into the long memory of a universal tradition. One and a half millennia of Benedictine history have been built on such humble, daily memories.

On 7 September 1851, the *Libro di Memorie* in Santa Scolastica records the arrival of 'Canon Don Raffaele Martelli, professor of Eloquence, to spend a couple of years here giving a regular course of Rhetoric to our youths. He is a worthy subject, of devout genius, fine manners and exquisite education'.[1]

Martelli entered fully into the monastic routines. The Divine Office he used to pray with the dozen Canons of Santa Maria della Piazza, he now chanted with forty or fifty monks and novices. Seven times a day he joined the monks gathered in choir to chant the prayers using *recto tono* – on a single note with no deviations – standing or sitting erect, in a calm and dignified rhythm with long pauses. He learned that the communal recitation of the Office and regular periods of meditation were what powered the contemplative thrust of Benedictine life. Martelli found new inspiration to return to the *Imitation of Christ*. Casaretto encouraged the monks to read it every day, and even to substitute it for their *lectio divina*.[2]

Martelli taught language and literature in the lower high school. He had little freedom in choosing texts for his teaching, as Casaretto excluded anything that smacked of politics. He was never allowed to forget his liberal past. When he set out to visit the great abbey at Montecassino with two English companions, he found himself turned away at the border of the Kingdom of Naples and trudged back to Subiaco alone. The *Libro di Memorie* notes, with exquisite understatement, 'he did not have a passport for travel abroad'. Martelli must have known in advance that crossing a border between States required a valid document. The Kingdom of Naples was vigilant in keeping out anyone from other Italian States, including priests, who was even suspected of liberalism. Martelli was effectively stateless.[3]

His students came from all over Italy and from the two English-language seminaries in Rome: the English College and the Irish College. The English-speaking novices at Santa Scolastica gave Martelli conversation lessons, in exchange for private tuition in Italian.[4]

Casaretto was particularly attracted to the English-speaking world. He visited England and planned to send monks to the British colonies in Africa, India, the Far East and Australia. John Bede Polding, the first Archbishop of Sydney, appointed Casaretto his Vicar-General in Italy. When Casaretto opened his first College for Missions in Genoa in 1847, Polding arranged for four novices to be sent there from England.[5]

The Genoa College was Casaretto's first venture in preparing missionary monks, an undertaking that had the full backing of his spiritual director, Saint Vincenzo Pallotti. He was chaplain of the missionary seminary 'Collegio Urbano' in Rome and founded the missionary order that bears his name. In 1845, Casaretto introduced Pallotti to two Spanish Benedictines, Rosendo Salvado and José Maria Benito Serra. They were in Rome preparing to depart for Western Australia. Pallotti gave the young Spaniards an icon of 'Our Lady of Good Counsel', which today hangs in the Abbey church in New Norcia.[6]

When Casaretto took up his position in Subiaco, he wasted no time in transferring his twelve students from Genoa. The group included one Australian.

Martelli's dream of working with Aboriginal peoples in distant lands could not have taken more dramatic and unexpected shape. On his arrival in Subiaco, he met his first Australian. John David Murra was an Aboriginal boy from New South Wales. He was just nine years old. There is much that is uncertain about how he ended up on a boat bound for Italy. It seems his father may have given initial consent, only to have second thoughts, but by that time the boy was on his way to Europe.[7]

Martelli must have admired Casaretto's plan to train young Aboriginal men to become monks and priests. The development of an Indigenous clergy was a priority of Propaganda Fide from its earliest days, most recently restated in the 1845 Instruction to heads of mission territories, *Neminem profecto*: Indigenous and European clergy should be treated equally in every respect and Indigenous priests should be given adequate preparation for consecration as bishops in their own territories.

After Murra's arrival in Italy, nothing more was ever said about him by the Australian clergy, which suggests the initiative to bring him to Italy came not from Polding but from Casaretto. Casaretto begged Polding, in vain, to send a second youth from Sydney. His reasons were sensible and enlightened: a second youth would be a companion for Murra and would ensure he did not forget his native language. Casaretto wanted Murra to return to Sydney 'as an aboriginal missionary, and not as a black Italian'.[8]

There were other Australian connections waiting for Martelli at Santa Scolastica. Among the novices from the English College in Rome were three young nephews of Abbot Henry Gregory, Polding's Vicar General in Sydney and Prior of the Benedictine monastery attached to St Mary's Cathedral. The illustrious uncle visited Subiaco in 1852, and Martelli must have heard about his sister, Scholastica, who helped found the first community of Benedictine women in Australia, now Jamberoo Abbey. All this must have confirmed the stories Martelli had read about Australia in *Il Piceno*.[9]

Then, when he had been in Subiaco barely a month, came the encounter that set the direction of the rest of Martelli's life. On 15 October 1851, Rosendo Salvado arrived at Santa Scolastica with his secretary, Venancio Garrido. Salvado and Serra had established the mission of New Norcia in 1846 but a lack of resources brought them back to Europe to gather funds and personnel. Serra returned quickly to Australia but Salvado was ordered to remain in Europe while Propaganda decided where to send him, either back to Perth and New Norcia or to open a new mission at Port Victoria (Darwin). Salvado visited Subiaco at the request of the Pope. Pius wanted Salvado to confer with Abbot Casaretto.[10]

No records survive of the meeting between the Spanish missionaries and the Canon of Ancona. But during the week he spent at the abbey, Martelli must have heard Salvado's story: how he had been forced to leave his monastery in Spain by a liberal revolution; how he followed Serra to Italy, where they completed their monastic formation in the Abbey of the Holy Trinity at Cava de' Tirreni, near Naples; how they offered themselves to the missions and on their departure received a blessing from Pope Gregory XVI himself.

Salvado must have told Martelli how he arrived with Serra in Western Australia in 1846; how they were the first Catholic missionaries to venture into country north of the Swan River Colony, where they befriended the Noongar people, learned their language and attempted to adopt their nomadic hunter-gatherer lifestyle; how, when this proved unsustainable, they evolved a plan to establish a village at New Norcia for monks and Aboriginal people, introducing agriculture and a stable style of life.

Before coming to Subiaco, Salvado had used his time in Rome to write an account of his Australian adventures, to encourage donations from wealthy donors. The *Historical Memoirs* were completed in the summer of 1851 and, by late October, Salvado was back in Rome presenting printed copies to the Pope and others. Now Martelli could relive the thrill of the adventures he had heard directly from Salvado: stories of encountering 'Australian savages', of eating grubs and mouthfuls of lizard pre-chewed by a Noongar companion, of the intense heat and enormous distances to be covered on foot. He read with fascination the descriptions of Noongar society, customs, diet and spirituality. The professor of Rhetoric must have pored over the chapter on 'Australian philology' with its word list of two Noongar dialects, probably Yued and Balardong, transcribed using Italian and Spanish spelling conventions, and with Italian translations.[11]

Martelli heard of the first steps towards establishing an Indigenous clergy in Western Australia. Salvado had shrewdly sold the idea to the Perth establishment by calling it 'the grand experiment of the civilisation of the aborigines', a phrase he coined for a letter to the *Inquirer* but never used again. Priests and nuns in Western Australia had already brought five Aboriginal children to Europe, but all died within a few years of arrival. Salvado and Casaretto realised how unrealistic it was to bring children so young (around ten) to places so foreign and far from home. Salvado decided any other Noongar youths would have to be at least fifteen or sixteen years of age and have already received some education in Australia.[12]

In 1851, however, things must still have looked promising. On 27 December, in Santa Scolastica, Martelli attended the ceremony in which John David Murra was clothed in the Benedictine habit. His black gown had the red trim and sash that marked the youths training for work in the missions.[13] Though he seemed to settle in well at Subiaco, Murra too died in Italy, aged fifteen, in 1857.

Australia came a step closer to Subiaco in 1852. A meeting in Montecassino brought together monks of the Cassinese

Congregation from all over Italy. The 'Congregation' is the basic unit of organisation of the Benedictines. All monasteries are autonomous units, though since the fifteenth century they have associated freely in Congregations. At the 1852 meeting, the Cassinese Congregation elected Casaretto as its Abbot President and unanimously approved a proposal put forward by Salvado. The New Norcia mission was affiliated to the Congregation and a novitiate was set up in Subiaco to prepare students for Australia. The other Italian monasteries of the Congregation pledged financial support.[14]

After his first year of teaching, Martelli spent the 1852 autumn break in Subiaco. Salvado's visit had given him a new direction. He 'looked at Australia from afar with love', wrote Dom Antonio De Riso, director of the *scuola inferiore* in which Martelli taught. He was writing to Salvado, who was in London preparing to set sail for Australia.[15]

Salvado and Garrido had been busy. In France, Spain, England and Ireland, they recruited workers for the mission. Garrido assembled the group in Cadiz, at the southern extremity of Spain's Atlantic coast, while Salvado found a ship in London, made the payments for the trip and made his own way to Cadiz. He calculated there would be just a few days to wait for their ship to arrive, enough to complete the final fitout. However, winter storms damaged the ship and it would take five long months and considerable extra expense to make it seaworthy again. For Martelli, the delay was providential.

As the new academic year began at the end of 1852, Martelli spoke to Casaretto about securing a posting to a foreign mission. The conversation, far from calming him down as Casaretto hoped, left him 'in a state of restlessness'. He was becoming impatient. On 10 January 1853, he lodged a written request for permission to go to Rome, to consult with 'certain other persons, equal to yourself in their benevolence to me and trustworthiness'.[16]

Casaretto must have turned him down, since Martelli wrote again a fortnight later. This carefully crafted letter offers precious insight into Martelli's state of mind. It is an excellent example of how he dealt with superiors, with deference, playfulness and a dogged persistence that will be a feature of his correspondence in later years.[17]

The first card he plays is friendship. After opening with the usual 'Most Reverend (*Reverendissimo*) Father Abbot', he stops after just one sentence and addresses Casaretto with unaccustomed familiarity, 'Dear (*Caro*) Father Abbot': 'allow me to speak to you with affection more than with reverence, since your present status of Superior cannot make me forget the older one of friend'.

Now he takes his superior/friend through the steps of the journey that have brought him this far, at every turn reminding Casaretto of the promises he had made:

Remember, I beg you as warmly as I am able,

remember that two, nearly three, years ago I revealed to you my plan to dedicate the rest of my days to apostolic life in some foreign land; that you had the goodness to promise to help me with that plan; and to this end you opened your home here to me and in order to give me a legitimate reason for being here, despite the rules that prohibited it, you entrusted me with the teaching position in the school;

remember, I beg you, that when I sought the counsel of pious, prudent and eminent persons they encouraged me to pursue my plan as an inspiration that came from the grace of God and not to look on it as a mere whim;

remember, finally, what I have told you several times, that if I remain here any longer, I am afraid of losing my vocation for the reasons I have mentioned to you, and therefore I believe I am obliged to use every means to accomplish my plan as soon as possible.

The most powerful means I believe is the protection Your Reverend Paternity has promised me several times, and I firmly trust that you will grant this to me wholeheartedly even in the face of any slight inconvenience my departure might cause you.

After this rhetorical tour de force, he drops the bold familiarity and returns deftly to his usual punctilious courtesy, signing off with a formal flourish:

Allow me to kiss your hand with all reverence and believe me, unalterably, Your Reverend Paternity's
Most Humble and Most Devoted Servant
Raff. Martelli

Casaretto was in no hurry to allow his talented and popular teacher to leave at the beginning of a new academic year, despite Martelli's puzzling protestation that he feared losing his vocation. And so Martelli waited.

Just a few days after Martelli wrote to him, Casaretto received a letter from Salvado. It was all about Salvado sending more novices to Subiaco and said nothing about his departure. But it was written from Cadiz: he was still in Europe! His ship was still in dry dock in London and was not expected to reach Cadiz before March, another four or five weeks at least. Martelli made his decision. He was going to Australia. In a few frantic days, he obtained permission from Casaretto and made his arrangements.[18]

In great agitation, he wrote to Abbot Angelo Pescetelli in Rome. Pescetelli held the important position of Procurator of the Cassinese Congregation and was undoubtedly one of the persons Martelli had intended to consult in January. Like Martelli, he was a former Professor of Rhetoric and English Literature and had had his own troubles because of his liberal views. They were close: Martelli addressed him as *affezionatissimo amico*, 'most affectionate friend', the only abbot he ever dared address as 'friend'. On 9 February, Martelli wrote breathlessly, 'Dear Father Abbot, Great news! Mgr Salvado is still in Spain ... I am flying to join him in Cadiz, to go to Australia with him.' He says nothing about Salvado expecting him, simply: 'We met when he was last here'.[19]

The next day was the feast of Saint Scholastica. Martelli obtained a formal licence stating he was authorised to 'celebrate the Holy Sacrifice of the Mass and carry out other ecclesiastical functions' in any other place, with the permission of the local Ordinary. He saw Casaretto for the last time that evening. The Abbot had taken to his bed, weary and unwell, but received Martelli and gave him his blessing. Martelli left the next day.[20]

Everything happened so fast he did not have time to collect his personal papers, and Casaretto promised Salvado he would forward them at a later date. Martelli travelled light. The only books he packed were for his spiritual edification – the Divine Office, the *Imitation of Christ* – while all his beloved 'profane' texts, even Dante, he left behind. Not because this was a merely spiritual quest: what he was seeking to recover was his sense of himself.[21]

For his unannounced encounter with Salvado, Martelli collected a set of glowing recommendations from leading Benedictines. Casaretto commended him as a 'worthy priest, in excellent health, highly educated, he speaks English and French and has lived in the monastery with great edification'. He was reluctant to let him go, since Martelli was more use to him as a teacher of future monks in Subiaco than as a missionary in Australia. Yet he gave him up 'willingly, because such is the will of God'. Casaretto's secretary, Alfonso Salomone, recommended Martelli as 'respectable in every way'.[22]

In Rome, Martelli visited the Abbey of St Paul Outside the Walls. He collected two letters for Salvado, one a business letter from the Abbot, and the other a warm letter of recommendation from Pescetelli. The liberal-minded Abbot knew all too well the ambiguities of Martelli's recent past and makes a point of praising Martelli's 'exemplary virtue, firm willpower and capacity for the most heroic sacrifices'. He pays Martelli a rare compliment: 'he is a Benedictine at heart, though he does not wear the habit'. Pescetelli hopes that 'in the land of kangaroos' Martelli will find in Salvado 'a special friendship to take the place of many others that he is leaving behind in Italy'.²³

Martelli did not have a passport. The French Ambassador was willing to help, but only nationals could receive a French passport, so he arranged an introduction to the formidable Director-General of Police, Monsignor Antonio Matteucci.²⁴

From Civitavecchia, the Papal States' port on the west coast, Martelli caught the *Requin* to Marseille and Barcelona. The ship's pilot turned out to be a former student of his, Giovanni Giacchetti from Ancona. Martelli's French lessons had helped him find work on the French steamer. The two corresponded in later years.²⁵

Arriving in Barcelona on 4 March, Martelli met Fr Pedro Naudó, a young diocesan priest in the city's splendid Gothic basilica of Santa María del Mar, a short walk from the harbour. Fr Naudó worked as an agent for Bishop Salvado, as Martelli would later do in Fremantle. On this occasion, there were letters and gifts for Salvado that he entrusted to Martelli.

There is no evidence Martelli had been in touch with Salvado after the days they spent together in Subiaco in October 1851. Perhaps he had a sort of standing invitation to join the missionary party whenever Casaretto agreed. Perhaps he took a calculated gamble. Even so, his rushed departure shows not only Martelli's ability to act decisively when he had made up his mind, but also his absolute confidence that he would find a welcome into Salvado's band of missionaries.

The first letter from Martelli to Salvado that has survived is a short one he dashed off in Barcelona the day he arrived there. The language recalls the statements he made to Casaretto two years earlier, when he was examining his conscience and searching for a way forward. He begs Salvado to entrust to him 'those tasks that will be appropriate for my weak capabilities' and adopts Salvado as the 'model' missionary whose example he will attempt to emulate. He begs to be allowed to join his Australian mission:

> I bless those storms which forced you to return to Europe, thus providing me with the opportunity to join you before you once again set sail for the Benedictine Mission, that I beg you to allow me to join, giving me those tasks that will be appropriate for my weak capabilities. Who would have said, a year ago, when I had the good fortune of meeting you in Subiaco, that I would become one of your missionaries! Then I only longed for this secretly in my heart, scarcely daring to hope that my desire would be fulfilled. And now in a few days my joy will be full, as I place myself in your arms. On the 6th I will leave this city on the Balear, which will arrive there on the 13th or the 14th, which will be one of the most beautiful days of my life. May I always be your faithful companion in the labours that accompany the life of a missionary, just as I am certain that I will always find in your person the model of the virtues that are required in a missionary![26]

As he begs to be taken into Salvado's arms with paternal affection, he implores his blessing, recognising him as he always would, as first and foremost a consecrated bishop, an authority and guarantee that Martelli's path will continue within the one true Church.

> In the meantime, please deign to receive me even now with paternal affection and impart your blessing on one who is pleased to declare himself
> Your Right Reverend Excellency's
> Most devoted and humble servant
> Raffaele Martelli

From Barcelona the *Balear* took him via Gibraltar round to Cadiz, where he arrived on 13 March 1853. It was two days after his forty-second birthday.[27]

CHAPTER NINE

Amid the Immense Solitude of the Ocean

April–August 1853

In Cadiz, Martelli found Salvado and Garrido and their 'travelling family' assembled and waiting patiently to sail. There were thirty-seven 'lay brothers', skilled workmen who had taken partial vows. Their crafts would help build New Norcia – carpenters, stonemasons, wheelwrights, shepherds, millers, gardeners, tailors, cobblers, bakers, cooks, infirmarians.[1]

They had waited out the winter in the convent of Santo Domingo. Martelli saw how the Benedictines had creatively maintained their daily routines of prayer, work and study, even in unfamiliar surroundings. He heard inspirational stories of Spanish missions in the Americas, since missionaries leaving or returning to Spain would usually stay in the same convent.[2]

Martelli's position was, from the beginning, anomalous. The only non-Spaniard among them, he was also the only non-Benedictine. Yet in church hierarchy terms, he was second only to Salvado: he was a priest, older than Salvado, and bore the title of Canon, with a background as a seminary professor. His status commanded formal respect, but his humility and warmth quickly earned him affection. Everyone else in the party owed obedience to Salvado by virtue of a monastic vow, whereas Martelli's submission to his episcopal friend was a personal gesture.

A month to the day after Martelli's arrival, the *John Panter* finally docked in Cadiz. It brought the last members of the missionary party from Ireland, the young priest Thomas O'Neill and two lay catechists, Matthew Broderick and Michael Mulrooney.

Passenger ships to the southern seas were still not common. They became more frequent and more comfortable in the second half of the nineteenth century as steam replaced sail. In the middle of the century, it was still common practice to fit out a merchant ship with accommodation below decks, as required.

The *John Panter* was a barque, with three masts, the fore two square rigged and the mizzen, or aftermost mast, fore-and-aft rigged. Built in Newport in 1837, with a displacement of 272 tonnes, the ship was on the smaller side of average. Solid and reliable, to Martelli it seemed 'more of an ox than a horse'. For this voyage, a section of the tween deck aft was partitioned off as a rudimentary dormitory for all but the captain and 'gentlemen passengers'. Conditions in steerage were basic. Above decks, at the stern, the raised quarterdeck contained cabins.[3]

A sailing ship had its own hierarchies of authority, and the arrangement of the spaces on board reproduced the social world of its passengers. The bishop, Salvado, had a cabin to himself, next to the captain. The four priests – Martelli, Garrido, Ribaya and O'Neill – were two to a cabin. First-class passengers were served a bottle of beer each at dinner but no wine. The other cabin above deck was occupied by an Englishman, Henry Robert Grellet. He came to Western Australia to manage the Geraldine lead mine, north of Geraldton, and earned some distinction by surviving the shipwreck of the *Leander* near the Irwin River. He seems to have kept himself to himself during the voyage.

It took two days to load the material for the New Norcia mission, all forty tonnes of it. There were the tools of the artisans' various trades, church vestments and sacred vessels, homeopathic medicines, clothes for Aboriginal people, a small church organ, fruit trees to plant in New Norcia — orange, olive, lemon, jujube — and two beehives.[4]

As the ship was loaded, Martelli wrote letters of farewell to his friends in Rome, Pietro Regnoli and Gaspare Finali, full of the sad presentiment that he was never to return.[5]

On the morning of the 16th, the missionaries processed from the cathedral to the docks. Behind a monk carrying a large cross, followed the missionaries in pairs, then Martelli and the other priests, and finally Salvado, accompanied by monks and clerics from the Cathedral. An 'immense crowd' of local clerics and lay people accompanied them to the water's edge. A cantor sang out the Litany of the Saints, calling on the intercession of Christians from down the centuries, and all chanted in response, 'Pray for us'. The *John Panter* set sail from Cadiz at 9.30 on the morning of Tuesday 19 April.

Martelli kept no written record of the voyage, except for a long letter he wrote to Casaretto during the stopover in Cape Town. Salvado and Garrido kept diaries, as did Manuel Martínez. He was a comb-maker but in Australia was ordained a priest and remained a lifelong friend of Martelli. When emigrants kept shipboard diaries in the nineteenth century, these were not primarily intended for posterity. They were a way to give a meaning to the extraordinary voyage and the migration experience. The diaries of missionaries are of a different kind. Salvado, Garrido and Martínez all knew their travel around the globe, whatever its final outcome, only made sense within the Benedictine tradition. The Australian project was another tile being added to the mosaic of Benedictine history, that lived on in them.

Martelli, for all that he admired and loved the 'Benedictine family', was not a member and his contribution was, as it were, from the outside. What is more, his love of words and writing were an integral part of the hubris that in Italy had led him to repentance and a new start. He took to heart the advice of the *Imitation of Christ*: 'Many words do not satisfy the soul, but a good life refreshes the soul, and a clear conscience leads to great trust in God' (I, 2). After leaving Ancona, he never wrote anything for any kind of audience, beyond church sermons.[6]

On board the tiny ship tossing on the great ocean, the missionaries rose early for morning prayer; the four priests and Salvado would each say their own Mass; towards evening, they would assemble again on deck to chant Vespers and sing the *Salve Regina* and the Litany of the Virgin. Martelli was deeply affected by the choral prayer: 'in that melancholy hour and amid the immense solitude of the ocean, this chanting inebriates the soul with a dear and holy sadness'. He remembered that Dante, in the *Purgatorio*, heard the pilgrim souls singing the *Salve Regina* and *Te lucis ante* ('Before the ending of the day'), a prayer for protection from the dangers of the night. Martelli felt the same nostalgia Dante so famously described:

> It was now the hour that melts a sailor's heart
> and saddens him with longing on the day
> he's said farewell to his beloved friends.
>   and when a traveller, starting out,
> is pierced with love if far away he hears
> a bell that seems to mourn the dying light.[7]

The irreligious crew of hardened sailors were bemused by the daily ritual of communal prayer. Martelli saw Salvado's diplomatic skills in an incident he recounted with admiration to Casaretto. One evening, as the missionaries began their chanting, the sailors started singing their own songs 'with an accompaniment of a demon-like noise and raucous laughter'. This despite a contract with the captain that guaranteed them freedom to carry out all religious practices. 'Monsignor, with his presence of mind, averted any danger', Martelli related with admiration:

> The next morning he went up to the head of the singing gang and complimented him on his fine voice and the good fun he had the previous evening. The good fellow was either satisfied or embarrassed to hear this. In any case he took no further part and the others quickly grew tired of it.[8]

After morning devotions and the Divine Office, the missionaries would study, read and write, and busy themselves with their crafts. Bishop Salvado and Brother Oltra led choir practice. All attended English language classes from Fr O'Neill and the two catechists. Just as in Subiaco, Martelli was learning his English from Irishmen, perhaps also picking up the lilting accent.[9]

Martelli had no craft to exercise, and he found it difficult to study on the rolling ship. At night, the lighting was not enough to read by. He could not tolerate being idle. The boredom, he dourly told Casaretto, was a 'serious matter'.[10]

He found distraction in the wildlife he saw for the first time. He told Casaretto about the sea birds, whales, sharks, dolphins and the Portuguese man-of-war jellyfish. The repetitive diet was varied by fish the sailors caught, mostly bonito. One day, a flying fish landed on deck and was found to be very tasty. As they approached Cape Town, the sailors tried to catch some albatrosses, luckily without success. They did manage to trap some cape pigeons, which made a good dish once their oily flavour was disguised by 'a sauce the English call *curry*'.[11]

The ship's captain was Master Robert Austin Clarkson – Salvado considered him 'sober and prudent'. According to Martelli's and Salvado's reports, Captain Clarkson planned to sail from Cadiz to Fremantle without stopping. The earliest sailing ships to Australia would round the islands off the west coast of Africa and then move away from the coast. This was to avoid the

'South Atlantic High', an enormous high-pressure system that could keep ships becalmed for days, even weeks. Prevailing winds took ships diagonally across the Atlantic to Rio de Janeiro. Since Rio is roughly on the Tropic of Capricorn, ships would swing south-east for Cape Town quickly, picking up the westerly trade winds. From there the Roaring Forties would bring them straight to Western Australia.

As the technology of sail improved, ships no longer used Rio as a stopping point. They followed the same route out into the Atlantic but turned east at the latitude of Rio without making landfall. By mid-century, ships could also cut out Cape Town and would follow 'the Great Circle', swinging out around the Cape of Good Hope to pick up the strong westerlies as soon as possible.

This seems to have been Captain Clarkson's plan. At the beginning of the journey, the weather had been mostly kind and they made good speed to the Equator. At the Tropic of Capricorn, 1500 kilometres out from Rio, the captain turned the helm. From south-south-west, he headed east-south-east. However, the South Atlantic High moves north as the southern hemisphere heads into winter. Perhaps Captain Clarkson had not allowed for the long delay in Europe, for he sailed right into the doldrums. If Martelli and Salvado were right and Clarkson had planned not to stop at the Cape, it was a serious miscalculation.

In his letter to Casaretto, Martelli described the terror of dead calm amid the endless ocean. On 4 June, they covered a mere 40 kilometres (compared to over 250 kilometres per day at the beginning of the trip) – and that was all in an easterly direction without moving a single mile south. Some days the calm was so complete the ship would not respond to the helm.

Martelli recalled the very real fear that the water would run out. The captain cut rations to a half and then to a third and then a quarter. By 15 June they were down to 19 gallons (85 litres) per day – for the sixty-one persons on board, to say nothing of the animals. They were still 3000 kilometres from the Cape. A triduum of prayer was answered in the form of an English steamer. The

Protomelia was carrying coal from Tyneside direct to Aden. At first it showed no interest in the *John Panter*'s signals, but luckily it needed a letter to be taken to Cape Town. Five of the *Panter*'s crew rowed over to collect the letter and explained the dire conditions on board. The captain relented and accompanied the crew back to the *John Panter*.

Benjamin Lodwick was just twenty-nine years of age and on his first voyage as captain. While the barrels of water were being transferred, Lodwick was treated to lunch with the captain and first-class passengers of the *John Panter*, proving a most agreeable companion. The company of the urbane young Englishman and the arrival of the water made 17 June, for Martelli, the 'happiest day of the journey'.[12]

Even so, when the lookout caught sight of Table Mountain on the feast of St Peter and St Paul, 29 June, they were down to their last barrel of rainwater, with just one barrel of salted pork.

The crew, with Salvado, stayed on board ship. Only the four priests were allowed ashore with the captain. It was cold, wet and windy, so Martelli and fellow priests Garrido, Ribaya and O'Neill spent just two days buying all manner of supplies. It was no weather for sightseeing but they did visit the newly constructed Cathedral, dedicated, like Martelli's church in Ancona, to St Mary – but here at the tip of Africa it was Our Lady of the Flight into Egypt – and able to hold no fewer than 2000 people. Martelli, the Canon, and Garrido, the monk, both observed approvingly that the Divine Office was recited daily in the Cathedral.

On Sunday 3 July, the weather lifted and with it the spirits of the missionary party. They woke to the spectacle of Table Mountain covered with snow, towering above the picturesque bay and city. The harbour revealed new delights: a large whale passed so close 'we could have jumped onto its back' and there was bird life everywhere – fowls, pigeons, ducks and geese, albatrosses and penguins. Martelli and the other priests returned from the city with several hundred oranges, four dozen 'beautiful, large cabbages' and fresh meat. The missionaries and the crew left on board had been fishing. Some caught small fish with lines; others improvised lobster pots from sacks, placing a cask hoop in the top and a weight in the bottom to make them sink. They caught a hundred lobsters in a single day and 'dined royally'.[13]

Out of Cape Town, they reached as far south as the 38th parallel, on the edge of the Roaring Forties, then turned east. The storm started to build almost as soon as they were on the open sea. By Sunday 10 July, the rolling of the ship made it impossible to say Mass or even to stand on deck. During the night of the 14th, the storm grew into a full hurricane and when they woke the following morning, Garrido recalled the sea 'was the very image of Hell'. They now knew the terror of a winter storm in the Southern Ocean. The captain trimmed all sails except one on the main mast. They were at the mercy of the mighty elements.

At 10.30 that morning, a massive wave broke over the stern. It took away part of the wooden superstructure, destroyed the compass and smashed the windows of the first-class cabins. It became difficult to control the helm. The *Panter* was running before gale-force winds. Wave after wave poured through the above-deck cabins and down through the hatches onto the monks huddled below. There was a real danger of being 'pooped' – overwhelmed by a wave from the stern and either swamped or turned broadside to the waves and rolled over.

The captain took evasive action. He veered sharply to starboard, cutting across the waves and the wind. The ship now took the full fury of the storm against its side. It pitched and rolled horribly: 'we continually found ourselves now in deep gullies between mountains of water, now touching the clouds with abysses to left and to right, so deep they filled us with terror'. The ship's bell rang out continually, like the tolling of imminent doom.[14]

Below deck, there was water everywhere and it was impossible to bail it all. Holes were drilled so that the water would collect in the holds and scuppers. The monks worked the pumps in half-hour shifts because water 'was pouring in everywhere'. Those who were not working prayed to Mary Help of Christians for deliverance:

Morning star, pray for us.
Health of the sick, pray for us.
Refuge of sinners, pray for us.
Comforter of the afflicted, pray for us.
Help of Christians, pray for us.

While Salvado tried to salvage his belongings above deck, Garrido and Martelli went below. They spent the long winter night in steerage, being tossed this way and that as the ship shook and shuddered. The battened hatches kept them locked in below but the huge waves still managed to pour through, soaking them in icy water. The noise down below in a sailing ship was deafening. The shrieking wind and the noises of the sea; the waves crashing against the ship, ringing out 'like cannon shots'; the great timbers creaking and groaning; the solitary stormsail on the main mast letting out a mighty sound like a clap of thunder: all the noises of the storm were horribly amplified in the cavernous, confined space below deck. As the storm raged through the endless night, the passengers lost hope. They recited prayers of contrition and penance, entrusting themselves to their Maker, and two English members of the crew, one of them a Protestant, approached Garrido to make their confession.[15]

Martelli rose early the next morning, the feast of Our Lady of Carmel. When a rainbow shone through the storm clouds, all were sure the Virgin to whom they had entrusted their journey would deliver them from mortal danger. By midday, the worst of the storm had passed, and the *John Panter* was able to reset its sails heading east to Australia along the 36th parallel. The storm would remain in their memories for ever: years later, Garrido reminded Salvado that 16 July was the day when 'we began to live again on the *John Panter* when, after the storm and threat of shipwreck, we were saved by the intercession of Mary'.[16]

The clear night skies at these southern latitudes now revealed something the missionaries could only have seen by crossing to this side of the globe, a constellation invisible in the northern hemisphere. Martelli must have shared the exultation and confidence that Salvado recorded at this 'splendid guide to mariners and consolation to every good Christian':

> We had the Southern Cross directly in front of us, perpendicular to our sight; it was wonderfully brilliant and its beauty gave us a symbolic ladder on which to climb to adore Him who on the Holy Cross redeemed the world from the bonds and power of the prince of Darkness.[17]

As they approached the Australian coast, the weather became more regular, progress was good, and daily routines of prayer and work were resumed. They enjoyed the company of dolphins and seals; on 12 August they saw a Cape Leeuwin pigeon, and the next day, fish appeared to jump out of the water around the ship. All augured well for their arrival. The winter sunset Salvado described as 'the most brilliant, beautiful and sublime I have ever seen. Such a sight as this is rarely to be witnessed in the Southern Hemisphere and never in the Northern. The vividness of the colours, especially the blues and violets, and the beauty of the small clouds formed an enchanting sight'.

Finally, at 1 pm on the 14th, 'Land ahoy!' rang out from the lookout atop the main mast. He had spied the lighthouse on Rottnest Island and by nightfall the passengers on deck could see its beam of light, revolving once a minute. Martelli concurred with his Spanish companions that the Blessed Virgin had arranged for their safe arrival on Australian soil to fall on the feast of her Assumption.[18]

The next day, 15 August, the pilot came out and guided them into Gage Roads, where they dropped anchor at 11.30 am. Bishop Serra came as quickly as he could but a strong sou'wester meant he could not make it out to the ship until after dark, at 8 pm. He greeted each member of the missionary party, asking their name and office, encouraging them in the work to which they were called. The strong winds kept them all on board all the next day, until finally, on Friday 17 August, they were rowed ashore. It was 'four months less three days' since they had left Cadiz.[19]

Raffaele Martelli stood for the first time on Australian soil. When all were on land, they recited together the *Te Deum*, the fourth-century hymn of praise sung in thanksgiving on solemn occasions:

> We praise You, O God; we acknowledge you as Lord [...]
> Every day we thank you. And we praise your name forever, for centuries of centuries [...]
> Let your mercy, O Lord, be on us, for we have hoped in you.
> O Lord in you have I hoped: let me never be put to shame.

No wonder Martelli always felt a unique bond to the men with whom he had stared death in the face, crossing the Southern Ocean in the middle of winter. It was common for the early colonists to 'quote the name of the vessel in which they sailed, almost as a certificate of membership in a special society'. Martelli would often refer to the 'band of *JohnPanterini*', those who like him had sacrificed everything to serve their God in unknown lands, those who with him had faced the terrors of the mighty ocean cooped up in their tiny ship, and with whom he now prepared to bring Christian faith and culture to the Great South Land.[20]

CHAPTER TEN

A Bare and Melancholic Shore

1853–1855

Raffaele Martelli's dream of sharing in Salvado's work of 'christianising and civilising' the Aboriginal people of the fifth continent was shattered even before he set foot on Australian soil. As they sat cooped up on the *John Panter* waiting to be rowed ashore, Bishop Serra brought the new arrivals up to date on the wash-up of Perth's 'ecclesiastical civil war'.[1]

When Serra took over the diocese of Perth in 1852, he became Apostolic Administrator, because the first encumbent, John Brady, refused to renounce his title as Bishop of Perth. Faced with crippling debt, Serra prioritised Church structures for the rapidly growing European population. He would not divert scarce resources to a mission aimed at the small number of Aboriginal people in the colony.

Serra had begun construction of a new monastery on land close to the city, called 'New Subiaco'. The name speaks of the location. Italian *Subiaco* is from the Latin *sub lacum*, 'below the lake'. When

Emperor Nero built himself a summer villa there, he made three artificial lakes, one of which survives as the Lago di San Benedetto. Serra dreamed that his New Subiaco, overlooking lakes Monger and Herdsman, would be the heart of Catholicism in Western Australia, just as Bishop Polding was developing Catholicism in Sydney on Benedictine foundations. All Benedictines in Western Australia were now based in New Subiaco, except for a skeleton staff running the farm at New Norcia, with all proceeds going to the Perth diocese.[2]

The missionaries on the *John Panter* were appalled. The Benedictines were bound by obedience. Salvado wrote immediately to Cardinal Fransoni, Prefect of Propaganda Fide, begging for his Bishop's title to be revoked, so he could dedicate himself entirely to the mission at New Norcia.[3]

But what about the two priests, Martelli and O'Neill, not bound by monastic obedience but badly needed in the diocese? Serra had come prepared. His secretary, Martín Griver – a Spanish priest and a non-Benedictine – had drawn up a document for the three priests to sign. The document bears the signatures of Raffaele Martelli and Thomas O'Neill, and of Griver. It is dated 16 August 1853.[4]

The signatories declare it is 'our intention and free will to contribute to the honour and Glory of God devoting ourselves to the service of these Missions under the direction of the Right Revd. Dr Serra Apostolic Administrator of this Diocese and Missions and of His canonical Successors'. In return, the Bishop would 'paternally take care and provide for all our temporal wants and that in lodging, in dressing and supporting us, as far as the circumstances of the mission will allow, will not permit us to be in want of any thing proper of a clergyman'.

The contract had a fixed term and a financial guarantee: the Ordinary of the diocese will not 'deny us the means for the passage to our own home, or to some another mission, in case of our requesting it, after having served ten years to this Mission'. Why ten years? This was common among Benedictines as a period for negotiating discernment and commitment: Abbot Casaretto sent missionary oblates overseas for ten years before allowing them to make their solemn profession, and Salvado introduced the practice of novices waiting ten years after simple vows before making their final profession.⁵

Serra saw, from their first dealings, that the Italian priest was intelligent and capable. He told Archbishop Polding how impressed he was by the 'very respectable looking Canon of Ancona'. While Martelli bowed to Serra's ecclesiastical authority, his affections were clearly for Salvado. This was the seed of future troubles.

So, Martelli moved to Perth and set about learning the ways of colonial Australian society. He offered priestly service in the three settlements on the Swan: Fremantle, Perth and Guildford.⁶

The pressures of running a growing diocese with insufficient resources and the inconvenient presence of the charismatic Salvado proved too much for Serra. On 15 October, the Administrator took afternoon tea in Perth with Salvado and three priests. Serra exploded in bitter resentment:

> It's a terrible thing. Everywhere I go, everyone I talk to, whatever place I am, all I hear about is Monsignor Salvado. Monsignor Salvado is the man of peace. Monsignor Salvado is the man of order. He is the Bishop. He is the Administrator. He is the one who fixes everything. He gets all the glory and I, after so much sweat and so many sorrows, I am nothing, I have become less than a shoemaker.⁷

Martelli may not have been present, since the three priests were probably all Benedictines, but he would have heard the news immediately. He must have been horrified, not just by the petty meanness, but rather by the threat to the unity among the small band of missionaries. First, the mission to the Aborigines had been abandoned, and now the 'Benedictine family' to which he had entrusted his destiny was tearing itself to pieces.

Salvado had not yet been allowed back to New Norcia. Serra promised to accompany him on a visit, but after his outburst he felt indisposed and gave Salvado permission to go without him.

Martelli may have gone with Salvado. In a letter of July 1854, Martelli recalls seeing a number of crucifixes 'at the Mission', on some earlier visit. It is odd, however, that Salvado's diaries make no mention of Martelli travelling with him in 1853.[8]

With Salvado out of town, Serra left for Rome to resign his responsibilities in Perth. By the time the news reached Salvado, Serra was on the road to Albany to catch the first boat from King George's Sound. All temporal and spiritual authority in the diocese was left in the hands of the reluctant Salvado, the 'Acting Apostolic Administrator'.

Salvado never wavered from his commitment to establishing the mission in New Norcia. However, Benedictine obedience taught him that the unwelcome task of developing the diocese in Perth and establishing the community at New Subiaco would, under the unerring guidance of Providence, ultimately lead to good. There was much to be done.

Perth was growing quickly. After its foundation in 1829, the Swan River Colony had struggled to establish a self-sufficient economy. Then, as New South Wales and Victoria repudiated convict transportation and in the West pastoralists and merchants clamoured for cheap labour, London redirected convicts to Perth. Between 1850 and 1868, the convict system transformed the face of the new colony. It brought 10,000 male convicts, the Pensioner Guards and their families (2500 in all), and 2000 serving girls.[9]

The arrival of the *John Panter* doubled the number of priests in the colony. Frs Martelli, Garrido, O'Neill and Ribaya joined Pietro Aragon OSB, Timothy Donovan and Martín Griver (and the Benedictines Ramón Terrés and José Pujades who left the diocese soon after). One of Salvado's first tasks was to assign his priests to the growing Catholic population.

The citizens of Fremantle were clamouring for a priest. The port was home to 258 Catholic residents as well as most of the 431 Catholic convicts in the colony. The present chaplain, Fr Timothy Donovan, would travel an hour or two on horseback from Perth. When Governor Fitzgerald received a petition with three hundred signatures, he allocated funding for two resident priests: Donovan for the free population and Thomas O'Neill as prison chaplain.[10]

O'Neill was young, not quite twenty-four years of age, and sincere but inexperienced. Barely a month into the job, he was suspended from all duties after an unseemly exchange of accusations with the Anglican chaplain. Catholic prisoners rioted, armed Pensioners rushed to the prison and the townspeople barricaded themselves in their homes. Over a hundred men were confined to cells on bread and water and six of the ringleaders were flogged. Bishop Salvado publicly distanced himself from O'Neill's actions and the whole matter quickly blew over. Salvado moved Donovan into the prison position, and Martelli was appointed town chaplain. So it was that, fully a century before the mass migration following the Second World War that brought 3000 Italians to Fremantle, the port settlement had its first Italian priest.[11]

In Fremantle, Martelli began learning the trade of parish priest. Everything was new: 'My tasks, which for anyone else would be a trifling matter, take up all my time, considering that I must pay attention to the smallest things since this is a new office for me'.

He moved into the priests' house on the corner of Henry Street and High Street. This was next door to the first St Patrick's. The rudimentary presbytery was cold, windy and prone to flooding when the sou'-wester drove high tides up from the Esplanade. Martelli lived in one room. He asked Salvado for a 'sacred image' or crucifix to hang above his bed, since 'I receive parishioners in the same room in which I sleep'.[12]

He found Fremantle unattractive, as many Europeans did, especially since he was separated from Salvado and his *John Panter* companions. He wrote to Garrido, 'Leaving superiors and friends in Perth was bitter for me and I was somewhat sad in this new and unlovable place'. Curiously, for one who had grown up in a port city, he added,

> I love seeing green fields and leafy plants up close: the sea I love to see at a certain distance as if in the background of a painting:

and here, it is only a bare shore, and a melancholic one too. Nevertheless, I am beginning to get used to it.[13]

With the move to Fremantle, Martelli's letters to Salvado begin to appear in the archive. The mail service was efficient, first by horse with riders exchanging mailbags halfway, then steamers began a twice-daily service between city and port. In the evening of 18 June 1854, Martelli wrote to Salvado in Perth and was disappointed not to receive a response the next day: 'Perhaps Your Excellency has already replied to my letter of last night, but your response has not arrived yet'.[14]

Martelli's letters have survived through Salvado's careful conservation of all manner of records to do with the mission. They give us Martelli's own description of his new life and a new appreciation of his character and personality. Salvado visited Fremantle from time to time, and Martelli would travel to Perth to see Salvado – with the latter's permission. They met on average once a month and, between visits, they continued the conversation on paper. Martelli wrote on average once a fortnight.

The mechanics of life were onerous and time-consuming, and everything had to be paid for out of a modest government salary and the meagre Sunday collection. Bread was expensive in Fremantle, so perhaps Salvado could send some from Perth and put books in the bread bag to save on postage. His gratitude to Salvado was not so much for the things he sent as for the confidence he showed: 'I thank you for everything. I shall not fail to take advantage of the freedom you so kindly grant me to ask you for anything I may need.'[15]

Most of his parishioners were Irish. Unlike other Australian colonies, the majority of Catholic clergy in Perth were not from Britain or Ireland, which meant Catholic-Protestant relations did not automatically have an ethnic or political dimension. Still, there were pastoral challenges and Martelli sought advice and permission on everything. The issue of 'mixed marriages' tested all missionaries: Propaganda issued universal guidelines in 1855. While some Australian bishops refused the sacraments to parents who sent their children to other schools when there was a Catholic school available, Martelli was happy that Salvado did not follow this approach.[16]

Martelli could be punctilious in following canon law. He would withhold absolution in the confessional if a Catholic in a mixed marriage failed to bring up their children as Catholics. Yet children should not be punished for the sins of their parents:

> You will recall the case of a certain man from Fremantle, who is sending his daughter to a Protestant School. The girl is at the age that she can make her first Communion and is at present coming to me for the necessary instruction. When this is done, I am inclined to admit her to that Sacrament, considering that her not coming to the Catholic school is not her fault, but her parents'. I will do nothing, however, without first having your approval.[17]

Martelli enjoyed teaching catechism to prepare children for the sacraments, but found many adults perfunctory in their faith, attending Sunday Mass but doing little more. 'Nevertheless if I ask them for some money for the expenses of the church, they do not deny it to me, and I must be satisfied with this.'[18]

He was also responsible for convicts in the North Fremantle hiring depot. They had a 'ticket of leave' allowing them to seek employment. Martelli would cross the Swan to say Mass at the depot on Sundays and Wednesdays. He noticed the difference between Irish and English: 'In North Fremantle, my small flock of Irish prisoners has disappeared. Now I only have nine ticket of leave men, English, all very cold, and tense, poor things, who do not seem to have the resolve of the earlier men.'[19]

Salvado told him that he was only required to visit the convict depot in North Fremantle on Sundays. Obedience did not exclude a little legalistic one-upmanship. Martelli argued that since Salvado had not told him not to visit the depot mid-week, just that he was not obliged to, he would continue exactly as before. To soften the nit-picking, he deftly describes his visits to the depot as a *passeggiata*, a word evoking the ritual twilight promenade in piazzas all over Italy.[20]

The weekly foray over the river to North Fremantle gave rise to an incident that Martelli recounted to give his friends a good laugh at his own expense. We can imagine Salvado reading the letter out to the community in New Subiaco, translating Martelli's Italian into Spanish for the lay brothers as they roared with laughter to hear of the learned and venerable Canon transformed into an incompetent instructor of horses. 'Most revered Monsignor, among your heavy and often thorny concerns', the letter opens with ironic gravity,

> may it not displease you to receive this letter, written with the intention of offering you and our common friends material for a good laugh. According to what Your Excellency had organized with Mr Ronayne, I received a horse from him this morning for my usual Sunday excursion, an old cart nag, heavy and bad-mannered, but good enough for my short trip. After arriving at the river crossing, I ask for the boat. The boat is not there: it has gone to Fremantle to be repaired, and may not be back for a month. What to do? Go back and take the horse back home, no, because I would have wasted too much time. And I could not leave the horse there either, since there was no one to leave it with. For a moment, I thought of crossing the river without getting out of the saddle: I am lucky that I did not let myself be convinced by such an ambitious thought, but reflected that, not knowing the beast, it should not be risked. Then one of the ferrymen suggested I get off, unsaddle the horse, get in the small boat and pull the poor beast behind while it swam across. Without hesitating I immediately accept the proposal, but what do you think? When the old animal felt the ground missing beneath its feet and himself being pulled by the boat, I think he thought he was lost, and I thought so too when I saw him with his feet almost in the air, and his head above the water only enough to be able to breathe, and I heard him moaning like someone who has come to their end. But, as it pleased God, we

reached the other side and I was freed of that anguish; and I easily reached my destination. After finishing my business, I returned: but having reached the river, we could not go through the same scene: the river was too rough and the horse would have been in too much danger. I had to give the horse to someone there and come back to town on foot, where I arrived more worn out than other times, and sorry for what had happened. I immediately told Mr Ronayne about it, so he could arrange to get his animal back, because later, when the wind had dropped, or so I thought, he could come back the way he went. But things happened differently. I heard, this evening, that Mr Ronayne had to send his horse to cross the bridge in Perth and that consequently, he will charge me both for the horse and for the man sent to bring it back. In conclusion, instead of enjoying a comfortable horse ride and going on my journey like a gentleman, I endured weariness, anguish, displeasure and, what is worse, I have caused the mission who knows what expense, to say nothing of the laughter that went on and continues behind my back as an excellent instructor of horses in the art of crossing rivers![21]

There was little work Martelli could do with Aboriginal people he encountered. He did what he could. A man called Jack ended up in the Military Hospital. He had an old wound from a gidgie (spear) which had not healed and he was facing a risky amputation. Martelli offered the man spiritual comfort and planned to baptise him, since Jack said he desired it – provided Salvado agreed:

I questioned him. He has lived a lot in the company of Europeans and, having served in a family, learnt some notions of Christianity and some prayers. I spoke to him about God, heaven, baptism, asking whether it would please him to receive this Sacrament. Since he answered yes, I would be happy to confer it upon him, in the case that, after the amputation, his death was certain. Tomorrow I will see the surgeon, who must operate on him. I would like to have your opinion before baptizing him.[22]

Two days later he wrote again. Things had not gone well. Because of his poor health, the doctors thought it unwise to give him chloroform and Jack refused the operation. The outcome was desperate:

> This morning poor Jack was lying in a field, abandoned like a dog; and I do not know whether he had fled or was sent away from the Hospital, where he had received shelter only in case they needed to operate. Poor creature! His body will perish and his soul will not be saved![23]

We hear no more of poor Jack.

Martelli was responsible for the local primary school. The Roman Catholic School for Boys had sixty pupils. Irish catechist Michael Mulroony was appointed full-time teacher. He was lax in accounting for moneys he raised for the mission, including funds he collected from the pupils (without authority) to pay for new desks. When Mulroony found out Martelli was asking around to check this story, he became insolent. He told his pupils they need recognise no other authority than his and that of the bishop. Martelli forwarded Mulroony's letters to Salvado unopened, 'for I am certain its content would embitter me' and prayed *'transeat a me calix iste* [let this bitter cup be taken from me]'.[24]

Two weeks later Mulroony was dismissed. As an act of spite, he locked all the children's schoolbooks in a chest, taking the key with him. In such circumstances, a sense of humour was a precious ally. 'Let us laugh', Martelli confided in Salvado, 'because if we get angry, as I am tempted to do, it will be worse for us'. When Mulroony opened his own school and attendance at Martelli's school plummeted, the bickering took on a dangerous ethnic dimension. Fr Donovan took Mulroony's side and Martelli referred to the Irish priest as Mulroony's 'compatriot': Donovan was English, not Irish, but Martelli clearly classified them both as British subjects. When Salvado ordered Martelli to announce from the pulpit that Catholic boys were not allowed to attend Mulroony's school,

Martelli expected trouble. In a letter to Griver, he underlined an incriminating phrase he must have heard:[25]

> I will comply with the orders of His Lordship: but I have ground to fear that two bad consequences will come of this measure, which I propose to your prudent consideration. The boys will not leave Mr. Moolrony's school; and a great noise will be excited throughout the Town against <u>foreigner clergy</u>.[26]

Sure enough, Martelli found himself reported to the magistrate for threatening excommunication and discrediting people's good names. In the end, Mulroony had a change of heart and came to Martelli on his knees begging for forgiveness. 'I picked him up,' he told Salvado, 'and embraced him, showing him the crucifix. He is the one, I said, you must ask for forgiveness'.[27]

In the port town, Martelli still had contacts with fellow Italians. The Benedictine lay brothers, based in New Subiaco, worked in Perth and Fremantle as directed. Martelli warmed to the half dozen 'Neapolitans' – Salvado's name for them as they were all from the monastery in Cava, near Naples. They were Giuseppe 'Joseph' Ascione the master mason, Pietro Ferrara the infirmarian, Mauro Rignasco the all-round handyman and later infirmarian, Costabile Turi the cook, Alferio Rizzo the gardener, and the two macaroni makers Agostino Balsano and Nicola Filomeno, who was also a tanner.

Nicoletta Salustri was the first Italian woman to migrate to Western Australia. She had a lot in common with Martelli. She was born in Ancona or nearby Senigallia in 1814. Her father, like Francesco Martelli, fought with the French under Napoleon and after Waterloo withdrew his family to English protection on Corfu. There, Nicoletta married an Irish soldier, James O'Byrne, who had to retire from the army for health reasons and signed up as a Pensioner Guard. Martelli baptised their children and grandchildren. He must have seen a lot of them yet they are absent from his letters: the Salustri-O'Byrne family clearly gave their parish priest no cause for concern. James died in 1871 but Nicoletta survived him until 1892, raising their eight children single-handed. In 1994, Salustri Place in North Fremantle was named in her honour.[28]

Letters from Italy were few and far between, and aroused contrasting emotions. In August 1854, as he celebrated his first year in Australia, Martelli received two letters containing the handwriting of fourteen different people:

> Some news was good, some bad. Two deaths of friends, one more painful than the other! *Nihil est ab omni parte beatum*. It is good for me that I receive letters only rarely. The day of their arrival is, for me, a day of emotions, in which bitterness is mixed in good measure with sweetness.[29]

Sometime early in 1854, Martelli wrote to Ancona, to renounce his place in the Chapter of Santa Maria della Piazza and make way for the election of his successor. He had already resolved to make Australia his home, with or without the ten-year contract to the diocese. The title and dignity of Canon he clung to all his life.[30]

His parish work was teaching him to be more tolerant of the foibles and failings of others. 'No stranger to misfortune', he quoted Virgil, 'I am learning to relieve the sufferings of others'. Already in April, Salvado told Garrido, 'Mr Martelli is proving to be a true missionary'. He drew inspiration from the stoical Benedictines who faced a winter under canvas while the new monastery was being built: 'their virtue is, for me, a guarantee of patience, thanks to which sufferings will be turned into a sort of satisfaction. As he mused to Garrido, he seems to be trying to convince himself:

> They are laying the foundation of a good work that, blessed by the Lord, will one day turn out both glorious for religion and useful for humanity: we cannot tell when this day will be, and who knows whether we will ever see it: but he who works for God is never in a hurry.[31]

At the same time, he knew exactly what his plans were when his ten years were up. He confessed to Fr Garrido that he was thinking already of his retirement to New Norcia but, recalling the chastening words of the *Imitation of Christ*, 'You were born to work, so why do you look for rest?' (II, 10), he expressed shame at his self-indulgence:

> Meanwhile I want you to know, Fr Garrido, that New Norcia will be, I desire and hope, the resting-place for my old age, if God grants me a long life. From time to time I dwell longingly on this project, but then I feel ashamed to be thinking of rest when I have scarcely begun the hard work.

With the dawn of 1855, Salvado rang the changes and Martelli and Donovan swapped roles. Martelli now had his first experience as chaplain to the Convict Establishment, as the prison was known.[32]

Martelli stamped his own authority on the chaplaincy position. He was unbending in defending the rights of Catholic inmates. When guards accompanied Catholics to Sunday Mass but remained seated throughout the service, he spoke to the Superintendent, 'who gave orders for this impertinence to be discontinued'. Catholic–Protestant relations were a minefield and Martelli's predecessors had taken opposite but equally unhelpful approaches: Irishman Fr O'Neill leapt imprudently to the defence of his convict countrymen, whereas Englishman Fr Donovan rebuilt the relationship with the authorities at the expense of the Catholic prisoners who felt undefended by him. Irish pioneer Joseph Thomas Reilly recalled that:

> Canon Martelli was as accomplished as he was learned, and his strong personality not only had an effect on the authorities, but also exercised a most salutary influence over the Irish convicts themselves. Canon Martelli comforted the men, defended the Church, and in a short time made the authorities clearly understand that the Catholic convicts should be perfectly free to exercise their religion.[33]

We know little else about Martelli's life in 1855. There is just a handful of letters to Salvado from January–February and then just a single letter in November. This is because they saw a lot of each other during the year and their conversation did not need paper to stay alive. Salvado was often in town and they also travelled together, including a week at New Norcia after Easter.³⁴

On 24 May 1855, Bishop Serra returned on the *Lady Amherst*, bringing more missionaries for the diocese. On the Fremantle wharf, Martelli recognised youthful faces from Subiaco: Spanish priest Ildefonso Bertrán and Irish novices Christopher Reynolds and Frederick Byrne. The novices were placed in charge of the Fremantle school and shared a room in the presbytery. Serra asked Martelli to take them 'under his care, fixing their timetable for rising, study, Mass, and recreation, and how to teach in the school etc'. This is a little surprising given that Martelli was not living by the monastic rule, but Serra told Salvado, 'the shadow of Martelli alone will help the boys' school go well'.³⁵

Also on the *Lady Amherst* were four young women of a new French order, St Joseph of the Apparition. Serra told Martelli his reason for bringing them to Perth was to 'hinder the Sisters of Mercy from becoming bold and to keep them in subjection', at least according to Reynolds and Byrne, who had their own troubles with Serra. Martelli and Salvado accompanied the nuns to the draughty, waterlogged residence in Henry Street, where they soon opened their first school. The four spoke no English and were directed to make their regular confession to Martelli, who spoke good French. The youngest of the group, Sister Zoe, could not get used to the Italian priest. Or perhaps, thought Serra, it was Martelli who could not cope with the zealous novice since 'she has the ability to make a confession of three or four days last for two hours!'³⁶

Serra resumed control of the diocese. He sent Salvado to visit locations outside Perth, preparing Martelli for a move out of the city.

CHAPTER ELEVEN

The Lord is Walking through Your Town

1854–1855

We do not know when Raffaele Martelli learned to ride a horse. In downtown Ancona, presumably, he had no need and there were carriages for travel to other cities. Horse-riding may have been one of the challenges he encountered in the southern hemisphere. That he never really mastered the art is well documented in his letters and in local newspaper reports which narrate various misadventures, even when he was in his sixties.

By the beginning of 1854, Salvado judged his equestrian skill sufficient to invite Martelli to accompany him on pastoral tours around the south-west of the colony, visiting the areas with Catholic populations: Dardanup, Albany and the Avon Valley.

Over half the Catholics in Western Australia lived outside Perth and Fremantle, yet there were still no priests stationed outside Perth. Salvado turned his attention to the Catholic population spread thinly across thousands of square miles. He travelled to several settlements, gaining first-hand knowledge of the need for a priest and offering the isolated settlers the rare religious consolation of the sacraments. Salvado made a point of taking a priest with him on these visits, for the company and to introduce the new missionaries to the realities of pioneer life outside the city. Martelli was a frequent companion.[1]

During Lent 1854, when he had been just six months in the colony, Salvado invited Martelli on a long tour of the South-West. Salvado sent a long and detailed report to the Society for the Propagation of the Faith in Lyons, which was a major benefactor of the diocese and the mission.[2]

They rode out of Fremantle on 21 March and headed first for Mandurah. Crossing the estuary by ferry, they followed the road recently opened by convicts that took them on the ocean side of the inlet, out along the narrow strip of land between the Indian Ocean and the 'magnificent view' of the estuary. Finding no Catholics in the area, they continued south, moving away from the sandy coastal plain into the forest country of the South-West. Here, all was unfamiliar: shapes, colours and foreign foliage 'that have no dear familiar names' but new names in Noongar to be learned.[3]

The road took them deep into the soft light of the tuart forests. The towering trees of dull-grey bark and pale-green leaves formed a beautiful open forest, kept clear by regular Aboriginal burning, so that visibility was clear for a half mile in any direction. On the inland side, they passed through areas of dark-red marri, named with the Noongar word for blood, that housed huge flocks of parrots and cockatoos. Most imposing of all, the stately jarrah, known to the two travellers as Swan River mahogany. The prized hard wood was already widely used in building. And roadmaking: Martelli had seen convicts laying jarrah slabs on the sandy track between Fremantle and Perth and covering them with limestone and gravel, to build the first road between the city and the port.

Halfway to Bunbury, they spent an hour with the first Catholics they met, Mr and Mrs Loughlin, who lived in a simple hut in the middle of the forest, dreaming of opening an inn for travellers. Approaching Bunbury, the missionaries headed for the home of

Irishman Thomas Little. Riding along the Leschenault Peninsula, they gazed back over the inlet. They had never seen so many sea birds – 'they numbered in the millions' – and marvelled at the black swans, such a contradiction in terms for the European mind.

They expected to find Little at 'Belvidere', the horse-breeding property on the peninsula he managed for Charles Prinsep, who was based in Calcutta. However, Little and his wife Eliza had recently moved to Dardanup, fourteen miles inland. Two of their sons welcomed Martelli and Salvado at Belvidere and the next day rowed them back over to the mainland at Wattle Point, while their horses were taken round the north end of the inlet.

William Little rode out with the two missionaries to his parents' new home on fertile pastoral country at the beginning of the Ferguson Valley. Thomas and Eliza were building a 'little palace of red brick', a solid two-storey residence surrounded by rose bushes and grape vines, with fig trees and stone fruit trees in a crowded orchard. The days in Dardanup were the highlight of the trip.[4]

Thomas Little sponsored Irish Catholic settlement in the Dardanup area, and by 1854, a quarter of its residents were Catholic, the highest concentration of Catholics in the colony. In 1852, Little had offered Bishop Serra land to build a church and the colony's third Benedictine monastery, but nothing came of it. The visit by Salvado and Martelli turned hope into reality. Little confirmed his offer of land and building materials, Salvado started a subscription with a substantial commitment of £25, and others agreed to contribute in cash or kind according to their means. It was all decided there and then.[5]

The next day, Saturday 25 March, was the feast of the Annunciation. The foundation stone was laid and the future church dedicated to Our Lady of the Immaculate Conception. The church, blessed and opened three years later by Fr Garrido, would be the first in the colony outside Perth and Fremantle.

It was Martelli who preached at the hastily arranged dedication ceremony, in front of nearly eighty people. He never forgot this first experience of establishing a church in rural Western Australia:

> In the middle of the bush, beneath the pavilion of the sky, encircled by a small but pious group of faithful, celebrating quietly but with sincerity, the sacred rite was completed, not with extravagant pomp, but with joy felt in the soul! May God grant that while he gives us the favour of opening new Churches on earth for him, he may not deny us the more desirable one of building him a living temple in our hearts and in those of others![6]

The next day being Sunday, Martelli and Salvado said one Mass each so all family members could attend. Martelli's sermon from the dedication ceremony has not survived, but his Sunday homily has. If the survival of so many of Martelli's letters seems a piece of improbable good luck, the existence of around twenty sermons from three decades looks more like a miracle. His letters to Salvado and others are conserved because of the Benedictine awareness that they were the carriers of a tradition, recorded by the faithful and patient collection of the written record of deeds great and small. But how did his sermons find their way to the archive of the mission? He must have sent them too to Salvado.

His surviving sermons are written out in full, on whatever sheets of paper he happened to have, complete with words crossed out, second thoughts, additions. One of the early sermons is written with cross-hatching: short of paper, he came to the end of the page, turned it ninety degrees and then wrote over the text at right angles. In his first sermons, his English is correct but uncertain and stiff, often betraying Italian structures from which he is translating. Though the grammar is not flawless, the content is authentic and genuine. He speaks directly to his listeners, relating the gospel of the day to the world they were building for themselves.[7]

His sermon of 26 March 1854 opens by connecting his tiny bush congregation to the universal church, reminding them of the worldwide community celebrating the same mysteries with them. It was the fourth Sunday in Lent, known as 'Laetare Sunday' from the opening prayer 'Rejoice [Laetare] o Jerusalem'. In churches all around the world and here in the Australian bush, the sombre mood of Lenten penitence lifts for a moment:

> The fourth Sunday of Lent is celebrated by the Catholic Church with greater solemnity than the others and with a kind of temperate joy, as becomes the penitential time of Lent. She borrows the most chearful expressions from the Prophets Isaias and David and allows the voice of the organ to break the long silence and rejoice again the vault of our temples.

It was also known as the 'Sunday of the Five Loaves' because the Gospel of the day was the story of Jesus feeding the crowd of five thousand with five loaves and two fishes (John 6:1-15). As Martelli unpacks the Gospel event, and in particular the reaction of the Jewish people present who wanted to make Jesus their king, we hear the former liberal wrestling with the true nature of Christian liberation:

> The Jews, who expected that Christ would restore temporal prosperity and political independence to his native country, were delightfully impressed by a miracle which showed so tender compassion for the temporal necessities of the people and so astonishing power of relieving them. And the thing went so far that, in the hope that Christ would be pleased with their design and put himself at the head of that multitude to begin his glorious career, they deemed that time was not to be left to proclaim and make him King. But Christ fled again to the mountain himself alone and they were disappointed.

Then, bringing the Gospel events into the life of his congregation, Martelli turned to the Eucharist. The new bread can 'restore strength to the fallen in order to rise again and redeem the misspent time'. He asks his Dardanup congregation, 'Now what return shall we make to our Lord for his gift?' and, in a rhetorical flourish, answers with words of St Augustine:

> Although the Lord is almighty, says St Augustine, he cannot give us any more;
> although he is the wisest of all, he knows not how to give more;
> although he is the richest of all, he has nothing more to give:
> what shall we then give to him?[8]

What we can do is conform our behaviour, our understanding and our will to the 'rule of the cross', what the *Imitation* (II, 12) called 'the royal road of the Holy Cross'. Coming now to his conclusion, Martelli looked squarely at the prosperous Littles and their family, friends and employees. All labour has an eternal dimension, he reminded them:

> You may work in building houses and clearing woods and filling lands as much as you like, to provide for your wants of life and improve the future condition of your children: but remember that we have not here a permanent city, as St Paul says, but are looking for a future and everlasting one... remember that our great business, whatever point of this globe we choose to inhabit, our great business is to save our soul.

Here is the plain talking of one who acknowledges the condition of his listeners without condescension and speaks to their circumstances out of personal conviction. The reminder about the accumulation of riches is directed to them – '*you* may work' – but he ends with the condition they all share – '*we* have not here'. He, like them, has chosen this part of the globe, and through all the travel and toil and trouble the 'great business' for him, as for them, is to save his soul.

The next day Martelli and Salvado rode into Bunbury where they met sixty-two Catholics from the surrounding districts. Everywhere, communities of Catholics begged for assistance in erecting their own chapel where, as Thomas Little put it, 'they could attend Mass without risk of catching a brain fever in Summer or of being drenched with rain in Winter'. Continuing south, they followed the sandy dunes to Ludlow where twenty-seven Catholics congregated to meet the visiting priests. The large number of families with young children meant a Catholic schoolteacher was needed. Some Catholics from The Vasse (Busselton) had not been able to come up to Bunbury or Ludlow, so the two rode on, following the slow sweep of Geographe Bay. They met up at Wonnerup, so there the missionaries made an end to their trip and turned for home.[9]

Everywhere, Martelli and Salvado were overwhelmed by the grateful hospitality of individuals who had not seen a priest in many months, including convicts working on road gangs. They gave instruction and administered sacraments. Martelli gave the statistics to Garrido with great satisfaction: 113 Confessions, 98 Communions, 22 Confirmations, three Baptisms and one Marriage. They were back in time to celebrate Holy Week in Perth and Fremantle respectively.[10]

It was not long after Easter that Martelli saw Salvado again, at the funeral of Fr O'Neill. The young priest was struck down by a fever on Holy Saturday and died after ten days of delirium. Many believed that his death was due to the shock of his treatment by prison authorities in January and the floggings administered to Catholic prisoners who rioted to defend him. O'Neill was the first of the band of *JohnPanterini* that Martelli was to mourn.

This tragedy provided the circumstance for Martelli's second journey to the hinterland. It would have been O'Neill's turn to accompany Salvado on the next round of visits. Martelli gladly took his place, and in late May rode out with Salvado to Guildford and the settlements over the eastern hills. They spent another fortnight on the road, visiting families, communities and prison depots in Toodyay, York and Northam. They heard confessions of convicts and counselled young Irish girls working in homes.[11]

The mutual respect and the bond of friendship between the two men grew strong through these weeks on the road. They travelled long distances on horseback, forty or fifty miles a day, sleeping in the homes of settlers or in the open with very few comforts. There was little opportunity for pretence or dissimulation. One got to know a lot about one's travelling companion.

Martelli and Salvado had much in common. Both were from comfortable backgrounds, Martelli middle class and Salvado landed gentry. Cultured and well educated, they spoke many languages between them and were at home with the classical tradition of European high culture. Both were music lovers, Martelli a conductor of choirs and Salvado an accomplished pianist. Martelli must have loved the story of Salvado's legendary impromptu recital in the Perth Court House. In May 1846, desperate for funds, Salvado had walked from New Norcia to Perth and improvised a three-hour fundraising concert for the Perth establishment. Martelli knew the popular melodies from Italian opera that Salvado played, especially from one of his favourites, Bellini's *Norma*. This opera was 'the representative masterpiece of its age' and Martelli had seen it on stage at the Teatro delle Muse in 1842 and 1845. He would have relished the ecumenical nature of the recital by the Benedictine Spaniard: the courthouse was made available by the Protestant Governor, the piano provided by the Sisters of Mercy, the programmes and posters were printed for free by a Protestant, and the advertising, also gratis, was in the hands of a Jew.[12]

Martelli admired Salvado's abilities as an organiser, motivator and diplomat. He must have been challenged and inspired by Salvado's cast-iron conviction that the work he was doing was not his own but the work of another. The guarantee of this was the human reality through which the Christian presence in the world continued to manifest itself: the Church. Martelli saw Salvado's unwavering obedience to the decisions Serra, his ecclesiastical superior, left in his hands. Even as Salvado watched his dream of a mission to the Aborigines crumble, he continued to serve the Church in Perth out of obedience.

Salvado was indeed the model of the ideal missionary that Martelli had longed to meet in 1853. As Abbot Pescetelli had hoped on Martelli's departure, Salvado also offered the special friendship to replace those he had left behind in Italy.

Salvado for his part saw Martelli's dedication and qualities in the way he dealt with challenges at the prison and on the long pastoral visits on horseback. From 1855 on, in letters to Propaganda Fide, Salvado would describe Martelli as 'truly most worthy', 'most zealous', 'indefatigable', one who was 'making a name for himself of immortal honour'. In years to come, he recalled Martelli's dedication and ability to endure discomfort:

> Riding with him through the Australian bush to attend to the poor Catholics scattered here and there, I saw how, though weary from riding as many as forty miles under driving rain or beating sun, after a night spent in the bush with no bed, no dinner, no breakfast or lunch than a cup of tea and a crumb of bread, he remained full of courage and energy to face another twenty or thirty miles on horseback.[13]

After these two trips to the South-West and the eastern hills, the next township on the list of pastoral visits was Albany, on King George's Sound. Martelli was sent to 'preach a mission' to reassure and encourage the small group of Albany Catholics, barely 190 of them. He sailed from Fremantle on 1 November.[14]

Three of Martelli's sermons from the Albany mission have survived. He was getting into his stride. The work of travelling long distances to tiny settlements with no resident priest was physically demanding but closer to the missionary ideal than having to deal with colonial administration in towns. He greeted his new congregation warmly:

> My dear friends, I think it is equally gratifying to you to see me as it is to me to meet you for the first time. Although I am unknown to you and you to me, I am aware that you have been long time anxious to see a priest coming to this place and administering to your souls the religious comforts which you have been deprived of for a long while.[15]

For the first sermon, he took as his text the encounter of Jesus with the tax-collector Zaccheus, from Luke 19. He offered the Albany faithful a powerful synthesis of the Christian claim: 'the Lord, I may say, is walking through your town just as he was walking through the city of Jericho'.

Martelli carefully draws the parallels between each moment of the story and the lives of his tiny Albany congregation. Echoes of the *Imitation of Christ* and of Martelli's own spiritual journey come through as he urges his listeners:

> in order to see and to know the Lord you must get out of the crowd by retirement, recollection and hatred of the wicked world; you must run to heaven by disengaging your heart from earthly affections; you must climb up to the tree of the cross embracing the humility and mortification of our Saviour.

He recommends using this mission for moments of self-examination, prayer and silence, in order better to hear the voice of God. He turns to his flock and speaks to them the words Jesus addressed to Zaccheus from the foot of the tree: 'Zaccheus, make haste and come down, today I must enter your house'. The good folk of Albany are urged to welcome Jesus, as Zaccheus did, into their home, rejecting 'any dishonest gain, any unlawful pleasure, any design or revenge, any vicious habit'.

How different are the content and the tone of this sermon from those he preached at the funerals of the young students killed in Italy's patriotic war, less than a decade earlier. And yet, there is the same sensitivity to the importance of social conditions in shaping a life and predisposing a soul: Zaccheus was 'very much attached to his riches which had been accumulated perhaps by violence and oppression of the poor, as the class of men to which he belonged used to do'.

The third and final sermon in Albany was based on the day's Gospel reading, 'The Kingdom of Heaven is likened to a grain of mustard seed'. The Church, from humble and inauspicious beginnings, had spread over the entire world, through the work of those who are 'weak, mean and contemptible in the eyes of men'. What does life in the Church mean for his small congregation in Albany?[16]

Italian Catholic spirituality in the nineteenth century was centred on the moral virtues. These were presented as not intrinsically supernatural but as natural, human virtues reinforced by supernatural intervention. Martelli urges his listeners to make themselves an example of Christian virtue, for all to see and admire. We must all live as 'models to our separated brethren', setting 'good examples of sobriety, justice and piety'.[17]

He encouraged his congregation to take the opportunity to approach the sacraments, to receive confession and communion. For their own good, to be sure, but also to spare him an awkward reckoning with an avuncular but stern Father Almighty:

> Well, Father Martelli, give an account of your stewardship: did all the Catholics at the Sound comply with their duty? To give them an opportunity of doing so has been the chief end of your excursion so long and expensive. Did Mr So-and-so approach the Sacraments? And did Mrs So-and-so? No, my Lord. How grieved He will be at my reply.

Martelli challenges his European listeners to remember they are 'living among a native population'. The contradiction at the heart of the missionary view of the Aboriginal population is already clear in this early reflection: the Noongar are 'our neighbours' yet 'poor creatures'; while they are 'creatures of God bearing His likeness', they are to European eyes 'disfigured'. His exhortation to charity is a response to the evil effects early contact with Europeans is already having on the Noongar:

> Do not fail to reflect that living as you are among a native population you should abstain through charity to them from every disorder which might be a scandal to those poor creatures.

> They are our neighbours, creatures of God bearing His likeness –
> disfigured as it might be – destined to the same knowledge of
> truth, ransomed by the same blood of Jesus Christ. What a crime
> it would be instead of instructing them to do good to teach them
> the evil they do not know, instead of leading them on to virtue
> to plunge them into depravation and sin, instead of gaining them
> to God to push them into the abyss of hell!

After a full month in Albany, Martelli opted for the overland mail cart to take him back to Perth. The trip took anything up to a week and passengers often slept in the open, cooking and eating food with the driver. A new route from Albany to Perth had just opened up, heading to Perth through Williams and Bannister. Martelli chose the older, slower route, so he could visit friends. After Kojonup, the mail cart headed north-west to Dardanup, where he called on Thomas and Eliza Little and admired the progress in construction of the church of the Immaculate Conception. In Bunbury, he blessed the marriage of a Catholic wife and Protestant husband who had earlier exchanged vows before an Anglican priest.[18]

He returned to Albany a year later. Pius IX had proclaimed the dogma of the Immaculate Conception of Mary at the end of 1854 and invited Catholics everywhere to celebrate a Jubilee. It had long been popular belief that Mary was, from the moment of her conception, without that limit on human freedom that tradition calls 'original sin'. Pius IX now gave official definition of the dogma on the traditional date of the feast, 8 December. Marian devotion was a strong feature of nineteenth-century Catholic piety. Benedictines too brought this devotion to the young Australian Church. In April 1854, Pius IX granted a request from Bishop Serra to place the diocese of Perth under the protection of Mary with her title 'of the Immaculate Conception'. That was the same month when the church in Dardanup was dedicated to 'Our Lady of the Immaculate Conception' and eight months before Pius defined the dogma.[19]

In June 1855, Bishop Serra read the Papal Bull to the faithful in St John's Cathedral, announcing that the mother church of the diocese would henceforth be known as the Cathedral of the Immaculate Conception of the Blessed Virgin Mary. A special three-month Jubilee would apply in the Perth diocese, from the feast of the Nativity of Mary on 8 September to the new feast day, 8 December. To obtain the special graces, Catholics were to take Communion, make their Confession and perform other tasks. Serra sent his priests off around the diocese.

Martelli went to Albany, and on his return to Perth he was on the road again, to preach the same mission in Toodyay, Northam and York. He made sure his return route was via New Norcia, since he knew Salvado would be riding to Perth for the celebration of 8 December. In his diary, Salvado noted Martelli's talent for friendship: 'Martelli did not want to miss such a good opportunity to make the journey in company'.[20]

When Martelli had visited York with Salvado the year before, he saw with admiration that some Catholics walked long distances to attend Mass from the visiting priests. Now Martelli reported to Bishop Serra that more than twenty people in York had abandoned the faith, the main reason being the lack of a resident priest. Serra immediately ordered that Martelli should relocate over the hills to establish a Catholic presence there.[21]

Another new beginning.

Lieutenant Edmund Henderson, Toodyay, Green Mount West Australia (1854)

CHAPTER TWELVE

Over the Hills

1856–1857

Dear Monsignor, the life I have begun to live could certainly not be called Epicurean: sleeping on the ground and eating potatoes with rotten eggs!

Raffaele Martelli arrived in Toodyay on 4 January 1856, empty-handed. Bishop Serra gave him nothing, and the £1 he received from Salvado was soon gone. He paid 14 shillings to feed his horse – 'in these parts a priest without a horse is little more than useless' – and soon had nothing left to feed himself.[1]

He celebrated his first Mass in Toodyay the following Sunday to a small congregation. News of his arrival had not spread. But there is no complaining here from Martelli as there had been about his first Fremantle congregations. Instead, he was struck by the kindness of those who did attend, since no one put less than a sixpence in the plate and he collected 5/6d. The next day he began knocking on doors and asking for donations. For meals, he survived on the hospitality of his parishioners. He would have lunch for a week in one house, breakfast in another and dinner in a third. He shared whatever his poor flock could put on their table.

The Catholics of Toodyay were grateful at last to have a resident priest and they welcomed the Italian missionary warmly. They had met him twice before, when he visited with Salvado in 1854 and when Martelli preached the Immaculate Conception mission in November 1855.

The Aboriginal people in the district were from three language groups that meet in the Toodyay area: the Whadjuk of the coastal plain, the Balardong east of the Avon River and the Yued north into the Victoria Plains and New Norcia. The non-Aboriginal population of Toodyay was 874, while at the south end of the valley in York, they amounted to 1100. Salvado selected Toodyay because of the higher number of Catholics, 263 compared to 135 in York. The Convict Hiring Depot brought Catholics among the convicts, Pensioner Guards and servant girls. The valley made the fortune of a few wealthy landowners, but Martelli saw that his parishioners were doing it tough, a few concentrated in the towns but most scattered on small farms across a large area. They were, Salvado recorded, 'very poor'.[2]

Martelli's brief was to establish Catholic infrastructure: church, school and a residence for a priest. In April, a meeting of parishioners voted to build a church in the village, rejecting Salvado's earlier choice of a plot at the Convict Depot, upstream and on higher ground. Martelli started more door-knocking to collect signatures to petition the Governor for a grant of land and contributions or subscriptions.[3]

He depended on the generosity of parishioners for accommodation as well as food. After a few months in straw huts at the Convict Depot, he had to move back down to the village as winter approached. He occupied an abandoned wooden house in the bend of the river that had been used as a stable and was now condemned: 'no windows, no lock, holes everywhere'. Martelli does not mention bed bugs but his successor in Toodyay found them the size of chickpeas. As the winter rains set in, he was exposed to the whims of the river.[4]

Toodyay was built, near the present West Toodyay bridge, on the great bend of the Avon River where it turns sharply south-west and heads towards the Swan. In both winters Martelli spent in Toodyay, the Avon burst its banks and the flat land in the bend of the river was under water for weeks at a time. The surveyors in the 1830s knew only dry years and paid no heed to stories from the Balardong about great floods. Ignoring Aboriginal knowledge would spell the end of the original Toodyay settlement.[5]

Martelli was marooned, a prisoner in the draughty, cheerless house. 'The river runs wild', he told Salvado, 'the water floods from every side and imprisons me for days on end in my solitary shelter'. Sometimes he had difficulty keeping a light burning, and with night-time temperatures plunging to freezing, 'if it were not for the fact that I maintain a hearty fire night and day I would die of cold'. His parishioners up at the depot could not cross the river for Sunday Mass and the collection plate suffered.

He knew such mortification was for his own good but struggled to find the virtue to embrace it. He sought inspiration in Fr Garrido, who had replaced him in Fremantle:

> I know you are quite unmindful of your own inconvenience, and perhaps where there is something to suffer, you will feel the happier. This is not the case with me, destitute as I am of virtue and love of mortification... I am very happy in my position, so quiet, so far any disturb: indeed if I do not turn it to the best advantage of my soul, I have to blame only myself.[6]

The heroism asked of the missionary was measured out in the minutiae of everyday life. What parishioners could not provide, he had to beg from superiors. One parcel from Salvado contained paper, envelopes, a razor, trousers and wine. When he asked Salvado for two pairs of socks and received four, he clothed his humiliation in irony and humour. 'Your Excellency imitates the goodness of God who always grants more than what is asked of him.'⁷

He was constantly on the move, ministering to his scattered flock and seeking the comfort of companionship. He would ride out to isolated farmhouses around Toodyay and down the valley to Northam and York. 'If I do not go, every now and then, in search of my sheep, they will not look for their shepherd by themselves.'⁸

On Sundays, his love of praying the Office in company took him far and wide. He would leave after morning Mass and ride all day to Perth, just to spend an evening with his 'religious family' and recite Vespers with them in the Cathedral. Or he would ride out to the Buckland farm, near Irishtown, for Evening Prayer or to celebrate Mass. The farm manager, James Dempster, was not Catholic, but allowed Martelli to minister to the Irish ticket-of-leave men working on the farm.⁹

Every two months, he rode over to New Norcia. At first, he took the old route via Bolgart, sleeping in the hut of Mr Higgins the shepherd, until he sold up and Martelli had to sleep rough: 'Mr Higgins has sold his place, and I am about to lose the comfort of being able to stop there half-way to Norcia. Never mind! In the bush!' After that, he travelled via Bindoon, saying Mass there. Salvado's diaries from this time often contain the phrase, 'Fr Martelli got lost in the bush again'. One of his bush rides was an opportunity to tell another tale at his own expense that must have lightened the long days of his missionary readers. A business-like letter about the building project ends with a quirky postscript:

> P.S. Yesterday after lunch, returning from the city, where I usually go on Sundays, my Prince pulled a fast one on me. Suddenly he made a sharp movement and abruptly turned around. I was thrown to the ground, where I found myself, I cannot say how, seated comfortably. Thank the Lord, I was not harmed, apart from an electric shock so to speak, which was in truth a little too violent. I was not scared, because I did not have time. The reason

why the horse took fright, can you believe, was the sight of a humble donkey that was calmly grazing along the road. So, in Australia donkeys are so rare that they cause fright! They would not believe it at the antipodes.[10]

The endless days on horseback, the rigours of dwelling and diet, the mortification of having to beg for everything, the battle to extract a land grant from the government, the relentless door-knocking to raise funds – it all took its toll. In that first winter, Martelli shared a misogynistic euphemism with Salvado to describe a persistent health issue that dogged him all his life. On this occasion, the problem had kept him in New Norcia longer than planned.

> The illness that you call the Young Ladies was bothering me and made a quicker return impossible: I stayed on for a week.[11]

Salvado used the word *señorinas* to refer to haemorrhoids. He eschewed the more elegant *señoritas* from official Castilian Spanish, in favour of the word from Galician, the local language of his region of Spain. This became *signorine* in Martelli's Italian and was their code name for that tiresome complaint, common among the missionaries. Treatments could be eye-watering by modern standards. Martelli's Neapolitan friend Mauro Rignasco worked as infirmarian at the mission and was understanding, though direct, in his instructions. 'If you do not wish to subject yourself to applying leeches to the anus because the pain is bad', he advised Salvado, 'at least apply them to your hip'.[12]

The matter was serious for those spending long days in the saddle. Once, he was ordered to ride to Albany only to be replaced at the last minute. He was mightily relieved:

> Travelling by horse, as he will do, for around thirty miles a day for a week is now, or rather would be for me now, a Herculean effort: the Young Ladies known to us would give me unbearable trouble.[13]

The life of the missionary was hard on the soul as it was on the body. The constant travelling to New Norcia and Perth was an attempt to keep at bay the feelings of loneliness that threatened to swamp him. He treasured visits by monks on their way between Perth and the Mission, even when they turned up by mistake, like Bishop Serra, who got lost in a fierce storm with Brother Manuel Martínez and Noongar lad John Dirimera. Martelli was overjoyed when his bedraggled friends turned up on his doorstep and he was able to ply them with large quantities of milky tea in front of a roaring fire.[14]

But such moments of relief were rare. As his first winter in Toodyay wore on, he opened his heart to Salvado: 'I thank you for your witty letter. I am very sad, and going to York does not cheer me up'. The Italian word he uses for the emotion he is feeling is *triste*. He used the same word when he was first posted to Fremantle and had to leave friends and superiors in Perth. The modern dictionary translates it as 'sad, melancholic' but nineteenth-century dictionaries pinpoint the feeling more accurately. While someone who is *melanconico* 'delights in unhappy thoughts', a person who is *triste* 'feels no delight at all'. What was at the heart of this feeling? Martelli knew from Thomas Aquinas that *tristitia* is the 'desire for an absent good'. Being alone in Toodyay meant being cut off from the family to whom he had committed himself and whose 'assistance, direction and protection' he could not do without. The absence could only be filled with letters.[15]

In letter after letter, he asks Salvado to write and to get others to write. He has no other way to keep in touch with friends and with the life of the mind and soul he had left behind. He makes his own the lamentations of Job: 'Here, I have no company, I have no books, miseremini mei, saltem vos amici mei [have pity on me, at least you my friends]'.[16]

Martelli needed no excuse to write. He wrote simply to stay in touch:

> Revered and Dear Monsignor, Although I have nothing important to say, I will write anyway. I am writing because in this

absolute distance from Superiors and friends, writing is a relief, and receiving replies is a real consolation.[17]

Such a confession was not disinterested, however. The mail arrived on Saturdays and Martelli does not hesitate to complain about an empty mail bag:

When the Post arrives here and brings me nothing from Superiors or friends, it is a disappointment that disheartens my spirit, especially when a reply is expected with great agitation, bearing in mind that for the next delivery one must wait for no less than another week.[18]

Letters also record his indignation in the face of injustice. When Bishop Serra's heavy-handed treatment of the Sisters of Mercy went too far, Martelli told their heroic superior, Ursula Frayne, that her plight reminded him of the life of St Francis de Sales, which he had been reading: 'The merciful God allows the souls which he calls to the highest pitch of perfection to be put to the highest trials'. This letter was sent to Propaganda Fide, with others from Salvado and the Spanish priests. It was a bold move to commit such views to paper, and years later, Frayne told Salvado she 'would never forget your or Fr Martelli's kindness'.[19]

At the end of that long, first winter came the welcome news that land was granted for a schoolhouse, presbytery and church, on the corner of the present Toodyay West Road and Picnic Hill Road. Martelli's door-knocking had raised £110, but there was still £50 outstanding. Impatient to start, he reduced the dimensions to just 28 feet long by 21 feet wide – keeping the fireplace – and gave the go-ahead.

By November, the walls were up. It was complete, except for the roof, in March 1857, when Bishop Serra laid the foundation stone. The short report in the *Perth Gazette* was likely penned by Martelli. The style is his:

On last Sunday, the eighth of March, the ceremony of laying the foundation stone of the new Roman Catholic Church of St Mary, at Toodyay, was performed, – if not with the solemnity prescribed by the Roman Ritual on such occasions, at least with the heartfelt joy and sincere piety on the part of the faithful who flocked from every part of the district to witness the long expected sacred rite.[20]

The report praises the generosity of his poor parishioners and especially of the Protestant gentlemen who had donated to the project. 'This edifice, which promises to cheer the loneliness of the Toodyay townsite', he gives away,

is the sheer result of private subscription, it having sprung, one might say, out of the small but cheerfully given contributions of poor labourers, a few pensioners and some gentlemen, who, although of different persuasion, were pleased to lend a helping hand to their fellow colonists, who are less stored [sic] with the good things in this world.

By May 1857, the promised £50 had not materialised, and debts were falling due. No funding could be got from official sources. Serra appealed to Governor Kennedy, praising Martelli as 'one of the most efficient clergymen I have, and gifted with manners which render him amiable, and respected by everyone no matter what faith he professes'. Martelli told the Governor he would be grateful for convict labour from the depot. The Governor declined.[21]

Martelli wrote to Ancona, to the Canons of Santa Maria della Piazza. The Toodyay church would also be dedicated to the Holy Mother, under the Latin title 'Sancta Maria'. He tried to shame them into paying, telling them it had been an Italian – Luigi (Louis) Giustiniani – who built the first Anglican church in Western Australia, the original St Matthew's in Guildford. Arriving in 1836, Giustiniani made enemies of the powerful families that ran the new colony, denouncing them in the press for their mistreatment of the Noongar. After two turbulent years, he departed Western Australia in official disgrace but leaving an honourable memory. For Martelli, the fact that Giustiniani had abandoned Catholicism to become an ordained minister in the Anglican church and take a German wife made him an 'apostate'. Surely the Ancona Canons would send money to 'atone for such impiety'. There is no record of any contribution.[22]

Martelli was now living in fear of being sued: 'I cannot bear to be in the debt of anyone.' What distressed him most was that the creditors might come after his committee of 'poor Pensioners', who stood to lose their properties. He felt responsible and out of his depth, as he confided to Fr Garrido:

> I have run into debts which I am unable to pay off... I have miscalculated the expenses, through want of experience... Perhaps it was not advisable to start the building, but I can plead in my defence that I was pushed on to do so, in high quarters [Serra?], where there must be more experience of such interprises... It is a sad, a very sad case, dear Father Garrido, and I earnestly beg the favour of your prayers to God to enable me to go through this serious ordeal with humble patience to the last and to rescue at least my friends at Toodyay from the danger of the impending storm.[23]

In August, he visited the Catholics of Perth and Fremantle and collected enough money to keep his creditors at bay. He never forgot the trauma. When his successor over the hills, Fr Francisco Salvadó, built St Patrick's church in York, Martelli warned him not to start until he had enough funds to complete the project. 'The lesson I had in Toodyay will be enough for me as long as I live.' Fr Salvadó completed the chapel after Martelli left the valley. St Mary's church was finally blessed by Bishop Serra in January 1859, Martelli recorded forlornly, 'on a working day and, as a consequence, without concourse of the faithful'.[24]

His enthusiasm could be stronger than his scruples. Even before the Toodyay church had its roof, Martelli began planning a church in York. A fundraising tea party planned for January 1858 never took place; however, notes have survived of a speech Martelli prepared for the occasion. It shows how he presented himself to his Australian congregations.

'Dear Christian friends', he planned to address all assembled in York, Catholic and Protestant alike. The Professor of *Eloquenza* opened with a ritual disclaimer: 'do not expect a fine speech from me: if you do, you will be sadly disappointed. I am not an eloquent man'.[25]

He draws a long bow to encourage the settlers to build a Catholic place of worship: 'I beg to remind you that my native land is Italy'. While Italy cannot boast the wealth or military might of other nations, its artistic heritage is unrivalled. This is the result of the fusion of artistic genius and religious faith. 'The far-famed names of Bramante, Michelangelo, Raffaele d'Urbino would not shine with half as much glory, had not Catholicity inspired their mind and guided their hand.'

Martelli backs up this claim with a bold quotation from an unlikely source. The largest art exhibition ever held in Britain had recently taken place in Manchester, 'Art Treasures of the United Kingdom'. There were entire rooms of Italian art. Martelli read of a Protestant gentleman who attempted to pour scorn on the Italian material and in the process captured an important truth: 'Take away Popery from this exhibition and very little of interest will be left'. Martelli picks up the antipapist jibe, directed at the 'so-called dark ages':

> Oh! I can assure you, when my thoughts go back to the beautiful land that gave me birth, what I most regret is not the unrivalled beauty of its climate, not the charming sight of its fertile soil where nature has been lavishing its choicest gifts, not the standing remnants of a greatness and glory which are no more. What I regret the most keenly is the unparalleled grandeur and comeliness of its temples which so perfectly harmonise with the

majesty of the Catholic liturgy and so powerfully help human minds to soar to heaven above.

This is Gioberti's neo-guelph vision, largely discredited by now in Italy but still alive for Martelli. At the heart of the Italian nation stands its Catholic faith. The union of faith and culture is what he misses most. As he concludes with a cry of nostalgia, he seems to know already that he will not see the land of his birth again:

Oh! The Churches of Italy, which I do not expect I shall see any more! I never admired them so ardently as I do now: I did not know before that I loved them so much!

It is to be regretted that this impressive oration was never delivered in the fledgling settlement over the hills.

The two years in Toodyay brought Martelli closer to New Norcia. Salvado was given permission to return in February 1857 and was building up the agricultural activities which would make the mission self-sufficient. Martelli watched in admiration as the monastery farm and schools for Aboriginal children took shape. Salvado was clearly the 'right man in the right place'.[26]

In the autumn of 1857, Martelli wrote from New Norcia to his Roman friend Abbot Pescetelli. His abbatial interlocutor brought out the florid literary style of Martelli's earliest writings, so different from the varied, chatty tone of his letters to Salvado and Garrido. He gazed out the window to

watch, in distant fields, no fewer than twelve ploughs, driven by as many monks, as with the sweat of their brow they make fertile a soil which they are the first to teach how to produce the grains on which man feeds himself.[27]

Martelli learned something else during those two years. We read no more of the complaints he made in Fremantle about former convicts being unfit to teach in the school or tailors who always have excuses for being late with their work. He relied on such people in order to learn 'the exercise of the priestly ministry': brickmaker John Bonser, a Catholic expiree who walked from Toodyay to Perth for his wedding in August 1853, or young ticket-of-leave man Michael Barry from Cork. Barry assisted Martelli with all manner of errands and fund-raising. When he drowned in the Avon during the 1856 floods, Martelli was badly shaken. Distressed that he had to be buried in unconsecrated ground, Martelli appealed for another plot of land for a Catholic cemetery.[28]

Martelli grew to love the people of the region. He made up a word to refer to the good folk of Toodyay. The Noongar name, also spelt Duidgee, was pronounced 'tood-jee' (where 'tood' rhymes with 'could'). Martelli spelled it 'Tuggi', which in Italian is pretty close, just as Garrido concocted a Spanish equivalent 'Tuchi'. Martelli's affection for the inhabitants shines through in the name he coined for them, 'Tuggini', like *Fiorentini* or *Triestini*.[29]

The Tuggini took the learned and energetic priest to their hearts. In 1964, historian Rica Erickson collected a reminiscence from Michael Murphy. He recalled stories from his father, William, who was a teenager during Martelli's years in Toodyay. This contains the only physical description of Martelli:

> He was a very short, dark man, scarcely five feet tall, impulsive in manner, and very quick in his speech. He was a great scholar and spoke five or six languages to perfection. [...] Despite his diminutive stature even the naughtiest urchins, as well as people of all denominations, were won over by his kindliness.[30]

The locals observed the warm friendship that developed between him and the Anglican priest Rev. Charles Harper. They had both come to parish ministry later in life – Harper was a London-trained barrister turned settler-farmer and was ordained a priest at age fifty. They shared an enlightened approach to inter-religious marriages, which became more numerous with the arrival of the Irish girls. Before Martelli arrived, Harper performed marriage services for Catholic couples, on the understanding they would later be solemnised by a Catholic priest. In one month in York, Martelli performed the 'legitimation' of seven couples who had married before Anglican or Wesleyan ministers.

The friendship between Martelli and Harper is said to have contributed to the climate of mutual respect among Christian denominations in the district. Funds raised by church stalls at the Toodyay Agricultural Show were sent in alternate years to the Protestant Orphanage in Perth and to the Catholic Church in Northam. Erickson observes, 'In those days of religious bigotry the tolerance of the people of the district towards denominations other than their own was a notable aspect of life in Toodyay'.[31]

The legacy of Martelli's two years in the valley was more than bricks and mortar. Bishop Salvado put it like this in a report to Propaganda:

> When obedience destined him elsewhere, a beautiful church and a moderately regular presbytery were a part, perhaps the smallest part, of the advantages his activity and zeal had brought to the Catholics of the District, who in truth were very poor.[32]

With its 'inns adorned with gaily painted swinging signs, thatched cottages surrounded by garden plots and fruit trees' and the sounds of 'lowing herds with their tinkling bells and the grunting droves of swine', early Toodyay 'resembled a small English hamlet'. Martelli did not stay long enough to bask in this idyll. His two energetic years over the hills were brought to a close as abruptly as they had begun. In Fremantle, Fr Donovan was going to Europe on leave of absence and Martelli was summoned to replace him.[33]

He left Toodyay the town in January 1858, taking a long detour through New Norcia. Fr Garrido was now in Dardanup and Bunbury, and Martelli would gladly have flown past Perth: 'I wish I could come on the wings of the cokotoos to pay a visit to you and both your congregations.'[34]

But he was bound for Fremantle. Back to prison.

CHAPTER THIRTEEN

The Prison Affects My Spirit as the Haemorrhoids Affect My Body

1858–1862

Fremantle was coming into its own. Western Australia was the only Australian colony where the port and the administrative centre were clearly separate in name and identity. Since 1853, the town's population had nearly doubled, to nearly 3000.[1]

To Martelli, it was still a 'disconsolate deserted shore'. Five months after he moved, he 'would go back over the Hills [in English] tomorrow if I were allowed: but I am settling into my new position and with each week that passes, I am here with less aversion'.[2]

Martelli's new position as prison chaplain did nothing to endear the town to him. He was now enmeshed in the colony's expanding convict system, unavoidable in the most visible public buildings in the port – the huge Convict Establishment, Commissariat, Round House. The Establishment now housed just under 400 inmates.

Religion played a central role in the convict system. Attendance at chapel was compulsory for prisoners and staff. The Anglican

Chapel was at the centre of the main cell block. Grand and imposing, it looks out through large, unbarred windows towards Fremantle and the sea, as if to say to the worshipping prisoners: reform and you may return to the free world outside, resist and you will remain in this world of confinement. On arrival at the prison, all convicts were handed a bible, a prayer book and a toothbrush. One in five convicts was Catholic. Martelli celebrated Mass in the corridor of the main cell block until a Catholic chapel was created in 1861.[3]

The first service the chaplain could offer the prisoners was the simple gift of his presence. Martelli reported to the Comptroller-General that he was 'at all times accessible to the prisoners during the hours they were permitted to see me'.[4]

Martelli offered the prisoners as much access to the sacraments and to communal prayer as he could fit into the week. On Sundays, he said Mass morning and evening, and on weekdays he led the prisoners in prayer, sometimes during the breakfast hour, sometimes at Evening Prayer. Every day at 11 am he read prayers for the sick in the hospital, and once a week he visited patients in the lunatic asylum. He formed a prison choir and taught them chants and hymns. He had texts set to music by Salvado, as he used to do in Ancona with Maestro Malucci, settings of the Mass, the Salve Regina, an anthem to Mary 'O Purissima, o sanctissima', and a 'Victoria Plains Litany', the prisoners' favourite. 'The harmony from the hymns set to music by Your Excellency', Martelli wrote to thank him, 'resounds throughout the walls of my prison and pours a drop of comfort into hearts troubled by remorse and sadness'. Unfortunately none of this music survives.[5]

The prison library was 'second in importance to the decent performance of the ordinances of religion'. He ensured there were books suitable for Catholic readers and demanded that anti-Catholic literature not be given to them. Many prisoners had low literacy skills and he had to write their letters for them. He held a daily class in his office 'for the express purpose of imparting religious instruction to the more ignorant of my flock'.

One curious incident reveals Martelli's generous concern for the convicts in his care and his careful attention to the niceties of the social hierarchies that he believed were essential for social order. The Governor made an unexpected visit to the Establishment. When Martelli found out, after the event, he was afraid he might have created a negative impression on the Governor. 'He cannot have failed to think of me', Martelli worried,

> for the strange reason that if he did not see me, he certainly saw my legs in one of the cells, and he must have been told who the owner of that pair of legs was and that he was in that moment in conversation with one of the prisoners, seated in his usual position, on the bucket with which every cell is supplied. *I* was the owner of those legs. The door of the cell was left ajar and in part was hiding my person. His Excellency must have been told that I was inside, and so he passed before it without the door being thrown open and without him speaking to that prisoner. I took no notice whatsoever of what was going on outside, thinking that it was the usual visit of the Superintendent or the Magistrate.[6]

The account captures an image of the diminutive chaplain in his long black robe, perched unceremoniously on the humblest of all seats, immersed in conversation with one of his unfortunate charges. Perhaps he was hearing a confession of sin and repentance, or was he simply listening to an outpouring of desperation, offering the solace of religion and human companionship?

Martelli was swamped by feelings of inadequacy for the demanding task. There was no other arena of colonial life where the 'two religions' – Anglicanism and Catholicism – found themselves in closer contact, where the 'antagonism' between them was more conspicuous to the public eye, or where 'the impressions made on the souls inside the prison have a greater influence outside'. The position required a missionary 'endowed with brilliant and equally solid qualities, a man with no less ingenious talent than faultless conduct'.⁷

The brutality of the convict system brought out the worst in people. 'Grim warder and ward were one', wrote political prisoner John Boyle O'Reilly. The lack of mutual trust and the absence of genuine religious sentiment wore him down. It seemed impossible to persuade prisoners to approach the sacraments: 'Fr Donovan used to give out communion to eighty at a time, me to not even ten. Each person sees things their own way.' He suspected Donovan made too many concessions and he 'could not in conscience do the opposite of what I am doing'.⁸

But there were positives. Martelli petitioned the Governor to provide the Catholic chaplain a residence within the Establishment, as was the case with all other officials. This never eventuated and Martelli's health benefited from the constant walking across town:

> Going from home to church, from church to home, from home to the prison, and from the prison to home; and then, again, from home to the prison, and from there to the church, and from the latter back home again, and doing this constantly every day, has produced a happy revolution in my blood system, increased my appetite, etc.⁹

The result? 'The young Ladies are bothering me much less, perhaps as a consequence of my less sedentary lifestyle'. He tried Salvado's homeopathic pills, nonetheless.

Hanging over everything there was 'the great matter of the language'. For the non-Anglophone clergy in the early Western Australian church, the weekly sermon in a foreign language was a major cause of anxiety. Martelli begged Salvado to time his visits to Fremantle for the start of the week, 'when the thought of the Sunday sermon does not weigh, like a nightmare, on my poor brain and does not dispose me well to enjoy some dear company'.¹⁰

Martelli worked hard to calibrate his sermons to his congregation. In Dardanup and Albany he encouraged small congregations battling to maintain their faith in the face of huge challenges. Over the hills, he adopted the approach popular in England, where, in the new climate of emancipation, 'Catholic preaching took a defensive posture in an effort to explain the teachings of the Church'. Sermons from Toodyay are full of references to dogma and the teachings of the Council of Trent, to equip his flock to rebut error and slander. Preaching in the prison required a different approach again. Martelli tuned his rhetorical gifts to those suffering the brutal hopelessness of the convict system. One memorable example is his 1859 sermon for the Eighteenth Sunday after Pentecost.[11]

The Gospel of the day opens: 'Jesus, entering into a boat, passed over the water and came into his own city (Matthew 9:1).' The whole sermon was developed out of this single image, following a method taught in the seminary of Ancona, based on *Meditations of the life of Jesus Christ for each day of the year* by renowned Jesuit preacher Ambrogio Spinola. Three simple steps – memory of the place, imagining the characters and final prayers – appealing to the three powers of the soul: memory, intellect and will.[12]

Martelli brings the scene close to his listeners. Jesus did not have to take a boat to cross the Sea of Galilee, and Martelli brings to mind other scriptural moments of aqueous transit. Jesus could have crossed 'by bidding the liquid element to withdraw before his steps and through the sandy bottom to open a pass to the divine traveller' or he could have 'glided over the tops of the billows as if they were solid enough to support the weight of his body'. But no. A humble vessel is available.

Into this boat, Martelli invites his flock, to sit alongside the Divine Traveller, as naturally as if they were crossing the Swan River at North Fremantle:

> Smooth is the face of the deep: a gentle breeze is swelling the sails; everything portends a speedy pleasant passage. How sweet to follow with our imagination the tranquil course of the little vessel, loaded with such precious cargo and gracefully advancing towards the harbour. I fancy the waves were reverently kissing

the ship as it passed along and that, clouds and storms having been chased far away, the sky was with unusual brilliancy smiling above in a silent homage to Him who made it. Lucky vessel indeed, to whose lot it fell to convey such a traveller and happy those who were admitted to share in the blessing of his company.

In the second step, Martelli imagines the characters in the story and unpacks the allegorical meaning of the event. The passengers in the boat with Jesus represent the 'good Christian sailing on the ocean of this life', happy because, with Jesus in the boat, he is sure of reaching his destination, 'the blissful city of God'.

What does it mean for the life of the Christian 'to take our Blessed Lord in his boat'? he asks, moving the focus closer to his convict congregation. Giving Jesus 'full dominion over his soul and squaring his life by the Gospel' brings the Christian the sweetness that comes from interior order and peace. The 'crew of the low passions is kept under due subjection'; the Christian steers around 'insidious rocks' and ignores the 'enchanted island, abundant with apparent delights' but steers straight 'for the land of the living and its neverending beauties'.

In reaching Spinola's third step – reflections directed to the will – Martelli turns to his specific goal to encourage the prisoners to attend the sacrament of confession more often. He returns to the allegory. Storms will come: furious winds and raging billows are the 'time of temptation'. The Christian must draw closer 'to his divine Pilot', redoubling vigilance and prayer, even throwing overboard any temporal goods which are distracting him from his journey. This brings a 'hundredfold reward' in the present and, as his journey draws to its close, his joy 'reaches its height':

> Either there is no joy in this world, or, if there be any, it is for the Christian, who on sailing over the perilous ocean of life, does not part company with Jesus. Quiet, undisturbed is his course: happy beyond expression is its end.

At this point, to explain why it is that Christians fail to accept this joy offered them, Martelli joins his listeners in the boat, with a bold first-person plural, 'Let us consider ourselves'. We all share a common baptism, we are all sinners and we must all confess our sins to regain our right relationship with ourselves. We have all 'compelled Christ to quit our vessel and the consequence was a melancholy shipwreck'. If we are not yet drowned, it is through Divine Mercy that keeps us afloat, firstly through our baptism but now through regular confession. Martelli is not afraid to cite historical authority: 'the Fathers of the Church assembled in Trent' described confession as the 'second plank [the first was baptism] after the shipwreck of salvation'.[13]

He concludes addressing the circumstances in which his congregation found itself. In the gospel story, when Jesus got out of his boat, he healed a paralysed man, not just in body as he requested but also in his soul. Likewise, Martelli was sure that if the convicts prayed at all, it was merely for physical deliverance from their bondage. He pleads with them to lift their gaze and pray for the higher gifts:

> For the state of your soul you have no concern: you have no recourse to your heavenly physician: your conscience is loaded with numberless sins for which sooner or later, you will be brought to account; and you do not hasten to disburden it with a sincere confession: you know you have suffered the shipwreck of sin, and do not stretch out your hand to seize the plank that can save you. May the merciful Lord bring you to a sense of your danger; may he prevail on you to provide in time for your eternal salvation; may he address to you the happy assurance he gave to the paralytic in the Gospel: 'Be of good heart, son, thy sins are forgiven thee'.

This is a long homily: it would have taken at least fifteen minutes even with Martelli's quick delivery. Methodical in its structure and clear in its development of the theme, it shows a free poetic imagination at the service of a heartfelt concern for his unhappy audience, who are addressed sometimes as 'you', but often with an inclusive 'we'.

Meanwhile, problems in the Perth diocese threatened to engulf Martelli. Bishop Serra was struggling to cater for the growing population with insufficient resources. His behaviour became erratic and alienated many. Martelli's young friends, Reynolds and Byrne, had abandoned their Benedictine training and sailed to South Australia: not, as Casaretto believed, because they were given insufficient monastic training – 'being left to nurse their own vocation, they lost it' – but because they found Serra impossible to work with.[14]

Serra began to see conspiracies among his priests. During 1856–1857, four Benedictines left the mission. Fr Benito Martín was ordered to leave for differences of opinion that Serra considered insubordination. A year later, two more badly needed priests, Aragon and Ribaya, and lay brother Micalet became so disillusioned at not being able to work with the Aborigines at New Norcia that they left the colony. They joined Fr Martín in Ceylon at the mission of the Sylvestrines, the Benedictine congregation known for its dark-blue habit.

It was over New Norcia that Martelli too fell foul of Serra. When Martelli heard Serra claim it was 'useless to work for the conversion of the savages, who are now few and are rapidly disappearing', he held his tongue but thought aloud to Salvado, 'May God forgive him'. In 1857, Serra demanded the entire wheat crop from the mission. Salvado decided the only solution was to have Rome declare New Norcia juridically independent from the diocese of Perth. He made formal representation to Cardinal Barnabò, Prefect of Propaganda.[15]

Serra suspected that senior clergy among the *John Panterians* – Salvado, Garrido, Martelli and possibly others – were impugning his reputation in Perth and in Europe. However, he could not afford to lose any more priests. At first he tried separating the conspirators – Salvado in Perth and New Norcia, Martelli in

Fremantle and Garrido in Bunbury. The arrival of Belgian priest Fr Adolphus Lecaille in February 1858 gave him room to move. On 9 April, he informed Garrido his services were no longer required. Fr Lecaille was being sent to replace him.[16]

Martelli had heard rumblings of Serra's displeasure with Garrido while still in Toodyay. Now, in Fremantle, he was devastated that the mission might lose so valuable a priest and that he should lose such a friend. On 21 April, he poured out his heart to 'Dear Father Garrido, my oldest acquaintance in the mission, my shipmate, my fellow-laborer, my edification and confort [sic]'. He praised Garrido's loyal obedience, knowing that if the same fate ever visited him, he would struggle to accept it with such virtue:

> Whilst bewailing your threatened departure as a calamity on this mission and as a dreadful trial, which the Lord has permitted to befall you, I cannot be without fear that when I expect at the least the same treatment may fall to my lot, and I am very much afraid that I could not put up with it in the same spirit of humble resignation as you did.[17]

Events moved quickly. On 24 April, Serra ordered Garrido to leave the mission. Martelli wrote to Salvado, using delicately oblique language that left no doubt as to identities but elegantly named no names and avoided rancour or bitterness:

> The thunderbolt that struck in the Dardanup area astonished me. I feel very great pity for the victim that was struck and the possibility of a similar accident causes me no little worry. Furthermore I cannot resign myself to the thought that the case allows no remedy and, although my mind is unable definitively to suggest any, it appears nevertheless that some attempt should be made. When I was still in Toodyay, I heard a thunderclap, but it was not clear which part of the country was threatened: the misfortune in Bunbury has revealed the enigma. I am much inclined to take the opportunity from that mysterious threat to

protest (for what it is worth) on behalf of the innocent victim and I am studying how to do it without touching the susceptibility of the Thunderer. It seems that I will feel remorse, if I do not take this defence, although it is with no hope of succeeding.[18]

As Garrido waited in Perth for a ship, Martelli could not bear to sit idly by in the face of such injustice. He wrote to Serra, flatly denying that Garrido had turned him against the bishop. By way of reply, Martelli was invited to Perth to see the evidence for himself, an invitation he was careful not to accept. He wanted to write to Thomas Little in Dardanup, to encourage a petition from Garrido's parishioners, but stayed his hand as he watched Garrido and Salvado, models of discretion both. Garrido chose not to give his Dardanup parishioners prior warning that he was leaving, to avoid gossip about Serra, and Salvado kept the news from the New Norcia community until the last minute because he knew the devastating effect it would have on morale.[19]

On 28 July, Garrido's ship was ready. The two Fremantle priests, Martelli and Thomas Lynch, accompanied him to the shore. Next morning, Martelli penned a moving description of the scene for Salvado:

> Revered and dear Monsignor, Two hours past last midnight, Fr Garrido, accompanied by me and by Fr Lynch, got into the small boat that took him to Garden Island where the *Indian Chief* was anchored. In this moment, I suppose it is setting sail. Your Excellency can imagine what state our hearts were in. I will not easily forget his last words when we separated on the beach. 'Perhaps it is for the good of this Mission'. He was deeply moved. Holding my hands in his, he added 'if it is not for punishment of my sins'. 'I think it is rather for a trial of your virtue', I answered, 'God bless you'. He let my hands go and jumped onto the sailor's back who put him in the little boat. When it started to move off, I called out 'Safe journey and speedy return'. I could not hear the answer that he gave: we were too far apart. The unusual hour, the

solemn calm of the night, a ray of very bright moonlight added interest to the touching scene. Fr Garrido leaves us examples of rare virtue. No shade of resentment could be noted in his words: there was no lament about his fate, so hard and, as I am persuaded, so keenly felt. He has an indestructible trust in Providence and in feelings of mercy towards this Mission. It seems that he does not doubt at all that one day he will return to these parts, although it could be, as he said, after a week of years. I felt great consolation in accompanying him to the shore and enjoying his company in the final hours of his residence in this country. Yesterday he wrote to Your Excellency, but he wanted to finish the letter on board the *Indian Chief* and from there to send it by way of the harbourmaster, through the post. Hence I suppose that it will reach you at the same time as mine. Another of the Missionary priests who came on the *John Panter* has disappeared. May God grant he is the last one![20]

Garrido too joined the Benedictines in Ceylon. He told Salvado that he would speak to no one about his Australian experience except Salvado and Martelli.[21]

With Garrido off the scene, Serra now levelled the same charges against Martelli: disobedience, which simply meant expressing views different to Serra's; disloyalty towards Serra in his letters to Europe about the mission; and turning others against Serra. When Fr Francisco Salvadó rode down to Perth, Serra forbade him to meet Martelli. He returned over the hills — Martelli uses a curious Italian saying to lighten the mood — 'with his bagpipes in his bag, as they say in my country'.[22]

Certain he was next to be expelled, Martelli's heart was 'often possessed by dark thoughts and sinister forebodings'. He took great care not to antagonise his bishop. When Serra wanted to cut his annual allowance and the debate became 'heated, too heated in truth, on my part', Martelli was quick to ask for forgiveness. To little effect: Serra refused to dine with his Fremantle priests. Martelli began to prepare for the inevitable. He was unmoved by invitations from Fr Ribaya to join the monks in Ceylon but applied to Propaganda to be transferred to another Australian mission in the event he was expelled from Western Australia.[23]

In the meantime, he prayed for the grace to accept such a fate with the same spirit he had seen in Garrido: an obedience that was not half-hearted, resentful or grudging. Garrido's humility was the stance of an intelligent, mature person in his prime, in full possession of his faculties and strengths.

Obedience lay at the heart of the imitation of Christ. Modern theologian Luigi Giussani grasps the link between obedience of superiors and personal conversion – 'following those recognised by the Church as the guarantors on her behalf of the truth of the Spirit's gift is an ultimate obedience that tries to incarnate the imitation of Christ and fidelity to the Church down to the last capillaries'. Martelli saw the Benedictine vow of obedience take flesh in his companions. Salvado described obedience as his 'anchor' which 'strengthened him by its power'. Garrido followed the counsel of a Spanish colleague that 'patience and obedience will always end in victory'. Martelli prayed to have some share of these Benedictine virtues and pondered his own lack of faith:

> Certainly, doing the will of God by obeying that of one's Superior is the most glorious, most useful and most desirable thing: but what a cost to this poor heart of ours![24]

The prospect of being sent away from Western Australia forced Martelli to be very clear about what he was doing here. He was not here to prove anything to anyone, least of all himself. His missionary labours, though often solitary and exhausting, were not a test of piety or perseverance. They only made sense within a larger story, that of the missionary church. While he prayed for the grace to obey his superior's orders, he also prayed to remain in the companionship that had brought him to Australia and still continued every day to show him the human face of his divine calling.

THE PRISON AFFECTS MY SPIRIT AS THE HAEMORRHOIDS AFFECT MY BODY

For four long years, as the huge limestone Establishment loomed over the tiny port settlement at its feet, so the convict system weighed heavy on the heart of its acting Catholic chaplain. Martelli felt St Paul's desire to dissolve, *cupio dissolvi*, a yearning to leave this present state. He dreamed of visiting New Norcia and shaking hands with Salvado's trusted friend Bigliagoro. In one letter, the 'realities of his life' burst into his elegant Italian with the alien English words that sum up the misery of the convict system:

> How the desire for a visit to Norcia grows in me, in proportion to the length of my fasting! How I would cherish to shake hands with the generous Bigliagoro! But these are poems...they are golden dreams...prisoners, dark cells, bread and water, flogging, lunatics, are the realities of my life.
>
> [Quanto mi cresce il desiderio di una visita a Norcia a proporzione che il digiuno si prolunga! Quanto mi sarebbe caro to shake hands con il generoso Bigliagoro! Ma queste sono poesie... sono sogni dorati... Prisoners, Dark Cells, Bread and Water, Flogging, Lunatics sono le realtà della mia vita.][25]

The prison affected his spirit as the haemorrhoids afflicted his body: 'These scenes in the prison produce the effect in my spirit that the Young Ladies produce in my body, a malaise, a sadness, in short, a bad mood.'

The Convict Establishment became a metaphor. When Salvado returned to New Norcia after a visit to Fremantle, Martelli complained, 'Your Excellency is on your way and you are leaving me in prison!' He longed to have his own 'ticket of leave'.[26]

In 1860 came the shocking possibility of a transfer to Champion Bay, present-day Geraldton, 400 kilometres to the north, when Fr Donovan returned from leave. There he would be alone again, required to build another church far from the capital. As it happened, Donovan did return but immediately resigned his formal appointment as prison chaplain. This let Martelli off the hook of moving to Champion Bay, but it seemed Donovan might leave the colony for good, condemning Martelli to the prison for ever: 'Farewell, hills of Toodyay! Farewell, plains of Victoria! Farewell, fields of New Norcia!'[27]

Another aspect of his work made Martelli's tenure at the prison even more unwelcome: he received no pay from the government and had to rely entirely on Griver for funds from the diocese coffers.

The payment of prison chaplains was a litmus test of the evolving relations between Church and State in the young colony. When chaplains began receiving salaries from the public purse, both bishops in Perth – José Serra and Anglican Mathew Hale – fought to maintain their independence from government control. Serra insisted that Catholic prisoners should receive religious instruction only from Catholic chaplains and these were responsible to their bishop, not to civil authorities.[28]

During 1858 and 1859, Martelli had been standing in for Fr Donovan. Donovan's salary, as the substantive appointee, continued to be paid to the diocese but when Donovan returned at the end of 1859 and resigned, the Governor said he could not pay Martelli because he was not 'a born British subject'. Fr Griver, however, wanted Martelli in the job. Martelli would have been pleased to know Griver told the Colonial Secretary that Martelli showed 'great zeal and patience'. So Martelli continued in the job, unpaid.

To break the deadlock, on 12 December 1860, Martelli became the first Italian in Western Australia to be naturalised as a British subject. *Congratulamini, civis Romanus sum!* he quoted Acts 22:26 with mock exultation: 'Congratulate me, I am a Roman citizen!' When he applied for a chaplain's salary, the Governor declined on the grounds that, though he professed respect for Martelli himself, *he* had not appointed Martelli to the position. Salvado told Cardinal Barnabò that Martelli was receiving no government pay because of Serra's poor relations with the Governor. Martelli survived on what Griver could give him out of diocesan funds, £100, half the government salary.[29]

Finally, Griver decided to ring the changes. On 1 April 1862, Martelli and Fr Lynch swapped places. The new Governor, Hampton, accepted Martelli's request for back pay for his two years and three months of service as a British subject, since December 1860. Hampton granted half the pay he would have been entitled to, which Martelli was pleased to use to repay Fr Griver for the support he had given him during that time.[30]

CHAPTER FOURTEEN

Informed on All Matters Happening in Rome

1859–1862

The monastery of St Benedict in New Subiaco was solemnly opened on 2 June 1859. Bishop Serra asked for one of the Fremantle priests to attend. Martelli had no interest in the monastery: he described it to Salvado as 'the sublime folly of Subiaco'. However, Serra was still refusing to eat with the Fremantle priests after a row with Martelli. So, Martelli attended, but during the ceremony was tempted by a thought – he knew not if it came from on high or from a low place – that whispered to him a question from the Gospel: 'ut quid perclitio haec? [What is the purpose of this waste?]'. When Serra told Martelli that one of the monks in Subiaco had had a vision of St Benedict, Martelli did not spare his sarcasm when he reported to Salvado, 'The great Patriarch St Benedict visibly visiting Australian soil for the first time would certainly be no small thing'.[1]

Barely six weeks after this milestone in his grand plans for the diocese, Serra had a bombshell land on his desk. Salvado's representations to Rome had achieved their goal. Martelli happened to be in Perth and was summoned to a meeting of priests. Serra read them the decree, dated 1 April 1859.

The New Norcia mission, while still part of the Perth diocese, was given exclusive control of the administration of the goods and property. All the Benedictines in the colony were free to decide whether to continue their monastic life at New Norcia under the authority of Salvado, or at New Subiaco under Serra. Before long, almost all the residents of New Subiaco had moved to New Norcia.

Martelli watched Serra's furious reaction to this news 'that reached him unexpected and terrible as a lightning bolt'. When Serra complained, 'If I am not fit to rule the Norcia Mission, I cannot be fit to rule the diocese', Martelli allowed himself a caustic jibe to Garrido, 'As far as this reasoning goes, I consider him to be perfectly correct'. Serra considered it a financial impossibility to manage the growing diocese, which now had churches in Perth, Fremantle, Dardanup, Bunbury, Guildford and Toodyay, new buildings under way in Fremantle and York and a church badly needed in Albany, and the new monastery in Subiaco – all this without the financial contribution from New Norcia. He left for Rome immediately to have the decree overturned.[2]

Serra told Fr Lynch he suspected Martelli of advising and encouraging Salvado to seek the juridical separation, and he would hold Martelli responsible for the dire consequences that would surely afflict the divided diocese. 'I knew that I was suspected of disaffection,' Martelli chortled, 'but I would never have dreamed that I would be accused of being nothing less than the principal cause of the Holy Father's Brief'. He wondered what fate would befall him if Serra ever returned to Perth. He still had four years left of his contract to serve.[3]

Fr Griver was left in charge, as Acting Apostolic Administrator of the diocese. He faced serious staffing problems. In 1859, Catholics in Western Australia numbered 3354 but were scattered over a thousand kilometres without an adequate system of communication. He set about recruiting diocesan priests, mostly from Ireland.[4]

Martelli could think only of leaving Fremantle and withdrawing to New Norcia. He became obsessed with bringing forward the expiry date of the contract he had signed on 18 August 1853. The irony was that the 1853 letter had also been signed by Fr Griver. But now Griver had a diocese to run. The good Canon was worth his weight in gold. New Norcia was drifting out of reach.

In the excitement of the transfer of the Benedictines from New Subiaco to New Norcia, Martelli somehow convinced himself that he too could simply leave the diocese and move to his 'earthly paradise'. In the second half of 1859, he bombarded Salvado, Garrido and Martínez with all manner of reasons why this would be a good thing. The prison chaplaincy work could be done by anyone else; he was getting old; the climate at New Norcia would be good for his health; Salvado could use an extra priest. He even played the ethnic card, noting that Irishman Fr Lynch's success in fundraising in the town 'is another example of the influence a priest from their own country can have over an Irish congregation'.[5]

By December, his patience had run out. He packed clothes for his first New Norcia winter into a suitcase (he appeals to Salvado by using the Spanish word *maleta*, though he misspells it, with Italian double consonants, *malletta*) and dispatched it to New Norcia. Salvado was in Perth and would be returning to the mission soon. What could be more reasonable than for Martelli to make the journey to the mission with him, once and for all?[6]

However, he would not make any move without Salvado's approval. He was prepared to assume responsibility for his own actions, but he needed to know that Salvado was not opposed to his plan: 'I am not asking for Your Excellency to approve my plan, it is enough for me that you do not oppose it'.[7]

Salvado was sympathetic but did not want to alienate Fr Griver, who had the unenviable task of keeping the diocese together during Serra's absence and was also Martelli's legitimate superior. Salvado must have advised Martelli to work with Griver to find a mutually acceptable outcome. This advice had the force of authority for Martelli, who told Abbot Casaretto in Italy, 'if I am still in my office at the prison, this is due to the authoritative advice received from His Excellency'. Martelli was learning the virtue of obedience from those he saw practising it. And prudence: 'I have never been a prudent man, but the good examples by which I am surrounded seem to have taught me something of that virtue'.[8]

Ten days after the suitcase headed north and while Martelli was still plotting his escape from Fremantle, Salvado left for the mission, alone. To defuse his disappointment, Martelli goes in for lyrical exaggeration. With tongue firmly in cheek, he makes his own the words of a love duet from Donizetti's *Lucia di Lammermoor*:

> So, Your Excellency is going, and is leaving me in prison! [...] Of course, since I cannot follow you in person, my thoughts will follow you: 'Verranno a te sull'aura, i miei sospiri ardenti etc.' [My ardent sighs will come to you on the breeze].[9]

There is more sighing as he begs Salvado to 'keep a little corner ready for the poor Canon and, when your eyes fall on my suitcase, offer a sigh to the heavens that my prayer be heard'. The poor battered suitcase, bearer of Martelli's misguided dreams, languished in New Norcia until April the following year, when Martelli conceded defeat, 'I hope my suitcase has returned from Norcia. If it were capable of shame, it would feel no small shame due to its haste.'[10]

By mid-1860, he was losing hope. The literary allusions in his letters to Salvado are no longer the flighty love duets of Romantic opera but the lofty devotion of the psalms:

> Poor me! Instead of getting closer to fulfilling my desire, I see myself getting further away from it. And when will the day come for me when I will be able to say in New Norcia: <u>Haec est domus mea: hic habitabo, quoniam elegi eam</u> [This is my home: here I will dwell, for I have chosen it]?[11]

In Rome, meanwhile, Serra's grudge against Martelli lingered. At an official luncheon, the bishop got himself seated between church heavyweights Cardinal Barnabò, Prefect of Propaganda Fide, and Monsignor Capalti, Secretary of the Congregation. He gloated to Griver, 'This will show you how things stand, so let Martelli and his friends say what they like'. A few weeks later, Martelli heard that one of his own letters had ended up on the desk of Pope Pius, no less. 'So it goes', he made light to Salvado of this curious honour and chuckled at the effects it had on Serra:

> What an uproar it caused! If Mgr Serra were able to get his hands on me, he would treat me no better than he treated the poor coffee-maker in Via degli Angeli Custodi in Rome. But this is all algebra to Your Excellency until you read the Roman letter, where you will find an anecdote, half comical and half tragic, that perfectly illustrates the Serrian character.[12]

The 'Roman letter' from Martelli's friend Pietro Regnoli is lost, so we can only imagine what passed between Bishop Serra and the hapless barista.

Martelli knew that if the 1859 decree were annulled, not only would Salvado's plans for New Norcia be scuppered, probably for good, but Serra could make life very difficult for his 'enemies'. Martelli saw himself living out the rest of his days as a parish priest or prison chaplain at the whim of the bishop of Perth. He swung into action.[13]

To support Salvado in countering Serra's efforts to have the separation decree rescinded, Martelli called on friends in high places. He wrote to Tommaso Gallucci, Vicar General to their old seminary professor, Cardinal Gaetano Baluffi. Baluffi was well acquainted with the Australian missions. In 1854, he published an encyclopedic account of Catholic missions around the world that was translated into many languages, including English, under the title *The Roman Church, recognised through its charity towards its neighbour as the true church of Jesus Christ*. Sydney had been saved from lawlessness and anarchy by 'a few Catholic priests'; on the western side of the continent, he cited Salvado's *Historical Memoirs* as evidence that it was only the missionaries who 'taught the savages of Oceania how to plough the field, clothe the desert in trees and govern the flocks and herds on mountains and plains'. When Baluffi wrote directly to Barnabò, Salvado had gained a powerful ally.[14]

Another old friend Martelli contacted was Pietro Regnoli. It is not known how Martelli and Regnoli first came to know each other. It must have been early, since in 1846, when Martelli's star student Gaspare Finali left Ancona to pursue university study in Rome, Martelli gave him a letter of introduction to Regnoli, 'his dearest friend'. Regnoli was six years younger than Martelli. He was from a liberal family in Forlì, in the northern Legations, and was with Martelli in the Roman University Battalion. He later built a successful career in the Roman civil service and wrote art criticism for influential journals. He had powerful connections that were useful to Martelli and Salvado. An uncle was a Canon of the Papal Basilica of St Mary Major and he was friends with liberal-minded Angelo Pescetelli, who was now Abbot of St Paul's. Martelli had a high opinion of his friend's political savvy: he thought Regnoli knew 'where the devil keeps his tail'.[15]

The two friends had written sporadically, but now began a regular correspondence, once a month. Martelli kept Regnoli informed of developments in Perth, including details that he knew Salvado was too polite to pass on, for example Serra's mismanagement of the diocese and the need of finance in Fremantle: 'Perhaps Mgr Salvado does not say these things, because he does not think it appropriate to say them'. Martelli had no such qualms. Regnoli passed all this on to Abbot Pescetelli and other contacts in the church hierarchy. His letters back to Perth provided invaluable intelligence on Serra's attempts to convince Barnabò, Casaretto and others. All this Martelli passed on to Salvado.[16]

Martelli knew that Regnoli was part of the 'left wing' of Catholic liberalism that was prepared to work for Italian unification 'at any cost', even renouncing the pope's temporal power. 'I beg you,' he warned Salvado, 'not to be scandalised if you sometimes encounter opinions, or aspirations, in his writing that do not sound good to a Catholic ear.' Salvado seems to have been unperturbed.[17]

Griver was well aware that Martelli was busy gathering intelligence for Salvado and New Norcia. He was piqued at being left in the dark and at the mercy of Martelli's version of things. 'It seems', he complained to Serra,

> that Fr Martelli is informed on all matters happening in Rome to do with the Mission and on every step Your Lordship takes. Since all things, including good ones as your Lordship says, can be mis-represented, would it not be better for Your Lordship to give us true and correct information, in order to contradict fake news?[18]

Rome was moving towards a decision. During 1861, word came that Propaganda had decided to initiate a formal review of the management of the diocese, an 'Apostolic Visitation' tasked with putting an end to the ongoing conflict between diocese and mission. Next came the shocking news that, without any Visitation, Bishop Serra would be allowed to return to Perth.

Martelli and three other priests took the very serious step of protesting directly to Cardinal Barnabò. The letter is in Italian, since Propaganda preferred correspondence to be in Italian or Latin. The handwriting is Martelli's. It carries the signatures of R. Martelli, Acting Chaplain of the Convict Establishment; Thomas Lynch, Chaplain of Fremantle; P. McCabe, Chaplain of Champion Bay; and F. Salvadó, Chaplain of York, Toodyay and Northam. The letter states that neither Salvado nor any other (Benedictine) priest in the diocese was consulted about the letter. Salvado would have been in an impossible conflict of interest, and the other priests could have faced serious consequences.[19]

The writers had heard, 'with surprise and regret', that Propaganda had decided to allow Serra to return. After 'mature deliberation', they agreed it was a duty of conscience to present 'certain considerations on this person' to the Roman authorities.

> The signatories are fully convinced that Monsignor Serra cannot resume the governance of this diocese without serious detriment to our holy Religion, since the vast majority of the faithful have a firm negative opinion of him, as a result of his personal character and various facts that left a sinister and indelible impression in their minds.

In seven tightly written pages, the letter sets out the case against Bishop Serra. With details of names, dates and places, the letter rehearses some of the sad moments of the church's first years in Western Australia that involved Serra: the conflicts with Bishop Brady, with the Benedictine priests who left the colony, with the Sisters of Mercy (and the difficult arrival of the Sisters of St Joseph), and with Governor Kennedy (and the position of the Catholic chaplain at the prison); the expenditure of funds on grand buildings in Perth to the detriment of much needed churches; the neglect of New Norcia and its work to 'convert and civilise the Aborigines'. With such a list of complaints, why had the priests kept silent till now?

> We thought it was impossible that we would be believed. We knew, or supposed, that Propaganda had received information from other sources. This was confirmed when we read that Monsignor had been asked in Rome to renounce the diocese. Now, however, we have heard, to our dismay, that he is allowed to return. We believe we cannot, without fault, fail to do what we can to save this diocese from the misfortune that threatens it.

This letter was dated 24 January 1862. The case had already been resolved. The letter and its reply crossed on the ocean. Propaganda realised that a compromise over the governance of Perth, New Subiaco and New Norcia was not possible with Serra. His resignation as Apostolic Administrator of Perth was accepted by the Pope on 15 December 1861. When the news reached Perth the following March, Martelli expressed the relief of all: 'May God be praised! Better for us, better for Mgr Serra, that he no longer has any ties to this Mission. He will be able to enjoy his peace and we are hoping to do likewise'. In fact, Serra retired to Spain, where he did much good, founding an order of nuns – the Oblate Sisters of the Most Holy Redeemer – which is still flourishing in fifteen countries, working with young women who have been victims of sexual abuse. He never returned to Australia.[20]

Griver was distraught but stoical when the news of Serra's resignation came to him second hand, via the usual suspects: 'Fr Martelli and Bishop Salvado learned from different channels that Your Excellency had resigned and that the Holy Father had accepted the resignation, but Your Excellency told me nothing. Praised be the Lord.' He now became Apostolic Administrator in his own right. Martelli felt Serra's resignation facilitated Griver's position. No longer obliged to 'consult his Superior at the antipodes [in Rome]' and able to 'follow the guide of common sense', Martelli thought he 'will be in a better position to manage our affairs with great success'. Griver's careful and prudent government would win him many admirers and he eventually became bishop of Perth in 1871.[21]

Salvado's work at New Norcia now proceeded with no interference from Perth. Since moving there in 1857, Salvado had built up the community – it now contained forty-seven monks – and was realising his vision of building a self-supporting mission, after the model of the medieval monastic towns of Europe. Monks and lay brothers would live a modified version of the Rule that would allow them to work alongside a community of Noongar families, all employed in the maintenance of the village. Houses were built for married Noongar couples, and residential quarters for Noongar youth, one for girls and one for boys. Fr Garrido was appointed Prior – Martelli welcomed him off the boat from Ceylon on the last day of 1859 and found his friend in excellent health, even putting on weight, after his exile – and Fr Bertrán became novice master.[22]

The diocese had a new, competent administrator. The mission at New Norcia was securely in the hands of the redoubtable Salvado. All Martelli had to do was find a way to secure his release when his ten years were up in 1863.

CHAPTER FIFTEEN

This Idle Paper Talk

Most of what we know of Raffaele Martelli in Australia comes from his letters. Their style tells us as much as their content; we learn as much about him from how he says things as from what he actually says. Though letters were a poor substitute for 'a chat as long as the road from Perth to New Norcia', they were a lifeline, especially when he found himself isolated in Toodyay, or in Fremantle threatened with expulsion. He poured his heart and soul into them. They show the educated, witty professor of rhetoric, and they reveal the lone missionary working through the consequences of commitments made in Italy and constantly in need of confirmation.[1]

Letters communicate facts, opinions, requests, replies and information of every kind. Most important, letters give expression to the relationship between writer and reader. What matters first of all is that you have picked up pen and paper to maintain the contact.

'I am writing', Martelli opens one letter to Salvado, 'for the sole purpose of saying I have nothing to write about'. To Garrido, he described his own letters as 'this idle paper-talk'.[2]

Letter writing in nineteenth-century Italy was the occupation of the few; it required education and training. There were rules to be followed. Martelli's colleague Giuseppe Montanari, professor of Rhetoric in nearby Osimo, wrote a popular textbook, *L'arte di scrivere lettere*. The subtitle shows the approach: *from the analysis of classical writers in Latin and Italian*.[3]

Martelli's first letters follow the rules. For example, he 'gives the line' in his first letters to Salvado. After the opening, 'Most Reverend Monsignor', he leaves four blank lines before beginning the letter proper. The blank space sent a message: the more important the addressee, the bigger the gap. Such niceties were disappearing in the socially mobile Europe of the time and in Australia there was no need for them. Besides, paper and ink were expensive. Before long, Martelli was cramming his pages full, even writing around the margins.[4]

The textbooks also taught different rules for different types of letter. But Martelli was a man of his time and embraced the new fashion of 'mixed letters'. He combines church politics and requests for clothing, questions of canon law and complaints about troublesome individuals, pastoral planning and hilarious tales of everyday mishaps.

He wrote to Salvado in Italian but in 1864 he switched to English. The other Spanish priests, Garrido and Martínez, did not know Italian and he did not know Spanish. Like any educated speaker of Italian (who also knows Latin and French), Martelli could certainly read Spanish without difficulty and also follow a conversation, especially through spending so much time with Spanish speakers. But he wrote to the Spanish priests always in English. His English is correct even in his earliest letters, though some spelling rules remained a mystery to him. Ever the language teacher, he wrote once or twice to Garrido in Italian and to Martínez in French, to keep them in practice.

Whatever language he is writing in, he enjoys inserting words and phrases from the other languages he shares with his interlocutors. This happens most often in letters to Salvado, as a light-hearted divertissement among friends who share the same knowledge of multiple languages and the same cultural formation to the highest level.

His letters in Italian are peppered with English words and phrases. Some refer to everyday objects that were new to him and were best expressed with the English word, e.g. *pensioner, fence, cheque, sheep station, raspberry jam*. He might drop an English expression into an Italian sentence for effect, though there is a perfectly good Italian equivalent, e.g. *paramount importance, envelopes, never mind*, or to anchor his remarks to the English conversations he hears all around him, e.g. *black fellow, cottage, lambing* or *lamming, parish priest*.

When he writes in English, his switching in the other direction is very limited. When he inserts Italian into his English, it is not for everyday objects — these are all English by now — but for expressive set phrases, e.g. *dolce far niente* 'sweet idleness', *così va il mondo!* 'that's the way the world goes'. The switch in language can have a euphemistic effect, as in *Now a bit of cronaca scandalosa clericale*, 'Now a bit of clerical scandalous news'. Individual Italian words are used only for some special connotation, e.g. *appartamentino* 'a little apartment', *villeggiatura* 'summer holidays'. A rarified word like *conchigliologo* 'seashell expert' to describe Vincenzo Rigacci is a kind of in-joke for the educated.

He suffered from the linguistic purism that afflicts many an educated bilingual speaker. When he used English words in his Italian, he was careful to underline them to maintain standards. He berated himself for forgetting everyday Italian words. 'Enough of these English lumps of lard: we are becoming barbarians and the *idioma del sì* is losing its grasp in our memory'. To rub it in, his definition of Italian is a phrase inspired by Dante's *De Vulgari Eloquentia*, meaning 'the sweet language that says *sì*'.

Memory was a problem. After nearly ten years in Australia, he could not summon up the Italian for 'eggplant'. When it finally came to him, he gave Salvado two versions for good measure, one in the dialect of Ancona and the second in Italian:

> Mi fa il favore di domandare se è possibile avere semenza del Eggplant? Mi è sovvenuto a qual pianta si applica questo nome. Le chiamiamo melanciani, o melanzane al mio paese.
> [Will you do me the favour of asking whether it is possible to have some eggplant seeds? I have remembered what plant this name refers to. We call them melanciani or melanzane in my hometown.][5]

He had the knack of finding a turn of phrase or proverb to sum up a situation and, by switching language, relieve tension with a wry smile. In his letters in Italian, we read of one person who was *cursed with a love of drink* (and yet elsewhere he uses the even more colourful expression *troppa devozione a Bacco*, 'too much devotion to Bacchus'). Criticism of Fr Griver is softened by using a common Italian saying like *the Apostolic Administrator is trying indeed* di cercar il pel sull'ovo [to search for the hair in the egg, that is, to split hairs, in archaic Tuscan spelling].

Switching languages made it difficult to keep boundaries. Once, when writing in English, Martelli mentions the Italian Brother Pietro Ferrara. Writing his title and name in Italian triggers a switch into Italian. Catching himself, he interrupts the sentence, with three dots, comments on the switch and meticulously backtracks to translate the Italian phrase into English. This was not for his reader's benefit, because Salvado would have understood perfectly anyway, but is all about Martelli's need to uphold standards.

> Fr. Pietro mi scrive da Nicol Bay poche righe [Fra Pietro writes me a few lines from Nicol Bay] … his name had betrayed me into Italian language. A few lines, then, he writes…[6]

In those early letters in Italian, everyday objects are sometimes given their Spanish names. This signalled a shared experience to his Spanish friend, especially in the minutiae of life: *calzoncillos* [misspelt as *calzoncillios*] 'underpants', *medias* 'socks', *cosilla* 'small thing', and *hermanos* 'brothers, that is, the monks'.

With his knowledge of so many related languages, he could be playful with new creations. The young boys in the New Norcia school he calls *muciaccetti*, from Spanish *muchacho*, but he spells it the Italian way and adds the Italian diminutive suffix *-etto*. For a humble phrase like 'jar of butter', he once wrote *Giarro di Butirro*. He is trying to use Galician, Salvado's home language, but his grasp of it is imperfect. 'Giarro' does not belong to any language: it sounds like a cross between English 'jar' and Galician *tarro*. *Butiro* is an old Galician word for 'butter', but with one r, not two.

That same letter contains phrases in Latin, French and English, including a very curious creation. Australian fences were like nothing he knew in Italy, so in 1854 he coined *la fensa* and that may be the first recorded use of a word famous among Italian migrants worldwide. But he needed a verb for the activity of 'fencing' a piece of land and produced a regular first conjugation verb *fensare*. From this it was a short step to form a past participle, and from 1856 Toodyay, we find this linguistic gem (the lack of underlining suggests the words were becoming integrated into his everyday language):

> uno dei lati lunghi del triangolo non esigerà fensa, poichè già si trova fensato
> [one of the sides of the triangle will not need a fence, since it is already fenced].[7]

As time went on, he became more playful in jumping from one language to another. His readers must have found it exhilarating. Three different languages – Italian, English and Latin – could be cobbled together in a sentence of just five words: 'Ma never mind, majora premunt', meaning 'but never mind, there are more pressing matters'.

Martelli's letters are also sprinkled liberally with quotations from literary works of all kinds. They clinched an argument or captured a situation with colourful accuracy. The quotations reference the educational formation and the cultural universe he shared with Salvado.

Quotations from the Bible are in Latin. He could blend a Latin clause seamlessly into his Italian. Gazing on New Norcia in the planting season, he pondered with the Psalmist:

> Che sarebbe del vederla quando in exultatione metent?
> What would it be to see it when in exultatione metent [they will reap in joy]?

Other Latin quotes are from St Augustine, but also Roman writers Virgil, Plautus, Phaedrus, Ennius and Horace. Italian authors he quotes from memory are Dante and Tasso, of course, but also Petrarch and Alfieri. His love of opera shines through quotation from Metastasio and Donizetti.

The language play extended to leaps of style, from the erudite to the everyday. He described one of his letters as 'una lunga cicalata de omnibus rebus et de quibusdam aliis'. This simply means 'a long natter about this and that', but he has boldly mixed a very colloquial Italian term *cicalata* – literally the noise made by *cicale*, cicadas – and the Latin title ('of all things that exist and a few more') of an encyclopedic work by Renaissance Humanist Giovanni Pico della Mirandola.

There is something acutely ironical about the way he uses metaphors from European high culture to refer to all manner of things in his new Australian world. Walter Benson, who painted a famous landscape of the mission, becomes 'your Raphael of Urbino', and Ceylon, where Fr Garrido and Fr Aragon 'met and ate the bread of exile together', he calls Patmos. When Propaganda planned to take action to end the impasse of 1862, Martelli expected a *Delenda est Carthago*, 'Carthage must be destroyed'. The irony here is humorous, to be sure, but it is sympathetic, not caustic. What he is really doing is not just interpreting his Australian experience throught the cultural framework of his European formation.

He is revisiting that formation through the eyes of his new Australian reality.

In Martelli's mix of language style, we glimpse the many levels at play in his relationship with Salvado — they were educated Europeans, missionaries, authority-subordinate, friends. A master of the classical tradition, Martelli's Italian ranges from the most elegant and formal construction of sentences and expressions to turns of phrase that come straight from everyday conversation.

He creates imagined dialogues with Salvado. This was a common device in nineteenth-century letters, to heighten the impression of overcoming distance. After a long vent of opinions on church-related topics, he 'hears' Salvado's impatient response and so comes to a humble close: '"Have you finished?" Yes, sir. I have only to kiss your sacred ring and ask forgiveness for such a long digression'.[8]

Relationships were also encoded in the way Martelli addresses his readers. He scrupulously follows the rules of social address. These rules were the linguistic representation of the hierarchical world in which Martelli was formed. His liberal convictions of reform, Christian progress and emancipation worked within, not against, the structures of social life into which he was initiatied from his earliest education.

Martelli never deviated from absolute respect for social position when writing to and about fellow clerics and civic authorities. Whatever the foibles of a given individual, they are named in Martelli's letters with deferential reference to their place in the social hierarchies that held the world together.

Martelli's letters to his closest friend always begin with some variant of 'Revered (or Reverend) and very dear Monsignor'. They invariably end with protestations of 'veneration and affection' from 'Your Most Reverend Excellency's most devoted and most grateful servant' or with kissing the episcopal ring or asking for blessing, or some combination of the above. Letters in English begin 'My Dear Lord' and close like the Italian ones.

Italian, like most European languages, has more than one way of saying 'you', as English did until the eighteenth century when *thou* dropped out of use. Different pronouns encode the status of the two persons in conversation and the nature of their relationship. They are crucial to maintaining social structure and establishing successful interaction with others.

Nineteenth-century Italian had three pronouns used for addressing one person. (Modern Italian has reduced this system to just *tu* and *Lei*, used in place of *Ella*: *voi* survives only in dialects and in Italian is only used in the plural.) Their spheres of use were clearly demarcated, though in flux due to profound social changes in progress:

tu: used by children and by adults speaking to children, and between close adult friends or colleagues.

voi: used between adult friends of equal status, who share social roles rather than family or personal affection; and by a superior to a subordinate.

Ella: used between strangers; between adults whose relationship is transactional, not personal; by a subordinate to a superior.[9]

It is quite unusual, in modern Italy, for pronoun usage to be asymmetrical. That is, once two speakers decide whether they will use *tu* or *Lei*, they will both use the same pronoun to each other. The only normal exception involves age. A younger person will call a much older person *Lei* to show respect due to age, but will receive *tu*.

In Martelli's time, however, asymmetrical politeness was the norm. Pronoun usage marked differences in social rank or role. Thus Martelli always addressed the bishops Salvado and Serra as *Ella*, while in their letters they called him *voi*. We know this from the times Martelli quotes the bishops in his own letters.[10]

Rules for pronoun usage intersected with rules for use of titles and modes of address to produce a complex and nuanced set of options which a competent social actor was required to know. Sex could be an additional variable, but all Martelli's correspondents were male.

It is difficult to generalise from the few letters that survive. However, Martelli only uses *tu* with friends he knew from childhood. He addresses Pietro Regnoli as *Caro Piero* or *Pierino*. Childhood friends – Regnoli and Tommaso Gallucci – use *tu* to him but none addresses him by his first name, perhaps in deference to his priestly status. Regnoli writes, in a jolly male way, *Carissimo Martelli*, but signs himself *Pietro*. Gallucci, who was also a cleric, addresses him *Carissimo Martelli* or *Carissimo Amico* and signs off 'all yours, Gallucci'. Another friend, Urbano Urbani, combines affection and respect in his *Carissimo Don Raffaele* and uses *voi*.

Among priests on friendly terms, the practice was *voi* with title and surname. Martelli opens his early letters to Garrido with a show of affection in the address, *Carissimo Padre Garrido*, but sticks to *Ella*. After ten years, however, the pronoun shifts to *voi*. In the letters he wrote to Fr Martínez in the 1870s in French, Martelli uses *vous*.

To religious superiors, Martelli follows the rule of maximum deference. Even to Abbot Pescetelli, whom he addressed effusively in 1853 as *Padre Abate Carissimo*, the pronoun is *Ella*. Abbot Casaretto is an interesting case, since they knew each other since childhood and their paths crossed in significant ways thereafter. The friendship can never have been particularly warm, since the pronoun in both directions is always *Ella*.

Of course, we have no direct evidence of how Martelli addressed Salvado or anyone else in face-to-face conversation. However, there is a suggestion in the written record. In an 1866 letter written to Salvado in English, Martelli abruptly switches to Italian to ask, 'Che ci fareste?' [What would you do about it?]. He seems to be imagining himself speaking directly to Salvado. If this is the case, it would confirm that in everyday conversation Martelli and Salvado used *voi* to each other. Spoken and written communication had their own rules.[11]

Hierarchical rules also governed expressions of friendship. Martelli knew that, from Cicero's theory of friendship onwards, the ideal of *amicitia* required equality of status among those who called each other 'friends'. So he happily calls Garrido *amico* even while still calling him *Ella*, he addresses Fr Martínez *mon cher ami*, and his old friend Tommaso Gallucci calls him *amico*.

Martelli and Salvado, however, close as they were, were not in any way equals. When Martelli interrupted a sentence to address Salvado affectionately, he calls him *Monsignore mio carissimo* 'my dear Monsignor'. He wrote to Regnoli about his friendship with Salvado, calling Salvado 'my buon Padrone ed Amico', though that letter was in English and he switches to Italian to soften the effect of such a confidence. He described Salvado once to Garrido as 'our good Rosendo'. But he would never address Salvado, on paper, as *amico*. The nearest he came was once in an upbeat letter from Toodyay. After asking to be allowed 'to kiss your sacred ring and please give me your blessing' he signs off with a quick *Obbl.mo Aff.mo S. e A*. This is short for *Obbligatissimo Affezionatissimo Servo e Amico*, 'most grateful and affectionate servant and friend'. He could not bring himself to write the whole word. Pietro Regnoli, on the other hand, was outside the ecclesiastical hierarchy. Thus, while he is obsequious to a fault in his letters to Salvado, Regnoli had no hesitation in signing himself 'Your most devoted Servant and Friend'.[12]

Letters sent and received were not merely conveyors of information and affection. A letter is a physical token of the relationship between writer and addressee. From the hand of the writer to the hand of the reader, a letter is a sign of absence, a bridge across distance, a continuation of presence, until such time as physical reunion is possible. The paper, the ink, the handwriting, are all traces of the writer that enter the physical world of the reader. Between physical encounters, letters allowed a 'continuation of conversation'.[13]

Letters can include or accompany gifts. Martelli's and Salvado's letters include quotes from letters of others or forward entire letters; they enclose newspaper cuttings; they accompany gifts of every kind. Later letters accompanied photographs of the writer.

Martelli used three different Italian words for gifts he received. Objects such as books, pictures, clothing, church supplies, food and wine, Martelli described as *presente* or *donativo*. But there is another kind of gift involved in epistolary correspondence and that is the letter itself. For this gift, Martelli always used a third synonym, *regalo*, the word he also used for the 'gift of a visit', *il regalo di una visita*. Again, nineteenth-century dictionaries shed light on the different emotions the words carry. Like the English verb 'to regale', the act of giving a *regalo* includes a component of affection lacking in the other two Italian terms: 'to give something which, if not valuable, is pleasing, or is supposed or claimed to be such'. The gift of a letter, or of a visit, is never just a *presente* or *donativo*, but always a *regalo*.[14]

The physicality of letters makes them potentially dangerous. During the heady days of the separation of New Norcia from Perth, Martelli began one letter, 'Reverend and dear Monsignor, I received your letter, I read it and I destroyed it'. Another ended, 'P.S. Your letters cease to exist shortly after they arrive.' Some of Martelli's letters to Salvado would meet the same fate: 'The letters from my Roman friend, you may consign them to the flames. Once Your Excellency has seen them, they have served the purpose for which they were written'.[15]

Letters can also be dangerous simply because they exist, not for their content but because they are a tangible sign of a relationship. When Fr Coll stayed in Fremantle in the difficult days of 1859, he would collect the mail from the convent. Martelli realised that Coll noticed how frequently Salvado wrote to Martelli. Martelli told Salvado he would change the collection process. The following week, 'I received your letter … I did not respond due to fear of the Pusillanimous, who could be scandalized by noticing, as you say, the close correspondence between us'.[16]

Though letters were usually addressed to only one person, they were often intended for multiple readership. Letters circulated freely among those in Salvado's network. Martelli and Salvado forwarded each other letters from others and, when Salvado was in Rome, Martelli and Garrido swapped letters they received from him. While Salvado was away, Martelli offered to forward items of news for general consumption directly to New Norcia, to Subiaco or to the Sisters of St Joseph, to save Salvado writing the same news twice. Letters of a confidential nature were treated with great discretion: 'We keep to ourselves what is to remain secret'.[17]

Why Martelli switched from Italian to English in his letters to Salvado is not easy to pinpoint. Not long after the expiry of his ten-year contract with the diocese, he wrote a four-page letter to Salvado – in English. From now on his letters to Salvado were all, with a very few exceptions, written in English.[18]

Around the time he switches language, his friends observed his decision to spend the rest of his days in Australia. Pietro Regnoli told Salvado, 'I am convinced it is because of the close bonds that tie him to Your Excellency, that he has resolved, ever more firmly, never to return to his homeland'. Garrido told Salvado that 'Martelli is very much wedded to New Norcia. Not only does he want to be buried there, but he wishes to spend the last third of his life there.'[19]

On a practical level, there were very few people in Martelli's daily routine with whom he spoke Italian. He had always spoken English with the Spanish priests. He took a keen interest in the welfare of the 'Neapolitan' lay brothers, but they were working in Perth now, not in Fremantle, 'Give my best love to my countrymen, Fra Costabile [Turi], Fra Pietro [Ferrara] and Fra Raffaele [Rizzo] and Fra Niccola [Filomeno]'. He must have seen Nicoletta O'Byrne née Salustri every Sunday at least, but she was immersed in the English-speaking lives of her eight children. Italians turned up from time to time by the most circuitous routes. Giovanni (or Jack) Marchetti was a seaman born in Venice and transported for life to Fremantle for stabbing another sailor in a fight in Liverpool. When he obtained his ticket of leave in 1860, Martelli recommended him to the priests of the outlying districts and was pleased to see him marry and establish a successful farm in Greenough. But Marchetti's life too was all in English.

Furthermore, Martelli's connections to Italy were growing weaker. One by one, news reached him of the death of his remaining family members in Ancona: his brother Antonio in 1863, a sister in Algiers in 1864, his 'dear old stepmother' Teresa Morelli early in

1865, his brother-in-law Aristide Tuzi in the cholera epidemic of the same year. 'And now I must prepare for my turn.' The only members of his immediate family left were his two stepsisters, the widowed Aldemira and Cleofina who had married one of the Morellis. He had never grown close to them: 'As they had not the same mother with me and grew up when I was already a man and I never lived under the same roof with them, there is no warm affection between them and me.' His absence of fifteen years had 'slakened even more the natural tie which binds us'.[20]

Other relatives and friends wrote less and less frequently: 'their silence is to me very painful'. Perhaps this was because he stopped writing to them. In June 1868, a priest from nearby Matelica, probably Oratorian Eugenio Maria Tommasi, wrote to Propaganda Fide asking for news on behalf of concerned relatives. A Propaganda official reassured him Martelli was alive and well since the Perth Administrator had requested renewal of priestly faculties for him. The official also asked Griver to encourage Martelli to stay in touch with his family more regularly.[21]

Early in 1866, Martelli stopped a letter to Salvado to add a note to Pietro Regnoli, also in English. He cannot explain why he has abandoned his first language – again described in Dante's words – for a tongue that he now lives in but is so inadequate for expressing his true feelings.

> My Dear Pierino
> This blessed English language is little adapted to the warmth of Italian feeling. It does not allow that dear, delightful pronoun Tu. You is very cold, and I almost feel repugnant in using it in these few lines. Why then I do not speak il dolce idioma del sì? I can scarcely assign a reason. 'Tis a frolic, I think.[22]

The frolic continued for a page and a half of news.

CHAPTER SIXTEEN

Labouring in a More Fertile Field

1862–1868

For the next six years, Raffaele Martelli was the chaplain of the largest parish outside Perth. He celebrated Mass and administered the sacraments, ran the church choir, supervised the two Catholic schools, visited parishioners, juggled finances and maintained buildings. He set up a Catholic lending library, aimed especially at young people.

Official duties were a chore: 'The older I get, the more unsociable I get, or rather I am becoming inclined to solitude and almost to misanthropy.' But there was always time to run errands for the New Norcia mission, visiting merchants to broker the buying and selling of tobacco or sheep, making payments and collecting monies for Salvado.[1]

'I think I have never been so busy', he told Salvado after just a month in his new position. The constant activity was good for his health: 'the Signorine have lately behaved with great bashfulness'. Martelli was now writing to Salvado in English. When writing in

Italian, the cause of his discomfort was <u>Young Ladies</u>, but now that he writes in English they have become *Signorine*: some things are best communicated under the veil of code-switching.²

His new position created ample scope for conflicts with the Apostolic Administrator. The Catholic Boys' School was run by the diocese but Martelli believed Fr Griver was not even-handed in his financial support for Perth and Fremantle. When two Christian Brothers arrived in 1864, one was appointed to Fremantle but quickly recalled to Perth. When Griver visited Fremantle at the end of March, Martelli and he had 'a little row' about the school. Griver put his views in writing and demanded that the letter be read from the pulpit. Martelli, as always, complied. Conflicts were always an opportunity to learn humility and obedience.³

The school for girls was an easier proposition. The Fremantle Saint Joseph of the Apparition Girls' and Infants' School was operated by the four nuns Martelli had known since they arrived in 1855. They had moved to new accommodation on higher ground, at the corner of Queen and High streets. Nevertheless, in the wet winter of 1862, Martelli still thought they were living 'like frogs, surrounded by water', all sick with rheumatic pains, and worse would come in the hot months when 'the air becomes filled with mephitic exhalations'.⁴

Martelli gave the Sisters regular spiritual direction, including their annual spiritual exercises every September. They sang with the church choir on feast days, adding to the 'solemnity' of the occasion. He gave practical assistance, accompanying them on visits, forwarding mail and helping out at their annual Bazaar, 'a tedious and dissipating business'. By spartan living and constant fundraising, the Sisters collected the impressive sum of £200 for a new convent and school. Fr Griver eventually contributed £300 from the central Mission Fund. The new building, next to the church and presbytery between Adelaide and Parry streets, was opened on 31 May 1863.⁵

Martelli preached at the opening Mass. On a subject as close to his heart as the education of the poor and in honour of the heroic

Sisters he admired so much, he prepared the homily with great care. His notes are covered with crossing out and rewriting.[6]

It was Trinity Sunday and he opened with a sustained meditation on this, the most profound of Christian mysteries. His point of departure and his horizon were as always the universal church spread across the globe:

> On this Sunday the universal Church pours out her feeling of profound adoration of the incomprehensible mystery of the Trinity of God and offers up a tribute of thanksgiving and praise to the Father who created the universe, to the Son who redeemed mankind, and to the Holy Ghost who has sanctified the Church. We adore the mysterious nature of God, we acknowledge the benefits which he has bestowed on his creatures.

His text, from the Epistle of the day, led him into the trinitarian mystery. His language is simple and accessible and, after all the hard work, his English flows effortlessly in triple repetitions of words and phrases, even triplets of triplets:

> 'Of him, says the great Apostle, and by him and in him are all things: to him be glory for ever (Romans 11:36).'
>
> Of him are all things: of whatever we possess God has the absolute dominion; of life, health, riches, power, we are only allowed but precarious tenure: they belong only to God.
>
> By him are all things: he made them out of nothing: from the most brilliant star of the firmament to the smallest grain of sand there is not a being that could come into existence, only for the creating will of God.
>
> In him are all things: he penetrates, he surrounds, he upholds the universe:
>> we breathe, we move, we live in God
>> like the bird breathes, moves, lives in the air,
>> like the fish breathes, moves, lives in the water.

> For of him, and by him, and in him are all things. How reasonable the conclusion which the apostle comes to: to him be glory for ever.

Martelli then turned to one of the subjects that most inflamed him, the false claim that the Catholic Church discouraged learning so that 'the less educated her members are, the more docile she expects to find them to follow her superstitious creed'. Here his polemical prose becomes heavier, the vocabulary more learned, the style combative:

> The reason which I prize this new building for is, above all, because it will be a standing protest against that false charge that is so often professed against the Catholic Church by her enemies, when they say that she neglects the education of her children, that she is unfavourable to the diffusion of knowledge, and that she courts the darkness of ignorance.

What answers can we give to this false charge? Martelli equipped his listeners to defend their faith. 'Teach!' was the commission Jesus gave to his disciples, and teach the Church had always done, sending religious orders – like the good Sisters – to all corners of the globe. In Western Australia, no Christian denomination 'has done and is doing so much as we Catholics do for the children of the poor'. Rounding on the ruling establishment, Martelli became openly sectarian: 'The Protestant Community has done nothing: the intellectual wants of the poor classes have found its purse closed all together'. The schools in Fremantle showed how Catholics – priests and people – valued education.

Still in polemical vein, he turned his animated attention to Catholic parents who sent their children to government schools. Surely they will now come to their senses: 'have they forgotten that the Almighty will one day ask an account of their children's soul at their hands?'

He knew he had gone far enough: 'But I do not like to discourse on so sad a topic on a day which calls forth sentiments of gratitude and holy joy.' His notes run out at this point and the final page is lost, so we do not know how he salvaged a mood of holy joy after such righteous and furious polemic.

The Sisters' school was situated on the Adelaide Street precinct, with its impressive new buildings. The first St Patrick's was a fine limestone building, in the Gothic Revival style, and the imposing presbytery next door was the second-largest building in town. Martelli spent the rest of his prison back-pay on the buildings and grounds. He planted four rows of Cape Lilac trees and 'plenty of roses' and then two dozen fig trees in the presbytery grounds with cuttings from New Subiaco. 'My successor will enjoy these improvements, not I; still, it is a pleasure to work for those who are to come, whether they will feel grateful or not.'[7]

St Patrick's was opened in August 1861, by Fr Griver, assisted by Martelli. Martelli saw that the church consisted only of the central nave, the transept being postponed for lack of funds. He feared at the time that it might never be finished. When he became Chaplain, he had the opportunity, and the duty, to bring the building to completion. He set about raising funds locally but relied on a top-up from Fr Griver. The Apostolic Administrator, however, was planning to provide Perth with a new Cathedral. A new phase of tug-of-war ensued.[8]

Martelli was passionate in representing his parishioners. They made sacrifices to raise the necessary funds but were frustrated that diocesan funds were spent mostly in Perth. Of the £862 spent on the church so far, over half was contributed by parishioners and local clergy, £150 from Governor Kennedy and the rest from voluntary contributions in several parts of the Colony. Fr Griver had dedicated a mere £50. Martelli outlined his parishioners' case in no uncertain terms: 'Do not, pray, think me arrogant in making these complaints: they are, I think, the echo of the sentiments of the people, and it is good for you to be made acquainted with them'.[9]

In 1865, Griver offered £100 towards building one of the church's two transepts. The uneven treatment was bad enough. Griver's piecemeal approach would produce a church with one transept built and the other missing, and 'the unfinished state of the edifice will be more strickingly apparent, after the addition'. Nevertheless, counting on Griver's £100 and the £68 from the monthly collection for the Chapel Building Fund, Martelli got the work done. When Griver paid up only £50 and said he would pay the other half when the *second* transept was also finished, it was too much for 'the irascible old Canon', who 'flew into a great fury'. When Griver changed his mind and paid the remaining amount, Martelli thought it was because he had seen how upset Martelli was.[10]

Martelli greatly admired Fr Griver as 'a prudent and pious man [who] governs the diocese well'. Their personalities, however, could not have been more different. Martelli preferred quicker decisions and decisive action: 'He is such a man for to raise objections, and I loose [sic] my temper with him.' Martelli confessed to Salvado he did not possess the virtue required to accept Griver as he found him:

After saying <u>yes</u>, he will, on reflecting, say <u>no</u>; then, reflecting again, he will utter a <u>perhaps</u>, and, lastly, he will wind up with a <u>I do not know</u>. I have seen this process of his thoughts, expressed exactly in the above quoted words. 'You ought to know him', your Lordship will say. Yes, but the circumstances in which I was entangled in the case were too painful for me to keep my temper.[11]

At the beginning of the transept project, Martelli hit on a memorable literary image to give respectful vent to his frustration. Archbishop Goody cites it approvingly in his short biography of Griver, noting that 'the meekness of Martín Griver clearly needed the occasional prod from the fiery, outspoken Italian Canon'. The image is from *The Liberation of Jerusalem*. In Tasso's epic, the sun rises after a night of hand-to-hand carnage between the Muslims who have occupied the Holy City and the Crusaders laying siege to it. Mighty Solyman, Sultan of the Turks, disheveled from battle and covered in blood, rides out alone in a fury to assess his options. Half-crazed with the shame of the night's losses and the thirst for revenge, he 'tosses in a great storm of thoughts', *in gran tempesta di pensieri ondeggia*. When Martelli wrote to Salvado that, when faced with competing demands from Perth and Fremantle, 'the Administrator "in gran tempesta di pensieri ondeggia" and keeps silence', the contrast between the fearsome Sultan and the cautious Administrator is so preposterous as to defuse Martelli's complaint. Salvado must have admired Martelli's ability to use his linguistic skill and literary knowledge to find ways to call a spade a spade without ever forgetting the proprieties required of his social world.[12]

For all that Griver's preference for Perth was a source of frustration, Martelli applauded his success in erecting a new Cathedral in the capital. The new Cathedral of the Immaculate Conception of the Blessed Virgin Mary was consecrated on 29 January 1865.

Martelli was disappointed the New Norcia priests did not take part (because of some miscommunication that has never been satisfactorily explained) since 'there is between the New Norcia family and the new sacred edifice, perhaps, more connection than people are aware of'.[13]

Local newspapers paid perfunctory attention to the event and a long letter from Martelli to Salvado in Rome is the only report that has survived:[14]

> Our Cathedral was solemnly blessed and opened on the 29th January amidst a gathering of some hundreds of people and nearly all the clergy of the diocese with the exception of the priests of New Norcia, who made themselves conspicous by their absence [...] What is certain is that, on so solemn an occasion, to miss a representative of New Norcia was very painful, at least to me; and I did not fail to complain to the Administrator, who, however, pleaded unguilty.

The interior of the building was lavishly decorated, a little too lavishly for Martelli's taste:

> The High Altar looks grand, but the altar furniture and decoration lacked that simplicity to which Roman eyes are accustomed. The principle "there is not too much of a good thing" had been blindly acted upon; and candlesticks and vases and alabaster jugs had been heaped upon with intemperate profusion. Besides, the three pedestals, originally intended to support the three statues, are in my opinion, an incumbrance and eyesore, at present, not doing duty for what they were meant.

After the solemn blessing at 10.30, the High Mass that followed was a multicultural affair, like the young West Australian church that joined together in celebration. Martelli, as the senior cleric in the diocese after Griver, acted as deacon. The Spanish Administrator was also assisted by the Irishman Fr Lynch as sub-deacon (the evening sub-deacon was the Belgian Adolphus Lecaille), while Irishman Matthew Gibney acted as Master of Ceremonies and preached the homily. Brother Odon Oltra from New Norcia played the organ, and a seventy-five-strong choir conducted by the German Christian Brother Botthian sang a Mass setting by English composer Samuel Webbe. Martelli gave more details to Salvado:

> The music was pretty good; sisters and brothers and laymen joining in it. A number of <u>Enfants de coeur</u> [altar servers], in red soutane and nice surplice, who had been previously trained and a company of girls in white with wreaths of flowers on their head, were not the least attractive feature of the ceremony. Fr Gibney altho' acting the Master of Ceremonies and directing everything, pronounced, after gospel, an impressive and able sermon, which he had prepared only the previous night. A collection was then made, which, joined to another collection at the evening sermon, given by Fr Lynch, has reached the amount of about £18. The

proceeds from the sale of the admission tickets was, I think, about £32.

The formalities resumed at sunset:

On the evening, after vespers and sermon, the Blessed Sacrament was transferred from the old chapel to the Cathedral, when a procession took place, with which people were delighted. It was after sunset. The Catholic Young Men's Society opened. They wore, for the first time beautiful sashes, the insignia of their body: schoolboys followed breast decorated with rosettes, altar boys came next with lighted tapers and then the whiterobed girls, some of them scattering flowers, and then the Fremantle Sisters and the Sisters of Mercy and the clergy and the canopy, under which the Bl. Sacrament was carried by the Administrator, the writer of this letter acting as deacon, as he had done at mass, and Fr Lecaille, subdeacon. All came off with all the decorum and pomp, which we could command; and I am sure that the 29th January 1865 will be long remembered with pride by all the Catholics, who attended the ceremony.

The architect and builder of the Cathedral, Benedictine lay brother Giuseppe Ascione, was well-known and popular. Martelli came to consider him conceited and, as the Cathedral was nearing completion, he told Salvado of rumours 'that our Michelangelo contemplates to leave this Mission, which I suppose has become too narrow a theatre to his glory'.[15] Ascione left Perth soon after the Cathedral opening. He travelled to South Australia, where he worked for old friends Christopher Reynolds, now bishop, and Fr Frederick Byrne. In Adelaide, he married Mary Anne Doyle, of Perth, who it seems was expecting another man's child. Martelli was harsh: Ascione 'has been satisfied to receive both cow and calf, as goes the phrase in my country'. When Ascione wrote from Adelaide, it seems Martelli did not reply.[16]

The opening of the Cathedral was all but ignored in the city's two newspapers, just a 'few dry words' in the *Perth Gazette*. It must have been this that prompted Martelli to take up writing for newspapers, something he had not done since the ambiguous days leading up to the 1848 war. In Risorgimento Italy, moderate liberals believed the press had a moral responsibility to inform and educate. Here, in Protestant Western Australia, it was important to keep Catholic news before the public eye: to reassure Catholics of the glorious achievements of their religion and to counter anti-Catholic prejudice.[17]

Unsigned announcements of Catholic events began to appear in local newspapers. It is likely that Martelli was the author. For example, a report in the *Inquirer* repeats many of the phrases from Martelli's report of the event to Salvado:

> CATHOLIC YOUNG MEN'S SOCIETY The soirée which was given by this Society in their Hall on Wednesday evening, and the 'good things' which were so liberally provided appeared to afford satisfaction. The pleasure of the evening was much enhanced by some of the Christian Brothers' pupils singing several amusing Negro Melodies...[18]

> Three days later, the Young Men's Society had their first tea-party, in the old Chapel, now transformed into a boys school. All the clergy attended: the good things were abundant: no lack of toasts proposed and responded to, the health of the Pope being the first. The boys performed several dialogues and gave Niger's songs: Other songs were sung, all came off with general satisfaction. So pleasant an evening I had not spent since I landed in Swan River.[19]

The *Inquirer* was the 'loyal mouthpiece' of Perth's Anglican establishment. An alternative voice was heard in 1867. The Fremantle *Herald* was founded by James Pearce and William Beresford, both ex-convicts and Anglicans, but with a liberal position on religious issues. The *Herald* was 'from the outset a decidedly radical and outspoken newspaper'. Martelli became a regular contributor.[20]

In March 1867, the *Herald* carried an announcement of the profession of vows by Mary Butler at the convent of St Joseph. The editors commented that the author was 'Canon Martelli, a Reverend gentleman well known to, and much beloved by, every member of our limited community', and added a long reflection on 'Sisterhoods'. The benefits and supposed dangers of female religious orders had recently been debated in the London *Pall Mall Gazette*, but the editors fearlessly recommended them to 'those who, though their aspirations are strongly Protestant, are still actuated by charities equally as Catholic'.[21]

Martelli would not suffer attacks on charitable works by the Catholic population. In February 1868, the Sisters of Mercy opened St Joseph's Orphanage for Girls in Perth. Eleven girls were moved there from the State-run Poor House, with some financial support from the government. In Fremantle, the *Herald* simply reported that several ladies at the Anglican cathedral were hoping to establish a similar institution for girls of the Protestant faith.[22]

The *Inquirer*, however, published a letter signed by 'A Magistrate'. The Catholic orphanage was the result of advantages the Catholic population had over the Protestants: 'they receive aid from abroad; they are inspired with the hope of strengthening their cause and increasing their converts; they have holy men and women ready for the work; they have orthodox modes of levying needful contributions from every member of the church.'[23]

Martelli was incensed and sent a long reply, dripping with sarcasm, not to the *Inquirer*, but to the *Herald*. If someone can explain what these *orthodox modes* are, he retorted, 'I might find it easier to complete the construction of St Patrick's'. Then he took a wider aim, at bigotry grounded in ignorance. He had read of the campaign waged by English MP George Whalley, *alias* Patrick Murphy, against the evils of Catholic confession. Many things, even absolution in the confessional, could be bought. Martelli cleverly insinuated that the 'Magistrate' was peddling the same 'old and wide spread prejudice'.[24]

Another attack on the Catholic orphanage came from the *WA Church of England Magazine*, summarised in the irrepressible *Fremantle Herald*. Anti-Popery polemic was one thing. The accusation that 'deception was practised' by Catholic fundraisers was too much. Martelli penned another lengthy reply, ending with an appeal for mutual respect:

> Is it possible that [the accuser] cannot even leave his neighbours in peace, who engaged in an enterprise of charity, which has enlisted the sympathy of colonists of every creed? Shall we then be compelled to remark with the French satirist, *Entre-t-il tant de fiel dans l'ame des dévots* [Can such bitterness enter into the heart of the devout]?[25]

This goaded the Editor of the *Church of England Magazine* into action. Catholics asked for donations for an orphanage, he rather lamely argued to the *Herald*, but diverted those donations to the Mercy Convent, and in this way got money from Protestants who would never otherwise have supported such an edifice. His parting shot merely echoed Martelli:

> I will not close this with the satire charitably applied by the Rev. Canon Martelli at the end of his letter, the question so ingenously [sic] asked by him. But I can justly repeat: 'Why will not these gentlemen leave their neighbors alone.'[26]

Martelli made no reply. Perhaps he recognised a moral victory, or perhaps it was a case of 'least said, soonest mended'. When the Catholic Orphanage Committee met for the first time early in 1869, it paid warm tribute to Protestant donors, agreeing that 'the heartfelt thanks of this meeting be tendered to the subscribers, but especially to their Protestant fellow-colonists for their support and assistance in this laudable undertaking'.[27]

The other side of Martelli's public defence of Catholicism was a growing fear of public scandal among clergy or people, which might give ammunition to the Church's enemies. When cases of sexual misconduct arose among clergy, Catholic or Protestant, he mused to Salvado, 'God protect us all, because we are all of the same clay and liable to the same miseries.'[28]

He became uneasy with his position as spiritual director to the Sisters of St Joseph. He told Salvado the small community of four sisters was 'unsound': two of them had received inadequate formation and did not submit to their superior. Martelli was preoccupied with the risk of scandal: if the discontent within the convent became publicly known, 'will not the Protestant notion receive a confirmation, that is, that the inmates of our Convents are no better than prisoners?' But he was troubled by deeper scruples, the chance that discontent might lead to some 'scandalous event': 'we must thank Providence that does not seem to permit temptation to approach the Convent Wall'.[29]

There is no hint from any other records of such a possibility within the Fremantle convent. Yet Martelli became agitated as he told Salvado how incompetent he felt. He seems uncertain even of himself:

> I have no experience of Convents. I am unfit for having any part in their direction; and I am frightened, to tell the truth. Have mercy on me. We have had a bad case among the priests. God preserve us from something of the kind in other quarters.

Yet, in other situations, his appreciation of human frailty was outweighed by an intransigent attachment to church teaching. In January 1865, a parishioner, one Mrs Barker, was found dead in her home. She suffered from alcoholism and the coroner ruled death was a result of her state of intoxication. Because of this, and the fact that she failed to attend church the previous Easter, Martelli felt 'bound to apply the censures of the Church by refusing Christian burial'. Her Protestant husband arranged for a burial by a Protestant minister, which was well attended – and by many Catholics, 'I am sorry to say'. Martelli was unmoved and had Griver's support. In defiant mood, he told Salvado, 'Fiat justitia, ruat coelum is the principle which has guided me [Let justice be done, though the heavens may fall]'.[30]

Still, while he waged these public battles to defend the church's public image, Martelli built genuine and productive friendships with the Protestant pastors in Fremantle, Anglican Rev. George Bostock and Congregational Rev. Johnston. The three clerics were on the committee organising the Fremantle welcome to the Duke of Edinburgh and together penned a united protest at the violation of the Lord's Day by boat crews training – during the hours of divine service – for the Foundation Day regatta.[31]

The collegial companionship of his fellow Catholic priests was one of his great pleasures. He enjoyed the quarterly meetings of the priests Griver instituted: 'Uniformity in certain practices is promoted and friendly feelings are kept up among the laborers of the same field'. And he always found time to share a humorous anecdote with the priests, especially at the mission. Martelli's knack for self-mockery never left him. Convicts built a bridge over the Swan at its mouth and in 1866 Martelli crossed it even before it was completed. A late-night sick call was a pretext for another tale of high drama:

> By climbing up a step ladder, I crossed it at midnight. It was rough and wet and the boards very slippery. Only for the company I had, I should not have ventured to have the honor of being among the first who have crossed it. I did not dare look down on the water. It seemed frightful. The danger of being blown away, in stormy whether [sic], is not very remote.[32]

Conversely, the lack of collegiality in those with whom he was called to share his life was the cause of real suffering. For all his ten years in Fremantle, Martelli shared the presbytery with Fr Lynch. Relations were never more than cordial. It is not clear what caused the difficulty. Perhaps Lynch resented being moved to the prison chaplaincy in 1862, because that is when the tension surfaces in the archive. In official prison correspondence, Lynch was fulsome in praise for his 'indefatigable predecessor', but in his first annual report, he made a rather pointed remark about levels of religious conviction at the prison: 'To me, who till lately had the consolation of labouring in a more fertile field, it is truly saddening to witness a barrenness of belief that tells of an almost utter extinction of Faith as a Principle of Recovery'.[33]

Arguments blew up over the most trivial matters of housekeeping. An ethnic dimension emerged when Fr Patrick Gibney (brother of future bishop Matthew) arrived in February 1864 and Lynch invited him to stay in the presbytery without saying anything to Martelli. When both Gibneys were in the house with Lynch, Martelli felt himself 'shut out' by the three Irishmen and begged Fr Griver to transfer him back 'over the hills'. The problem cannot have been totally ethnic, however, since Lynch had an equally stormy relationship with Martelli's successor, Irishman Anselm Bourke. By the end of 1864, Martelli and Lynch were barely on speaking terms: 'My confrere and I meet only once in the day, at dinner time. I make almost always two or three attempts to introduce some topic of conversation; I get an answer in the laconic style, and often a monosyllabical one, and then silence until we meet again'. Martelli knew his own failings and appealed to Garrido for encouragement: 'The older I grow, my dear friend, the more disagreeable and irritable I become. I stand in need of your prayers and exhortation'. Garrido was lapidary in response: 'the world is itself a continual disappointment'.[34]

His six years as Chaplain to Fremantle were busy, challenging and productive. Universally recognised for his compassion towards those in need and his cordial good will towards those of other faiths, Martelli formed strong bonds with his parishioners. But his heart was elsewhere. Letters to priests at New Norcia contain ironic and unflattering descriptions of Fremantle. These were not so much a judgement on the town as a way of relieving his frustration at not being free to retire to the mission. 'I have a great wish to get out of this sand', he wrote to Martínez in December 1864. In February 1868, after his summer month in New Norcia, he told Garrido he was returning to his 'Sheep Station'. A new priest had arrived in the diocese and Martelli wondered whom he would replace, 'who will be the first soul drawn out of this Purgatory? Not I, I am sure. <u>Fiat voluntas tua</u> [Thy will be done].'[35]

By 1868, the end of his Purgatory was in sight.

CHAPTER SEVENTEEN

My Ten Years Are Up

1862–1868

Martelli, my friend, pray to the Lord for me – a lot. I lead a life that is quite useless: oh if only I could at least do something for the Lord in the few years of life left to me! 47 or 48 have gone by in dreams and plans and nothing has come of them.[1]

Martelli's childhood friend, Tommaso Gallucci, must have struck a chord. To all appearances, Gallucci had built a successful ecclesiastical career: he was now Vicar General to Cardinal Baluffi in Imola. This letter is from 1860, when Gallucci, like Martelli, was approaching fifty. Both men seemed obsessed. They did not want to live uselessly.

When Martelli took up the position of town chaplain in March 1862, he reminded Fr Griver that in just over a year's time, 'my ten years are up'. Surely now he could join the mission and do the useful work he had come to Australia to do. Fr Griver laughed off suggestions Martelli might leave and advised him to pray for the strength to continue his labours in the vineyard of the Lord. On the day the contract expired, 18 August 1863, Martelli informed Griver that he now considered himself free from all obligation to the diocese. However, to allow time for finding a replacement, he offered to stay in Fremantle until the end of September.[2]

Martelli's position in the diocese was uniquely ambiguous. When New Norcia was separated from the diocese in 1859, only two Benedictine priests remained at the service of the diocese, Fr Bertrán in New Subiaco and Fr Bourke in York. If priests were to be moved, Martelli could hardly expect to take precedence over the two Benedictines.[3]

In theory, Martelli was free to move as he wished. Salvado did not have the authority to order him to stay or to leave and could only advise him not to leave the diocese. For Martelli, this advice was as good as a command. He knew there was no realistic prospect of leaving Fremantle until new priests came to Western Australia.

He became so discouraged that he began to look elsewhere. He knew from Fr Christopher Reynolds that Adelaide was short of priests. In Ceylon, the Vicar Apostolic in Colombo, Bishop Sillani, a fellow *marchigiano* from near Ancona, would accept him, provided Propaganda agreed. Martelli appealed to even higher authorities. The monks owned a painting of the Archangel Raphael, from the seventeenth-century Seville School. When Garrido sent greetings on his feast day, Martelli felt the saint was 'calling me to New Norcia from the fine painting you have up there'.[4]

Two years into his time as Fremantle Chaplain, however, a new crisis threatened New Norcia. Any thoughts Martelli had about acting on the expiration of his contract were put on hold.

Abbot Casaretto, Martelli's friend who was abbot of Santa Scolastica, wanted to bring New Norcia under the direct control of the Cassinese Congregazione and bring the mission into line with European monastic practice. He allied himself with Bishop Serra. If Serra succeeded in getting the 1859 decree of separation rescinded and returned as bishop of Perth, it would be easier for Casaretto to assume effective control of New Norcia. Martelli believed that

School of Bartolmeon Estaban Murillo, The Archangel Raphael

Serra had imposed Casaretto's strict 'Primitive Observance' in the New Subiaco monastery as a way of gaining Casaretto's support.[5]

Martelli was writing regularly to Casaretto during this period and may have unwittingly contributed to these developments. In late 1859, Martelli confided in Casaretto about the difficulties facing the West Australian church. This letter has not survived, but Casaretto's reply was to the point: 'Your letter confirmed my belief that things in the missions [New Norcia and Perth] are not prospering as well as had been communicated here. In fact, they have reached the point to make one fear for the very survival of those missions.' He made a visceral appeal to Martelli: 'if [Salvado] has not received my recent letter, beg him by the bowels of J.C. [Jesus Christ] not to oppose the union of his monastery of New Norcia with our Subiaco Province'.[6]

In July 1864, Cardinal Barnabò informed Salvado that Propaganda had appointed Casaretto as Superior of New Norcia. Salvado was summoned to Rome to put his case.[7]

Martelli was devastated. As the departure loomed, he asked to be buried at New Norcia if he should die during Salvado's absence. From Albany, Salvado wrote to Martelli and Garrido and sailed on 24 September 1864.[8]

In Rome, Salvado called on Martelli's old friend Pietro Regnoli. He became a frequent guest at Sunday lunch in the Regnoli home in central Rome. Pietro's brother, Lieto, was a doctor and treated Salvado for minor ailments, and his daughter and nephew took Salvado sightseeing around Rome. Regnoli told him he became 'one of the most important members of the family'.[9]

Martelli was delighted to know his dearest friends had become friends with each other. He imagined them together in the comfortable Regnoli home he knew so well: 'I wish I were in a corner of that drawing room and have my share in the laugh of the company'. From afar, he could relive the relationship with his old friends vicariously, through Salvado. He switched to Italian to pass on thanks to the Regnolis, knowing that Salvado would communicate the sentiments in the original language:

I beg you to express my heart-felt acknowledgements to my Pierino and his good sister for the gentilezze che prodigano, com'Ella dice, a V. Eccellenza [kindnesses they shower, as you say, on Your Excellency]. I look upon them as if they were done to myself.[10]

Regnoli brought Salvado into his network of influential friends – artists and scientists – who would be useful to the mission in many ways. The cultured Spaniard moved with ease among Rome's elite. Friendships were cemented by the exchange of gifts. Martelli sent curiosities from Australia, both flora and fauna.

The gift-giving was two-way. Martelli asked Salvado for a set of Stations of the Cross for St Patrick's, a Bambino for his Christmas crib, and incense: 'I am fond of perfumes as a Parisian dandy and ready to pay for them, but they must be good indeed'. And books: 'I have no Italian books here.' He asked for Regnoli to send a 'pocketable' edition of Dante and Tasso. Regnoli added Petrarch and Ariosto, an old Risorgimento favourite, Silvio Pellico's *Le Mie Prigioni*, and two books on religious topics.[11]

Another gift that circulated between Martelli, Salvado and their Italian networks was photographs. Back in 1862, Martelli received a photograph of Pietro Regnoli and his family. He forwarded it to Salvado in New Norcia with a witty covering note:

> Revered and dear Monsignor, I have the honour to present to you a party of Ladies and Gentlemen [these three words in English], who have come to visit me at the Antipodes and now wish to see N. Norcia, about which they have heard so much in Rome. Mr Pietro Regnoli is accompanied by his venerable mother, by his sister [Malvina] now a widow and, I believe, the mother of the boy [Scipione], and lastly by his daughter Emilia, who had the good fortune to receive Confirmation from Mgr Serra, as you will recall. What do you think of this surprise? Please extend a warm welcome to these dear strangers and after they have stayed an appropriate period with you, please send them to me.[12]

Six weeks later, 'our Roman friends have returned to Fremantle safe and sound, and I have kept a spot for them in my bedroom'.[13]

Salvado was quick to grasp the potential of the new technology and sent photographs of himself and the mission to friends and donors far and wide. Martelli, on the other hand, was strangely reticent about having his own photo taken, even when the women of the Regnoli household asked for it. He tied himself in knots trying to justify his excess of bashfulness. At the root of it, perhaps, lay his growing feeling of detachment from Italy:

> I am in a dilemma. To refuse them seems to be ungracious. I almost feel I am guilty of ingratitude. On the other hand I feel so repugnant to have myself multiplied by photographic process and reappear in the old world to serve no useful purpose. Will you undertake to apologise...?[14]

Their correspondence from this period contains a rare record of emotion. In early 1866, Martelli failed to mention New Norcia at all in a couple of letters and Salvado deduced he was thinking of staying in Fremantle after all. 'Well, well, well', Martelli was put out, 'this I did not expect. How can your Lordship harbour any doubt about my wishes on the subject of joining the Native Mission of N. Norcia, I am at a loss to understand'. What he added next must have really surprised Salvado. Martelli was writing to old friends, Reynolds and Byrne, about joining them in Adelaide. After a year or so there he would transfer to New Norcia *from South Australia* so Griver would have no grounds for complaint. The shortest road from Perth to New Norcia was via Adelaide.[15]

This misunderstanding elicted words of 'glowing friendship' from Salvado that deeply affected Martelli, 'What a treasure the Lord has bestowed on me in your affectionate friendship, you do not know, nor can I appreciate it in an adequate manner.' He shared Salvado's letter with Garrido and confessed to being 'not a little confused at being the object of so much undeserved affection'. Indeed, he wryly added, 'I cannot regret the gentle remonstrance

I made to him, since it has had the effect of eliciting from him the manifestation of so kindly feelings'. Salvado's letter has not survived but we can judge the tone from something he wrote to Garrido two days earlier:

> May the Lord enlighten him and guide him to the correct decision. I could not hold him in higher esteem if he were my own brother, nor wish greater things for him than those I wish for myself. And I am firmly convinced that I am only fulfilling a duty of mutual and fraternal obligation.[16]

As these expressions of affection were flowing back and forth, Salvado took a major step in Rome. He had with him a letter Martelli had written on the eve of Salvado's departure. Reverting to Italian, Martelli set out his position with respect to New Norcia in very formal language, asking Salvado to put his case to the Prefect of Propaganda Fide. Here is the text of the letter in its entirety (translated from the Italian):

> Before Your Reverend Excellency departs for Rome allow me to remind you of my desire, manifest to you already many times, to be received into the Benedictine Community of New Norcia. The time of my ten-year-long engagement in this Diocese expired in August last year, as you well know. The Apostolic Administrator of this Diocese, Fr Martin Griver, has refused so far to assent to the execution of my plan; and Your Excellency, for reasons of prudence, has not believed it appropriate to receive me without the assent of said Administrator. I now make bold to ask you to deign to propose my case to His Eminence the Prefect of Propaganda, so that he may wish to use his authoritative influence with Fr Griver, in order that the latter may desist from making further opposition to my desire.[17]

His Eminence the Prefect had no intention of forcing Griver's hand at a time when relations between Perth and New Norcia were under negotiation. This is why Salvado sat on the letter for two years. Then, in April 1866 (when Martelli was threatening to move to South Australia), he presented the letter to Cardinal Barnabò in person. Barnabò reminded Salvado of his canonical obligations. The bishop of Martelli's home diocese had to give approval. Salvado wrote to Archbishop Antonucci, with a brief but glowing testimonial:

> He left Europe in 1853, in my company, for those regions almost at the antipodes, and I am delighted to be able now to testify not only to his excellent and exemplary conduct, but also his great zeal for the salvation of the souls entrusted to him and the singular disinterest and rare abnegation with which he has always discharged all and each of the various difficult tasks placed in his care [...] In any case, the fact that His Eminence Cardinal Baluffi honours Martelli with the title 'excellent friend' would be for me a more than satisfactory recommendation.[18]

Salvado's letter contains two definitions of Martelli's intention. He 'desires to join the monastic community' and then Salvado would be prepared to 'admit him to the religious habit in the monastery'. This second expression is Benedictine language. When they enter the novitiate, future monks 'take the habit' or 'are clothed in the habit'. Martelli never used such language. He spoke of 'entering the community', 'living under the shadow of St Benedict' and so on, but made no mention of professing vows or 'taking the habit'. In 1851, he told Casaretto he was too set in his ways to bend to the rule of cloistered life. Salvado seems to have respected this. The Benedictine family was always able to welcome within its embrace persons of various identities. Salvado's letter must be referring to this warm welcome, not to the taking of vows.

Antonucci, however, took Salvado literally. 'His decision to become a Benedictine Religious edifies me greatly and moves me,' he wrote, 'and I cannot but bless the Lord who brings his servants to perfection in marvellous ways.' He happily approved Martelli's decision and congratulated the Benedictine Order for 'in this worthy churchman it acquires a person of virtue, knowledge and learning that are out of the ordinary'.[19]

It is strange that Martelli makes no mention of these developments in any of his correspondence. He clearly was aware of them, since he pressed Garrido to declare if he would have any difficulty in admitting him to the mission if Cardinal Barnabò was satisfied, to which Garrido answered 'None'. Yet, his letters contain no further mention of the possibility of 'joining the Benedictines'.[20]

In Fremantle, meanwhile, Martelli continued to pepper Fr Griver with requests for release from the diocese. He tried to force Griver's hand by demanding their 1853 contract be honoured. Griver repeated that Martelli was free to leave at any time. As for money, the diocese was no longer bound to pay Martelli any removal expenses. In 1853, priests kept no moneys for themselves but gave everything 'to the Administrator to make a common Mission Fund'. Since some priests 'felt dislike for that common manner of life', Bishop Serra had granted them a salary and allowed them to keep donations from their congregations for themselves. So 'when we accepted this new arrangement, it may be said that we renounced the hope' that the Administrator would pay their exit from the diocese.[21]

Martelli's sense of fair play was affronted. But what kept him in the diocese was the strategy Griver used. If Martelli left, the Administrator would, most regrettably, be 'obliged to ask Fr Martínez' to replace him. Martelli told Salvado that Griver was 'playing with me a game of chess':

> When I check his queen, he guards off the blow by, as it were, checking my own queen; that is, when I say I am going, he writes to New Norcia to summon Fr Martinez to take my place; and then, of course, I am compelled to retract my word and resign to my fate. But the game, I hope, will shortly be at an end.[22]

Griver knew all along that Martelli would never accept this. A big part of Martelli's reason for going to New Norcia was to be in the company of his Benedictine friends, especially Martínez and Garrido. He had grown fond of the younger priest, telling Garrido in 1862, 'How much I admire and love him'.[23]

It was Martínez who replaced Martelli in Fremantle every January so he could take his annual summer holiday in New Norcia. Those weeks at the mission were for friendship. Martelli would go for long walks with Garrido, morning and evening, 'on the hills surrounding the Mission', just as he loved a sunset walk in Fremantle, out to the Hampton bridge across the mouth of the Swan.[24]

As his own frustrations simmered, Martelli was learning forbearance for the faults of others. Salvado stayed at the monastery of Sant'Ambrogio in Rome and was surprised when Casaretto presented him with a bill for expenses. Martelli seems less judgemental than sad at such petty meanness in his old friend: 'I am not a little shocked at the niggardly way in which you have been treated by your host. I can only say that the best men have their weak points'.[25]

The New Norcia case was decided on 12 March 1867, entirely in Salvado's favour. New Norcia was raised to the status of Prefecture Apostolic and Abbey Nullius, its territory separated from the Perth diocese. Salvado was appointed Abbot for life, with all Benedictines in Western Australia under his authority. Martelli rejoiced that this would guarantee the mission 'stability, independence and tranquillity', and give him the chance to retire there.[26]

The see of Perth remained under the temporary authority of Fr Griver. The separation of diocese and abbey was a delicate process. Salvado received explicit instructions from Propaganda that 'the priested monks currently serving the diocese should not leave for New Norcia immediately or all together, but should do so in a staggered manner to be arranged amicably in consultation with the Perth Administrator'.[27]

Martelli knew his transfer to New Norcia was just a matter of time and all he had to do was wait. Even as Salvado stayed on in Europe for two more years, Martelli seems to have relaxed into a state of confident expectation.

Certain of the eventual outcome, his horizons seem to have shrunk to his immediate surroundings. Connections to Europe grew more tenuous. Regnoli received fewer letters and was forced to ask Salvado for news of his old friend. When Salvado left Rome for Spain, Regnoli signed off, 'Regards to Martelli, as I will be hearing his news less often now'. Martelli's letters to Salvado continued their monthly rhythm, but now the tone is lighter, concerned with news and people in Perth and in Europe, with scarcely a complaint or request about his entry into the mission.[28]

He was now in his mid-fifties and becoming obsessed with the passing of time. 'I am growing old and thin shocking fast,' he told Salvado. 'Mr Harris, the magistrate of the Vasse, met me this afternoon, after one or two years that he saw me last, and unceremoniously remarked upon the unpleasant fact.' The haemorrhoids 'make a man irritable and unpleasant, unless he has learned to conquer himself; a science in which I am not proficient at all'. The thought of two days riding 'nearly unmans me' and he would face the ordeal only to enjoy the peace of New Norcia.

If you wait any longer, he warned Garrido in May 1868, 'the old Canon will be good for nothing, he will be only a nuisance at the Mission. You remember what old Horace says of the faults of old people: difficilis, querulus, censor, castigatorque minorum [difficult, quarelsome, censorious, punisher of youth]'. It was not just the demands of running the parish that was wearing him down. The situation in the presbytery had become intolerable.[29]

In October 1868, Martelli told Salvado he must leave Fremantle immediately. Since the gates of New Norcia were closed to him, he would go elsewhere.

The relationship between Martelli and Fr Lynch had broken down. For two months, they stopped eating together and things of a 'disedifying nature' took place between them. Persons outside the presbytery 'were becoming aware of the situation' and friends told Martelli that either he or Lynch had to leave Fremantle. We will, mercifully perhaps, never know the details, since neither priest recorded his grievances on paper. They both confided in

Fr Garrido in face-to-face meetings. Lynch stressed he only asked for 'fair play' and 'tried hard, did much violence to myself, and made many sacrifices'. Martelli told Garrido simply, 'I do not like to commit to writing details and explanations.'[30]

Martelli also informed Griver that he could take no more and would leave within a month. With Garrido, he was blunt: 'Do not undertake to alter this my resolution, it is time lost. I cannot, I will not, and I think I should not go on. Matters are gone too far.'[31]

A month later, Martelli rode over to Perth to speak with Garrido, who was in town on business. It was Friday 6 November. He planned to leave for Adelaide with the next colonial mail, on the 14th. South Australia? Garrido asked, why do you not go directly to New Norcia? 'Because I am not wanted there', replied Martelli. Garrido's remonstrations could not dissuade Martelli from leaving Fremantle, but did change his destination. Martelli would leave the following week as planned, but directly for the mission. He would announce this to his congregation immediately, at Sunday Masses 'the day after tomorrow'.[32]

That same evening, however, a tragedy occurred that made him delay yet again. Fr Lynch's niece was admitted to the Lunatic Asylum. Mary McCann came to the colony in 1865 to join the Sisters of Mercy in Perth, but left the convent in March 1868, claiming (with her uncle's support) she was mistreated there. Lynch planned to take her back to England himself and entrusted her to the Sisters of St Joseph while he waited for a boat. Martelli thought the Superior showed lack of prudence in admitting the girl without getting advice.[33]

As he returned from Perth that evening, the two Fremantle priests were called urgently. Mary was admitted to the Asylum suffering 'under religious delusions', a not uncommon diagnosis for the time. Martelli was involved because the imposing limestone building was the responsibility of the town chaplain. She recovered quickly and was discharged into Lynch's care. By January, she was on a boat for Ireland. After the night of Mary's breakdown, Lynch spoke not another word to Martelli, except in the presence of

Garrido, nor did he speak to the Sisters of St Joseph, even as they were caring for his niece.[34]

Martelli decided to say nothing to his congregation that Sunday, lest people should deduce that his decision to leave was influenced by the tragedy. He waited for his replacement, Fr Bourke, to arrive from York, but he was delayed and Garrido was leaving soon for New Norcia. The day before Bourke was due to arrive, Martelli caught the steamer to Perth.[35]

There was no time to organise a farewell function. An effusive 'Address of the Roman Catholics, Fremantle, to the Very Rev. Canon Martelli, on his returning to the Victoria Plains Mission, in December 1868', appeared in the *Herald*, along with a reply from Martelli. 'Very Rev. and Dear Father Martelli,' his parishioners began, dropping the official 'Canon' for the more intimate 'Father', 'we cannot allow you to leave without a public expression of deep and sincere regret at parting with, not only a zealous and devoted pastor, but also with a kind, wise and fatherly friend in our worldly troubles.' He would take with him 'the affection and esteem of your congregation' and 'the respect of all classes of the community'. The parishioners singled out 'your ever watchful care in the moral training and improvement of the schoolchildren and rising youth' and their gratitude for 'completing the building of St Patrick's', Martelli must have relished the recognition of prudence as one of his legacies:

> your committee had daily opportunities of witnessing the prudence and energy with which you met the many difficulties arising during the progress of that work, and now heartily congratulate you on its successful completion.[36]

In reply, he thanked the writers for 'the affectionate address' and, anxious to avoid any self-satisfaction, added, 'As to the flattering terms in which you have made allusion to my humble service during the period of my pastoral ministrations, all I can say is, that I wish I were deserving of them'.

The editors of the *Herald* added their own warm and ecumenical vote of thanks:

> Had an opportunity been afforded we are satisfied his Protestant fellow-citizens would have borne testimony to the many excellent qualities of this accomplished gentleman, scholar and christian minister, so truly catholic in his sympathies and charities. He carries with him into his comparatively less laborious sphere of action the best wishes of every member of the community.[37]

Fellow priests sent good wishes. At the mission, Fr Martínez told Garrido 'our good friend the Canon' would be welcomed by the Community 'with sincere cordiality'. Fr Gibney wished Martelli the *paix d'esprit* 'peace of spirit' he had so long desired.[38]

CHAPTER EIGHTEEN

To Convert and Civilise

The reader may have been surprised in earlier chapters to see Canon Martelli referring to Aboriginal Australians as 'savages'. Now, as we follow the good Canon on the road to the 'mission to the Aborigines' at New Norcia, is a good time to pause and consider the words he used to refer to the Aboriginal people of Australia and what this tells us about the world view he shared with other educated nineteenth-century missionaries.

The Italian word Martelli uses most frequently to refer to Aboriginal Australians is *selvaggio* 'savage'. Out of fifty references in letters written in Italian, *selvaggio* occurs twenty-six times. Other words are: *aborigeno* 'Aborigine', *nativo* 'native', *negro* 'black/negro', *australiano* 'Australian'. Salvado in his Italian writing used the same words in roughly the same proportions. The word 'Noongar', the name used by Aborigines in the South-West for themselves, is rare in colonial documents of the time and does not appear in the writings of Martelli or Salvado.[1]

What did Martelli mean by the term *selvaggio*? For a highly educated Italian, the word was etymologically transparent. It is derived from Latin SILVATICUS, an adjective from the noun SILVA 'forest', and described humans who lived a nomadic way of life in a forest or, in Australian terms, in the bush. 'Savage' formed a pair with its opposite, 'civilised'. Equally transparent, this adjective derived ultimately from Latin CIVES, a citizen, and means therefore a human person who belongs to a sedentary, urban social grouping, a CIVITAS 'city'. The semantic pairing of 'savage' and 'civilised' is evident in dictionaries of the time. One Italian dictionary defines *selvaggio* as 'the opposite of *civile*'.[2]

It is important here to consider another term, also current at the time. The word 'barbaric' has now, in the twenty-first century, become barely distinguishable from 'savage'. Two centuries ago they carried very different meanings, inherited from the Enlightenment. Voltaire distinguished between '*savages*, characterized by isolation and love of independence, and *barbarians*, who have coarse and rude customs'. In the same way, for the Italian- and Spanish-speaking missionaries in early Western Australia, 'savage' denoted a way of life, while 'barbaric' was a moral judgement that could be applied to a person in any culture, nomadic or sedentary.[3]

The way these three terms were understood by nineteenth-century missionaries can be grasped in two letters Salvado received in the 1870s. The first was written by Dom Michele Morcaldi of the Abbey at Cava de' Tirreni. He praised Salvado's work of 'educating the *savages* to the truth by educating them to work'. This is the work, he told Salvado, that Benedictines did in medieval Europe: 'the *barbarism* of these places 1200 years ago – language, customs, laws – was tamed and then transformed into beneficial *civilisation* by the spirit of St Benedict'. Morcaldi uses the Italian *selvaggi, barbarie, civiltà*.[4]

The same three words italicised here – *savage, barbarism, civilisation* – appear again in a letter from Bishop Griver. He had heard from a priest in Queensland about the notorious Native Police, groups of Aboriginal men recruited at gunpoint and armed by government officers to eliminate Aboriginal resistance. And for what reason? Griver asked. 'It seems some of the *savages* killed a few head of livestock! It seems incredible that a *civilised* Government can be so *barbaric*.' Griver uses the Spanish *salvajes, civilizado, barbaro*.⁵

The Italian abbot and the Spanish bishop used the same words with the same meanings. Among these educated European clergymen, the term 'savage', which today offends our modern sensibility, was still a quasi-scientific description of a way of life, a culture, in opposition to the urban cultures of 'civilised' town-dwellers. Morcaldi and Griver describe Aboriginal Australians as savages since they are, literally in their eyes, 'forest-dwellers'. When 'civilised' is given a moral overtone to mean refined and well-mannered, its opposite is not 'savage' but 'barbaric'.

The term 'savage' was also used in Britain during the eighteenth century, but by the end of that century the settlement of the so-called 'New World' had begun. Their inhabitants were less interesting in moral or cultural terms: they had become a legal and political problem. The term 'savage' was replaced in British discourse by 'native'. This is a term of territoriality: the inhabitants of Australia were relevant in so far as they had, or might have, property rights by virtue of having been born here, being 'native', from Latin NATUS, 'born'.⁶

The Spanish and Italian missionaries in Western Australia did not have *nativo* as part of their intellectual lexicon. When Martelli uses *nativo* in Italian, it was to translate something he had read in the local Australian press. He begins to use the term 'native' when he starts writing to Salvado in English, adopting the language of the place and the vocabulary of the time. In the same way, Salvado uses 'savage' in his Italian-language letters to Propaganda Fide, but in the 1864 report to the Colonial Secretary, he refers to Aboriginal Australians as 'natives', 'aboriginal natives' and 'aborigines', never as 'savages'.⁷

Martelli knew that, among his cultured friends in Italy, there was huge interest in the Aboriginal peoples of Australia, their way of life and the artefacts their culture produced. In 1862, in the midst of Roman negotiations about the decree of separation, he wanted to repay Pietro Regnoli for his help in gathering information and promoting the cause of New Norcia through his many well-positioned contacts in Rome. Perhaps Aboriginal artefacts?

Salvado was happy to oblige. He had tried taking a set of Noongar artefacts to Europe during his first return trip in 1849, but he could arouse no interest in them and ended up disposing of them. Now he and Martelli compiled a consignment containing samples of copper ore and lead, a large opossum skin rug, a sandalwood table, a dozen stuffed birds, a thorny devil lizard preserved in alcohol, fresh flowers in a basket and two large seashells. It took a year to assemble the items and six months for the collection to travel from Fremantle, via London, to Rome. Regnoli opened the case of wonders in his home in June 1863.[8]

Regnoli's daughter Emilia and nephew Scipione were thrilled to see objects that came 'from the other world, or hemisphere'. His sister Malvina found the pages in Salvado's *Historical Memoirs* which named all the objects and explained their functions.

At lunch in the Regnoli home one Sunday in 1867, Salvado met Luigi Pigorini, the rising star of Italian archeology, or paleoethnology as it was called. Together they admired the Noongar objects on display and swapped publications: Salvado's *Historical Memoirs* for Pigorini's groundbreaking report 'Paleoethnology in Italy'. This was the beginning of a long friendship.[9]

Pigorini used the objects as the basis of two public lectures he gave in his native Parma, on 'Gli Australiani'. The local newspaper reported that 'from comparisons between the weapons and tools of the Australians and the prehistoric weapons and tools that have been found all over Europe, Pigorini concluded that our first fathers, who lived in the Archeolitic Age, must have had the same customs as living Australians'. This was the new 'comparative ethnography', the new way to uncover the 'history lost in the darkness of most remote times'.[10]

Martelli sent a second consignment of Aboriginal artefacts to Italy in 1871. These were for one of Pigorini's collaborators,

Don Gaetano Chierici from Reggio Emilia, near Bologna. He too was part of Regnoli's endless network of influential friends. The priest's brother Alfonso was a modestly successful artist in Rome and Regnoli wrote flattering reviews of his work. Like Martelli, Don Gaetano was a seminary professor of liberal views before 1848 and was removed from his teaching position for a time. He defined himself as a 'priest and prehistorian', a bold oxymoron for the times.[11]

Martelli sent newspaper articles about the Aboriginal people of the North-West so that Regnoli could translate them for Chierici. When Chierici asked if he too could have some of the objects described in the *Historical Memoirs*, Salvado, in Rome, forwarded the request to Martelli. The consignment, sent via a Dr Ludovico Carbonieri of Fulham Road, London, reached Chierici in August 1871. The objects are now housed in the Museo 'Gaetano Chierici' di Paletnologia in Reggio Emilia. They enjoyed wide publicity in Italy's scientific establishment.[12]

In 1875, Pigorini and Chierici, together with Pellegrino Strobel, founded the *Bullettino di Paletnologia Italiana*, the first journal in Europe dedicated to the prehistory of a single country. The first issue opened with a paper by Chierici. He analysed eleven Stone Age flints unearthed in central Italy, which had been sharpened, he believed, to be used as spear tips. He proposed a startling comparison: 'The Museum in Reggio has a similar weapon belonging to the savages of the west coast of Australia. They call it a *ghici*. It is a slender pole made of strong wood, 2.12 metres long. On one side near the pointed end, it is embedded with glass slivers that, after contact with Europeans, replaced flints.' The Italian weapons were a later development of the type whose oldest examples came from 'the most savage tribes of Australia'. This is a textbook example of the 'comparative method' championed by the first Italian archeologists.[13]

That same year, Pigorini was appointed director of the new Museum in Rome that now bears his name, the Museo Preistorico Etnografico 'Luigi Pigorini', and became the University of Rome's first professor of paleoethnology. The museum illustrates the Three-Age System of prehistory. This was developed in Denmark and, in the English-speaking world, Scotland. There were strong links between the archeologists of Copenhagen and Edinburgh. Pigorini had visited the archeological museum in Copenhagen designed by Christian Jürgensen Thomsen around the theory of the three ages – stone, bronze, iron – through which humanity developed.[14]

This theory of human development was based on a belief in unilinear cultural evolution, that is, all human societies developed along a common track from hunter-gatherer (savage) to agricultural (civilised) cultures. While Europe represented the most advanced stage, other stages of human development were represented on the earth in contemporary cultures, understood to be 'living fossils' of European cultures, which had already progressed through these developmental phases in earlier times.[15]

To illustrate the oldest known culture on earth, Pigorini convinced Regnoli to donate to the museum the Noongar objects Martelli had sent him in 1863. A contract listed the objects and the page number in Salvado's *Memoirs* where they are described. He brought his students into the museum to examine examples of 'primitive' cultures that illustrated stages of development through which Europeans had passed. The oldest geological period with a modern example was the Quaternary, now visible in the Aborigines of South-West Australia; the Late Quaternary could be seen in the 'Eskimos' of polar regions; the Neolithic in modern Tahitians; and so on.[16]

Martelli's two consignments of Noongar artefacts and a third one Salvado sent Pigorini in 1882 are significant because they were intended to promote scientific research into the deep history of humankind. Later consignments from New Norcia were sent to the Vatican, and for different reasons. The Vatican collected artefacts from all mission lands in the late nineteenth century but this 'was focused on culture and spiritual life; there was no intention of using the material culture as a tool to learn about the distant past of humanity'.[17]

Martelli was excited to make his own contribution to scientific knowledge. He told Chierici he considered himself fortunate to 'assist your zeal for scientific discoveries in defence of revealed truths'. The discoveries of archeologists were a support to his understanding of human origins and progress. By informing Europeans about the Aboriginal cultures of Australia, he was helping overcome ignorance and advance progress.[18]

One of the revealed truths that Martelli found confirmed by new discoveries was the doctrine of monogenesis, that all human groups had developed from a single source. The opposing theory, of polygenesis, held that different races had different origins. Martelli had witnessed this debate within Risorgimento thinking while a seminary student in Ancona. In 1832, his Rhetoric Professor Gaetano Baluffi published *Sulla unità della razza umana*, 'On the unity of the human race'. This contested the claim by some Risorgimento writers that the Italian race derived its right to self-determination because it was born autochthonously on Italian soil and had not migrated there.[19]

Australia was a challenge to European ways of seeing and understanding the world in every possible way. Faith in the theory of monogenesis was shaken by the failure of colonial authorities to subdue and Europeanise Aboriginal peoples. This challenged the Enlightenment certainty that humankind was one and that 'all civilized peoples had been savages and all savage peoples were destined to become civilized'. By the middle of the nineteenth century, a soft version of polygenism began to circulate in Australia, claiming that humankind was either divided into separate species or at least 'that the differences between the races were so unalterable as to be fixed for all time'.[20]

This was the context within which Martelli used words and expressions that are so distant from our own to refer to the Noongar with whom he longed to work. As Salvado put it, 'the human race is all one species' and all peoples are destined to follow the same path of progress.

This can shed light on the paradox whereby these missionaries could, on the one hand, describe Australian Aborigines as being on the 'lowest rung of development' while on the other hand they did all in their power to offer them opportunities to accelerate their journey along the universal path of development. Much of Salvado's work at the mission was directed at convincing sceptical colonial authorities that Aboriginal people had the same innate potential as Europeans: witness his insistence on education in trades and crafts at the mission, the appointment of Noongar women as postmistresses, the formation of an Aboriginal cricket team, and so on.[21]

Such work was audacious and slow. In 1861, for example, something unpleasant happened at New Norcia involving some Aboriginal persons (details have not survived). 'It was a bad business, any way you look at it,' Martelli reflected to Salvado, 'but not such as to give discouragement. The moral regeneration of this degraded race can not be the work of just a few years, and those who lay its foundations are not, perhaps, destined to see its fulfilment.'[22]

If Martelli's faith in the ability of the Benedictines to 'convert and civilise' Aboriginal Australians wavered in the years before he joined the mission at New Norcia, there were two causes: the indifference of colonial authorities and the hostility of so many settlers.

At the very least, Aboriginal people were already becoming invisible. In 1859, Martelli complimented Salvado on his census of '555 black fellows' – Martelli used the English expression in an Italian sentence – and hoped this would silence those who claimed, 'the Aborigines have disappeared from the face of Australia'. In 1861, Martelli read a report of explorers who encountered 'numerous Australians' in the wheatbelt. 'In all reports of expeditions, large or small', he told Salvado, 'I always note that Aborigines are encountered everywhere. This proves the falsity of those who deny it and thus unintentionally seek to impede the eternal salvation of so many souls.'[23]

At worst, however, violence by unscrupulous settlers was spreading. Martelli knew of the ill-treatment of Noongar around

Perth. In May 1865, he heard a report from one of the Neapolitan monks, Brother Pietro Ferrara, about the La Grange massacre, the first such event to occur in the North-West. When three white explorers were killed by Aboriginal people, a group of settlers in retaliation slaughtered between fifteen and thirty Yawuru and Karajarri persons. Brother Pietro, who worked on De Grey Station in the Pilbara, sailed back to Fremantle on the boat that brought the bodies of the explorers together with the leader of the punitive expedition, Maitland Brown, who was hailed as a hero.[24]

Martelli had come to see frontier violence by Aboriginal people against settlers as self-defence against an armed occupying force. He was appalled, he told Garrido, at the 'murder of thirty natives, in avengement of an attempt made by them to repel from their native land a foreign invader'. He was equally categorical in his condemnation of the Anglo-Maori war in New Zealand, telling Regnoli, with a mix of anti-British prejudice and Risorgimento patriotism, 'It is no little humiliation for John Bull, as well as being in contradiction to the principle, promulgated elsewhere, that each people has the right to choose its own rulers'.[25]

Closer to home, Martelli saw state-sanctioned violence against Aboriginal people as he visited the colony's prison island. Twenty kilometres off the coast, Wadjemup had been renamed 'Rottnest' to immortalise Vlamingh's mistaken description of the native quokkas. The uninhabited island had been used as an off-shore detention centre for Aboriginal men since 1839, and during Martelli's time the island held between fifty and one hundred prisoners at any one time. They were brought there, in chains, from as far away as Esperance to the south-east or the Pilbara region 2000 kilometres to the north. Fr Anselm Bourke told Salvado the island was 'no great honour to a Christian government'. As Fremantle chaplain, Martelli would travel across on the government boat every month or two, simply to spend time with the prisoners. He could do little more.[26]

In November 1866, Martelli heard that Salvado's Noongar friend, Bilyagoro, was sentenced to two years on Rottnest for assault. Bigliagoro, in Martelli's Italian spelling, had been a close companion of the Benedictines since they first arrived on the Victoria Plains. He was fearful of being banished to the island, since his own brother Mori Mori had died there four years earlier.[27]

In December, Martelli sailed to the island with Garrido to visit Bigliagoro. 'I will not easily forget the scene I witnessed', he reported to Martínez. When Martelli called out Bigliagoro's name and the two priests greeted him warmly, Martelli was struck by the look of amazement on the faces of the other Aboriginal prisoners. 'I dare say since the prison was built', he related with a mixture of pride and anguish, 'it was the first time that a black fellow received such a mark of attention as a visit from a clergyman, going purposedly to say him a word of confort.'[28]

The priests feared that Bigliagoro would not survive the winter and arranged for Mrs Jackson, the Catholic wife of the new superintendent, to baptise him in case of emergency. He was released, however, on 30 June 1867, into the care of the mission under threat he would be sent back to the island for any further misdemeanour. Martelli sent Mrs Jackson a photograph of Bigliagoro to thank her for all she had done for him.[29]

As well as violence by settlers and colonial authorities, there were more subtle and insidious forces threatening the wellbeing, even the viability, of Aboriginal communities. Martelli knew the threat that introduced diseases posed to the Noongar. In the 1860s, whooping cough, measles and smallpox caused many deaths. Martelli warned Salvado to vaccinate Aborigines at the mission. He followed with keen interest Salvado's correspondence with Florence Nightingale between 1860 and 1864. The Spanish bishop and the English nurse shared the same concern, which Salvado put bluntly in his 1864 report to the Colonial Secretary, 'Can we civilize the Aborigines without killing them?'[30]

Martelli expressed similar doubts. In late 1862, a young Noongar woman named Maria Louisa Clemina (or King) came to Perth for convalescence. She was married to Benedict Cuper, who later married New Norcia's first postmistress, Helen Pangieran. In January 1863, Benedict took Maria Clemina back to their home in

New Norcia where she died shortly after. Martelli was troubled by her fate and pondered what it meant for the mission project: 'May Heaven enlighten Your Excellency to know in what way we can avoid the danger that seems to threaten the life of the savages when we help them move to civilized life. It is a great problem.'[31]

After a decade and a half in Western Australia, Martelli's faith in the civilising project was shaken. He now would have to work through these doubts in the mission to the Aborigines he was finally able to join.

CHAPTER NINETEEN

My Earthly Paradise

1868–1870

The years Raffaele Martelli spent in New Norcia are the time about which one would want to know the most. After fifteen years of patient service to the diocese, in town, country and prison, he could now fulfil the promise that had brought him to Australia. From his first letters from Fremantle, he had longed for the day when he could 'withdraw myself from the world into that solitude' and 'my earthly paradise'. Yet these years at New Norcia are the time about which we know the least.[1]

What we do know is the reason why Martelli came to New Norcia. Not simply to withdraw from city life, to live with men whose friendship he cherished, and to work with Aboriginal people. Above all, he came to New Norcia to prepare for death. 'As an inmate at New Norcia, I can lead a life of recollection and prayer, better than I could anywhere else, in preparation to my death, which cannot be very distant.'[2]

The nineteenth century was the last century when the preparation for a happy death was a universal Christian practice. It is a frequent theme in the correspondence in the New Norcia archives, by clerics and lay people. The approach was no longer the medieval terror of sudden death depriving us of the chance to put our affairs in order, but the insight that the key to dying well is living well, and to live well we must 'die to the world' a little every day. Death is not the opposite of life but an integral part of life itself. To prepare for one's own death was the most natural thing in the world.[3]

As he embraced this new life of recollection and prayer, Martelli moved into his own room, on the first floor of the north wing, above the refectory. He entered fully into the alternating rhythm of prayer, work and study that defines the Benedictine day. All meals were taken in common, with up to eighty men in the refectory. He preached at Mass when it was his turn and attended to the Catholics in the area when required. In short, Salvado reported to Propaganda, 'he leads the life of a monk although he is not one'.[4]

The monastery horarium at this time is described by Martelli's Neapolitan friend, Fra Mauro Rignasco. He wrote to a monk at Cava de' Tirreni to assure him that the New Norcia Benedictines were faithful to tradition, even in the Australian missionary setting. The day's work and rest were structured around the seven moments of community prayer in the chapel. The exact times of the horarium changed over time. This is the weekday routine Martelli made his own in 1868:[5]

> 3.00 am The bell rings to summon the monks to the chapel for *Matins*. The Office is chanted, standing. It takes up to an hour and a half. After a short break,
> Holy Mass, with two moments of meditation, and followed by 'the hymn of our Great Father St Benedict', *Laudibus civis*
> Short break for making bed and work
> Breakfast: tea with sugar and bread, as much as one wants, but without milk or butter.

Sunrise	In chapel for *Prime*
	Work
9.00	In chapel for *Terce*
	Work
11.15	In chapel for *Sext*, reading on the saint of the day, examination of conscience and the Angelus
12.00	Lunch (the main meal) offered variety from day to day: a rice soup with vegetables, or potatoes, legumes, with a piece of meat or some other dish (eggs on Fridays) and bread. Liquid refreshment is water. On the six main feast days of the year we have a third course and enjoy wine 'thanks to the sweat of the Brothers and the care of Him who rules all things'. After lunch, in chapel to recite the Five Psalms of the Most Holy Name of Mary [the Magnificat and psalms 119, 118, 125, 122: the first letters of these prayers spell the name MARIA]
1.00	In chapel for *None*
	Rest
	Work
Sunset	In chapel for *Vespers*
	Recitation of the Rosary and visit to the Blessed Sacrament
	Dinner, a repeat of breakfast: tea and bread.
	In chapel for spiritual reading
	Compline (always chanted)
	Examination of conscience, a few prayers (on Friday, discipline)
	Silence
8.00	The bell sounds for sleep

On Sundays and feast days, time for work was replaced by extra time for 'reading, writing, praying or resting'.

Martelli's work was to teach in the schools for Aboriginal children. Garrido joked that he had become 'Minister of Public

Instruction' of Victoria Plains. Martelli taught the boys at St Mary's at the northern end of town. It had opened in 1847 on the auspicious date of 8 December. Fr Martínez taught in St Joseph's school for girls, which opened in 1861.[6]

Girls and boys, around fifty in all, followed similar daily timetables. Rising at dawn, the children attended Mass and sang Psalm 116 'Praise the Lord, all you peoples, for great is his love towards us and his faithfulness lasts forever' before breakfast. Mornings were for learning trades and school lessons were in the afternoon. There was lots of singing, during classes and at other times: the children sang hymns and 'school songs', songs in their native languages and God Save the Queen. On Saturdays and Sundays, they would join in chanting parts of the Mass. Before dinner, the children would play or go on a walk until sunset. Martelli taught night school after dinner to boys who had worked all day. Thursdays were a break in the weekly routine. The children would go into the bush and hunt for food.[7]

The regular rhythms of monastic life were interrupted by happy events at the end of his first six months. Salvado returned to the mission, after five years in Europe. His return is the first moment when Martelli emerges into the light of the archives. And what an odd appearance he makes.

Garrido was in Perth on business and invited Martelli to join him to welcome their mutual friend home. In a long, wordy letter from the mission, Martelli tied himself in knots to decline Garrido's invitation. His convoluted explanations – 'if you ask the Canon to explain the matter, he cannot give a satisfactory account of himself' – show he is lucid enough to analyse his own foibles but not free to act on them.[8]

Garrido guessed the problem was that he had invited Martelli not directly but via Martínez. A personal approach did the trick. Martelli always was a stickler for correct procedure and respect for persons. But in this case, it is as if the monks were treating Martelli with the same informal trust they used among themselves. He seems unable to enter fully into membership of the community.[9]

Martelli arrived in Fremantle with days to spare and spent the time helping Fr Bourke and visiting old friends. In January, Bourke had told Garrido that Mass attendance was high because of Martelli's good work, and he was 'copying Fr Martelli's manner of conducting affairs and, although I can't do as well as Fr Martelli did, I am trying'. Bourke even heaped ironic praise on Martelli, painting a memorable picture of the ageing professor standing rather helplessly in the fields at New Norcia in the middle of summer, harvesting hook in hand: 'It must have been hard on him to stay out under the blazing sun, but I suppose he did not work very hard. His reaping must have been for ornament and fashion's sake rather than for its real utility'.[10]

On 21 May 1869, Salvado and thirty-two Spanish missionaries disembarked from the *Robert Morrison*. They were lay brothers except for the two priests, Francisco Goicoechea and Salvado's brother Santos. They all headed up to New Norcia, except for Salvado, who asked Martelli to stay behind with him to attend to mission affairs in Perth and Fremantle.[11]

Perhaps Martelli's status as a non-professed member of the New Norcia community gave him more freedom to stay outside the monastery? Or was it just that Salvado relished the time with a close friend and respected confidante? Together, they met with church authorities, visited priests and nuns in Perth and Fremantle, celebrated High Mass and gave First Communion to children. Martelli sent Garrido an express letter without telling Salvado, so Garrido could organise the community's welcome.

When Martelli and Salvado rode up to New Norcia together, they were met four miles out from the mission by delegations of local families, then Aboriginal children with their teachers. They entered the mission on foot as the community lined both sides of the road; bells rang out, gun salutes were fired. After prayers and chants in the church, including the Te Deum and a pontifical blessing from Salvado, speeches were made by an Aboriginal boy and girl and by Mr Butler.[12]

Salvado had returned home. With his friend and mentor back at the head of the mission, Martelli must have felt that New Norcia had become a little more his own home.

This new-found tranquillity was short-lived. Even before he returned, Salvado had committed to sailing straight back to Rome for the First Vatican Council. In fact, Salvado received permission not to attend the Council, but this reached the mission after he had left. Garrido thought Salvado's prompt departure was providential, but Martelli was blunt, 'Your being over punctual has been the cause of the contretemps.' He consoled himself with one of his favourite English sayings, 'What can't be cured, must be endured'.[13]

Salvado left the mission in September. His departure coincided with the arrival of the new Governor. In King George Sound, the abbot welcomed Frederick Weld – they had met before and Weld offered to help the mission in any way he could – and his wife Mena, whom he found 'young and graceful'.[14]

The Welds were of impeccable Catholic heritage. Martelli noted they shared his friendship with Australian Benedictines and deep attraction to their charism. Mena was confirmed by William Ullathorne OSB, who had returned to England after fifteen years in New South Wales. Sir Fred was a second cousin to the Benedictine Roger Vaughan, who came to Sydney in 1872 and succeeded Archbishop Polding five years later.[15]

The couple were popular everywhere. The papers waxed lyrical in praise of their charm, Martelli told Salvado, but what they do not report is how sincere the Welds are in their religious commitment. They received rare permission directly from the Pope to have a priest celebrate Mass and give them Communion in Government House, as often as they wished. Last Sunday, Martelli wrote breathlessly, they attended the Cathedral for 7 o'clock mass, High Mass at 11 o'clock and evening Vespers. Mrs Weld played the harmonium.[16]

Two months after taking up his position, the new Governor set out to inspect the northern districts. When the party arrived in New Norcia, Martelli and Garrido organised a welcome along the same lines as Salvado's recent return. When the Aboriginal children sang the national anthem and made speeches of welcome, Weld replied that the Queen commissioned all colonial governors to attend to the spiritual and human welfare of the different native races, and that he would do his best in this regard.[17]

Martelli was responsible for organising the visit and sent Salvado the long account of it published in the *Inquirer*. He was worried about the food and drink offered to their 'distinguished Guest'. A visiting Spanish sailor who had worked as a cook on an English boat proved useful in the kitchen, but the only liquid refreshment offered the visitors was home-made beer, and then at dinner, home-made wine, which 'the guests did not relish'. Salvado, on the other hand, was pleased to hear that the food and drink were not 'English style but monastic style'.[18]

Martelli watched in awe as Weld rose at 3 am for Matins, attended Mass and Rosary and made his confession. Colonial Secretary Frederick Barlee, an Anglican, also attended Matins, twice. He was 'much struck', he told Martelli, 'by the scene he witnessed, reminding him of what he had read in books, but never before seen with his own eyes'. Weld was given Salvado's room during his stay and told the monks, 'in a monastery I feel in my own element'. He knew Cardinal Barnabò personally and sent him his first impressions of the colony. Canon Martelli, he wrote, 'strikes me as a very superior man in every way'.[19]

Mrs Weld was every bit as capable as her husband, and as pious. Martelli's admiration for the couple reached its zenith in Perth that Christmas, when Mrs Weld told him she too wished to visit the mission and 'attend Matins with her husband!' The ecumenical scope of her Christian charity, however, challenged Martelli at the beginning. She attended a bazaar run by the Independents, or Congregationalists, in the company of Barlee, and made purchases. Martelli pondered to Salvado on the fact that Catholics were taught it was 'not lawful' to encourage such commerce 'as it would be to support a religious system which we hold to be false'. Salvado did not seem concerned and Mrs Weld's charisma seems to have won Martelli over. He called on her whenever he was in Perth.[20]

Martelli was in Perth when the Welds arrived because he was to accompany Griver on a pastoral tour – to the Avon Valley, the South-West, and Guildford and Fremantle – to preach a Jubilee celebrating Pope Pius' fifty years as a priest. The tour was postponed because of the arrival of the new Governor and Griver lost no time in renewing his invitation to Martelli to assist the diocese. Would he stay in Perth, or move to Toodyay for six months, or replace Fr Lynch, who was taking a year's leave from the prison chaplaincy?[21]

The decision to refuse the prison job was easy: 'one of my happiest days in W. Australia was when I got rid of that situation, seven years ago'. It was not so easy to refuse Perth and Toodyay, but Martelli worked out his scruples in a long letter to Salvado and quickly returned to the mission. He visited Perth twice in 1870, but only for short periods. He spent Holy Week at the Cathedral because of the shortage of priests. He was in Perth again at Christmas time to accompany Fr Garrido to the doctor.[22]

For some time, the priests at the mission had noticed that Garrido was 'not taking care of his corporal health'. By December 1870, his fevers were so frequent and so debilitating that he agreed to see Dr Ferguson in Perth. Martelli went with him and recounted the trip with gusto to Martínez. On the second night, they slept at Frazer's place, eight miles out of Guildford. 'The absence of every accommodation', Martelli wrote, 'was the least inconvenient to put up with'. At a time when Garibaldi's bands of Redshirts were planning an attack on the Eternal City in the final stages of Italy's struggle for national unification, the missionaries faced their own implacable foes. Martelli sought refuge from the ubiquitous bed bugs in their cart outside:[23]

> An army of those <u>Red-shirts</u> which love to inhabit in the abode of men who are not very particular about cleanness rushed upon the newly arrived travellers, for whom sleep became, since that moment, out of the question. I got a scent of their approaching and by no means would I consent to lay down, except in the

Spring-Cart, and altho' I was not delightfully situated, yet I would have not changed it with that of my fellow-travellers.[24]

The ailing Garrido must have spent an uncomfortable night inside. They fled at first light without eating or drinking and waited until they made Guildford before taking breakfast.

Garrido was not a good patient. It took six days to convince him to see Dr Ferguson. When he did, Martelli was in Fremantle on other business. He wished he could have been present during the examination because he suspected Garrido did not reveal the full extent of his ailments to the doctor. Garrido was on daily quinine and the bouts of fever robbed him of strength. He was keen to get back to the monastery.[25]

During this trip to Perth, word arrived of Martín Griver's elevation to bishop. When Griver sailed to Rome for his consecration and to attend the First Vatican Council, he asked Martelli to take over the administration of the diocese in his absence. Griver knew Governor Weld would prefer to deal with the older Italian than with young Fr Gibney. Martelli once described Gibney as 'this zealous, but not very prudent young man' and Weld's first impression of Gibney, he told Cardinal Barnabò, was that he was 'hot and pushing'.[26]

Martelli, however, declined, as he always did when offered any role that would have brought him into the public arena. He knew the advice of the *Imitation* (I, 9), 'It is much safer to obey than to rule'. The wounds of 1848 ran deep. To 'consecrate the rest of my life to the priestly ministry' and to live 'usefully' meant simply being of service. It is as if he did not trust himself to enter the public fray. So Fr Gibney became Acting Apostolic Administrator, the first step on a career in pastoral responsibility that culminated in his consecration as Bishop of Perth, succeeding Griver in 1886.[27]

In the Catholic world the announcement of the Council intensified the conflict between liberal and ultramontane currents. Devotion to the Papacy had grown enormously in the first half of the nineteenth century, so that when the doctrine of papal infallibility was proclaimed in 1870, it was almost universally accepted and applauded. All the Australian bishops present, including Salvado, voted in favour. Martelli thought the Council would produce much good: 'like the Council of Trent, the fruit the Vatican Council will produce in the world, will be slow and in the course of time. The present generation will not realise it, in its fullness at least'.[28]

While Salvado was at the Council, he received a request from Propaganda Fide for information about certain members of the New Norcia community, including Martelli. The Canon's anomalous situation – living in a monastic community but as a secular priest – meant that updates would now be requested from Salvado rather than Griver. The abbot was lavish in his praise.

> I have known him for seventeen years and in all these years I have never observed anything but irreprehensible conduct, great zeal for the salvation of souls, exemplary disinterest, sublime abnegation, obedience and humility that are in truth out of the ordinary. This is no exaggeration.

He then singled out the cardinal virtue for the lack of which church officials had once reproached Martelli, adding an adjective that would later adorn his tombstone:

> His personality, which is kind and loving, and marked by special prudence, have gained for him universal respect and esteem in these parts. He is in fact a true Apostolic Missionary.[29]

CHAPTER TWENTY

Et Nihil Coepimus

June–August 1870

For their 1866 summer holidays, the Aboriginal students at New Norcia spent a fortnight on Country. The girls went inland and the boys, in the care of Fr Martínez and some of the brothers, followed the Moore River to its mouth. The country, Martínez told Martelli, was beautiful and fertile. In the Mediterranean climate, the gentle, rolling fields were still green after the spring rains. The river had swamps and lakes along its banks, teeming with life. On the first day, the monks and students caught twenty-eight tortoises, one kangaroo and a few cockatoos, the next day three more kangaroos. Their hunting was so successful they 'did not need to kill any sheep'. They reached the ocean at Gabbadah, later renamed Guilderton, and returned to New Norcia on the feast of Saint Scholastica, 10 February, the girls having arrived the previous day.[1]

Martelli was delighted at the stories Fr Martínez told. He rejoiced that his young friend was able to 'hallow with the celebration of the Holy Mysteries, those wild regions whence no homage rose before to the throne of the Almighty.' However, the description of the rich pastoral country along the Moore also provoked an intriguing reaction. 'I was not aware', Martelli admits,

> that at so little distance from the Mission there are to be found sights so new, so different from what we see in this neighbourhood. I do not wonder that the Aborigines can seem and be so confortable in their nomadic life, even after having tasted the conforts of a civilised life.[2]

It is as if he is considering, for the first time, that the Noongar might have preferred their traditional ways even after encountering the civilisation that European, Christian missionaries brought them. Up to this point it had been difficult for him to understand why the nomadic Noongar were not quicker to abandon their own culture when offered the comforts and benefits of civilised life. Now in the face of the description of life in a different district, his belief in the irresistible superiority of European ways of life seems to be wavering.

The two schools for Aboriginal children between them housed around fifty children. At first, the children were all from Yued country, the Victoria Plains, but as illness and epidemics devastated the local population, the schools kept numbers up by taking children sent from other districts. Sometimes the children or their families begged for the missionaries to take them, or children would be sent with a guarantee they would be returned in a defined time period, say two years, and in some cases money changed hands. Children began arriving in the 1860s, sent by missionaries in Bunbury, the Avon Valley and the northern Champion Bay district.

Fr Adolphus Lecaille, a Belgian, came to Australia to work with Aboriginal Australians but, like Martelli, was assigned to parish work outside Perth. In Bunbury, he set up a 'native school' and translated the Creed and the Our Father into the local language. When he was transferred to Champion Bay, 400 kilometres north of Perth, he moved from Noongar to Yamaji country. He could not speak the local language – he told Cardinal Barnabò the two languages are 'as different as German and Italian' – and all he could do for the Aboriginal people was send their children to New Norcia to receive education, training and religious instruction. This is what brought Lecaille and Martelli together on a project as significant as it was traumatic.[3]

In early winter 1870, Lecaille reported that a number of Aboriginal children wished to move to New Norcia. Garrido asked Martelli to travel north to bring the children back to the mission. It would not be a difficult task and Martelli should be back 'soon'.[4]

Martelli was enthusiastic about the trip. He knew full well that the children would be moving 350 kilometres away from their home, onto the country of another Aboriginal group with a different language, where they would become full-time residents of a strictly organised European institution. What did he think he was doing with such a move?

Martelli took the educational principles he developed in Italy and applied them to colonial Western Australia. Children left untended would follow 'brutal instincts' or 'bad examples'. Christian schooling should offer them a safe and wholesome environment and equip them with good habits and values for when they 'move into the corruption of society'.[5]

This was how he put it in his 1848 speech in Rimini. If this was the great responsibility of education in Italy, how natural it was to extend that same protection to Aboriginal children in colonial Western Australia. How much more urgent, since these children were at risk of being 'corrupted by contact with the Europeans' as the colonial frontier advanced. The protection of such children was a noble task and Martelli was pleased to accept it.[6]

He had two travelling companions. One was Brother Agustín Cabané. He had sailed with Martelli on the *John Panter*. A proud Catalan, Brother Austin, as he was known in English, was a capable and trusted leader among the lay brothers. He worked closely with the Noongar farm labourers, and in 1867, a group of Noongar shearers, including Benedict and William Monop, handed over their pay to him for safe keeping, to avoid wasting or losing it all.

The ambiguities of the venture were already incarnate in Martelli's second companion, an Aboriginal boy called Jimmy. He was originally from the Northampton area, near Champion Bay. He had been at New Norcia for eight years and was now in his late teens. The missionaries thought Jimmy would be able to induce other Aboriginal youth in the area to come south to the mission as he had. They were badly mistaken.

The three travellers set out on Monday 13 June, in a spring cart. This was a light cart, drawn by a single horse. The suspension made it infinitely more comfortable than the saddle, especially for those with debilitating health conditions, but even in a spring cart, 40–50 kilometres a day for several weeks was a significant physical undertaking.[7]

Their first stop was Marah, the pastoral outpost recently established by the monks ninety kilometres north of the mission. Then they followed the mail run, north to Coorow station, on to Duncan Macpherson's homestead at Carnamah Springs, then to the coast at Dongara and up to Greenough. They slept in the open but with 'very little discomfort', or in hotels free of charge 'in consequence of the good repute in which New Norcia seems to stand for hospitality towards travellers of all classes'.[8]

The mishaps began as soon as they reached Greenough on Monday 20th. Fr Lecaille was up at Northampton, then called 'The Mines', looking for Aboriginal boys for the mission. He had written to New Norcia weeks earlier, telling Martelli to postpone his departure by a month, but the boy entrusted with the letter failed to deliver it. He was not due back until the end of the week.[9]

As Martelli waited, he could not even visit Catholic families in the district because of the bad weather. He knew Fr Garrido's health was declining and wrote him an upbeat report. After the unattractive sand plain north of the Victoria Plains, they were now on the rich alluvial flats of the Irwin district, the most fertile area of the colony. Even in the winter storms, the climate was warm and temperate. 'After crossing the long and dreary sandy plains, it is such a relief to reach this Promised Land,' Martelli reassured his friend.[10]

When Lecaille turned up, he headed back up north with Br Austin and Jimmy, leaving Martelli at the Greenough chapel. What unfolded on the road to Northampton showed immediately how delicate and fraught encounters at the frontier could be. Fr Lecaille recorded the bizarre chain of events in a letter to Fr Martínez.[11]

Before reaching Northampton, the three travellers came across a large number of Jimmy's relatives and friends at a corroboree. They were overjoyed to see him after so many years and begged him to stay with them. Jimmy said he preferred to stay with Lecaille and Austin and rode on to Northampton with the two missionaries. All the following day, Jimmy 'was in such a state of fear and gloomy apprehension' – who knows what conflicting emotions the young lad must have been feeling – and Lecaille was worried that Jimmy's mob would try to take him back 'by force'. With troubling candour, he admits to Martínez that 'we could have not prevented Jimmy's friends to take him away if they had been at the Mines, without using fire-arms by ourselves or by the Police'.

The next morning, Lecaille left Brother Austin at Northampton and made his getaway with Jimmy, stealing away before daybreak and taking back roads to avoid meeting Jimmy's relatives. They rode eighty kilometres, reaching Greenough late at night, where Lecaille recounted the misadventure to an incredulous Martelli and then rode on to Dongara where the Thursday mail cart would take Jimmy back to New Norcia.

More unsettling details emerge from a letter Martelli wrote to Martínez. Jimmy told him he had never asked to be sent to the North, and that the superiors sent him 'almost against his will'. Lecaille conceded the point: 'if so, I think the superiors may assure themselves for the future, that in my opinion, if there be any thing to gain by sending such youths to their native country to see their friends, there is much more to fear for'. The children who were in the area when Jimmy left for New Norcia were now too old to join the mission and the children in Northampton young enough to come to the schools (twelve years or younger) had never seen Jimmy before. Lecaille changed tack and planned to ask local Aboriginal men to help him convince children to relocate to New Norcia.[12]

This troubling debacle did nothing for Martelli's confidence in the project. He was beginning to grasp how complex such ventures were, how deep could run the ambiguities in relationships between missionaries and Aboriginal people. He asked Martínez for prayers and, barely two weeks into the trip, he was already pessimistic, 'Let [the mission] be prepared for a failure. So far, the prospects are gloomy'.

When Lecaille returned from Dongara, he and Martelli rode up to Champion Bay. Martelli celebrated the Mass there on Sunday 3 July.

They separated again. Lecaille headed straight to Northampton to join Brother Austin. Martelli followed alone, taking two weeks to visit Lecaille's parishioners along the way. Everywhere, he rejoiced to hear the settler families speak fondly of Fr Garrido. He had been the first priest to visit the area in 1857. Martelli gave photographs of the mission to the families, who treasured them in family albums. He quickly ran out and asked Martínez to send more pictures, of Salvado and Garrido, and also of the Pope – 'you cannot imagine how much people appreciate them'.[13]

When he met up with Lecaille and Brother Austin on Saturday 16 July, his misgivings only grew on hearing Lecaille's reports: 'The natives are running away from us into the far bush just as the shades of night are flying at the approach of daylight, and I fear that we have but little chance of succeeding in obtaining any'. After dinner that evening, Martelli sat down to gather his thoughts and write a report to Martínez.

The gospel reading of two weeks earlier came to his mind. When he said Mass in Champion Bay on 3 July, it was the Fourth Sunday after Pentecost and the gospel was the story of how Jesus called his first disciples, from Chapter 5 of Luke's Gospel. The fishermen had caught nothing all night but, at Jesus's bidding, they put out their nets one more time and netted a huge catch. This is the Gospel passage, with the key phrase italicised:

> Jesus said to Simon, 'Put out into deep water and pay out your nets for a catch.' Simon replied, 'Master, we worked hard all night long *and we caught nothing*, but if you say so, I will pay out the nets.' And when they had done this they netted such a huge number of fish that their nets began to tear, so they signalled to their companions in the other boat to come and help them; when these came, they filled both boats to sinking point. When Simon Peter saw this, he fell at the knees of Jesus saying, 'Leave me, Lord; I am a sinful man.' But Jesus said to Simon, 'Do not be afraid; from now on it is people you will be catching.'[14]

'Fishers of men': this and 'shepherds of the flock' are the foundational metaphors that define the identity and role of Catholic clergy. The image of the fisher in particular has a strong missionary connotation. These images flashed before Martelli's eyes that evening of Saturday 16th. He had given his life to following Jesus's instruction to become a 'fisher of men', but right now he identified more with Simon, dejected after a night's fruitless fishing. In the Latin text Martelli read out at Mass, Simon Peter's statement 'and we caught nothing' is *et nihil coepimus*. Martelli made it his own. 'My dear Father Martinez', he wrote,

> I wish I could communicate better news. The result of our efforts in the fishery of Native children is just the same with that of Simon Peter: et nihil coepimus. Fr. Lecaille and the Brother have returned from the Geraldine Mine, 40 miles at the North of this place, with empty nets.[15]

Martelli was certain this was apostolic work, 'fishing' like the apostles for the souls of those who had not yet encountered the Christian event and offering them companionship, hospitality and life in a Christian community. How could so noble a task prove such an abject failure?

Over dinner, the three missionaries had searched for answers. Martelli drew the threads of their conversation together for the benefit of Fr Martínez. Had they picked the wrong time of year?

> Perhaps the shearing season should have been a more propitious time, when the Natives are attracted by the expectation of gaining something at the Shearing Shed;

Or were they using the wrong methods of approaching the natives, an 'inprudent modus agendi'?

> perhaps it should be advisable for the recruiting Missioner not to show himself and his designs, but to use the instrumentality of other zealous men (but where shall we find them?) who might cox the parents to part with the children;

Or were they being thwarted by forces beyond their control, 'inimical agencies'?

> lastly, the selfishness of the Settlers, who draw an advantage from Native labour, especially the youths, has, we have reason to surmise, spread alarming and false rumours and frightened the Aborigines away from us.

They had come as far north as they planned. They seemed to be surrounded by nothing but abandoned mines. 'It is so gloomy to go around and see nothing but ruins of cottages in every side and only vestiges of works which have stopped.' Martelli informed Martínez that he and Brother Austin would turn for home. They would be back at New Norcia by the end of July.

At some point, however, Martelli added a P.S., two fresh pages that show a change of heart. The band of three decided to make one final attempt. Would Martínez give them permission to spend another week away? The shearing season in the north was a month earlier than on the Victoria Plains. In just a few weeks, Aboriginal people would come to the sheds looking for work. This was the last opportunity to find children. They would approach farmers they knew – 'Brown, Davis, Drummond, Burgess, etc' – since they had successful farms with big sheds and were sympathetic to the missionaries' cause.[16]

After posting that letter with its P.S., they rode out to Willow Gully to say Mass at the home of Mrs Williams. Martelli found it gratifying and edifying to see how families on remote stations kept their commitment to the faith alive, though weeks or months might pass before they could see a priest or approach the sacraments.

Word reached them that at Port Gregory, 30 kilometres to the north, 'a lot of Natives had congregated from various parts of the country, as far as the Murchison and Shark's Bay'. They had come looking for work with Bateman's whaling party. John Bateman, son of the Fremantle merchant of the same name, used to bring crews up to the Pakington whaling station operated by the Fremantle Whaling Company. The three missionaries headed out to the coast. Martelli recognised some of the whalers from his Fremantle days, some had even attended the Catholic school, and they proved willing helpers in the missionaries' efforts to approach the children.

What unfolded next lies somewhere between farce and tragedy. In his report to Martínez, Martelli's feelings are of utter failure and self-doubt. He is still thinking through the implications of the debacle that ensued. The military phrasing he uses – 'went to the attack' – and the cliched approach to the children with 'tobacco, lollies and sixpences' give a grotesque tone to its bitter self-irony.

> This morning we came hither and certainly never did we think ourselves so near the object of our expedition. We went to the attack stealthily, hiding our intentions and, apparently, desirous simply of entering into conversation with the Natives. We employed tobacco, lollies and sixpences to make friends. Some sailors of the Whaling Party, old my acquaintances and ex-pupils

of my Fremantle School, took interest in our undertaking and gave us help. But as soon as the secret was revealed, I mean to say, as soon as the rumour got abroad that we wanted the Picchinini [an Italian spelling of piccaninies], a general clearance of the youngsters was made, through fear, as it appears, that we were to take them away by force. Little talk could be employed to disabuse them, as they cannot understand much, and the conclusion was, or rather, is that we are now preparing to leave this horribly stinking whaling camp.[17]

In this letter Martelli is replaying the encounter in his mind from the point of view of the Aboriginal group. He is horrified to see himself cast in the humiliating role of kidnapper. The realisation that the local people suspected that he and Lecaille might resort to taking children *by force* traumatised him. Was this what being fishers of people looked like at the missionary frontier? How could the beauty of Jesus's call to follow the way, the truth and the life have been reduced to such squalor? The men with whom he laboured, both here and at the mission, were good and honourable men: how did they end up entrapped in such a travesty? It was thoughts such as these, and not merely the stench of the whaling camp, that made Martelli anxious to get away as soon as he could. He entombs the failure with a Latin epitaph, 'we are coming back re infecta [with the matter unaccomplished]'.[18]

A week later, they were back in Greenough and still no reply from Martínez. Martelli made up his mind anyway. The Shearing Shed Plan was doomed to fail, as their earlier ventures had failed. He had lost all confidence in their modus agendi for attracting students to the schools. 'Native parents', in the shearing sheds,

> would object to the giving up of their children to us on the same reasons which the natives of Port Gregory have alleged. They do not part with the few children they have, both through natural feeling and prejudice against the mission, besides the obstacle of

the great distance and the fear that they will never see again their children's faces.[19]

Martelli was exhausted and dejected: 'I am tired of being so long from my home. I wish much for my corner room at N. Norcia.' Two days later, he and Brother Austin bade farewell to their redoubtable Belgian companion and turned for home.[20]

They spent four days at Marah with the lay brothers, because their horses were 'knocked up' and the rivers were running high. There the news reached them that Fr Garrido had died on 12 August and was buried the next day. Martelli was distressed at not being able to participate in the funeral rites: 'To attend the funeral of our dear Father Prior would be to take part in a duty which is a kind of relief to the sorrow of our great loss.' They returned to New Norcia on the evening of the 15th, the feast of the Assumption.[21]

In those two months away from the mission, he had brought spiritual comfort to Catholic families scattered through the Mid-West and was edified by their stoical Christian hope. But the reason for the trip was to bring Aboriginal children to the mission schools. The failure to bring a single child and, moreover, the trauma of their disastrous attempts caused him to think hard about what the mission was doing and what his contribution could be.

He had come to the logical conclusion: 'since the Natives refuse to go to the Mission, the Mission must go to them. It will be necessary, sooner or later, to establish Branch Missions in the far North; and, if possible, out of reach of the settlers'. The strategems and tactics they had tried on this trip were at best ineffectual. At worst, they were demeaning to both Aboriginal people and missionaries and created mistrust. The only basis for meaningful coexistence between Aboriginal and European persons in Australia was long-term relationships, such as Salvado had built up at New Norcia with the Yued people of the Victoria Plains. He knew this was 'up-hill work' and at best 'partial, very partial, success can be expected and that at a great cost of patient labour'. But it was the only realistic way to achieve his aim in coming to Australia, to offer 'conversion and civilisation' to Aboriginal Australians.[22]

Settling back into his corner room, Martelli summed up the whole two-month-long exploit to Salvado: 'It was a fiasco, un fiasco solenne'. Those at the mission were not to blame. Fr Lecaille had been overly optimistic. Martelli was more pessimistic than ever about the chances of keeping the Aboriginal schools going. The evil effects of contacts with Europeans were spreading faster than the mission's ability to compensate:

> The keeping up of the numerical strength of our schools will be a difficulty, increasing in proportion that the aboriginal race is dwindling, towards its extinction, at least in this part of Australia.[23]

He shared with Salvado his sorrow at Garrido's death. The trip north, which prevented Martelli from assisting his friend during his final days and which had all been for nought, had been Garrido's noble idea and he was in no way responsible for the disastrous outcome. 'One of his last acts as a superior of the Mission, in your absence', he told Salvado,

> has been an attempt to increase the number of our Native children. It is to be hoped that his prayers in heaven will succeed better than the last effort of his zeal on earth.

CHAPTER TWENTY-ONE

Insignificant Service

1871–1872

Santos Salvado was three years older than Rosendo, founder of New Norcia. He was an imposing presence. Cultivated and self-assured, he had been a chaplain to the Spanish royal family.

On the death of Fr Garrido, Santos Salvado took charge of the mission as Prior, reluctantly but in obedience to the wishes of Rosendo. Martelli, ever conscious of the burdens of office, congratulated Martínez of avoiding a heavy responsibility: 'Should I congratulate you also on your escape?'[1]

When Garrido fell seriously ill in February 1870, Salvado had advised him to hand over his heavier duties as Prior to Fr Martínez and 'place another person in charge of the parish'. Garrido selected Martelli. Martínez and Vicar General Matthew Gibney agreed that Martelli would take up the role in August.[2]

However, around the time Martelli returned from the trip north, Santos told Martínez of a letter he had received from Rosendo, written in June or July. The abbot wanted Santos as Prior and Martínez to remain as parish priest. The good Fr Martínez demurred: 'But what will Fr Martelli say?' Santos was focused on the community, not on individuals: 'I will tell Fr Martelli there is no need for him to bother, since you are doing an excellent job'.

Santos told Rosendo that he had disapproved – but kept obedient silence – when Martelli had originally accepted the role of parish priest on condition that he have a horse at his disposal 'so he could go out every Thursday' when the schoolchildren had a day without lessons. Was this to visit parishioners? Or was it an escape valve from the disciplined life of the cloister? Did Santos think Martelli wanted his cake and to eat it too?[3]

Martínez was aware of Martelli's special status. During the trip north, Martelli told Martínez bluntly to stop addressing letters to him with the title 'Colonial Chaplain'. This was the title reserved for priests serving the diocese of Perth. Martelli's testy reaction shows his determination to be identified not with the diocese but with the mission. Martínez was probably at a loss, quite innocently, as what Martelli's status actually was.[4]

It was not a question of Martelli's abilities. The two Salvados, like Griver, had a high opinion of his skills and judgement. His capacity for obedience was never in question, either, but his was a personal commitment. For the Benedictine monk, obedience is one of the three solemn vows of profession. Cuthbert Butler explains that 'normal Benedictine obedience lies within the limits of normal Benedictine cenobitical life', that is to say, obedience has its fullest meaning in a life defined by the other two vows, of stability (life-long residence in the community that witnessed the profession) and the conduct of one's life in accordance with the Rule. Martelli had taken none of these vows. The ambiguity and limits of his position in the mission were set clearly before his eyes.[5]

In the weeks following this new arrangement, Martelli was tormented not just by the failure of the trip north but by a deeper malaise. On his next birthday, he would turn sixty. In October, he told Martínez, 'I render no service, or a very insignificant one, to the Mission'.[6]

He was adamant that he had no intention of leaving New Norcia. He reminded his young friend that, on arriving at the mission nineteen months earlier, he had recited a verse from Psalm 132, the same line he quoted to Salvado years before as he dreamed of the day when he would move to New Norcia: 'Haec est domus mea: hic habitabo, quoniam elegi eam [This is my home: here I will dwell, for I have chosen it]'.⁷

It rather seems he protested too much. He was anxious to find a way of making a difference, of providing significant service. He was getting invitations to leave the mission and serve elsewhere and he was finding it increasingly difficult to say no.

Fr Lecaille was using every possible way to convince Martelli to come north and work with him, wherever he wanted and for as little as six or twelve months. 'He has been pelting with letters the Superiors of New Norcia', Martelli complained to Salvado, 'he has made arrangements with the Authority in Perth [Fr Gibney], and he is continually at me, arguens, obsecrans, increpans [arguing, begging, reproaching].' The Latin phrase is from 2 Tim 4:2 and is high praise: this is the behaviour required of those dedicated to preaching the word of God in the face of all obstacles. The phrase was familiar to Benedictines: it is found among the 'qualities of the abbot' in Chapter 2 of the Rule.⁸

Martelli had a high regard for Lecaille, and had become his spiritual director. He did not dismiss Lecaille's requests lightly. But, once again, Martelli seems enmeshed in 'a scruple of conscience' about leaving New Norcia. God had allowed him to retire to New Norcia. Who was he to reject such generosity?

He worked out his scruples on paper to Salvado, who was still in Rome at the Council. He had told Lecaille that he would 'readily give up the quiet life I enjoy at the Mission and come to help you for the period you ask'. But to be sure that this was the will of God, it must be confirmed by ordained authority. Martelli resolved to accept Salvado's decision, whether a directive as abbot or advice offered as a friend. Meanwhile, for the four months it would take to get a reply to his letter, 'my good friend in the North will, I hope, leave me alone'.

Soon an invitation came from closer to home. Toodyay was left without a priest through illness. 'This is a case quite different from that of Greenough', he reasoned with Martínez, 'and I would feel justified in abandoning my solitude, for a certain time, for the sake of a parish in a state of destitution'. As it happened, Fr Gibney found an alternative solution, but Martelli was clearly open to the idea.[9]

Martelli settled back into life at the mission, with its rhythms of prayer and work. His status as a non-professed member of the community debarred him from taking on any extra responsibilities at the mission. He had failed to add to the number of students at the schools and all he could do now was teach. Though he complained about his advancing years and indifferent health, the duties assigned to him were not enough. He looked for other ways to live usefully, especially in education and the care of the young.

In March 1870, before the trip north, he had established a lending library for workers at the mission. It was widely patronised. At the end of the year, Governor Weld launched two intiatives that occupied Martelli through spring and summer. With the end of the convict period in 1868 and a general improvement in the economic state of the colony, demand grew for representative government. Elections were called for November 1870. A key issue in the election was State aid to Catholic schools. Weld devised legislation to ensure private as well as government schools would be funded from the public purse. His efforts bucked the national trend and helped avoid the sectarian strife that troubled the eastern colonies, which were moving away from a dual system of education.

In Western Australia, the matter divided candidates, voters and the press. Martelli reported to Salvado that the *Fremantle Express* was 'dead against us' and in Perth the *Inquirer* 'advocates pure secularism' while the *Herald* had not taken a stand. Martelli's attitude echoes the rejection of modernism with which Pius IX opened his pontificate. The campaign was 'the battle of the Church against the world, which is conspiring, in so many countries, against the influence of religion in training the rising generation'. Above all, though, he longed for rational debate above sectarian jealousies and historical hatreds: 'What I would deprecate is excess of heat and bitterness in discussion. The irons are getting too hot, as we say in Italy. It is jealousy, religious antipathy, national antipathy, that take the place of calm reasoning.'[10]

With Salvado and Griver still in Rome, it was up to Martelli and Gibney, the senior clergy in the colony, to identify pro-Catholic candidates and mobilise voters. Martelli took charge of the Victoria Plains and spent a fortnight in May travelling to farms and settlements as far south as Bindoon. For companionship, he invited Aborigines from the mission: William Monop, who lived with his wife Scholastica Nangulan in one of the married couples' houses, and, on another trip, Thomas Cayanga.[11]

Martelli's status as a non-professed member of New Norcia may explain why it was he, along with Benedict Cuper, who accompanied newly consecrated Bishop Griver on his first pastoral visit to the Plains that November.[12]

The end of 1871 saw another educational initiative that consumed Martelli during the following year. While the mission offered primary education to Aboriginal children, there was little education provided for the children of the farming families of the Victoria Plains.[13]

A Building Committee was formed of landowners, with Fr Martínez as the elected chair and treasurer. Land at Yarawindah was donated by the Clune brothers, and funds were gathered from Griver, Salvado and landowners in the district, and via tea meetings. Those who could not give cash offered their labour to the project. Victoria Plains historian Rica Erickson attributes the idea of the school to Martelli. It is clear that he and Martínez, the two teachers at New Norcia, did the lion's share of the planning. However, Martínez was the parish priest and Martelli remained in the background during the entire process, not a member of the committee and never mentioned in the minutes.[14]

St Joseph's School, also known as the Victoria Plains School, was opened on the last Sunday of September 1872. It was a festive event for the entire district. At 2 pm, guests of honour Fr Martínez and Canon Martelli were driven through the thronging crowd by Jeremiah Clune in his cart. When they were led through an arch of flowers and branches constructed in front of the doorway, members of the Native Volunteer Force fired a salute, which they continued to do at intervals during the proceedings. Martelli formed a procession of all the children from the mission schools and the intended pupils of the new school. He conducted the children as they sang several hymns.

Among the many speeches, Jeremiah Clune thanked Fr Martínez, who had worked 'for the good of all, white and black'. Martínez overcame his natural reticence and spoke at length. His remarks would not be of direct concern here, except that they mirror exactly the speeches Martelli had given on similar occasions. Phrases seem inspired by Martelli: 'Ignorance is a pest to Religion and Society'; 'Reading, writing and arithmetic is very useful indeed: but this was not the chief object of man's sojourn upon earth. We have been created for a much nobler end [...]. Religion is to be instilled into the human mind from the very commencement of infancy'.[15]

Martínez guaranteed freedom of conscience in his speech: 'Religious education must, of course, be given to Catholic children, but without violence to the conscience of those of other creeds, and none need be afraid that liberty of conscience will not be respected within these walls'.

So attuned were the two priests that when Martelli rose to speak, he 'found the rev. pastor had forestalled him and had said all that he intended to say'. It is interesting that he was invited to speak, despite having had no formal role in the project, but in recognition perhaps of his authoritative, though hidden, contribution. All we know of his remarks is the brief report in the *Inquirer*: 'Canon Martelli should not think of travelling over the same ground [as Fr Martínez] but would strongly advise the parents to send their little ones to school, and not blame the teacher if they found their children dunces'.[16]

To qualify as an 'assisted school', a manager had to be appointed for all dealings with the Central Board of Education. Martínez did not want the job, so in November, Griver offered it to Martelli. Martelli too declined, justifying his refusal to Martínez because of his insufficient experience but then contradicted himself by suggesting that if Martínez studied the rules he would find the job was less complicated than he thought. The school operated off and on until 1899. The building still stands, in a paddock on the corner of Great Northern Highway and the Mogumber Road.[17]

For this period at New Norcia, especially after Salvado's return in October 1870, there is only a handful of letters by or to Martelli in the archives. These must have been passed on to Salvado for perusal. Luckily for the biographer, Salvado conserved everything.

These letters reveal Martelli through the eyes of persons who valued his friendship even as he enjoyed the companionship of the community at New Norcia. He kept in touch with friends in Perth and Fremantle, and with former students and young people who had been in his care in the youth groups and sodalities of which he was chaplain. One of these was Kate Jackson, daughter of the Rottnest superintendent and Mrs Catherine Jackson, who cared for Bigliagoro. Now aged eighteen, 'your little Katie' told Martelli breathlessly that at her first ball, in Government House, she was under the patronage of Mrs Mena Weld and there she met Peter Gugeri, whom she later married. In Fremantle, she caught up with her former teacher, Sister Emily (Sr Émilie Petit), with whom she conversed in French. They recalled the time when, on hearing that the laundress used blue to turn their clothes white, Kate applied it to her own face hoping to have the same effect. 'The lecture I received that day [from Sr Emily] has cured me of all vanity for the future.'[18]

His special status at the mission kept coming up. When Pius IX lost his remaining temporal possessions – the city of Rome – in September 1870 and retreated into the Vatican, Salvado joined clerics around the world in expressing support to the Holy Father. He records in his diary that the Address was signed by 'all the monks of New Norcia and also by Canon Martelli'.[19]

During his four years at New Norcia, Martelli was happy to help out in the diocese, for short periods and urgent reasons, and always with the approval of the mission superior – but only for pastoral work. In July 1871, at the height of the political campaign on education funding and on the eve of Griver's return from Rome, Vicar General Gibney wanted Martelli to come to Perth to help with 'ecclesiastical affairs', but Martelli would not budge.[20]

Then, in 1872, as he worked on the Yarawindah school and wrestled with scruples about how to make himself useful, what finally convinced Martelli to 'abandon his solitude' was his former parish of Toodyay. After the 1850s floods that kept Martelli trapped in his draughty home, a new townsite was established in 1860 on higher ground. It was called Newcastle, after the Secretary of State for the Colonies, but revived the name Toodyay in 1910 to avoid confusion with the New South Wales city of the same name.

On 21 February 1872, Fr Gibney asked Salvado to send Martelli to Newcastle for a short time. The young Fr Michael Kirwan had been there for just two years but was returning to Perth in poor health. The people of the town received only occasional visits from Fr Patrick Gibney (brother of the Vicar General), who was stationed at York 60 kilometres away, and a woman had died in Newcastle recently without receiving the sacraments. Gibney was sure Martelli would not be reluctant 'as he has the sanctification and salvation of souls as much as heart as I do'. Within twenty-four hours, Martelli had accepted, but only until Easter.[21]

Martelli rode over on 27 February. He stayed until the end of the Easter Octave and then a little time to arrange his departure and replacement, and returned to the mission in the evening of 15 April. He cut a sorry figure, Salvado records, 'with one tooth less and saying that he could not stay there any longer because of his age and his haemorrhoids'.[22]

Almost immediately, Bishop Griver asked Martelli to return to Newcastle since he was still short of a priest. Martelli insisted that he took his instructions from Salvado, and 'if you prevail on Monsignor

Salvado to send me back again for a longer period, I will readily obey him'. When Griver asked Salvado to use his influence, the abbot declined but promised to send Martínez instead. He needed Martelli for the New Norcia schools, and, in any case, he was too unwell. In his diary, Salvado noted that Martelli's haemorrhoids were so painful he could not stand for more than a quarter of an hour at a time. Griver was sympathetic to his health problems – to a point. If Martelli settled in Newcastle for a time and spent less time in the saddle, the haemorrhoids might subside. This was a little disingenuous, since most parishioners lived not in town but on farmsteads, and a conscientious priest could not avoid long hours on horseback.[23]

It seems that Martelli did travel over to Newcastle a number of times during 1872. One curious incident during the time he spent there involved Governor Weld, who was inspecting the proposed rail route from Newcastle to the head of the Swan River. After an overnight stop at the Baylup Inn, he rode into Newcastle on the morning of Sunday 2 June. The account of what ensued was published in an anonymous obituary of Weld in 1891 in *The Universe*, a British Catholic newspaper, and reprinted in the Melbourne *Advocate*:[24]

> One bright but cold Sunday morning in the year 1872 I found myself at the picturesque town site of Newcastle, Swan River. I had had my breakfast early and was strolling about enjoying the scenery and the glow of the keen, fresh mountain air; being a guest of the good priest, the late Canon Martelli. After a time I entered the little reception room, which served as dining and drawing room in this humble priest's bush cottage, and was seated by the fire reading, awaiting the ringing of the bell for the one Mass to be celebrated at ten o'clock.

The anonymous writer had decided to forgo Holy Communion that Sunday. At this time, Catholics fasted from food and drink from midnight before receiving Communion, and the good writer was wary of a hunger-induced headache. When there was a gentle rap at the door,

> I said, 'Come in,' at the same time rising to see whom it might be. The door opened and the genial face of Governor Weld appeared. After the usual salutations he asked me if I knew where the Rev. Canon Martelli was. He had ridden in (on horseback through the bush) from Baylup (twenty-two miles) that morning, and wished to go to confession and to receive Holy Communion at Mass.
>
> I sought out the venerable canon, who was surprised and delighted to see his Excellency. How well do I remember the meeting of that dear, good Italian priest, so much loved in that district, now long since gone to his eternal reward.
>
> The mounted constables and his Excellency's suite now moved off to the town, leaving the Governor with the good priest in the church.
>
> At the Mass I saw this good man receive his heart's desire – our Blessed Lord in the Holy Eucharist. Ah, how ashamed I felt of myself, how mortified! His Excellency, though unaware, had taught me a lesson that morning which I shall never forget.

In July, Fr Bourke, who had been released from his Benedictine vows and was under Griver's authority, asked if Martelli could relieve him in Fremantle so he could visit friends in Adelaide, but Salvado declined to release Martelli 'due to his infirmities and advanced age'. In September, Bourke was still asking and Griver wanted to let him go: he even asked the diocesan priests to donate part of their Ecclesiastical Grant to assist 'the New Norcia priest that Salvado designates to attend to Catholics in the Victoria Plains'.[25]

It must have been concern for his old friend Fr Bourke that did it. Martelli agreed to move to Newcastle, but on strict conditions: (1) he would go for three months exactly – the time Bourke was taking off for his trip to Adelaide, (2) Griver would give him a good horse and saddle, (3) he would live in the house alone and (4) his salary must be no lower than the present priest.[26]

Martelli rode over on 8 October 1872 with Bigliagoro, who took his mission horse back to New Norcia. He would spend his remaining years, almost a decade, back over the hills.[27]

CHAPTER TWENTY-TWO

Ripening for Glory

1872–1878

The first thing the Catholics of Newcastle noticed was that the church was now open for Mass every day of the week. Not content with the obligatory Sunday and once during the week, Canon Martelli celebrated Mass every day whether he had a congregation or not. This was the new church of St John the Baptist. When it was consecrated in 1864, Martelli admired its restrained Gothic design. He would have appreciated the small round window incorporated in the rendered cross at the gable end of the building, reminiscent of a nearly identical window in the Sancta Maria he built in Old Toodyay.¹

The church also served as a school. A room behind the altar became the classroom. After Pensioner David Gailey, Martelli hired female teachers: Mrs Kirk, Miss Keefe, Louisa Roe, and others. The presbytery was a simple house to the front and side of the church. Martelli kept it scrupulously clean.²

The Catholics in the district appreciated their new priest's regular visits to their farms and homes. The Toodyay district had a non-Aboriginal population of around 2,000, but only 200 people lived in the town of Newcastle and another 200 in Northam. Just a week after he arrived in Newcastle, Fr Martínez was full of admiration that Martelli had already visited the growing town of Northam, 25 kilometres south: 'You will always be the same – always busy, never idle'.

His horsemanship never improved: his frequent falls were related to friends, and when he got lost in the bush, as missionaries often did, the story would make the newspaper. One winter, he got lost on the track from Newcastle to Bindoon, 'among the Bindoon mountains', Salvado recorded ironically. The local press reported with dramatic understatement how Martelli spent a night in the open under torrential rain: 'Without a fire, his horse his only companion, with wild dogs howling all around him, the rev. gentleman's situation must have indeed been an unenviable one'.[3]

An obituary that appeared in the *Inquirer* in 1880, a week after his death, recalled him as a peripatetic chaplain. He is described as tall, unlike Michael Murphy's recollection of him being 'scarcely five feet tall'. Perhaps the saddle gave extra height:

> How familiar was his tall, white-headed figure, clad in a coat that it was difficult to believe had ever been black, for sun and rain had bleached it into variegated hues, riding a slowly trotting horse, that he evidently had only partly under control! Many a bad fall did the old man sustain, but as soon as his horse was caught he always remounted without hesitation.[4]

The author of this tribute claims he had 'the privilege of an increasing intimacy' with Martelli and learned to look upon him as 'the ideal of a Christian minister'. This was in all probability Newcastle's Anglican minister, Rev. Hugh Pidcock. Excerpts from the obituary appear in Napoleone Ascoli's 1881 memorial eulogy, since Salvado sent the text to Pietro Regnoli and he passed it on to Martelli's former student. Ascoli vouched for the reliability of the tribute: since it was written by a 'Protestant priest' its assessment of Martelli was 'above suspicion'. Perhaps the 'C.' with which the original eulogy is signed refers to 'the Cascades', the house the Pidcocks built in Newcastle.[5]

William Hugh Pidcock was of impeccable Anglican credentials; educated at Winchester and Cambridge, his father and two of his brothers also priests. Ordained in 1864, he moved to Western Australia ten years later because of his wife Elizabeth's delicate health. In Newcastle, he replaced Martelli's old friend Charles Harper. Martelli formed an equally strong friendship with the new parson, nearly thirty years his junior.[6]

Martelli and Pidcock both followed the evolution of the Oxford Movement with keen interest, though from opposite sides. In October 1874, just six months after Pidcock arrived, Martelli invited him to visit New Norcia for the first time. The two clergymen spent a day riding on the Old Plains Road, enjoying the elevated sections that afford beautiful views of the Victoria Plains and the extravagant showings of spring wildflowers. Pidcock recalled this trip as the beginning of his path to Rome. He visited the mission three or four times a year, often with Martelli, but many times alone or with his wife.

In January 1876, the two rode over for the feast of the Epiphany. The visit of the Magi, universally celebrated as the manifestation of Jesus to the Gentiles, was for Salvado 'the anniversary of the call of the savages to the Christian faith'. Pidcock attended Mass and Divine Office, following them closely in a missal. He watched in admiration as Aboriginal children from the mission schools sang the High Mass and a number of children, Aboriginal and European, received the sacrament of Confirmation. Salvado noted in his diary that evening, 'he told me in clear words that if he had a livelihood he would cease to be what he is and would become a Catholic', adding with sharp irony, 'so he is a Protestant for his daily bread! But for conviction he is a Catholic'.[7]

The friendship with Martelli and with the Benedictines became the space within which Pidcock could work through his conflicting loyalties. He formed a special bond with Fr Martínez – they were roughly the same age – and when he and his wife were received into the Catholic church in Sydney in October 1882, he wrote with effusive thanks, 'my dear Father Martinez, how can I thank you, and his Lordship, and the other Fathers, and Brothers too, for all your great and many kindnesses to us for so long a period?' It was eight years almost to the day, Pidcock remembered, since Martelli accompanied him to New Norcia for the first time: 'Through him primarily I believe I owe the fact that I am a Catholic now: and after him to you all at N.N. and more especially to yourself'. The Pidcocks remained in Sydney. For a new livelihood, Rev. Pidcock taught in Catholic schools. After his wife's death, he entered the Society of Jesus and was ordained a priest in 1893.[8]

Martelli was initially reluctant to accept that he would not be returning to New Norcia any time soon. After six months, he told Griver he would stay on 'for a little longer', but Santos Salvado reported a conversation with the frustrated Canon: 'Blessed three months! Not a day more, said Fr Martelli, and it has already been very close to seven more months.' It took a year for Martelli to send for a heavy crate of his personal effects from New Norcia.[9]

On the other hand, Santos Salvado seemed in no hurry to recognise Martelli's ongoing status as a member of the community. In a letter of June 1873, he confessed to his brother, the abbot, 'I still need to send Father Martelli the breviary that he wants'. Benedictines used their own version of the Breviary for Divine Office. A new edition reached New Norcia in 1864, and Martelli gained permission to use it while at New Subiaco or New Norcia. In Newcastle, he must have reverted to the standard Roman Breviary until Santos sent the Benedictine version. Then at last he could reduce the distance from the community by praying the same daily prayers from the same text.[10]

After two years in Newcastle, Martelli told a confrere in Italy, 'Monsignor Salvado has, as the English say, loaned me to the Bishop of Perth for an indefinite period'. He says 'as the English say' to echo the transactional, secular phrase that he heard in Perth, in place of the more appropriate language of canon law used by Italian and Spanish speakers. He embraced his new position, but because Salvado had agreed to it. His spiritual home was New Norcia.[11]

It is striking therefore, and a source of frustration for the biographer, that there are almost no letters from Martelli in the New Norcia archive dating from his time in Newcastle. From his first fifteen years in Western Australia until he retired to the mission, the archive averages twenty-five letters a year. From his eight years in Newcastle, we find a total of merely ten letters.

The epistolary silence with Rosendo Salvado is especially perplexing. It is true that they saw each other whenever Martelli visited New Norcia – three or four times a year and in 1876 seven times – and when Salvado visited Newcastle. It is also true that after 1874, Martelli no longer needed pen and paper for business messages, as the New Norcia telegraph office had opened the year before. But this does not explain the lack of letters between old friends.

Martelli and Salvado were now both in their sixties, devoted, in the fullness of their lives, each to his own station. Martelli knew the people of Newcastle needed his presence and Salvado was the leader of an abbey nullius with a thriving agricultural business. Perhaps the best explanation of the lack of letters is that their long friendship had matured into a companionship of deep spiritual understanding, that could be nourished by occasional visits but no longer needed the frequent exchange of written communication.

Instead, the Newcastle years have conserved Martelli's image for us. Three photographs survive. Two were taken in the same setting. The frame around one of them identifies the photographer as James Manning, son of the prominent citizen of the same name. He operated a successful studio in King William Street in Perth. In November 1874 and again the following year, Manning visited Newcastle with Alfred Chopin. They set themselves up in the Freemasons' Hotel on Stirling Terrace to 'take likenesses'.[12]

In one portrait, Martelli looks into the camera, a little stiff, having finally acceded to having his image recorded and not at all comfortable with the new technology. The second photograph is identical except that Martelli is looking away and the book has

Canon Raffaele Martelli, c. 1875

been turned over to show the pages not the spine. This photo was a gift to Miss Louisa Roe, who taught at the Catholic school at Newcastle during 1878. On the back of the photograph she has written 'Rev. R. Martelli' and '1876'.[13]

The image constructed in these two portraits is the conventional portrait of a simple priest, in regulation soutane, without adornment. He sits, quiet and collected, his hand resting on his copy of the Divine Office. This was a frequent pose in priestly portraits and must have been an obvious choice for Martelli. He had learned the stability that came through the discipline of the 'work of God' while a Canon of Santa Maria della Piazza in Ancona. Among the Benedictines in Subiaco (Italy) and then in New Subiaco and New Norcia, he loved the unity expressed and created through choral recitation of the Hours. Now, as a missionary chaplain, it was his daily duty to recite the Office alone. The regular recollection of his origin and destiny was the heart of all his doing and being and he never failed to remind himself, through regular contemplation, of the meaning of his life and work. The obituary in the *Inquirer* would include this vignette of the ageing priest:

> Often have I met him at friends' houses at a distance from Newcastle, and, as either of the canonical hours approached, would he ask to be let alone, and withdrawing himself to the end of the verandah, or a corner of the room, he would draw forth his Breviary and quietly recite his appointed office.[14]

One other photograph of Martelli survives. At the bottom of the frame we read 'Canon Raffaele Martelli' and the date 'About 1875', written in a hand that resembles the writing of Dom William Giménez. The top of the frame gives this information about Martelli in a different hand: 'Accompanied Salvado 1853'. The image is printed on one of Santos Salvado's blank cartes de visite, and has 'R[everen]do S. Salvado, New Norcia, Australia' printed on the back. No further information is recorded. It may have been taken at New Norcia. The blank background is common in the photographs taken by Santos Salvado, since he often took portraits outside, against the walls of the church, to catch the light.[15]

Canon Raffaele Martelli and unidentified youth, perhaps Frederick Mead Caranet, c. 1875

Equally unknown is the identity of the young boy who stands calmly at Martelli's side, as the priest's hand rests lightly on his shoulder. He is wearing the simple shirt worn by students in the mission schools. Salvado records that on 3 October 1876, Martelli rode over to New Norcia to visit Bishop Griver, who was convalescing after a serious illness. He brought with him a young Aboriginal youth from Beverley at the southern end of the valley. Salvado believed he was the brother of Gregorio Mayacan, who was already at the mission, and records the boy's name as Caranet, but he became known as Frederick Mead. Caranet had begged Martelli to intercede with Salvado so that he too would be accepted into the mission. He agreed to stay, signing with X. Could Caranet be the boy in this photograph?[16]

During the 1870s, Salvado became more involved in the development of policies to protect Aboriginal women and children from the more violent consequences of expanding settlement. Martelli brought two more children from the Avon Valley to the mission.

On 14 November 1876, he accompanied a thirteen-year-old girl named Chuberan, also known as Mary Ann, from Northam. Mary Ann's father was English and her mother was Noongar. It is worthy of note that in his diary entry, Salvado uses the racial profiling terminology that was becoming normal in the colonial administration, and describes Mary Ann as *de media casta*, 'half caste'. This may explain why Martelli brought her: as a young girl entering puberty, he may have feared she was at risk. Mary Ann was baptised at the mission the following year and three years after that married Frederick Blurton. The second youth was taken to the mission in early 1880 by a local non-Aboriginal youngster who did jobs for Martelli, Tommy Williams. This was Willie Nanonga, and he came to join his brother Willie Willyway, who had recently wed Eliza Tainan.[17]

There was little else Martelli could do for the Aboriginal people in the area. As the colonial frontier advanced, the destructive effects on the Noongar became more grievous and more stark. When archeologist Gaetano Chierici wrote in 1874 asking for a second set of Aboriginal artefacts, Martelli was unable to help. The traditional way of life was now impossible, he told his Italian confrere, and the corrosive effects of European contact were depressingly evident:

Savages appear here in numbers only for the annual fair, horse race, etc, and they offer humiliating evidence of the degree to which contact with Whites has corrupted them. To study usefully the primitive state of the Aborigines now, one would have to travel hundreds or thousands of miles from the European settlements. Even at New Norcia, little may be gathered for the benefit of science. That Mission is, above all, an educational institution for youth. The life of the bush is completely forgotten. Only a few nomadic savages pass through, and rarely at that. Indeed, the race is gradually but rapidly dying out everywhere the Whites have penetrated.[18]

Martelli became more and more pessimistic about the future of Australian Aborigines. To his old friend Pio Urbani, in Ancona, he wrote in 1878, 'I say nothing of the Aborigines, they are a race condemned to extinction'. This sounds like the 'doomed race' theory that was now firmly fixed in colonial thinking. Enlightenment ideas about race and progress justified the belief that the extinction of the Aborigines was inevitable. However, Martelli gives no indication that he shares the world view of social evolutionism, that 'less developed' cultures were destined to be superseded by 'more developed' ones. His pessimism is rather a description of the evolving conflict at the colonial frontier.[19]

What threatened the future of the Aborigines was not the evolutionary struggle between savage and civilised but the ongoing effects of British conquest and the destructive actions of rapacious and unscrupulous settlers. He knew that Fr Bourke had sent teenage girls to New Norcia from York, some with venereal disease, 'the victims of the fierce passions of evil white men'. He told Pio Urbani with bitter sarcasm, 'Everywhere the Whites penetrate with their civilisation and their vices, the Blacks gradually disappear. This is what has happened along the coasts. The same thing will happen in the interior.' Martelli's conclusion, that New Norcia was the only institution dedicated to the welfare and education of the Aborigines, would be echoed a century later by Jack Davis: 'Mission ground was the only place left as a haven from the murderous onslaught of White settlers'.[20]

His passion for education and literacy, even now that he was no longer in the classroom, inspired various initiatives. He tried to establish a 'liberal Catholic library' in Newcastle but without success, because of the 'paucity of Catholic readers living within the immediate vicinity'. He served on the school boards established as part of Governor Weld's educational reform. He was elected in November 1874 to the Northam District School Board, polling the highest number of votes, and later also to the Newcastle Board, along with Rev. Pidcock. The two priests visited bush schools in isolated settlements, examining the children, presenting prizes and distributing sweetmeats to them. Martelli also served on the Central Board of Education based in Perth.[21]

His parishioners were found more in isolated farms and tiny settlements than in Newcastle itself, so his days were spent on horseback. His devotion to those who looked to him for the ministrations of Christian charity was always a priority. In January 1880, he arrived at New Norcia in days of 'suffocating heat'. When a telegram informed him two days later that someone in Newcastle was ill, he left the mission immediately, knowing he would have to ride through the night and sleep where he could by day:[22]

> No man ever led a more active life. He was not content with being the nominal pastor of a district the settled portions of which are considerably larger than the whole of Middlesex. [...] Up to the last day or two of his pastorate the aged man would set forth, in all weathers, on horseback, to hold service in some outlying part of his district, or to visit the sick and afflicted. So tender and comforting was his sympathy that I have known the staunchest Protestants express a wish for his visits, when in distress and anxiety.

Hugh Pidcock, if indeed he was the author of the *Inquirer* obituary, remembered that the Catholics were among the poorest of the community and some of the bush-houses in which Martelli regularly stayed were rough 'and worse than rough, I fear'. Martelli was once seen ordering a pair of trousers with extra length in the leg so that they would fit closely under his socks and stop the 'nocturnal vermin' crawling up his legs while he slept.

The physical effort was taking its toll. His first letters from Newcastle sound weary: the trips to Northam and York 'tired me greatly'. His list of health complaints grew more varied. The haemorrhoids worsened, though some days he covered fifty miles on horseback. By 1878, he could walk barely a mile without difficulty. His eyesight had never been strong. Early in his Australian years, he lost his glasses and told Salvado, 'I feel like I am without eyes'. By early 1880, he seems to have lost most of his teeth, since he thanked Salvado for giving him the name of the famous cure for toothache, 'Bunter's Nervine', hastening to point out it was for friends, not for himself, since 'my teeth have taken the French leave with me'. He wrote a whimsical note to Pio Urbani, 'If you send me a photograph of yourself, I will send you one of me. We shall see who is withstanding better the destructive action of time.'[23]

At Easter 1877, Martelli was in Perth at the Cathedral, while Fr Carreras supplied in Newcastle. Henry Spencer, who was the same age as Martelli, was received into the Church during the Vigil Mass and told Salvado he was 'much impressed with his [Martelli's] appearance'. When he met Martelli again six months later, he found him 'much aged in appearance since I last saw him. As I saw him at Mass this morning I thought as the corn gets yellow when it is ready for the sickle, so he is ripening for glory'.[24]

CHAPTER TWENTY-THREE

Always on the Move

1878–1880

As his strength declined, he found the energy for one final project. Newcastle had adequate Catholic facilities. Martelli had added a choir loft to the church in 1876 and two years later consecrated the Catholic cemetery. For his final exertion, he turned his attention to Northam. The town had grown quickly and was now more populous than Newcastle. Northam had no Catholic building. Martelli celebrated Mass and other sacraments in the Mechanics Institute Hall, which was used on Sunday evenings for Anglican services. He would now build a church and dedicate it 'to the great St. Joseph'. There was a strong and vocal concentration of Catholics in nearby Irishtown, but Martelli pushed ahead with a site in the middle of Northam on Wellington Street.[1]

He galvanised all sections of the community, Catholic and Protestant alike. Martelli's identity as a Catholic was never out of public view. When he was called to give evidence in court, he insisted on swearing the oath on a Catholic Bible. However, a clear sense of his own identity was never a barrier to encountering those of other convictions. Rather, it seems to have opened him to others, in respect for the search for truth that motivated all according to their circumstances and their backgrounds. Mutual knowledge was the path to breaking down prejudice.[2]

As building contractor, Martelli appointed George Throssell. Known as 'the Lion of Northam', he was the dominating personality in the district and became town mayor, member of Parliament and the second Premier of Western Australia. Throssell did not have sufficient funds available at the start of the project and Martelli insisted he accept £100 to get the job started. An active Anglican, he would remember Martelli as 'one of the finest Christian gentlemen he had ever the pleasure of being acquainted with'. Throssell's daughter Evelyn remembered Martelli at the family dining table, alongside the Anglican chaplain Stephen Brown, in a remarkable scene:

> Our parents were very broad in their religious beliefs & although the Church of England came first they were ever ready to offer hospitality to the other denominations who came to Northam to establish their churches. I recall one day when the Church of England minister & the Roman Catholic priest (the only churches at that time) were dining with us, father asked one to say grace & the other to return thanks. That was the first priest established at Northam, the Rev Father Martelli from New Norcia, who was beloved by everyone.[3]

Such generosity was not unique. Early settlers were so grateful to see a Christian priest of any denomination that, for example, Fr Griver stayed with a number of Protestant families during his 1858 tour of Champion Bay, and Anglican Lockier Burges asked him to bless the meal in his house. Even against such background, a meal framed by prayer from an Anglican minister and a Catholic priest is a memorable event in early Western Australia.[4]

The project architect was Peter Anthony Gugeri of Perth. He was born in London to a Swiss-Italian father and English mother, and studied with the founder of the Gothic Revival, Augustus Pugin. In 1873, he married Martelli's young protégée Kate Jackson on Rottnest Island. Martelli saw him regularly at meetings of the Perth Board of Education. For Northam, Gugeri designed a small neo-Gothic structure in local brick with four buttresses on each wall. The area behind the altar was divided into a sacristy and a bed-sitting room containing a camp-stretcher, table, chair and fireplace for the visiting priest.[5]

Martelli made sure he had the funds before building started. Local Constable John Maher collected most of the £210 donations, a substantial part of which was from Protestants of the town. Bishop Griver promised £150. Martelli thanked generous friends in Perth and Fremantle in a letter to the *Record*. He even enlisted Salvado to the cause. One family has passed down the story of the Abbot riding over from New Norcia and putting on a concert in Northam. Salvado stayed with the Morgan family at 'Bardeen' near Irishtown. The family loved music-making on Sunday evenings. Salvado played the Morgans' organ, Abraham (father of the family) got out his piano accordion, and a good time was had by all. Martelli must have ridden out for these soirées whenever he could; he would have loved them.[6]

Martelli laid the foundation stone of the new building on Easter Monday 1877. An anonymous 'Northam correspondent' in the Perth *Inquirer* encouraged all to attend, with words of warm appreciation for the indefatigable priest:

> Father Martelli is a pattern to ministers of other denominations. He may in fact be called an itinerant minister, for he is nearly always on the move – the poorest of his people are sought out, the children's welfare looked to, and steps taken to secure to them that religious instruction forbidden in the public schools. This is as it should be.[7]

Another anonymous correspondent to the *Inquirer*, this one from Newcastle, could find no more fitting praise of Martelli than the description of the village preacher in Goldsmith's 'The Deserted Village':

> Thus to relieve the wretched was his pride,
> And even his failings leaned to Virtue's side;
> But in his duty prompt at every call,
> He watched and wept, he prayed and felt, for all.
> And, as a bird each fond endearment tries,
> To tempt its new fledged offspring to the skies;
> He tried each art, reproved each dull delay,
> Allured to brighter worlds, and led the way.[8]

When the day came, Martelli found himself addressing a crowd of no fewer than four hundred people. The surviving scraps of his speech notes show his overwhelming gratitude and joy: 'My dear friends, at this moment, my feeling is one of heartfelt gratitude to Almighty God, my heart is overflowing with joy.' His remarks were widely quoted in the press, including the *Western Australian Times*:

> I believe that I echo the sentiments of the whole Catholic district when I say that this is one of the happiest days in our lives; that after long waiting, we are going at last to have here in this townsite a place of our own, a house of prayer, an altar at which to offer up the sacrifice of the Holy Eucharist; a house where the sinner may be reconciled to his Maker; a place where in the dark and lowering hours of adversity you may come to look for comfort; a house in which to render thanks to that God who is the Giver of all good gifts.[9]

He confessed to the crowd that he had been sceptical about the poor Catholics of the area being able to build their own church. 'But I now admit I was mistaken. I was too timid.' He was effusive in his thanks to those who had made this wonderful occasion possible by covering the projected cost of £500: Constable Maher, Bishop Griver and 'our good Protestant friends who have also responded nobly to our call, and I take this public occasion to offer to them our gratitude and our thanks'.

George Throssell rose to speak, opening with thanks on behalf of 'his brother Protestants' for the 'compliment paid them by the Rev. Father Martelli'. With the straight-talking that betokens real friendship, Throssell looked forward to the erection of a Protestant church in the town, certain that their Catholic friends 'would not withhold their hand'. Throssell led the temperance movement that sought to curb excessive drinking in the town. He knew Martelli was sympathetic to the cause but could not participate in an initiative of the International Order of Good Templars. He hoped that the day would come when the priest could join him on a common platform to advocate a practice that 'in the cottage or the mansion, brings peace, good will and prosperity in its train'.

A year later, again on Easter Monday, Martelli organised a fundraising day for the St Joseph's building fund. The whole town turned out for merriment and entertainment – a bazaar with the drawing of fourteen raffles, a tea-meeting at the Mechanics Institute, a performance of readings and music by 'dark minstrels from York' and an Irish balladeer, finishing with a dance that evening. Fr Martelli thanked all involved, stating that 'on all occasions when he had solicited assistance from his congregation in and around Northam, he had always found them ready to respond, and that too with the utmost cheerfulness'. The press reported that he left the stage 'amidst loud cheering, evidently called forth from the conviction that the success of the day's proceedings throughout was owing to Father Martelli's action and kindly exertions'.[10]

The local fundraising could not cover the decoration and furnishings for the interior of the church. Martelli appealed to Rome, reminding the authorities how generous the Western Australian faithful had been to Pope Pius earlier that year on the golden jubilee of his episcopal consecration. He sent Pietro Regnoli a petition for church vestments – to be presented 'to I know not whom' – together with a supporting letter from Bishop Griver. He even asked Abbot Pescetelli to use his influence: 'I do not ask for money, or for objects of precious metals or rare workmanship. Any article, simple in nature and required in the liturgy, especially in the Holy Sacrifice, will be received with joy and profound gratitude.' Regnoli, with the help of Gaspare Finali, now a Senator, mobilised a group of Roman ladies working with the order of St Joseph of the Apparition, and not long after the official opening a set of vestments and sacred vessels duly arrived. The good Sisters also prepared a second set of liturgical objects for Northam. After Martelli's death, Regnoli sent them to New Norcia: vestments, vessels, images of saints and medals of Pius IX, and devotional books.[11]

The next Easter Monday, 1879, saw the opening. It was a grand affair. Visitors of all denominations flocked in from Newcastle, York and the surrounding district. The church could not hold the crowd and half had to stand outside. After a procession around the building, Martelli officiated, assisted by Fr Anselm Bourke, who rode over from York and preached a fine sermon on 'My house shall be called a house of prayer'. Martelli had helped the local choir prepare Webbe's Mass in G, perhaps the same as the consecration of the Cathedral. After Mass, a bazaar in the Temperance Hall, a tea-meeting in the Mechanics Hall and a concert of dramatic farces and comic songs raised £61. Martelli made a point of thanking 'the ladies who had kindly given trays etc.'[12]

Martelli installed a bell in the church. This, so the story goes, was a gift to him by prisoners in the Fremantle Establishment. There are other stories that account for the presence of the bell. In 1884, the Colonial Secretary acceded to a request from Bishop Griver that the bell of the old police station and prison, no longer in use, be given to the Catholics of Northam. Wherever it came from, the bell now hangs in the entrance to the new St Joseph's, built to replace Martelli's church in 1901, and a plaque records the local folklore, that the bell used to inform parishioners that the priest had arrived from Newcastle to say Mass and to find a meal:[13]

This bell has been erected to mark the centenary of the blessing and opening of St Joseph's church. The bell belonged originally to the Very Rev. Canon Rafael Martelli, the first priest to minister to Northam on a regular basis in the mid 19th century. Tradition has it that it was presented to him by the convicts of Fremantle Gaol, in recognition of his kindness to them and his advocacy on their behalf. It was reputedly brought to Fremantle by a convict transport ship, from whence it found its way to the prison.

Martelli's attention to Northam in this period seems to have been almost at the expense of Newcastle. In March 1880, for example, the *Record* lists subscriptions he collected in Northam for the Irish Famine Relief Fund but no word of Newcastle.[14]

At Easter 1880, Martelli made a kind of unofficial farewell to the Avon Valley and the people he served and loved. By now he was organising his retirement to New Norcia. This would be his final public appearance. He said the first Easter Mass in the new St Joseph's. To celebrate the greatest of all Christian feasts in the new church was the conclusion and culmination of his final exertion on behalf of the people of the valley.

With great care, he prepared a long sermon for the occasion. 'This is the day that the Lord has made: let us be glad and rejoice': this text from the Gradual prayer of the Mass opens his reflection on the Easter events. 'By these words our Holy Mother Church announces to us the anniversary of the Resurrection of our Lord and Saviour Jesus Christ. The history of this, the greatest of miracles, is as follows' – for half a page he takes the congregation step-by-step through the Easter events, from the burial of Jesus, to his rising to the announcement by the women, to the encounter on the road to Emmaus, right up to the appearance of Jesus in the upper room and the first commissioning of the apostles: 'Peace be to you. As the Father hath sent me, so I also send you'. There could have been no more fitting reflection on his twenty-seven years in Western Australia. He had spent those years comforting the faith of

Catholics in this foreign land, preaching the gospel to those who knew nothing of the Christian event, laying the first foundations of the church in a place so distant and different from his own, spending every ounce of his strength for the mission entrusted to him by his Lord. As he described the mission entrusted to the apostles, he was summing up his own life's work:[15]

> What a sublime mission: a mission similar to that of the Son of God. To preach the gospel to the nations of the earth, to lay the foundations of the C. Church, and to shed their blood, to immolate their life in the cause of J. Christ.

The Christian call invites an answer. Speaking to his congregation as one of them, in the first-person plural 'we', he did not shrink even now from calling the baptised back to their responsibilities:

> The Church comands us all to confess our sins at least once a year, and to receive worthily the Holy Communion at Easter, or within the time appointed. Easter has come. How many among you have complied with their duties? There are not a few who have turned a deaf ear to the voice of the Church. Why? Either because they have lost their faith and are Catholics only by name, or because they are living in sin and have no desire of changing their life. Both classes are to be deeply deplored, and which more, I do not know.

He knew the faith of his people; they had built the church with the generosity of their offerings. Theirs is the credit if now they stand in a building of which he can say, 'God is worshiped in it with the worship that Jesus Christ has taught us. The sacraments instituted by Jesus Christ are administered in it. Here, he stopped and looked around the building, pointing one by one to the sacramental sites within the building, the same sites he had touched and kissed in Santa Maria della Piazza in Ancona when he became a Canon of that church. First, the ambo at which 'the life-giving bread of the word of God is broken'; then the confessional, 'the tribunal of penance at which repentant sinners recover peace of conscience and the friendship of God'; then the altar, 'the holy Table, at which we feed on the flesh of the Spotless Lamb'; and back to the congregation and to himself, and their common need for 'the Mercy of God'.

The following day, Easter Monday, he held another Mass in St Joseph's to give thanks for the first anniversary of the opening. Mass was followed by another successful bazaar. The sermon for this Mass is merely a page long, brief words to remind his congregation of the history of their practice of the faith in the town and how grateful they all should be:[16]

Beloved Brethren

What is our object in assembling today at the foot of the altar? To offer the Eucharistic sacrifice in thanksgiving. In thanksgiving for what favour? For the favour which has enabled us a year ago to erect this sacred edifice exclusively to the worship of God. To duly appreciate this favour we are only to recall to our memory past times, when we were obliged to have our religious meetings in places so much out of harmony with the august character of our sacred rites.

I remember very well, and you remember too, the time a small thatched cottage, lent to us no doubt with the best feelings and adorned for the occasion as well as the poverty of the owner allowed, was made the dwelling house of Him who the heavens cannot hold. We afterwards considered as a great privilege when we were allowed to erect our altar in the court house of this town where the associations of the locality used to make our assembling there anything but agreeable.

We made, then, another step towards improvement and obtained leave to hold our religious assemblies in the hall of the Institute, which was a great gain indeed on the score of space and confort [sic], but a painful thought used to haunt us that the room was occasionally used for worldly entertainment, parties, balls and theatrical performances.

At last we have seen this building raised, dedicated solely to prayer and religious worship. To rejoice in this accomplishment and to tender our thanks to God for it is the object which has called us together today.

Now, more funds were needed to make the building truly fitting for its sacred purpose. This was work for other hands, not his:

Some improvements have been effected, since we opened this church twelve months ago. Hence the necessity of raising funds to liquidate some debts contracted. A harmonium has been purchased, the sanctuary has been carpeted, the seats have been more confortable and some altar furniture is to be paid for. I have no doubt that you will come forward today and by patronising the usual contrivances for the raising of funds, you will show your approval of what has been done, and your willingness to contribute to the further embellishment of the house of God.

There. His work was done. The three major centres in the Avon Valley – Toodyay, York and now Northam – all had their own Catholic church. Ongoing funding and maintenance could be entrusted to others. For the good Canon, it was time to leave.

CHAPTER TWENTY-FOUR

To Lay My Bones in New Norcia Ground

1880

Three months had turned into eight years. The old Canon had served the diocese faithfully and well for long enough.

He had only agreed to move back over the hills, in 1872, because the Catholics of the district had been left without a pastor and he would not leave without identifying a successor. In the spring of 1879, Martelli heard that a replacement was due to arrive in the colony. This was another Father Martelli, who also left a happy memory in early Western Australia. His origins are clothed in mystery.

The new priest first wrote to Salvado in June 1879, from the Malabar mission on the south-west coast of India. He introduced himself as a secular priest, forty-two years of age, who spoke English, French, Italian and several Indian languages. He was working at Mahé, a French settlement, after thirteen years as chaplain to English forces in India. He wanted to move to a less humid climate for health reasons. Recently, in London, he had met

Fr Rafael Carmona, who was sailing to New Norcia and advised him to contact Salvado. Salvado passed his letter on to Griver, who invited the new priest to come as soon as he could, with good testimonials from his ecclesiastical superior.[1]

The new Father Martelli's first letter – to the Spaniard Salvado – was written in Portuguese and he signed himself 'Luiz Martelli'. In Western Australia, he was believed to be Italian and is usually remembered as Luigi. He gave Daisy Bates Italian lessons in 1899.[2]

Bishop Salvado thought Luigi was Raffaele's nephew, and this idea has been repeated in several histories. After meeting Luigi on his arrival in Perth, Salvado told the Prior of New Norcia that Luigi's father was Raffaele's brother and his mother a Portuguese woman from Lisbon. In Rome, Pietro Regnoli was very surprised to hear this and made enquiries among Raffaele's relatives in Ancona and Rome, who also contacted two unrelated Martelli families in Ancona. No one had ever heard of Luigi or of any member of the family called Antonio Ciriaco (the name of Luigi's father). It is curious that Raffaele did have a brother Antonio (who had a daughter but no sons), and Ciriaco is the patron saint of Ancona. However, neither Luigi nor Raffaele ever mention in correspondence that they were related. Until some definitive evidence settles the question either way, it may be best to put it all down to an uncanny coincidence.[3]

Raffaele Martelli also wrote to the new Martelli directly, asking him to come to Newcastle as his replacement. There is no trace of this correspondence between them but, according to Griver, Luigi replied to Raffaele quickly in December 1879. He would come as soon as he could raise the funds for the trip.[4]

As it turned out, Luigi Martelli did not arrive in Perth for two more years. However, his letter of December 1879 gave Raffaele Martelli the first concrete opportunity to guarantee a priest for his beloved parishioners in the valley as he retired to New Norcia.[5]

He was already withdrawing from worldly activities and relationships. In 1879, he resigned from all Boards of Education. Old friends were disappointed that their letters went unanswered.

In 1879, his old friend Christy Reynolds, now Bishop of Adelaide, begged Salvado to 'give my affectionate regards to the good Fr Martelli. He never writes to me'. Louisa Roe was also in South Australia, where she had followed one of her brothers and taught for a time. His letters to her, though full of affection – 'Dear Child in J.C.' – express melancholy and resignation. He was delighted that Louisa had met Fr Frederick Byrne, now Reynolds' Vicar General. As he passed on affectionate greetings, he could not disguise his detachment from the power structures of the world, even of the Church:

> If you see the Vicar General again, tell him I entertain for him all the esteem and affection of the old times with the addition of the respect due to his position in the Church, and the sympathy demanded by the arduous duties and responsibilities of the same.[6]

This mood of withdrawal from the cares of the world was shattered in early 1880. The Vatican was considering making him a bishop – in North America. The always well-informed Pietro Regnoli heard that Martelli was the preferred candidate for a province – perhaps Oregon – 'where Catholic affairs have gone badly for forty years because of disagreements between English and French bishops'. Propaganda was looking for a priest who was fluent in French and English, but was not English, French or German in nationality. He had to be prudent and competent in administration.[7]

In February 1880, Cardinal Simeoni, Prefect of Propaganda, asked Griver for an assessment. The bishop's reply was a measured but hardly effusive recommendation. Martelli met the essential criteria:

> I am pleased to state that he is sufficiently expert in the English and French language, of good customs, of acclaimed prudence and urbanity and, what is best, of commendable priestly virtues.[8]

On the question of Martelli's administrative competence, Griver knew that Martelli had declined all positions of responsibility offered to him. His assessment is tactfully phrased:

> As for his competence in managing affairs of great importance, I do not hear much, since he has held no office here where he might have demonstrated it. However I can say that in ordinary affairs he is affable and of not insignificant ability.

Griver knew that Martelli was set on retiring to New Norcia and told Salvado he 'would be very pleased if Martelli were given the honorary title of Archbishop, or at least Bishop, *in partibus infedelium*'.[9]

Martelli suspected that his friend Pietro Regnoli had a hand in the Vatican's offer. He wrote letters which Regnoli described as 'heated and to the point', demanding that his friend 'make good the wrong I had done him'. The underlining is Regnoli's, as he told Salvado of the agitated tone of Martelli's letters. Regnoli admitted he may have been partly to blame because the new Secretary of Propaganda Fide, Ignazio Masotti, was an old friend. When he congratulated Masotti on his appointment, Regnoli recommended his Australian friends 'for any eventuality'. On 31 July, Regnoli wrote to his old friend in Australia, unaware that he was near death, reassuring him, on the basis of recent conversations at Propaganda, that there would be no further talk of new destinations for him.[10]

Masotti was 'very sorry' at Martelli's refusal. Santos Salvado may not have been aware of all this, because he wrote after Martelli's death to tell his brother that Canon Martelli had the virtues and knowledge needed to become a bishop, but 'he was a liberal and Rome has never liked that'. It seems rather that Rome had forgotten, or at least forgiven.[11]

When this storm abated, Martelli had only to wait for a replacement to materialise. There was no more news of Luigi Martelli. Finally, at the beginning of June 1880, he heard that

Fr Joseph Keating had arrived in Perth from Melbourne. 'His arrival will enable me to retire to New Norcia', he confided in Louisa Roe, 'where your next letter will probably find me.' He did not inform Bishop Griver, but packed his bags.[12]

In Northam, the Anglican Throssells were dear friends and it was a tearful parting. The occasion was remembered half a century later by one of the Throssell sons, perhaps the eldest, Lionel, who was seventeen when Martelli left. 'The contract for the building was left to my father,' he recalled, 'and thus I saw much of this good old man':

> Between him, my parents and my grandmother, there was more, vastly more than friendship, there was that love that passeth man's understanding – and with the building of his church completed, feeling the infirmity of years and strain of hard work, the time came for him to lay down his work. This final farewell, and parting from my people is impressed upon my memory as one of the most beautiful and pathetic memories in my life. He rode up to our old home, tied up his pony to the fence and came in to have a few last words – saying to my mother: 'Mrs. Throssell, I have finished my work, I am now going home to die'. It was a touching scene; together they all walked out to his pony. Then came the final wrench, all so clear to me to-day. This saintly old man and gentleman, as he put the reins over his arm, hat in hand, he grasped my father's in deep and reverent silence, then turning, took my mother's and my grandmother's, holding each a little longer than usual, his lips quietly moving in silent prayer. Then, endeavouring to smile through his tears, he turned and rode away.[13]

Salvado's diary records that in the midst of the autumn work, Father Martelli arrived at the mission, unannounced, on the morning of Friday 11 June. His belongings arrived that afternoon.[14]

Griver knew nothing about it. On 16 June, he told Salvado he was planning to send newly arrived Fr Keating to Newcastle to relieve Martelli, 'since he wants to retire to New Norcia'. Martelli had been at the mission for five days already.[15]

Martelli told Salvado he had no intention of leaving. Salvado remembered later, with irony and admiration and just a little exaggeration, 'He went to Newcastle to do Monsignor Griver a favour but only for a few months. Since Mgr Griver never managed to find another priest, or rather did not want to find one, the few months turned into ten years!'[16]

If Martelli knew he was ill, he told no one, but the monks soon noticed something was wrong when, only eight days after he arrived, he was confined to bed. Salvado thought it was the haemorrhoids and applied leeches. This caused some shrinking, which brought relief and general improvement, but his condition was obviously much worse. It was diagnosed as dropsy, since he showed enormous swelling in the lower body, from the navel to the feet. Martelli knew he was dying. 'He was convinced there was nothing the doctors could do', Salvado told their mutual friend Abbot Pescetelli,

> and from the beginning he told me, 'This is my first and my last illness here in Australia'. Several times he repeated 'I thank God for the grace he has granted me of bringing me here to die in New Norcia, as I always wanted to. The idea of dying in the Newcastle hospital horrified me'.[17]

Salvado knew that Martelli had always wanted to 'lay down my bones in New Norcia ground'. Indeed, he told Pescetelli, 'if the illness had taken hold of him in Newcastle, I would have brought him here because I knew well how much he desired to die among us'.[18]

His condition deteriorated so quickly that Bishop Griver, who was in Newcastle introducing Fr Keating to the congregation, rode over in the spring cart. He came, he told the Prefect of Propaganda, 'out of friendship, for his solace and for my own'. On 9 July, Martelli was so weak Griver gave him the viaticum. Before receiving it, Martelli asked to say a few words to the many members of the community crowded into his room. He spoke many words of 'thanks, gratitude and praise', Salvado told Pescetelli, 'that reduced us all to tears'.[19]

Salvado began homeopathic treatment, since 'with allopathic [i.e. traditional] medicine we did not know what else could be done'. He administered arsenic, four globules every four hours dissolved in distilled water, and then alternated arsenic and sulphur, three doses of each, every twenty-four hours. By the 13th, the ailing Canon was given Extreme Unction, the sacrament of Anointing of the Sick. The next day he rallied a little and ate a hearty meal, a pigeon. A week later his condition deteriorated again, the leeches were applied, but Salvado knew that by now medical treatment could do nothing but prolong his life a little.

On 1 August, the New Norcia community gathered in prayer to commend his soul to God. Martelli could not speak but, Salvado recorded in his diary, 'we presume he can hear and understand what is said to him'. The following day, he lost consciousness, and at 10.30 pm entered his final agony. He died peacefully, just after midday, on Tuesday 3 August. Salvado's diary says simply 'Fr Martelli died at 12.30. R.I.P.' The sentence is written in large, heavy handwriting, underlined.

In the report on the mission that Salvado wrote for Propaganda Fide in 1883, he remembered Martelli's death as 'most edifying, just as his entire life as a missionary had been'. He summed up his memory of the man: he was 'humble, unselfish, zealous, hard-working, constant, well-educated, kind, in a word, an exemplary figure every missionary could model himself on'. A circle had closed. The disciple had become the master. Each had seen in the other a Christian witness to follow, a friend to walk with.[20]

Salvado wrote to Abbot Pescetelli of a friendship that had sustained him for nearly three decades. 'In him', Salvado wrote, 'I have lost a true friend, a personal friend of mine and a cordial friend of the mission. May God take him into glory'.[21]

In preparing his body for burial, the monks clothed him in the Benedictine habit, a detail Salvado noted in his diary and repeated in his letter to Abbot Pescetelli. Salvado always counted Martelli as a member of the New Norcia community. At the beginning of the year, he had sent a description of the community to Abbot Boniface Wimmer, who was compiling a directory of Benedictines worldwide. Martelli is described simply as 'Not Professed'. The gesture of clothing a body in the habit was an honour bestowed on special friends of the community. In 1890, a New Norcia labourer William McKay, a Scottish convert, was buried 'in the holy Benedictine habit, at his request'. In Martelli's case, this loving gesture was not his request but a spontaneous expression of affection from the community.[22]

Bishop Griver had offered to hold the funeral in the Cathedral. However, it was held in New Norcia the day after his death. His friend Fr Martínez had given Martelli the final viaticum and heard his final confession and now he celebrated the funeral and burial. In heavy rain, a large number of people came from near and far, Catholic and Protestant. A week later, Bishop Griver celebrated a High Mass in the Cathedral for the repose of his soul. In Ancona, the Canons of Santa Maria della Piazza held their own ceremony.[23]

Father Martelli was buried, as he had always wished, in the New Norcia cemetery. The one-acre plot of land was granted to Salvado in 1860 and consecrated in 1864, on the feast of the Nativity of Mary, 8 September. Nineteenth-century depictions of New Norcia show a large cross standing in the centre of the cemetery and a smaller cross at each corner. Martelli's friend, the saintly Fr Garrido, was buried in the centre of the cemetery, 'at the foot of the large cross', just to the left. Martelli was now buried next to his friend, at the foot of the cross and to the right (north).[24]

When the second Abbot, Fulgentius Torres, died in 1914, his monumental tomb was placed where the cross had stood. So now the burial plots of Martelli and Garrido lie at the foot of the large tomb. Like all graves of priests, monks and nuns buried in the cemetery, their plots are marked with a simple cross bearing name and dates. There are two errors on Martelli's cross. His dates are given as 1810–1880, whereas he was born in 1811. His name is followed by the letters 'OSB', the post-nominal given to

New Norcia Cemetery. At the foot of the monumental tomb of Abbot Torres we can read the gravestones of Venancio Garrido (left) and Raffaele Martelli (right).

Benedictines since the beginning of the eighteenth century. The oversight simply reveals the esteem and affection that led to him being dressed for his burial in the Benedictine habit.[25]

Martelli and Garrido are given a unique honour in the cemetery. Alone among all the priests buried here, the two friends have their own granite gravestones, on which a memorial dedication is inscribed. The two are neatly symmetrical in their wording:

Here lies	Here lies
Venancio Garrido O.S.B.,	Rev. Dom. Canon
a Spaniard,	Raphael Martelli,
the first Prior of New Norcia.	an Italian,
	a learned and apostolic man.
By working and praying for twenty-one years for the conversion of the Aborigines, he deserved very well of the Mission.	He died in this mission of New Norcia, Western Australia, on the third day of August, 1880, in his seventieth year.
He died on 12 August 1870, in his sixtieth year. Pray for him.	

It is no surprise to see Martelli memorialised for his learning, in the Latin *doctus*. The description of him as 'apostolic', *apostolicus*, is a special expression of praise from the monks who buried him. The apostolic dimension was central to Salvado's vision of monastic life. He once advised a monk who aspired to missionary work: 'A good monk will also be a good missionary'. The word *apostle* is Greek and means 'one who is sent, one on a mission'. The Gospels spell out the two characteristics of the apostle: 'Jesus appointed twelve, whom he also named apostles, to be *with him* and to be *sent out* to proclaim the message'. The apostle adheres to friendship with Jesus as the exhaustive meaning of their existence and, because of that relationship, lives the mandate to be sent.[26]

Life goes on. In his record of 4 August 1880, Salvado noted: 'Having concluded the funeral ceremony, we continued our usual labours with the extra task of washing wool that we call "dead" – this is skin wool that is taken from the skin of a dead animal.'[27]

Letters of condolence poured into New Norcia. Everyone was sure Martelli had gone to his eternal reward. Sister Julie Cabagniol wrote from the Albany convent of St Joseph of the Apparition. Martelli was the first priest she met when she arrived at Fremantle twenty-five years earlier and she told Salvado, 'I have lost a good friend and the death of any of my family would not have saddened me more'.[28] From Italy came letters from the Regnolis. Martelli's half-sister Aldomira asked Pietro Regnoli to obtain a reminder of her brother.[29]

The *West Australian Catholic Record* of the following week published a long and moving obituary, unsigned:

> Not only those who knew him well but even those but slightly acquainted with him were impressed with the conviction that Father Martelli was a holy priest and a cultivated gentleman. His piety, gentleness and grace of manner were unmistakeable [sic], and conciliated favour for him with all classes and, we may add, with all denominations. He endeavoured to gain the good will of all men, not for a selfish motive, but for their own good.

He wished to please all, to win all goodness. But above aught else he strove to please God and do His holy will. Through all these seven and twenty years which we have known him, he was faithful, gracious and just. He has now gone to his reward. May he rest in peace.[30]

The long obituary that was probably written by Hugh Pidcock appeared in the *Inquirer*. Writing it, the author states, was a 'labour of love'. In the light of Pidcock's later entry into the Catholic Church, it is interesting that the opening text is from the Book of Wisdom (5:4-5), which, though included in the Anglican lectionary, is counted by the Church of England among the apocryphal books of the Bible:

We fools counted his life as madness, and his end to be without honour; now is he honoured among the children of God and his lot is among the saints.

Pietro Regnoli passed on a request from Gaspare Finali, Martelli's former student, now a decorated Senator of the Kingdom of Italy. He longed to have some object of Martelli's, something he had often held in his hands. The anti-clerical Senator asked for Martelli's copy of the *Imitation of Christ*.[31]

CHAPTER TWENTY-FIVE

Conclusion

As the first anniversary of Martelli's death approached, Napoleone Ascoli delivered a commemorative oration on his former teacher to the Circolo Filologico in Ancona. The published text was dedicated to Senator Gaspare Finali, 'whose love and reverence for Raffaele Martelli was exceeded by no one', and the proceeds of the booklet would fund a plaque in Martelli's honour. Ascoli's sudden death in 1909 caused the project to lapse but he had already drafted the inscription for Ancona's Civic Library:

> This plaque remembers Canon Raffaele Martelli, who was an exemplary priest, a distinguished man of letters, a talented teacher and a proven patriot. In 1848 he fought with the volunteers of the Marche for the independence of Italy. In Australia he lived and died spreading, with apostolic fervour among a primitive and uncivilised people, all the works of civilisation together with faith in Christ.[1]

Regnoli told Salvado of Ascoli's oration and warned him it was 'of liberal flavour'. Liberal it was, full of the fervour of the 1848 campaign against the Austrians and confident in the construction of a new, unified and secular Italy. This became the memory of Martelli that was handed down in the histories of Ancona. Martelli the liberal man of letters. Martelli the educator of patriots. Martelli the military chaplain. The recognition of his missionary work that was to be included in Ascoli's memorial plaque faded in official memories.[2]

In 1960, to celebrate one hundred years of Italian unification, the city of Ancona renamed a number of streets and squares. A large open area in front of the Caserma Villarey, the splendid military barracks built in the 1860s and now (2025) home to the Università delle Marche, was named 'Piazzale Raffaele Martelli'. On the street signs in the Piazzale, Martelli is remembered as a 'man of letters', *letterato*. There is no reference to the fact that he was a priest, or a missionary.[3]

In the City Council documents that gave the historical background on the persons being honoured, however, Martelli was remembered both for his patriotic activism in Italy and for his selfless work in Australia. The website that recorded the deliberations is no longer available, but the citation documented the memory that was celebrated in the city. It quotes the phrase from Giangiacomi's list of 'brazen enemies of the government':

> Born in Ancona on 13 March 1811, he was a Canon and professor of rhetoric in the seminary and taught many youths national Italian pride. The police depicted him as one of the most passionate and brazen enemies of the government. He took part in the Veneto campaign of 1848 and then distinguished himself in the siege of Ancona in 1849 for his humanitarian work. He left Ancona in 1851 and joined the Benedictine mission of New Norcia in Australia where he remained twenty-seven years living a life of poverty and hardship. He died on 3 August 1880 at 70 years of age.[4]

In 1859, ten years after the disastrous events of 1848–1849, Martelli wrote to Gaspare Finali, full of enthusiasm for the victories of the Piedmontese army over the Austrians. The mighty foe who had crushed the 1848 rebellion was now swept aside as Italy strode inexorably to independence and unification. But the unification of the country was in the hands of liberals with whom Martelli could have little in common. He watched aghast as the new government turned on the church, marginalising the Papacy and seizing church assets. After Italian armed forces burst through the walls of Rome in 1870, Finali, now a Senator, begged his old teacher to return: 'Come back, come back to this Italy, now free and united, that you taught me to venerate and love'. Martelli declined with bitter regret: 'ah no, I am old and in bad shape, *malandato*; but even if I could, I would not return to Italy to look like an enemy'.[5]

The actions of the first Italian governments of the 1860s were bad enough. The new ruling class, from Piedmont, had been attacking Catholic institutions in the Kingdom of Savoy since the 1840s and now applied its religious policies to the peninsula. Monasteries and convents were dissolved, their resources confiscated. But the loss of the temporal power – first the central Italian regions and then Rome itself – was for Martelli the final tragedy, the ultimate betrayal of the liberal ideals on which he had staked his priesthood and his reputation in his Italian years. Martelli was at one with the official church position as he watched Pius IX retreat into isolation in the Vatican, issuing a decree *Non expedit* ordering Catholics not to vote or stand for election for the new Italian Parliament. It would be a century before Cardinal Montini, the future Pope Paul VI, acknowledged that though the end of the temporal power 'seemed a collapse', it proved with time to be providential, ushering in an era of greater spiritual authority of the Papacy.[6]

Catholic liberals had moved on. The more conservative gradually withdrew from political life. Others argued for a purification of religion itself, untying religion from temporal affairs, and rejected any form of 'political Catholicism'. Others still carried on the legacy of Gioberti's vision, of an Italian identity in which Catholicism occupied a central place. From Australia, Martelli failed to see the seismic shift that was happening in Italian Catholicism, in the form of the emergence of the laity, educated, informed and active in all levels of the new Italian State.[7]

The irony of Martelli's political stance is that he remained obstinately true to Gioberti's vision of the mid-1840s, while no one in Italy, least of all Gioberti, kept faith to his original neo-guelphism. Gioberti's movement was, in the colourful Italian expression, a 'fire of straw', that burned bright but quickly faded in the events of 1848. In his determination to show the mutual identity of religion and civilisation, Gioberti ended up over-emphasising the social function of religion and devaluing its transcendental dimension. Religion became primarily a political tool for asserting Italian civilisation and the superiority of Italian culture over others. The guelph vision of an alternative idea of nation, based on religious tradition, persisted in Italy in different forms up to the late twentieth century. However, in its original formulation, the one to which Martelli held fast, it was utterly unworkable. A century and a half after Italian Unification, Pope Benedict XVI reflected on Gioberti's theocratic proposal. If Pius had let himself become the leader of a united Italy, he observed, 'the papacy would have come to an end'.[8]

Times had changed and Martelli could not change with them. The ideas and ideals that had him branded as a liberal in 1846 eventually saw him playing the part of the 'intransigent'.

The same strength of character and single-minded commitment to principle saw Raffaele Martelli labour selflessly for fifteen years in Western Australia – Fremantle, the Avon Valley and then Fremantle again, prison and town – as he argued, cajoled and threatened his way to retirement in New Norcia. During the ten years he pledged to the diocese of Perth, his longing to join the mission had the tone of a hopeless dream, one he knew he could not fulfil until he had honoured his commitment. When Fr Griver argued that changed circumstances absolved the diocese from keeping its side of the bargain, Martelli's sense of fair play was affronted. Yet his decision to spend five more years in the service of the diocese reflects the lessons he was learning from Bishop Salvado and the Benedictine community and from his own humble, constant discipleship.

Above all, he learned a life-changing lesson in the power of obedience. He saw up close the foibles and failures of the men to whom the universal mission of the Church was entrusted in this far-flung corner of the New World. He saw the injustice of decisions taken against colleagues and close friends, and for a time he feared he was next to be expelled from the colony. Yet he saw also that those who succeeded in building a Christian presence that endured were those who subordinated their own plans, desires and even rights to a story of which they were humble servants. The saintly Fr Garrido was an inspiration, and Martelli prayed to imitate the way Garrido offered all of himself, not with passive acquiescence or begrudging resignation but with mature, intelligent and freely offered submission.

Martelli's relationship with Salvado is at the heart of his every decision. The precise nature of the relationship is tantalisingly out of reach, because we only have Martelli's letters and none of Salvado's and because Martelli left no other written traces. Nevertheless, the reverence Martelli expressed for the indomitable, multi-talented bishop in his first letter, of 1853, never abated during their long years of friendship. The friendship grew into a bond of close personal affection built on mutual respect and honesty. Yet to the end, Martelli's letters to Salvado are couched in observance of their hierarchical roles: 'My Dear Lord'. This is of a piece with his understanding of the Church as the defining frame of his identity in all its respects.

When, after fifteen long years, he achieved his dream of withdrawing from the diocese to serve the mission at New Norcia, Raffaele Martelli found himself again the victim of changing times. Since 1853, the population of the colony had nearly doubled and the relentless advance of the colonial frontier threatened the livelihood of Aboriginal populations further and further away from the new urban settlements. The disastrous Northampton trip in search of children to bring to the mission's schools was a humiliating demonstration of just how fraught relations between Aboriginal people and Europeans had become. Martelli never wavered in his belief in the mission entrusted to Salvado by Pope Gregory: to 'convert and civilise' the Aborigines of Australia. In his later years in Newcastle, he sent or accompanied children at risk to the safety of the mission. But when he moved to New Norcia, he had been an outsider for too long. He felt incompetent to negotiate the minefields of cultural contact and saw little scope for making a concrete contribution to the life of the mission. When he could not become parish priest of New Norcia since he was not a professed member of the community, there was little he could do at the mission beyond teaching in the schools.

What form of priestly work, then, was open to the good Canon as he entered his sixties? Though he complained during his first year over the hills, the complaints soon stopped. This was to be his lot. His memory of Garrido's example and the ongoing companionship of Salvado and the young Martínez taught him to go beyond the English proverb he was fond of quoting, 'What cannot be cured must be endured'. He learned rather to embrace this new situation as the locus of his priestly mission. His decision to consecrate the rest of his life exclusively to the exercise of the priestly ministry took shape in Salvado's 'conversion and civilisation' of Aboriginal people. Now, after two decades in Western Australia, circumstances landed him in the role of parish priest to a predominantly Irish flock in the scattered towns and farms of the Avon Valley. And he had learned that circumstances, even the most unexpected and unwelcome, were both the means through which the will of his God revealed itself to him and the path through which he fulfilled his destiny.

The politics of the old world and the new brought only strife and disillusion. How often he heard Fr Garrido repeat, 'the world is a continual disappointment'! The social order he saw emerging in Italy, that denied the religious ground of human coexistence, was impossible for him to contemplate. Instead, he learned a deeper lesson. His hidden ministration to the humble people he served was not a retreat but a fulfilment. His horizon became universal; the church was no longer merely the embattled institution of the old world but a worldwide community of people of all classes and qualities. Many of his homilies begin by reminding his tiny congregations that the liturgy they were celebrating connected them to Christians all around the world, all united in the same work of living out their faith in whatever circumstances they found themselves in.

It was in this spirit that he took on his final work as a humble country priest. His eight years over the hills were years of withdrawal and preparation for death. But he could not live half-heartedly, and so threw himself into the many tasks required of a priest serving a flock scattered over distances he had to cover uncomfortably on horseback. The circumstances he traversed had all been for his maturation. He knew himself and he knew his craft and this was where he would live out his final years of service.

It is this decision that explains two persistent puzzles about Martelli's presence in the archive. There are virtually no letters at all written from Newcastle, because he withdrew into his own interior life, safe in the knowledge that the community he considered his own was always there and secure in his ability to live what he was now asked to live, alone.

The mystery remains as to why no letters that Raffaele Martelli received from anyone in Western Australia have survived. The very few exceptions are letters that he passed on to someone else at New Norcia. Around four hundred letters by Martelli are conserved in the New Norcia archive, so we can confidently guess that he received approximately the same number. Surely he treasured the correspondence with friends in Australia and Italy? Surely the record of his friendship with Salvado, that brought him to Australia in the first place and sustained him through nearly three decades, surely this would have been among his most treasured personal effects?

Yet, when his personal belongings arrived at New Norcia for the last time, his letters cannot have been among them. If they had, Salvado would have kept them. Did he leave them behind in Newcastle, where they gathered dust and were eventually disposed of by someone who did not appreciate their significance? Did he destroy the letters himself? As he retired to New Norcia that last time, did he free himself of all earthly attachments, even the written record of his years here? Did his humility and his scruples prevent him from seeing the precious legacy he left behind?

It is for others who knew him or studied his work to record the quality of the man. Martelli would have resiled from the judgement of Dom William Giménez, a historian monk of New Norcia, who wrote on the back of one of Martelli's studio portraits in the archive, 'the greatest of Western Australian priests'. But perhaps he would accept an assessment that refers, if not to prudence, then to another of the cardinal virtues: justice. Long-time Fremantle parishioner J.T. Reilly remembered him with well-known lines from Jacobean dramatist James Shirley:

> Only the actions of the just
> Smell sweet and blossom in the dust.[9]

The early promise of a brilliant career came to nothing in Italy. In three decades of almost anonymous missionary work in Australia, we look in vain for the singular feat, the lasting monument, the pose of the protagonist. We will see great things, though, if we recall the words of a great missionary of the twentieth century, St Teresa of Calcutta: 'There are no great things, only small things done with great love'.

Notes

Notes to Preface

1 HIC JACET REV. DOM. CANONICUS RAPHAEL MARTELLI, ITALUS, *VIR DOCTUS ET APOSTOLICUS*. OBIIT IN HAC MISSIONE NOVAE NURSIAE, *AUSTRALIA OCCIDENTALIS*, DIE TERTIA AUGUSTI, MDCCCLXXX. AETATIS SUAE ANNO LXX. R.I.P.
2 John J. Kinder and Joshua Brown, *Canon Raffaele Martelli in Western Australia, 1853–1864: Life and Letters* (Melbourne: Abbey Press, 2014).

Notes to Chapter One 'Ancona'

1 'In cima al Guasco drito / 'l domo de la città / tuto bianco arefito / 'nt'un scoio d'eternità', from Franco Scataglini, 'I giorni popolari', in *So' rimaso la spina* (Ancona: L'astrogallo, 1977); Thomas Trollope, *A Lenten Journey in Umbria and the Marches* (London: Chapman & Hall, 1862).
2 Roberto Domenichini, 'Il Dipartimento del Metauro nell'età napoleonica (1808–1815)', *Atti e Memorie della Deputazione di Storia Patria per le Marche* 92 (1987), 463–517.
3 Information on the Martelli family was compiled from *Registro Generale di popolazione fatto nell'anno 1812*, no.5953, ASAn; *Rubricella Generale per lo Stato di Popolazione del Comune di Ancona fatto nell'anno 1812*, no.3837, ASAn; *Stato delle Anime 1812* and parish registers, ASDAO; *Registro delle nascite 1811*, no. 336, ASAn; on Santa Maria della Piazza see Rosario Pavia and Ercole Sori, *Ancona* (Roma-Bari: Laterza, 1990).
4 Palermo Giangiacomi, *Ancona: sua storia* (Ancona: Libreria Editrice Giuseppe Fegola, 1923); the 1811 battle of Lissa (now *Vis* in Croatia) is not to be confused with the better-known battle of the same name of 1866.
5 Michael Broers, *The Politics of Religion in Napoleonic Italy: The War against God* (London and New York: Routledge, 2002); Riccardo Benzoni, 'Il culto di San Napoleone. Ricerche erudite nella Milano napoleonica', *Giornale di Storia* 14 (2014), 1–32.
6 *Regolamento disciplinare per le scuole pubbliche della comunità di Ancona* (Ancona: Sartori, 1822).
7 *Il Secolo di Leone X o sia il Risorgimento delle Lettere e delle Arti in Italia. Accademia che danno al pubblico nel giorno 6. di settembre 1827*, Fondo Seminario, ASDAO; Leo X was the son of Lorenzo the Magnificent and the first of the Renaissance Medici popes.

8   Raffaele Martelli to Rosendo Salvado, 23 May 1865, NNA 2234A-20-107.
9   Agostino Peruzzi, *La Chiesa anconitana, dissertazione. Con note e supplementi di Luigi Pauri e di Sebastiano Petrelli* (Ancona: Gustavo Sartorj Cherubini, 1845).
10 Luca Da Monterado, *Mons. Tommaso Gallucci (1813–1897). Prete anconetano, diplomatico, vescovo di Recanati-Loreto* (Loreto: Congregazione universale Santa Casa, 1997); Gianfranco Brocanelli, *Seminari e clero nelle Marche nella seconda metà dell'Ottocento* (Roma: Herder, 1978).
11 Agostino Peruzzi, *Cenni biografici intorno al sacerdote Don Mariano Bedetti, Arcidiacono della Chiesa Anconitana* (Modena: Reale Tipografia Eredi Soliani, 1834).
12 Rosendo Salvado, 'Historical Sketch of the Monastery and Community of New Norcia', *Tjurunga* 11 (1976), 30–41.

Notes to Chapter Two 'Your Probity and Virtue'

1   Lorenzo Bonomelli, 'Il colera del 1836 e il corpo francese d'occupazione di Ancona', *Il Risorgimento. Rivista di Storia del Risorgimento e di Storia Contemporanea* 68, no. 1 (2021), 34–66; Mario Natalucci, *Ancon dorica civitas fidei: uomini e monumenti della Chiesa* (Ancona: Cassa di Risparmio di Ancona, 1980); Emiliano De Laurentiis, 'L'Abate D. Pier Francesco Casaretto e la sua Opera 1832–1839', *Il Sacro Speco di S. Benedetto* 41, no. 2 (1935), 34–46.
2   Giovanni Lunardi, 'Giovinezza e formazione di Pietro Casaretto', *Studia Monastica* 14 (1972), 349–374.
3   Cuthbert Butler, *Benedictine Monachism: Studies in Benedictine Life and Rule*, Second ed. (London: Longmans, 1924).
4   *Costituzioni dell'Insigne Capitolo della Chiesa Collegiata e Parrocchiale di S. Maria e S. Rocco della Città di Ancona 1819*, Fondo Parrocchia di S. Maria e S. Rocco, ASDAO; Giuseppe Bolis, et al., *Le pietre raccontano. Santa Maria della Piazza* (Castel Bolognese: Itaca, 2011).
5   *Bullarium ab anno 1832 usque ad annum 1842* 16 January 1837, ASDAO.
6   'The Late Canon Martelli', *The Inquirer & Commercial News*, 18 August 1880, 2.
7   Frances O'Donoghue, *The Bishop of Botany Bay: the life of John Bede Polding, Australia's first Catholic Archbishop* (London and Sydney: Angus and Robertson, 1982).

Notes to Chapter Three 'Food of the Mind'

1   Raffaele Martelli, *L'eloquenza cristiana: inno* (Ancona: Sartorj Cherubini, 1843).
2   Alberto Mario Banti, *La nazione del risorgimento: parentela, santità e onore alle origini dell'Italia unita* (Torino: Einaudi, 2000).
3   Michele Luzzati, 'Per la storia dei cognomi ebraici di formazione italiana', in *L'Italia dei cognomi: l'antroponimia italiana nel quadro mediterraneo*, ed. A. Addobbati et al. (Pisa University Press, 2012), 497–509; Napoleone Ascoli, *Raffaele Martelli: discorso* (Ancona: Stab. tip. dell'Ordine di E. Sarzani e Comp., 1881).
4   Gaspare Finali, *Le Marche: ricordanze* (Pesaro: Istituto per la Storia del Risorgimento italiano, 2010 [1897]). The expression is from Dante, *Inferno* XV,

    82–85, in the translation by Robert Hollander and Jean Hollander (Anchor Books, 2000).
5   Gregorio Penco, *Storia della chiesa in Italia. Volume II: Dal Concilio di Trento ai nostri giorni* (Milano: Jaca Book, 1978); Banti, *La nazione del risorgimento*, 44–49.
6   Finali, *Le Marche*, 171–172; Maurizio Isabella, *Risorgimento in Exile: Italian Émigrés and the Liberal International in the Post-Napoleonic Era* (Oxford: Oxford University Press, 2009).
7   Poem 128, in Petrarch, *Canzoniere*, trans. J.G. Nichols (Manchester: Carcanet, 2006).
8   Da Monterado, *Gallucci*, 42; Giacomo Martina, 'Il clero italiano e la sua azione pastorale verso la metà dell'Ottocento', in *Il pontificato di Pio IX (1846–1878)*, ed. Roger Aubert (Torino: Editrice S.A.I.E., 1969), 761–857; Palermo Giangiacomi, *Tre Patriotti: Faiani, Giannelli, Buglioni* (Ancona: Tipografia Sita, 1938).
9   'Viaggetto autunnale alla montagna del Catria nell'ottobre del 1842', *Il Tiberino*, Year 9, nos. 18–21 (26 July, 2 August, 9 August, 16 August 1843), 142–143, 150–151, 158–159, 167; Raffaele Martelli, *Viaggetto autunnale alla montagna del Catria nell'ottobre del 1842* (Loreto: Tipografia dei Fratelli Rossi, 1844). The episodes in *Il Tiberino* were unsigned, as most contributions to the journal were, and the author of the monograph identifies himself merely with the initials 'R.M.' in the opening dedication, 'To the loving tutor of his adolescence Monsignor Luigi Canon Pauri, Rector of the Seminary of Ancona, R.M., as a sign of a grateful heart'. In the Diocesan Archive of Ancona, Martelli is given as author.
10 Daniele Barbadoro and Franco Barbadoro, *A Fonte Avellana e sul Catria. Un monastero e la sua montagna: storia e memorie* (The authors, 2008); *Paradiso* XXII, 106–111.
11 *De Imitatione Christi*, trans. Ugo Nicolini (Milano: Edizioni Ares, 1996); Peter Burke, 'Cultures of Translation in Early Modern Europe', in *Cultural Translation in Early Modern Europe*, ed. P. Burke et al. (Cambridge: Cambridge University Press, 2007); Thomas à Kempis, *Solitude and Silence*, trans. Robert Nixon OSB (Gastonia NC: TAN books, 2023).
12 Pietro Regnoli to Salvado, 9 October 1880, NNA 2234A-35-180; Peruzzi, *La Chiesa anconitana*, 237; Pietro Regnoli to Salvado, 12 March 1881, NNA 2234A-36-36.

Notes to Chapter Four 'To Be Pope, the Pope Must Be King'
1   Roger Aubert et al., *The Church between Revolution and Restoration* (New York: Crossroad, 1989); Domenico Spadoni and Giovanni Spadoni, *Uomini e fatti delle Marche nel Risorgimento italiano* (Macerata: Unione Tipografica Operaia, 1927).
2   Giovanni Spadoni, 'Il primo processo politico nelle Marche dopo la restaurazione del 1815', *Le Marche nel Risorgimento* (January); Gualtiero Santini, *Anconitana Gens*, MS, ASAn.
3   Different accounts in Giangiacomi, *Tre Patriotti*, and Gualtiero Santini, *Ancona nel 1848–1849* (Macerata: Tip. P. Colcerasa, 1927).

4   Gualtiero Santini, *Anconitana gens*, MS, ASAn; Mario Natalucci, *Ancona attraverso i secoli. III: Dal periodo napoleonico ai nostri giorni* (Città del Castello: Unione Arti Grafiche, 1961); Giangiacomi, *Ancona: sua storia*, 318–319.

5   Claudio Desideri, ed., *Gualtiero Santini, La Giovane Italia in Ancona* (Ancona: Istituto per la Storia del Movimento Democratico e Repubblicano nelle Marche, 2003); Donatella Fioretti, 'Persistenze e mutamenti dal periodo giacobino all'Unità', in *Le Marche*, ed. Sergio Anselmi (Torino: Einaudi, 1987), 33–119.

6   Maurizio Isabella, 'Religion, revolution and popular mobilization', in *Re-Imagining Democracy in the Mediterranean, 1780–1860*, ed. Joanna Innes et al. (Oxford: Oxford University Press, 2018), 231–252.

7   Martelli to Pietro Regnoli, March 1862, cit. in Ascoli, *Raffaele Martelli*, 23–24.

8   Giacomo Martina, 'Formazione del clero e cultura cattolica verso la metà dell'Ottocento', in *La Chiesa in Italia dall'unità ai nostri giorni*, ed. Elio Guerriero (Cinisello Balsamo: San Paolo, 1996), 120–206; Martelli to Salvado, 14 December 1859, Kinder & Brown, letter 98; Martelli to Salvado, 16 January 1861, Kinder & Brown, letter 116.

9   Gaetano Baluffi, *La Chiesa Romana riconosciuta alla carità verso il prossimo per la vera chiesa di Gesù Cristo* (Imola: Tipografia Galeati, 1854); *The Charity of the Church, a Proof of her Divinity*, trans. Denis Gargan (Dublin: Gill and Son, 1885); Martelli, Sermon for the Twelfth Sunday after Pentecost, [31 August] 1862. NNA 02129-010.

10 Pietro Zovatto, 'La spiritualità dell'Ottocento italiano', in *Storia della spiritualità italiana*, ed. Pietro Zovatto (Roma: Città Nuova, 2002), 478–532; Giacomo Martina, *Pio IX (1846–1850)* (Rome: Università Gregoriana Editrice, 1974).

11 Michele Maroni, *L'Arsenale di Ancona. Reminiscenze storiche* (Fano: Società Tipografica Cooperativa, 1901); Raffaele Martelli, *Relazione della sacra cerimonia onde fu inaugurato l'Arsenale anconitano dall'Eminenza Reverendissima del Cardinale Antonio Tosti Pro Tesoriere della Reverenda Camera Apostolica il 12 Marzo 1843 fatta pubblicare dalla Camera Primaria di Commercio in Ancona* (Ancona: Gustavo Sartori Cherubini, Tipografo Vescovile, 1843).

12 Martelli, *L'eloquenza cristiana*.

13 *Anconetana Commissaria Politico-Militare di aggregazione alla setta carbonica onde preordinare e promuovere la ribellione / Processo contro Schiavoni, Mariani, Vernizzi, Maccari ed altri/ 498*. Tribunale civile e criminale di prima istanza in Ancona, n. 498, ff. 148–149, ASAn; *Turno Speciale. Anconitana Commissaria Politico-Militare di aggregazioni alla setta Carbonica onde preordinare e promuovere la ribellione. Relazione* (Roma: Nella Stamperia della Rev. Cam. Apost., 1844).

14 Palermo Giangiacomi, 'Patriotti anconitani nel Risorgimento', *L'Ordine* (24 May 1918), 4; Santini, *Ancona nel 1848–1849*, 40. Santini copied out the phrase in his huge manuscript compilation of notable citizens, Anconitana gens, n.d., Biblioteca Benincasa (Ancona), but the phrase does not appear in the published version *Gente anconitana* (Fano: Sangallo, 1969); Natalucci, *Ancona attraverso i secoli*, 134–135, and *Ancon dorica*, 205; Piazzale Raffaele Martelli was gazzetted

in August 1960, cf. Delibera n. 261 del 16/5/1960, Pref. no. 18395/2 del 8/8/1960. The 1844 phrase appeared in an official web site of street names in Ancona, which is no longer available: http://www.comune.ancona.it/ankonline/it/uffici/statistica/stradariostorico.html.

15 Lucy Riall, *The Italian Risorgimento: State, Society and National Unification* (London: Routledge, 1994).

16 Raffaele Martelli, *Versi in morte di Antonio Malaccari, studente di rettorica e alunno nel venerabile Seminario S. Carlo di Ancona* (Loreto: Tipografia dei Fratelli Rossi, 1844); Raffaele Martelli, *Per la solenne apertura dell'Istituto Riminese di educazione gratuita pei figli del povero. Discorso letto dal Canonico Don Raffaele Martelli Professore di Rettorica nel Ginnasio di Ancona il 30 Gennaio 1848* (Rimini: Tipi Orfanelli e Grandi, 1848).

17 Natalucci, *Ancona attraverso i secoli*, 125–126; F.A. Gualterio, *Gli ultimi rivolgimenti italiani. Memorie storiche* (Firenze: Felice Le Monnier, 1852).

18 E.E.Y. Hales, *Pio Nono* (London: Eyre & Spottiswoode, 1954); Mario Natalucci, 'Ricordi di Pio IX in Ancona', *Pio IX. Studi e ricerche sulla vita della Chiesa dal Settcento ad oggi* 8, no. 2 (1979), 245–255; Martina, *Pio IX (1846–1850)*, 91.

19 Ignazio Veca, *Il mito di Pio IX: storia di un papa liberale e nazionale* (Roma: Viella, 2018).

Notes to Chapter Five 'The Lively Leader of the New Things'

1 Giacomo Martina and Wiktor Gramatowski, 'La relazione ufficiale sul conclave del 1846: nel 150° anniversario dell'elezione di Pio IX', *Archivum Historiae Pontificiae* 34 (1996), 159–212.

2 Domenico Spadoni, 'Morelli, Ercole', in *Dizionario del Risorgimento nazionale: dalle origini a Roma capitale. Fatti e persone* (Milano: Vallardi, 1930–1937), 647; Sandro Morachioli, *L'Italia alla rovescia: ricerche sulla caricatura giornalistica tra il 1848 e l'Unità* (Pisa: Edizioni della Normale, 2013).

3 Celso Battaglini, *Il prodigio della Madonna del Duomo: Ancona 1796* (Ancona: Arcidiocesi Ancona-Osimo, 1996); Massimo Cattaneo, 'Maria *versus* Marianne. I 'miracoli' del 1796 ad Ancona', *Cristianesimo nella Storia* 16 (1995), 45–77.

4 Natalucci, *Ancon dorica*, 205; Francesco Borioni, *A Dio conservatore che per intercessione di Maria regina di tutti i santi ha liberi gli anconitani da orribile flagello* (Ancona: Sartorj Cherubini, 1836).

5 '17-18-19 agosto', ASDAO, Libro del Capitolo 1846; Raffaele Martelli, *Preghiere da recitarsi alla Regina d'ognissanti nella cattedrale di Ancona in un triduo di ringraziamento per l'amnistia accordata dall'immortale Pio 9. scritte dal canonico Raffaele Martelli* (Ancona: Sartorj Cherubini, 1846). Reprinted in Benedetto Monti, ed., *Componimenti raccolti in occasione delle feste fatte in Ancona ad onore dell'immortale Pio IX Pontefice Massimo* (Ancona: Sartorj Cherubini, 1846).

6 Ignazio Veca, 'Oggetti animati. Materialità, circolazione e usi della figura di Pio IX (1846–1849)', *Il Risorgimento. Rivista di Storia del Risorgimento e di Storia Contemporanea* 64, no. 1 (2017), 63–97.

7   Francesco Scarabicchi, *Una città di scoglio. Breve viaggio ad Ancona* (Ancona: affinità elettive, 2016).
8   Marcello Conati, 'Ernani di Verdi: le critiche del tempo. Alcune considerazioni', in *Ernani ieri e oggi* (Parma: Istituto di studi verdiani, 1987), 207–272; Carlotta Sorba, '*Ernani* Hats: Italian Opera as a Repertoire of Political Symbols during the Risorgimento', in *The Oxford Handbook of the New Cultural History of Music*, ed. Jane F. Fulcher (Oxford: Oxford University Press, 2011), 428–451.
9   Alessandro Alessandrini, *Relazione delle Feste Anconitane nella occasione dell'amnistia a' politici conceduta dall'immortale PIO IX gloriosamente regnante* (Ancona: Sartorj Cherubini, 1846).
10 See Monti, *Componimenti raccolti*, Parte Seconda; *Raccolta dei poetici componimenti già pubblicati in Bologna e di molti degli inediti venuti in luce per l'avventuroso Pontificato di Pio Nono* (Bologna: Marsigli e Rocchi con Giuseppe Tiocchi, 1846); 'Epigrafia', *L'Educatore storico e varietà di scienze, lettere e belle arti (Modena)* III, no. 2 (1846), 97–100.
11 'Nella Facciata della Scuola Israelitica', Monti, *Componimenti raccolti*, Parte Seconda, 139; Mrs G. Gretton, *The Englishwoman in Italy. Impressions of life in the Roman States and Sardinia, during a ten years' residence*, 2 vols. (London: Hurst and Blackwell, 1860); Valerio De Cesaris, *Pro Judeis. Il filogiudaismo cattolico in Italia (1789–1938)* (Milano: Guerini, 2006); Raffaele Martelli, 'Un benefattore dell'umanità. Biografia del P. Nicola Tommasi di Ancona, fondatore di un conservatorio di fanciulle nel 1794', *L'Artigianello*, 2 (23 January), 145–147, 161–163, 333–335.
12 Antonio Maria Cadolini to Vincenzo Gariboldi, 29 July 1846, cit. in Mario Rinaldini, *Le scuole notturne instituite in Ancona da Carlo Faiani. Noterelle storiche* (Ancona: Venturini, 1897); Martelli to Pietro Casaretto, 2 January 1851, ASA.
13 Martina, *Pio IX (1846–1850)*, 52; Roger Aubert, 'La Chiesa in Italia fino al 1870', in *Il pontificato di Pio IX (1846–1878)*, ed. Giacomo Martina (Milano: Edizioni Paoline, 1990), 119–182.
14 Martelli to Salvado, 2 April 1861, Kinder & Brown, letter 119.
15 Minute of letter of 5 October 1846. *Minutario Curia 1824–1847*, no. 997, ASDAO.
16 Gualtiero Santini, *Le Marche e il Risorgimento* (Macerata: Tip. P. Colcerasa, 1927); Ascoli, *Raffaele Martelli*, 9, cit. also in Spadoni and Spadoni, *Uomini e fatti*, 117.
17 Michele Millozzi, *Antonio Giannelli. Luoghi, clima, vita di un patriota del Risorgimento* (Ancona: affinità elettive, 2004); for national figures see Tullio De Mauro, *Storia linguistica dell'Italia unita* (Bari: Laterza, 1963), and for the Marche, Brocanelli, *Seminari e clero*, 36–37.
18 Natalucci, *Ancon dorica*, 195 & 205; Giangiacomi, *Tre Patriotti*, 6.
19 Carlo Rinaldini, 'Esequie al benemerito italiano Carlo Fajani di Ancona', *Il Fanfulla* (10 July 1847), *Nelle esequie di Carlo Fajani, ai concittadini* (Ancona: Sartorj Cherubini, 1847), *Narrazione degli onori funebri resi alla memoria di Carlo Fajani nel giorno XXVIII giugno 1847* (Ancona: Sartori Cherubini, 1847).
20 This is a question mark in the archival record that has become another building block in Martelli's reputation. An anonymous text entitled *Elogio di Carlo Fajani*,

'Eulogy of Carlo Faiani', is believed by some to be the text Martelli delivered at the Mass. Napoleone Ascoli quoted liberally from it in *Raffaele Martelli*, 10–12, and Palermo Giangiacomi believed it was by Martelli, cf. *Carlo Faiani* (Ancona: Stab. Tip. Cooperativo, 1921); however in *Tre Patriotti*, 11, Giangiacomi first attributed it to one Filippo Fiorenzi, about whom little else is known apart from a short encyclopedia entry by Giangiacomi himself, 'Filippo Fiorenzi', in *Dizionario del Risorgimento Nazionale. Dalle origini a Roma Capitale*, ed. Michele Rosi (Milano: Vallardi, 1931–1937). The Italian National Library Service cautiously attributes the text to Fiorenzi. Other evidence also points away from Martelli. The date '15 July 1846', printed at the end of the text, would mean it was delivered at Faiani's Month's Mind, instead of his burial a year later. Carlo Rinaldini wrote an account of the 1847 anniversary service for the Roman newspaper *La Fanfulla*, in which he claims the *Elogio* was published in March 1847, three months before the memorial service. The choice of the publisher Fabiani, in Corsica, would have been most irregular for a Canon. On balance, it seems unlikely Martelli was the author.

21   Archbishop Antonio Maria Cadolini, *Acta in vita et visitationibus Pastoralibus ab Antonio Maria Cadolini Episcopo cardinali*, 42. Fondo Visite Pastorali Cadolini, ASDAO.

22   *The Catechism of the Council of Trent*, trans. Rev. J. Donovan (Baltimore: Lucas Brothers, 1829), 212–213.

23   Martelli, *Per la solenne apertura*, 7.

24   'Avviso agli Associati', *L'Artigianello*, 2, no. 2 (10 January 1846), p. 16; Ferrante Aporti, *Elementi di pedagogia ossia della ragionevole educazione de' fanciulli* (Roma: Tipografia della Società Editrice Romana, 1847), 5.

25   Emilio Re, 'L'Artigianello', *Strenna dei Romanisti* 8 (1947), 246–254.

26   Raffaele Martelli, 'Un benefattore dell'umanità. Cenno necrologico intorno a Nicola Rossi, benefattore insigne dell'Ospizio de' Poveri in Ancona', *L'Artigianello* 1, no. 41 (18 October 1845), 333–335; 'Un benefattore dell'umanità. Biografia del P. Nicola Tommasi di Ancona, fondatore di un conservatorio di fanciulle nel 1794', *L'Artigianello* 2, 19 (9 May 1846), 145–147, and 2, 21 (23 January [sic but May] 1846), 161–163; 'Il fanciullo buon cittadino', *L'Artigianello* 2, no. 49 (5 December 1846), 385–386; 'Beneficenza. Azione generosa di un giovane patrizio', *L'Artigianello*, 3, 6 (6 February 1847), 44–46.

27   Natalucci, *Ancona attraverso i secoli*, 123; *Il Piceno*, 9 October 1847.

28   *Regolamento per l'Istituto di Educazione Gratuita pei figli del povero da fondarsi in Rimini da una Società di Contribuenti* (Rimini: Tipi Orfanelli e Grandi, 1847).

29   Carlo Tonini, *Compendio della storia di Rimini. Vol. 2: Dal 1500 al 1861* (Rimini: E. Renzetti, 1895), 529–530.

30   *Il Piceno*, 22 February 1848.

31   Enrico Morelli, *Benedite Gran Dio l'Italia Pius PP IX*, Roma, Paolo Guglielmi, 1848. Milan, Museo del Risorgimento, Civica Raccolta Stampe Achille Bertarelli, no. 3790.

Notes to Chapter Six 'A Holy Crusade: God Wills It!'

1. Martelli, *Per la solenne apertura*, 4, 19.
2. Natalucci, *Ancona attraverso i secoli*, 131.
3. Filippo Zamboni, *Ricordi del Battaglione Universitario Romano (1848–1849) per cura della vedova Emilia Zamboni* (Trieste: Parnaso, 1926); email from Ufficio Storico dello Stato Maggiore della Difesa, 7 March 2019.
4. Achille Maria Ricci, Proclama, 27 March 1848, ASDAO. Extracts in Natalucci, 'Ricordi di Pio IX in Ancona' 132–133.
5. Demetrio Diamilla-Muller, *Da Roma a Cornuda. Ricordi della Spedizione Romana nel Veneto (Marzo-Giugno 1848)* (Torino: Tipografia Fodratti, 1886).
6. Pietro Regnoli, 'Ultimo episodio dell'assalto di Vicenza, il 10 giugno 1848', *Il pensiero italiano* 17 (1896), 97–104; reprinted in *La Gioventù Italiana*, 2, no. 1 (1910).
7. Martelli to Casaretto, 2 January 1851. MSA.
8. Zamboni, *Ricordi*, 78.
9. The orations published are:
Raffaele Martelli, *Nel funere di Francesco Franceschi di S. Arcangelo, milite crociato nel Battaglione universitario romano, mancato in Ferrara il 27 giugno 1848. Parole lette dal cappellano Raffaele can. Martelli* (Bologna: Tipografia governativa alla Volpe, 1848);
Raffaele Martelli, *Nelle esequie rese all'anima di Luigi Gaudenzi senigagliese studente di legge in Roma, sargente nella prima compagnia del battaglione universitario morto in Ferrara il 27 giugno 1848, d'anni 21, reduce dalla guerra per l'indipendenza italiana. Parole di lode lette dal cappellano Raffaele prof. Martelli* (Publisher unknown, 1848); Raffaele Martelli, *Parole di funebre encomio lette in morte del milite studente di matematica Carlo Reali di Assisi mancato in Bologna il 3 luglio 1848 dal cappellano del battaglione universitario Raffaele prof. Martelli* (Bologna: Tipografia Tiocchi, 1848);
Raffaele Martelli, *In morte di Giuseppe conte Ferniani da Faenza milite del Battaglione universitario nella guerra dell'indipendenza italiana morto di sinoco in Bologna di anni 21 il 5 luglio 1848: cenno necrologico letto dal cappellano Raffaele can. Martelli* (Bologna: Tipografia Sassi nelle Spaderie, 1848);
Raffaele Martelli, *Nelle funebri onoranze rese al milite del Battaglione universitario Giuseppe Venturoli di Bologna, studente di matematica morto il di 6 luglio 1848. Parole di lode lette dal cappellano d. Raffaele prof. Martelli* (Bologna: Tip. Sassi nelle Spaderie, 1848).
The volume with all six orations is:
Raffaele Martelli, *Necrologie di alcuni giovani crociati militi del battaglione universitario romano nella guerra per l'indipendenza italiana combattuta l'anno 1848 lette nei rispettivi funeri dal cappellano Raffaele professore Martelli* (Loreto: Per le stampe dei fratelli Rossi, 1849).
10. *Il Piceno*, 25 April 1848.
11. Natalucci, *Ancona attraverso i secoli*, 143–146; Nicola Sbano, *Lorenzo Lesti, patriota, il suo tempo e la processura "anconitana di più delitti"* (Ancona: Il lavoro editoriale, 2016).

12 Boncompagno Da Signa, *L'assedio di Ancona. Liber de obsidione Ancone* ed. and trans. Andrew Stone (Venice, Filippi Editore, 2002); Francesco Pirani, *Medievalismi nelle Marche* (Fermo: Andrea Livi, 2014).

13 Santini, *Gente anconitana*, 112; Geltrude Franceschini, *Gli avvenimenti di Ancona negli anni 1848–49* (Roma: Forzani e C., 1899); Gualtiero Santini, *Diario dell'assedio e difesa di Ancona nel 1849* (Aquila degli Abruzzi: Officine grafiche Vecchioni, 1925).

14 Ascoli, *Raffaele Martelli*, 19.

15 Enea Costantini, *Il decennio di occupazione austriaca in Ancona (1849–1859). Ricordi aneddotici* (Ancona: Stabilimento Tipografico del Commercio, 1916); Gretton, *The Englishwoman in Italy*, 210–211; Santini, *Gente anconitana*, 134 and 211.

16 Ascoli, *Raffaele Martelli*, 20.

17 Ascoli, *Raffaele Martelli*, 18; *Bullarium* 8 July 1850, ASDAO; for charitable institutions in Ancona see Natalucci, *Ancon dorica*, 217–219, and Ercole Sori, *Ancona 1848–1870. Storia narrativa della città* (Rimini: Bookstones, 2017); Martelli to Pietro Casaretto, 31 January 1851. MSA.

18 Maria Lupi, 'Vescovi 1: dal 1848 alla fine del secolo', in *Cristiani d'Italia. Chiese, società, Stato 1861–2011*, ed. Alberto Melloni (Roma: Istituto dell'Enciclopedia italiana, 2011), 807–825.

19 Josef Metzler, ed., *Dalle missioni alle Chiese locali (1846–1965)* (Milano: Edizioni Paoline, 1990).

20 *Il Piceno*, 11 April 1850; This excerpt, undated, is cited in Ascoli, *Raffaele Martelli*, 21.

21 Thomas à Kempis, *The Imitation of Christ*, trans. Robert Jeffery (London: Penguin, 2013).

Notes to Chapter Seven 'To Consecrate the Rest of My Life to the Exercise of the Priestly Ministry'

1 Martelli to Salvado, 26 August 1867, NNA 2234A-22-216; Da Monterado, *Gallucci*, 68–88.

2 Martelli to Casaretto, 2 January 1851, ASA.

3 Daniel Rees, 'The Benedictine Revival in the Nineteenth Century', in *Benedict's Disciples*, ed. David Hugh Farmer (Leominster: Gracewing, 1995), 324–349; Giulio Fabbri, 'Il monastero di S. Scolastica in Subiaco durante il pontificato di Pio IX', *Atti e Memorie della Società Tiburtina di Storia e d'Arte* 40 (1967), 58–173.

4 Gregorio Penco, *Storia del monachesimo in Italia nell'epoca moderna* (Roma: Edizioni Paoline, 1968).

5 Martelli to Casaretto, 2 January 1851. MSA; John J. Kinder, 'Rosendo Salvado and Raffaele Martelli: friendship and vocation', *New Norcia Studies* 22 (2015), 1–11.

6 Martelli, *Per la solenne apertura*, 23; Aubert, 'Il pontificato di Pio IX'; Brocanelli, *Seminari e clero*, 15–16.

7 Martelli to Casaretto, 2 January 1851. MSA.

8   Giovanni Lunardi, 'The Missionary Spirit of Abbot Casaretto', *Tjurunga* 8 (1974), 35–56; *La congregazione sublacense O.S.B.* (Noci: Edizioni La Scala, 2003).
9   Martelli to Casaretto, 31 January 1851. MSA.
10 Martelli to Casaretto, 31 January 1851. MSA.
11 Martelli to Casaretto, 3 February 1851. MSA.
12 Martelli to Casaretto, 11 April 1851. MSA.
13 Martelli to Casaretto, 18 July 1851. MSA.
14 Martelli to Casaretto, 1 August 1851. MSA.
15 Martelli to Casaretto, 24 August 1851. MSA.

Notes to Chapter Eight 'A Benedictine at Heart Though He Does not Wear the Habit'

1   *Libro di Memorie dal 1851 al 1861*, 7 September 1851, ASS.
2   Lunardi, *La congregazione sublacense*, 238; Lunardi, 'Giovinezza e formazione', at p. 353; Mariano Dell'Omo, 'Ordini monastici II', in *Dizionario Storico Tematico: La Chiesa in Italia. Vol. II: Dopo l'Unità Nazionale*, ed. Roberto Regoli et al. (Roma: Associazione italiana dei professori di Storia della Chiesa, 2015).
3   *Libro di Memorie,* 28 October 1851, ASS.
4   Fabbri, 'Il monastero di S. Scolastica', 111–116; 'Obituary. Death of the Very Rev. R. Martelli', *The Record,* 12 August 1880.
5   Ambrose Flavell, 'Subiaco Congregation missionaries and the British Empire in the nineteenth century', in *La congregazione sublacense: inizi, ideali e attività missionaria*, Subsidia Monastica, 25 (Montserrat: Publicacions de l'Abadia de Montserrat, 2012), 67–93.
6   Fabbri, 'Il monastero di S. Scolastica' 119; Jesús-Angel Barreda, 'I rapporti di mons. R. Salvado OSB con san Vincenzo Pallotti', *Apostolato Universale* 16, no. 34 (2014), 4–13.
7   Terence Kavenagh, 'Distant echoes: Aboriginal and Islander boys at St Mary's Sydney in the mid-nineteenth century', *Tjurunga* 76 (2009), 60–96; Flavell, 'Subiaco Congregation missionaries'.
8   'Neminem Profecto: Instruction de la Propagande du 23 novembre 1845', *Mémoire Spiritaine* 3, no. 3 (2019); Flavell, 'Subiaco Congregation missionaries', 80.
9   Mary Shanahan, *Out of Time, Out of Place. Henry Gregory and the Benedictine Order in Colonial Australia* (Canberra: Australian National University Press, 1966).
10 George Russo, *Lord Abbot of the Wilderness: The Life and Times of Bishop Salvado* (Melbourne: Polding Press, 1980).
11 E.J. Stormon, ed., *The Salvado Memoirs* (Perth: University of Western Australia Press, 1977); for the language varieties, see Ronald M. Berndt, 'Salvado: a man of and before his time', 267–274. In Stormon's translation the chapter on 'Filologia australiana' is given the more prosaic title 'Two native dialects of the New Norcia district'.
12 Rosendo Salvado, 'Advertisement: To the Editor of the Inquirer', *Inquirer* (23 February 1848), 2; Benedict Upumera: Salvado, 'Advertisement'; John Baptist

Maria Dirimera and Francis Xavier Conaci: Stormon, *Salvado Memoirs*, 89–100; Dirimera's brother, Placid Cantagoro: Katharine Massam, 'The Spiritual and the Material: Women & Work in the Benedictine Mission of New Norcia 1860–1910', *New Norcia Studies* 22 (2015), 53–61; Mary Catherine Ballomara: Catherine Kovesi Killerby, *Ursula Frayne: a biography* (Fremantle: The University of Notre Dame Australia, 1996); Salvado to Casaretto, 20 January 1853. ASA.

13 *Libro di Memorie*, 27 December 1851, ASS; for the novice dress, Lunardi, *La congregazione sublacense*, 102.

14 Stefano Girola, ed., *Report of Rosendo Salvado to Propaganda Fide in 1883* (Melbourne: Abbey Press, 2015).

15 Antonio De Riso to Salvado, October 1852, NNA 2234A-7-174; 10 February 1853. NNA 2234A-7-28.

16 Martelli to Casaretto, 10 January 1853, ASA.

17 Martelli to Casaretto, 25 January 1853, ASA.

18 Salvado to Casaretto, 20 January 1853, ASA; Salvado to Alessandro Barnabò, 19 January 1853, ASPF, SC Oceania 5, 132–133. Salvado's letters to Propaganda Fide are now available in critical edition, in Federica Verdina, 'The correspondence of Rosendo Salvado to Propaganda Fide' (PhD thesis, University of Western Australia, 2018).

19 Pescetelli to Salvado, 31 July 1876, NNA 2234A-31-126; Paolo Carosi, 'La provincia sublacense (1851–1867)', in *Pietro Casaretto e gli inizi della Congregazione Sublacense (1810–1880). Saggio storico nel I Centenario della Congregazione (1871–1972)* (Publicacions de l'Abadia de Montserrat, 1972), 405–459, 407; Salvado to Casaretto, 20 January 1853, ASA; Martelli to Pescetelli, 9 February 1853, ASPFM.

20 Pio Bighi, licence, 10 February 1853, NNA 2234A-8-42; Martelli to Casaretto, 29 June 1853, ASA.

21 Casaretto to Salvado, 11 Feburary 1853, NNA 2234A-8-44.

22 Casaretto to Salvado, 9 February 1853, NNA 2234A-8-41; Alfonso Salomone to Salvado, 10 February 1853, NNA 2234A-7-28.

23 Angelo Pescetelli to Salvado, 17 February 1853, NNA 2234A-8-57.

24 Martelli to Casaretto, 12 February 1853, ASA.

25 Ascoli, *Raffaele Martelli*, 21; Martelli to Salvado, 24 October 1867, NNA 2234A-22-269; Salvado brought a letter from Martelli to Giacchetti in November 1869: Rosendo Salvado, Diaries, Vol. 8, 69 (26 November 1869), NNA 2234A-8.

26 Martelli to Salvado, 4 March 1853. In Kinder and Brown, *Raffaele Martelli: Life and Letters*, letter 1.

27 Salvado, Diaries, Vol. 2, Insert no. 2, NNA 2234A-2.

Notes to Chapter Nine 'Amid the Immense Solitude of the Ocean'

1 Martelli to Casaretto, 29 June 1853, ASA; Judith Woodward, 'Formation of Benedictine Identity and Kinship: Nineteenth Century Preparation of Monks for the Mission of New Norcia', *New Norcia Studies* 3 (1995), 29–38.

2 Manuel Martínez, Diary, 20–30, NNA 2234A-30.

3   *Lloyd's Register of British and Foreign Shipping from 1st July 1838 to the 30th June 1839* (London: Cox and Sons, 1838); Martelli to Casaretto, 29 June 1853, ASA.
4   Girola, *Report 1883*, 51; Garrido, Apuntes de viajes, 129, NNA 2234A-21 (G2 1846–1853).
5   Ascoli, *Raffaele Martelli*, 21–22.
6   Andrew Hassam, *Sailing to Australia: Shipboard Diaries by Nineteenth-Century British Emigrants* (Melbourne: Melbourne University Press, 1995).
7   *Purgatorio* VIII, 1–6.
8   Martelli to Casaretto, 29 June 1853, ASA.
9   Salvado to Theodoli, 4 July 1853, ASPFM.
10 Martelli to Casaretto, 29 June 1853, ASA.
11 Salvado, Diaries, vol. 3, 14, NNA 2234A-3.
12 Martelli to Casaretto, 29 June 1853, ASA.
13 Salvado, Diaries, vol. 3, 18, NNA 2234A-3; Garrido, Apuntes de viajes, 159, NNA 2234A-21 (G2 1846–1853).
14 Salvado to his mother, 17 August 1853, NNA 02953-7.
15 Garrido, Apuntes de viajes, 162, NNA 2234A-21 (G2 1846–1853).
16 Garrido to Salvado, 16 July 1867, NNA 2234A-22-159.
17 Salvado to his mother, 17 August 1853, NNA 02953-7.
18 Venancio Garrido, Apuntes de viajes, 164, NNA 2234A-21 (G2 1846–1853).
19 Salvado to Fransoni, 18 August 1853, ASPF, SC Oceania 5.
20 Rica Erickson, *Old Toodyay and Newcastle* (Toodyay: Toodyay Shire Council, 1974), 7.

Notes to Chapter Ten 'A Bare and Melancholic Shore'
1   Girola, *Report 1883*, 50–51; D.F. Bourke, *The History of the Catholic Church in Western Australia* (Perth: Archdiocese of Perth, 1979); Christopher Dowd, *Rome and Australia: The Papacy and Conflict in the Australian Catholic Missions 1834–1884* (Leiden: Brill, 2008).
2   Fragment of letter of Bishop Serra to unnamed Cardinal, undated, CCA, Serra Correspondence 1850–1855, 1-003-15; Patrick O'Farrell, *The Catholic Church and Community in Australia: a History* (Melbourne: Thomas Nelson, 1977).
3   Salvado, Diaries, vol. 4, p. 2, NNA, 2234A-4; Salvado to Cardinal Fransoni, 18 August 1853, ASPF, SC Oceania, 4, 972.
4   Odhran O'Brien, *Martin Griver Unearthed. The Life of a Spanish Missionary Priest Who Became a Bishop in Colonial Western Australia, 1814–1886* (Sydney: St Pauls, 2014); statement by M. Griver, T. O'Neill, R. Martelli, 16 August 1853, CCA, Bishop Serra Pastoral Letters 1851–1859, Stack 1 Box 003-1.
5   Lunardi, 'The Missionary Spirit of Abbot Casaretto', 42; Girola, *Report 1883*, 92.
6   Serra to Archbishop Polding, 25 August 1853, CCA, Bishop Joseph Serra Letter Book 2 1850–1853, A3-24.
7   Girola, *Report 1883*, 52.

NOTES

8 Martelli to Salvado, 4 July 1854, Kinder & Brown, letter 26; David Barry, 'Shall we walk or ride? Take the spring cart or coach? Perhaps the train? New Norcia-Perth-New Norcia with Dom Rosendo Salvado 1846–1899', *New Norcia Studies* 22 (2015), 86–92.
9 Geoffrey Bolton, *Land of Vision and Mirage: Western Australia since 1826* (Perth: University of Western Australia Press, 2008).
10 Odhran O'Brien, 'Cash, Convicts & Catholicism: Catholic Ministry to Convicts and Church-State Relations in Colonial Western Australia', *New Norcia Studies* 23 (2016), 75–92; Bourke, *History*, 56–57; Geraldine Byrne, *A Basilica in the Making: the centenary of St. Patrick's, Fremantle* (Fremantle: Mazenod Press, 2000) see also Appendix 2.
11 Donovan to Salvado, 10 January 1854, NNA 2234A-9-12; 12 January 1854, NNA 2234A-9-15.
12 Martelli to Salvado, 4 July 1854, Kinder & Brown, letter 26.
13 Martelli to Garrido, 16 April 1854, Kinder & Brown, letter 9.
14 Martelli to Salvado, 19 June 1854, Kinder & Brown, letter 22.
15 Martelli to Salvado, 22 February 1854, Kinder & Brown, letter 5.
16 Polding to Serra, 26 July 1853, NNA 2234A-8-156; Salvado to Barnabò, 17 June 1854, ASPF SC Oceania 5, 554–556; Letter from Prefect, Propaganda Fide, to Bishops of Mission Countries, 27 June 1855, NNA 2234A-10A-56; Martelli to Salvado, 11 May 1854, Kinder & Brown, letter 16; Martelli to Salvado, 2 January 1855, Kinder & Brown, letter 38.
17 O'Farrell, *Catholic Church and Community*, 174; Martelli to Salvado, 28 August 1854, Kinder & Brown, letter 36.
18 Martelli to Garrido, 16 April 1854, Kinder & Brown, letter 9.
19 Martelli to Salvado, 17 April 1854, Kinder & Brown, letter 10.
20 Martelli to Salvado, 28 February 1854, Kinder & Brown, letter 8.
21 Martelli to Salvado, 22 January 1854, Kinder & Brown, letter 24.
22 Martelli to Salvado, 19 February 1854, Kinder & Brown, letter 3.
23 Martelli to Salvado, 21 February 1854, Kinder & Brown, letter 4.
24 John Rikkers, *Western Australian Schools 1830–1980. Part One: Schools and Teachers 1830–1871* (Perth: Education Department of Western Australia, 1984); Donovan to Serra, 12 September 1853, NNA 2234A-8-170; Martelli to Salvado, 9 May 1854, Kinder & Brown, letter 15; Mulroony to Martelli, undated letter, early May 1854, NNA 2234A-8-219; Martelli to Salvado, 11 May 1854, Kinder & Brown, letter 16: 'let this cup pass from me' (Matthew 26: 39).
25 Martelli to Salvado, 27 May 1854, Kinder & Brown, letter 19; 22 June 1854, Kinder & Brown, letter 23.
26 Martelli to Griver, 7 June 1854, NNA 2234A-9-123A.
27 Martelli to Salvado, 18 June 1854, Kinder & Brown, letter 21; 10 August 1854, Kinder & Brown, letter 32.

28 John Robert Cook, 'An account of the lives of James O'Byrne, 1806–1871, soldier, and Nicoletta, nee Salustri, 1814–1892, his wife, 1987', Q B/OBY, State Library of Western Australia, Perth.
29 Martelli to Salvado, 8 August 1854, Kinder & Brown, letter 31; the Latin phrase is from Horace's *Odes* (2.16): 'Nothing is blessed in every respect'.
30 'Il Signor Canonico Martelli rinunziò il Canonicato li 29 luglio 1854', Puntature 1854 ASDAO.
31 Martelli to Salvado, 15 January 1855, Kinder & Brown, letter 39, the quote is from *Aeneid*, I, 630; Salvado to Garrido, 20 April 1854, NNA 2234A-9-97; Martelli to Garrido, 16 April 1854, Kinder & Brown, letter 9.
32 Martelli to Salvado, 2 January 1855, Kinder & Brown, letter 38.
33 Martelli to Salvado, 15 January 1855, Kinder & Brown, letter 39; Joseph Thomas Reilly, *Reminiscences of Fifty Years' Residence in Western Australia* (Perth: Sands & McDougall, 1903), 133–135.
34 Salvado, Diaries, vol. 5, p. 38 (16 April 1855), NNA 2234A-5; Salvado, Diaries, vol. 2, p. 16 (24 May 1855), NNA 2234-2.
35 Serra to Salvado, 8 June 1855, NNA 2234A-10A-49; 9 June 1855, NNA 2234A-10A-50.
36 Letter from Christopher Reynolds and Frederick Byrne to unknown priest, 27 May 1856, in Brian Condon, ed., *Letters and Documents Supporting Historical Studies of the Catholic Church in Australia* (Adelaide: South Australian College of Advanced Education, 1983); Serra to Salvado, 30 May 1855, NNA 2234A-10A-40.

Notes to Chapter Eleven 'The Lord is Walking through Your Town'
1 Salvado to Barnabò, 1 May 1855, ASPF SC Oceania 5, 773–774.
2 Rosendo Salvado, Report to the Society for the Propagation of the Faith, 1 August 1854, NNA 2234A-9-154.
3 Elizabeth Deborah Brockman, 'On Receiving from England a Bunch of Dried Wild Flowers' (1868), in John Kinsella and Tracy Ryan, eds., *The Fremantle Press Anthology of Western Australian Poetry* (Fremantle: Fremantle Press, 2017).
4 Dom William OSB, 'Birth of the Catholic Church at Dardanup (Albany, Bunbury and the Vasse), with Topics of Colonial Interest', *Early Days: Journal of the Royal Western Australian Historical Society* 5, no. 6 (1960), 14–30; Anon., 'Settling Migrants. How Thomas Little of Dardanup Fared Years On', *The Skeleton* March (2003), 2.
5 O'Brien, *Martin Griver*, 112–113.
6 Martelli to Salvado, 8 April 1856, Kinder & Brown, letter 48.
7 Martelli, Dardanup Sermon, 26 March 1854, NNA 02129-008; Martelli, Sermon for the First Sunday of Advent, 5 November 1854, NNA 02129-019.
8 These lines were often attributed to Augustine but are not found in any of his works. Martelli may have read them in Giovanni Battista Pagani, *L'anima divota della Ss. Eucaristia* (Vigevano 1835), a text widely used in seminaries at the time.

9   Thomas Little to Archbishop J.B. Polding, 11 July 1856, in Sr M. Xavier Compton et al., eds., *The Letters of John Bede Polding OSB* (Sydney: Sisters of the Good Samaritan, 1996).
10 Martelli to Garrido, 16 April 1854, NNA 2234A-9-94.
11 Salvado, Diaries, vol. 2, Insert no. 2, NNA 2234A-2; Report to the Society for the Propagation of the Faith, 1 August 1854, NNA 2234A-9-154.
12 Stormon, *Salvado Memoirs*, 42–43; *The Inquirer*, 27 May 1846, 3; Eladio Ros, *La musica en Nueva Nursia* (Madrid: Ministerio de Asuntos Exteriores, 1992); David Kimbell, *Vincenzo Bellini, Norma* (Cambridge: Cambridge University Press, 1998); Ottaviano Morici, *I cento anni del Teatro delle Muse di Ancona* (Ancona: Nacci, 1927).
13 Salvado to Barnabò, 1 May 1855 and 27 January 1857, SC Oceania 5, 773–774 and 1296–1298; Salvado to Giovanni Simeone, 20 April 1870, ASPF SC Oceania 9, 757–760.
14 Polding to Salvado, 22 April 1854, NNA 2234A-9-101; Bourke, *History*, 55.
15 Martelli, Albany Sermon 1, November 1854, NNA 02129-014.
16 Martelli, 'Sermon for Dom VI post Epiphaniam', 19 November 1854, NNA 02129-018.
17 Zovatto, 'La spiritualità dell'Ottocento italiano'.
18 Irma Walter, 'Early Mail Services in the South-West of WA (1829–1901)', *Harvey History Online* (2019), ; 'Catholic Church – Marriages – Perth – 1849–1870', SLWA 2961A/4; Salvado, Diaries, vol. 2, Insert no. 2, NNA 2234A-2.
19 Roger Aubert et al., *The Church in the Age of Liberalism*, (New York: Crossroad, 1989), 224–226; Lunardi, *La congregazione sublacense*, 38–39; John N. Molony, *The Roman Mould of the Australian Catholic Church* (Melbourne: Melbourne University Press, 1969), 49–100; Fabbri, 'Il monastero di S. Scolastica', 110.
20 Martelli to Salvado, 13 November 1855, NNA 2234A-10a-98; Salvado, Diaries, vol. 5, 109–125, NNA 2234A-5.
21 A.M. Clack, *Glorious Apostle. A History of the Catholic Church in York* (York: St. Patrick's Roman Catholic Church, 2009); Serra to Garrido, 9 December 1855, NNA 2234A-10A-90.

Notes to Chapter Twelve 'Over the Hills'
1   Martelli to Salvado, 8 January 1856, Kinder & Brown, letter 46; 27 July 1856, Kinder & Brown, letter 59.
2   For the Noongar population, Erickson, *Old Toodyay and Newcastle*, 4; for the non-Aboriginal census of 1854 and numbers of Catholics, Bourke, *History*, 54–55; Salvado to Giovanni Simeone, 20 April 1870, ASPF SC Oceania, 9, 757–760.
3   Dom William Giménez, 'Toodyay of the Mudbricks', c. 1962, SLWA Rica Erickson Papers, 8588A/10.8; Martelli to Salvado, 8 April 1856, Kinder & Brown, letter 48.
4   Martelli to Salvado, 19 May 1856, Kinder & Brown, letter 55; F. Salvadó to R. Salvado, 17 May 1858, NNA 2234A-13-50.
5   Erickson, *Old Toodyay and Newcastle*, 81.

NOTES

6   Martelli to Garrido, 2 June 1856, NNA 2234A-11-72.
7   Martelli to Salvado, 21 April 1856, Kinder & Brown, letter 52.
8   Martelli to Salvado, 19 May 1856, Kinder & Brown, letter 55.
9   Martelli to Salvado, 19 May 1856, Kinder & Brown, letter 55; Rica Erickson, *The Dempsters* (Perth: University of Western Australia Press, 1978).
10   Martelli to Salvado, 19 February 1856, Kinder & Brown, letter 47; 14 April 1856, Kinder & Brown, letter 49.
11   Martelli to Salvado, 23 August 1856, Kinder & Brown, letter 62.
12   Rignasco to Salvado, 9 May 1860, NNA 2234A-15-68.
13   Martelli to Salvado, 11 January 1858, Kinder & Brown, letter 67.
14   Manuel Martinez, Diary, NNA 2234A-30.
15   Martelli to Salvado, 23 August 1856, Kinder & Brown, letter 62; Niccolò Tommaseo and Bernardo Bellini, *Dizionario della lingua italiana* (Torino: Unione Tipografico-Editrice, 1861–1879), s.v. tristezza.
16   Martelli to Salvado, 27 July 1856, Kinder & Brown, letter 59: Job 19:21.
17   Martelli to Salvado, 27 April 1856, Kinder & Brown, letter 53.
18   Martelli to Salvado, 5 May 1856, Kinder & Brown, letter 54.
19   Martelli to Ursula Frayne, 11 February 1856, ASPF, SC Oceania, 5, 897; Ursula Frayne to Garrido, 28 May 1869, NNA 2234A-24-69.
20   'Toodyay', *Perth Gazette*, 13 March 1857.
21   Martelli to Garrido, 18 May 1857, NNA 2234A-12a-5; Serra to Colonial Secretary, 30 March 1857, SRO CSR 380/277–278; Martelli to Colonial Secretary, 27 October 1856, NNA 2234A-11-145.
22   Bourke, *History*, 72; Martelli to Salvado, 14 December 1857, Kinder & Brown, letter 66; Lesley J. Borowitzka, 'The Reverend Dr Louis Giustiniani and Anglican Conflict in the Swan River Colony, Western Australia 1836–1838', *Journal of Religious History* 35, no. 3 (2011), 352–372.
23   Martelli to Garrido, 10 May 1865, NNA 2234-20-97; 18 May 1857, NNA 2234A-12a-5.
24   Griver to Salvado, 19 August 1857, NNA 2234A-12-40; Martelli to Salvado, 20 January 1859, Kinder & Brown, letter 76.
25   Martelli, Address at the first Catholic Church Tea Party at York for the Erection of a Church, 1857, NNA 02129-011.
26   Salvado, Diaries, vol. 5, p. 8, NNA 2234A-5; Griver to Salvado, 19 August 1857, NNA 2234A-12-40; Martelli to Salvado, 20 January 1859, Kinder & Brown, letter 76; Martelli to Garrido, 18 May 1857, NNA 2234A-12a-5.
27   Martelli to Pescetelli, 25 May 1857, ASPFM, Fondo Salvado.
28   *Ireland-Australia Transportation Records*, National Archives Ireland, TR 10, P 256; Martelli to Salvado, 23 August 1856, Kinder & Brown, letter 62.
29   Martelli to Salvado, 14 October 1859, Kinder & Brown letter 90; Garrido, Apuntes para el uso de Fr. Venancio 130 (9 January 1855), NNA 2234A-24 (G5 1850–1861); Salvado to Bérengier, 24 April 1875, NNA SAVE 2054–2057.

30 Rica Erickson, 'If It Hadn't Been for the Murphys', *Early Days* 9, 6 (1988), 52–64; Erickson, *Old Toodyay and Newcastle*, 134. The original notes are in Rica Erickson Papers, SLWA Acc. 8588A/1.2, notebook 36.
31 Rica Erickson, 'Friends and Neighbours: The Irish of Toodyay', in *The Irish in Western Australia. Studies in Western Australian History Vol. 20*, ed. Bob Reece (Nedlands: Centre for Western Australian History, 2000), 49–58; 'Marriages-Catholic Church-York', SLWA Acc. 2961A/8; Erickson, *Old Toodyay and Newcastle*, 134.
32 Salvado to Giovanni Simeone, 20 April 1870, ASPF SC Oceania, 9, 757–760.
33 Erickson, *Old Toodyay and Newcastle*, 136.
34 Martelli to Garrido, 25 January 1858, NNA 2234A-23-41.

Notes to Chapter Thirteen 'The Prison Affects My Spirit as the Haemorrhoids Affect My Body'

1 F.J.A. Broeze, 'From the Periphery to the Mainstream: The Challenge of Australia's Maritime History', *The Great Circle* 11, no. 1 (1989), 1–13; R. T. Appleyard, 'Western Australia: Economic and demographic growth 1850–1914', in *A New History of Western Australia*, ed. C. T. Stannage (Perth: University of Western Australia Press, 1981), 211–236.
2 Martelli to Salvado, 18 May 1858, Kinder & Brown, letter 69.
3 Luke Donegan, *Fremantle Prison: Convict Daily Life* (Perth: Government of Western Australia, 2009); Olimpia Cullity, 'Reform and punishment: Fremantle Prison, 1850 to 1890', *Studies in Western Australia History* 31 (2016), 63–79.
4 Martelli to Comptroller-General, 28 January 1859, *Accounts and Papers of the House of Commons. 7: Colonies*, vol. XLV (1860), 46.
5 Martelli to Martínez, 23 November 1859, NNA 2234A-15-151; Martelli to Salvado, 28 July 1858, Kinder & Brown, letter 73; 25 March 1859, NNA 2234A-13-138; Martelli to Martínez, 17 October 1859, NNA 2234A-15-129; Martelli to Salvado, 6 May 1859, Kinder & Brown, letter 81; Ros, *La musica*, 53.
6 Martelli to Salvado, 1 October 1860, Kinder & Brown, letter 107.
7 Martelli to Garrido, 9 July 1858, Kinder & Brown, letter 71; Martelli to Salvado, 18 May 1858, Kinder & Brown, letter 69.
8 'The Gaol', in Kinsella and Ryan, *Anthology*, 66–67; Martelli to Salvado, 1 December 1859, Kinder & Brown, letter 93; 18 January 1861, NNA 2234A-16-182.
9 Martelli to Salvado, 18 May 1858, Kinder & Brown, letter 69.
10 Martelli to Salvado, 23 September 1860, Kinder & Brown, letter 106.
11 Jessica A. Sheetz-Nguyen, 'Catholic Preaching in Victorian England, 1801–1901', in *A New History of the Sermon: the Nineteenth Century*, ed. Robert Ellison (Brill, 2010), 207–232; Martelli, 'Tenth Sunday P[ost] P[entecosten]. On image worship', 20 July 1856, NNA 02129-004; Martelli, 'Eighteenth Sunday after Pentecost', [9 October] 1859, NNA 02129–003.
12 Da Monterado, *Gallucci*, 62–63.

13 Council of Trent (1547): DS 1542. The Council attributes the expression to St Jerome.
14 Flavell, 'Subiaco Congregation missionaries'; Margaret Press, *From Our Broken Toil. South Australian Catholics 1836–1906* (Adelaide, 1986).
15 Martelli to Salvado, 28 July 1858, Kinder & Brown, letter 73.
16 Ron Keightley, 'The Expulsion of Father Venancio Garrido: Causes', *New Norcia Studies* 12 (2004), 58–73.
17 Martelli to Garrido, 21 April 1858, NNA 2234A-13-32.
18 Martelli to Salvado, 18 May 1858, Kinder & Brown, letter 69.
19 Martelli to Salvado, 17 June 1858, Kinder & Brown, letter 70; Martelli to Garrido, 14 May 1848, NNA 2234A-13-49.
20 Martelli to Salvado, 28 July 1858, Kinder & Brown, letter 73.
21 Garrido to Salvado, 8 January 1859, NNA 2234A-14-5.
22 Martelli to Salvado, 19 July 1858, Kinder & Brown, letter 72.
23 Martelli to Salvado, 2 December 1858, Kinder & Brown, letter 75; 28 July 1858, Kinder & Brown, letter 73; 10 May 1859, Kinder & Brown, letter 82; Martelli to Garrido, 13 February 1859, NNA 2234A-14-020.
24 Luigi Giussani, *To Give One's Life for the Work of Another* (Montreal: McGill-Queens University Press, 2022); Girola, *Report 1883*, 106; Keightley, 'The Expulsion of Father Venancio Garrido: Causes', 65; Martelli to Garrido, 9 July 1858, Kinder & Brown, letter 71.
25 Martelli to Salvado, 4 December 1861, Kinder & Brown, letter 132; Phil. 1:23-24; 2 February 1859, Kinder & Brown, letter 77.
26 Martelli to Salvado, 14 December 1859, Kinder & Brown, letter 98; 4 October 1861, Kinder & Brown, letter 127.
27 O'Brien, 'Cash, Convicts & Catholicism'; Martelli to Salvado, 25 March 1859, NNA 2234A-13-138.
28 O'Brien, 'Cash, Convicts & Catholicism'.
29 Martelli to Salvado, 8 February 1860, NNA 2234A-15-185; Western Australia. Minutes of the Proceedings of the Legislative Council, 12 December 1860; Martelli to Salvado, 1 January 1861, Kinder & Brown, letter 115; 16 August 1861, Kinder & Brown, letter 125; Salvado to Barnabò, 19 December 1861, SC Oceania 7, 390–391.
30 Martelli to Comptroller General, 24 March 1862, TNA Series: CO 18/125, *Western Australia. Original Correspondence*. Despatches: Convicts January-June 1862 (AJCP ref: http://nla.gov.au/nla.obj-2039437227); Martelli to Salvado, 30 March 1862, Kinder & Brown, letter 142.

Notes to Chapter Fourteen 'Informed on All Matters Happening in Rome'
1 Martelli to Salvado, 4 October 1860, Kinder & Brown, letter 108; 10 May 1859, Kinder & Brown, letter 82; 15 June 1859, Kinder & Brown, letter 83: the question is from Matthew 26:8; 15 September 1856, Kinder & Brown, letter 63.
2 Martelli to Garrido, 14 August 1859, NNA 2234A-14-156.

3   Martelli to Salvado, 11 July 1859, Kinder & Brown, letter 84.
4   Bourke, *History*, 69.
5   Martelli to Salvado, 1 December 1859, Kinder & Brown, letter 93; Martelli to Martínez, 17 October 1859, NNA 2234A-15-129; 17 October 1859, NNA 2234A-15-129; Martelli to Salvado, 11 July 1859, Kinder & Brown, letter 84; 15 June 1859, Kinder & Brown, letter 83; 21 August 1860, NNA 2234A-15-192.
6   Martelli to Salvado, 5 December 1859, Kinder & Brown, letter 94.
7   Martelli to Salvado, 7 December 1859, Kinder & Brown, letter 95.
8   Martelli to Salvado, 17 June 1860, Kinder & Brown, letter 104; 25 April 1867, NNA 2234A-22-91.
9   Martelli to Salvado, 14 December 1859, Kinder & Brown, letter 98.
10 Martelli to Salvado, 24 April 1860, Kinder & Brown, letter 100.
11 Martelli to Salvado, 26 July 1860, Kinder & Brown, letter 105: Psalm 132:14.
12 Serra to Griver, 5 September 1861, CCA Serra correspondence 1861; Martelli to Salvado, 16 January 1862, Kinder & Brown, letter 136.
13 O'Brien, *Martin Griver*, 117.
14 Baluffi, *Chiesa Romana*, cit. from *Charity of the Church*, 373–374, 397–398; Tommaso Gallucci to Martelli, 6 September 1860, NNA 2234A-17-156.
15 Finali, *Le Marche*, 172; Martelli to Salvado, 25 September 1865, NNA 2234A-20-198.
16 Martelli to Pietro Regnoli, 24 August 1861, ASPF, SC Oceania, 7, 170.
17 Martelli to Salvado, 16 January 1861, Kinder & Brown, letter 116.
18 Griver to Serra, 24 June 1861, cit. in Maria Helena Braga de Silva, *Jose Maria Benito Serra: essays on his life* (Madrid Hermanas Oblatas del Santísimo Redentor, 2005).
19 Dowd, *Rome and Australia*, 67–68; Martelli, Lynch, McCabe and Salvadó to the Prefect of Propaganda Fide, 24 January 1862, ASPF, SC Oceania, 7, 382–385.
20 O'Brien, *Martin Griver*, 121; Martelli to Salvado, 30 March 1862, Kinder & Brown, letter 142.
21 Griver to Serra, 4 April 1862, cit. in Braga de Silva, *Serra: essays*, 353; Martelli to Salvado, 30 March 1862, Kinder & Brown, letter 142.
22 Martelli to Salvado, 16 January 1860, NNA 2234A-15-183.

Notes to Chapter Fifteen 'This Idle Paper Talk'
1   Martelli to Salvado, 16 October 1860, Kinder & Brown, letter 110.
2   Martelli to Salvado, 17 October 1861, Kinder & Brown, letter 128; Martelli to Garrido, 14 February 1866, NNA 2234A-21-45.
3   Giuseppe Ignazio Montanari, *L'arte di scrivere lettere dedotta dall'analisi de' classici scrittori latini ed italiani per opera di Giuseppe Ignazio Montanari* (Firenze: Tipografia Calasanziana, 1840).
4   Giuseppe Antonelli, *Tipologia linguistica del genere epistolare nel primo Ottocento. Sondaggi sulle lettere familiari di mittenti cólti* (Rome: Edizioni dell'Ateneo, 2003), 30–34.

5 Martelli to Salvado, 8 August 1862, Kinder & Brown, letter 150; Mario Panzini, *Dizionario del vernacolo anconitano* (Ancona: Controvento, 2008).
6 Martelli to Salvado, 5 January 1866, NNA 2234A-21-5.
7 *fensa*: Martelli to Salvado, 3 July 1854, Kinder & Brown, letter 25; *fensato*: 14 April 1856, Kinder & Brown, letter 49.
8 Antonelli, *Tipologia linguistica*, 75–84; Martelli to Salvado, 4 October 1860, Kinder & Brown, letter 108.
9 Annick Paternoster and Francesca Saltamacchia, '(Im)politeness Rules and (Im) politeness Formulae: Metadiscourse and Conventionalisation in 19th century Italian Conduct Books', in *Studies on Language Norms in Context*, ed. Elena Maria Pandolfi et al. (Frankfurt am Main: Peter Lang, 2017), 263–301.
10 Salvado: Martelli to Salvado, 10 November 1859, Kinder & Brown, letter 92; Serra: Martelli to Salvado, 6 May 1859, Kinder & Brown, letter 81.
11 Martelli to Salvado, 24 February 1866, NNA 2234A-21-53.
12 Martelli to Pietro Regnoli, 24 February 1866, NNA 2234A-21-53; Martelli to Garrido, 28 September 1864, NNA 2234A-19-213; Martelli to Salvado, 8 April 1856, Kinder & Brown, letter 48; Regnoli to Salvado, 1 August 1867, NNA 2234A-22-178.
13 Martelli to Salvado, 20 January 1859, Kinder & Brown, letter 76.
14 Martelli to Salvado, 28 March 1859, Kinder & Brown, letter 80; Tommaseo and Bellini, *Dizionario*, s.v. regalare.
15 Martelli to Salvado, 17 June 1858, Kinder & Brown, letter 70; 25 March 1859, NNA 2234A-13-138; 21 August 1860, NNA 2234A-15-192.
16 Martelli to Salvado, 11 July 1859, Kinder & Brown, letter 84; 5 August 1859, Kinder & Brown, letter 86.
17 Martelli to Salvado, 16 November 1864, NNA 2234A-19-243; 11 December 1864, NNA 2234A-19-266; 17 February 1865, NNA 2234A-20-47.
18 Martelli to Salvado, 23 December 1863, NNA 2234A-18-197.
19 Regnoli to Salvado, 21 June 1863, NNA 2234A-18-88; Garrido to Salvado, 24 October 1864, NNA 2234A-19-232.
20 Antonio and the sister: Martelli to Salvado, 16 December 1864, NNA 2234A-19-259; Teresa Morelli: Martelli to Salvado, 23 May 1865, NNA 2234A-20-107; Domenico Tuzi, Cleofina: Martelli to Pietro Regnoli, 24 February 1866, NNA 2234A-21-53.
21 Martelli to Salvado, 27 December 1866, NNA 2234A-21-281; Propaganda Fide to Don Eugenio Maria Filippo di Matelica, 20 July 1868, ASPF, LDB, 1868, 735; Propaganda Fide to Griver, 23 July 1868, ASPF, LDB, 1868, 751.
22 Martelli to Pietro Regnoli, 24 February 1866, NNA 2234A-21-53.

Notes to Chapter Sixteen 'Labouring in a More Fertile Field'
1 Martelli to Salvado, 2 February 1859, Kinder & Brown, letter 77; 2 July 1862, Kinder & Brown, letter 146; 24 October 1867, NNA 2234A-22-269.

NOTES

2   Martelli to Salvado, 1 May 1862, NNA 2234A-17-96; 16 December 1864, NNA 2234A-19-259.
3   Martelli to Garrido, 4 March 1864, NNA 2234A-19-313; Martelli to Salvado, 23 April 1865, NNA 2234A-20-88.
4   Martelli to Salvado, 21 July 1862, Kinder & Brown, letter 147.
5   Martelli to Garrido, 25 December 1867, NNA 2234A-22-368; Martelli to Salvado, 5 January 1866, NNA 2234A-21-5; 2 July 1862, Kinder & Brown, letter 146; Byrne, *Basilica*, 18.
6   Martelli, 'On the opening of the New Convent and Girls Schoolroom of St Joseph' [31 May 1863], NNA 02129-12.
7   Martelli to Salvado, 23 December 1863, NNA 2234A-18-197; 16 August 1862, NNA 2234-17-225; 22 August 1865, NNA 2234A-20-167; Martelli to Garrido, 29 June 1867, NNA 2234A-22-153.
8   Martelli to Salvado, 26 July 1860, Kinder & Brown, letter 105.
9   Martelli to Griver, 27 July 1864, CCA, Griver papers.
10 Martelli to Salvado, 23 October 1865, NNA 2234A-20-224; 24 April 1866, NNA 2234A-21-91.
11 Martelli to Regnoli, 24 August 1861, ASPF, SC Oceania, 7, 170; Martelli to Garrido, 13 December 1867, NNA 2234A-22-345; Martelli to Salvado, 24 May 1866, NNA 2234A-21-124.
12 L.J. Goody, *Martin Griver. Second Catholic Bishop of Perth (1814–1886)* (Perth: Vanguard Press, 1986), 40; Tasso, *Gerusalemme Liberata*, X, 3; Martelli to Salvado, 25 June 1865, NNA 2234A-20-127.
13 Martelli to Salvado, 25 January 1865, NNA 2234A-20-19.
14 Odhran O'Brien, 'Beyond Melbourne: Nineteenth-Century Cathedral Building in the Diocese of Perth', *Journal of the Australian Catholic Historical Society* 39 (2018), 45–54; Martelli to Salvado, 17 February 1865, NNA 2234A-20-47.
15 Martelli to Salvado, 12 October 1864, NNA 2234A-19-223.
16 Frances Stibi, 'Profile of an early church architect', *Australian Catholic Historical Society Newsletter* 19, no. 3 (2009), 4.
17 Maurizio Isabella, 'Freedom of the press, public opinon and liberalism in the Risorgimento', *Journal of Modern Italian Studies* 17, no. 5 (2012), 551–567.
18 'Events of the Month', *Inquirer and Commercial News*, 22 February 1865.
19 Martelli to Salvado, 17 February 1865, NNA 2234A-20-47.
20 Bob Reece, 'Fremantle's first voice: the Herald (1867–1886)', *Fremantle Studies* 6 (2010), .
21 'Local Intelligence' and 'Sisterhoods', *The Herald* (Fremantle), 23 March 1867.
22 *The Herald*, 25 April 1868, p. 3.
23 Reece, 'Fremantle's first voice'; A Magistrate, 'The Protestant Orphan Asylum', *The Inquirer and Commercial News*, 6 May 1868, p. 3.
24 R. Martelli, 'To the editor of The Herald', *The Herald*, 9 May 1868, p. 3.
25 'Review', *The Herald*, 29 August 1868, p. 2; Martelli to the editor of The Herald, 5 September 1868, p. 3; the French is from Nicolas Boileau, Le Lutrin

[The Lectern] (1683), a satirical poem about a quarrel between two ecclesiastical dignitaries.
26 *The Herald*, 19 September 1868, p. 3.
27 *The Herald*, 6 March 1869.
28 Martelli to Garrido, 21 April 1864, NNA 2234A-19-95; F. Salvadó to Garrido, 10 July 1864, NNA 2234A-19-173; Martelli to Salvado, 23 April 1865, NNA 2234A-20-88.
29 Martelli to Salvado, 23 April 1865, NNA 2234A-20-88; 23 January 1865, NNA 2234A-20-15.
30 Martelli to Salvado, 17 February 1865, NNA 2234A-20-47.
31 *The Herald*, 23 November 1867, p. 3; *The Herald*, 6 June 1868, p. 3.
32 Martelli to Salvado, 19 January 1867, NNA 2234A-22-8; 24 September 1866, NNA 2234A-21-204.
33 Thomas Lynch to Comptroller-General, 15 December 1862, report for the year 1862: TNA Series: CO 18/130, *Western Australia. Original Correspondence. Despatches: Convicts January-June 1863* AJCP ref: http://nla.gov.au/nla.obj-2039469813.
34 Martelli to Salvado, 24 February 1864, NNA 2234A-19-312; 6 April 1864, NNA 2234A-19-316; 7 March 1864, NNA 2234A-19-314; 16 November 1864, NNA 2234A-19-259; 9 February 1864, NNA 2234A-19-310; Martelli to Garrido, 22 February 1864, NNA 2234A-19-311; 8 April 1864, NNA 2234A-19-317.
35 Martelli to Martínez, 29 December 1864, NNA 2234A-321; Martelli to Garrido, 18 February 1868, NNA 2234A-23-87.

Notes to Chapter Seventeen 'My Ten Years are Up'
1 Tommaso Gallucci to Martelli, 6 September 1860, NNA 2234A-17-156.
2 Martelli to Salvado, 30 March 1862, Kinder & Brown, letter 142; Martelli to Salvado, 23 August 1863, Kinder & Brown, letter 166.
3 Martelli to Salvado, 16 December 1862, Kinder & Brown, letter 160.
4 Martelli to Salvado, 23 December 1863, NNA 2234A-18-197; Ilarione Silani to Garrido, 13 March 1864, NNA 2234A-19-62; Follower of Bartolomeo Estaban Murillo, *The Archangel Raphael*, New Norcia Collections 1975.701; Martelli to Garrido, 23 October 1864, NNA 2234A-19-230.
5 Lunardi, *La congregazione sublacense*, 122; Martelli to Pietro Regnoli, 24 August 1861, ASPF, SC Oceania, 7, 170.
6 Casaretto to Martelli, 25 March 1860, NNA 2234A-05392, cit. in Girola, *Report 1883*, 103.
7 Girola, *Report 1883*, 98.
8 Salvado to Garrido, 22 September 1864, NNA 2234A-19-207; Martelli to Garrido, 15 October 1864, NNA 2234A-19-224.
9 Martelli to Salvado, 24 March 1865, NNA 2234A-21-71; Regnoli to Salvado, 1 August 1867, NNA 2234A-22-178; undated letter, NNA 2234A-27-186.

10. Martelli to Salvado, 25 September 1865, 2234A-20-198; 20 November 1865, 2234A-20-249.
11. Martelli to Salvado, 23 April 1865, NNA 2234A-20-88; 24 March 1865, NNA 2234A-20-71; *La vita di Gesù Cristo e la sua religione* by Antonio Cesari and the bestseller by Martelli's old teacher Gaetano Baluffi, *La Chiesa Romana riconosciuta alla carità verso il prossimo per la vera chiesa di Gesù Cristo*.
12. This must be the photograph Regnoli mentions in his letter of 21 March 1863, NNA 2234A-18-71; Martelli to Salvado, 16 August 1862, NNA 2234A-17-225.
13. Martelli to Salvado, 2 October 1862, NNA 2234A-17-226.
14. Martelli to Salvado, 24 February 1866, NNA 2234A-21-51; 24 September 1866, NNA 2234A-21-204.
15. Martelli to Salvado, 24 March 1866, NNA 2234A-21-76; Garrido to Salvado, 6 March 1866, NNA 2234A-21-59.
16. Martelli to Salvado, 2 July 1866, NNA 2234A-21-168; Martelli to Garrido, 13 July 1866, NNA 2234A-21-159; Salvado to Garrido, 19 May 1866, NNA 2234A-21-118.
17. Martelli to Salvado, 22 September 1864, NNA 2234A-19-320.
18. Salvado, Diaries, vol. 17, 33 (17 April 1866), NNA SD 2234A-17; Salvado to Antonio Benedetto Antonucci, 9 August 1866, ASA, Fondo Salvado, also in NNA 05392.62.
19. Antonio Benedetto Antonucci to Salvado, 15 August 1866, NNA 2234A-21-174.
20. Garrido to Salvado, 13 June 1866, NNA 2234A-21-134.
21. Griver to Martelli, 25 May 1866, CCA Bishop Serra Pastoral Letters 1851–1859, Stack 1 Box 003, 1.
22. Griver to Martínez, 6 February 1865, NNA 2234A-20-32; 26 July 1866, NNA 2234A-21-163; Griver to Barnabò, 27 July 1866, ASPF, SC Oceania 8, 563; Martelli to Garrido, 6 March 1862, NNA 2234A-17-223; O'Brien, *Martin Griver*, 114; Garrido to Salvado, 26 August 1866, NNA 2234A-21-182; Martelli to Salvado, 26 August 1866, NNA 2234A-21-184.
23. Martelli to Garrido, 6 March 1862, NNA 2234A-17-223.
24. Martelli to Garrido, 21 April 1864, NNA 2234A-19-95.
25. Martelli to Salvado, 2 July 1866, NNA 2234A-21-168.
26. Martelli to Salvado, 22 May 1867, NNA 2234A-22-109.
27. Barnabò to Griver, 22 March 1867, NNA 2234A-22-71; Salvado to Garrido, 23 March 1867, NNA 2234A-22-73; Propaganda Fide to Salvado, undated, NNA 2234A-22-382.
28. Regnoli to Salvado, 1 August 1867, NNA 2234A-22-178.
29. Martelli to Garrido, 25 May 1868, NNA 2234A-23-223: the quotation is from Horace, *Ars Poetica*, 173.
30. Martelli to Salvado, 16 June 1868, NNA 2234A-23-249; Martelli to Garrido, 13 July 1868, NNA 2234A-23-303; Martelli to Salvado, 17 July 1868, NNA 2234A-23-312; Lynch to Garrido, 24 August 1868, NNA 2234A-23-377; Martelli to Garrido, 8 October 1868, NNA 2234A-23-452.

31 Martelli to Garrido, 8 October 1868, NNA 2234A-23-452.
32 Garrido to Martínez, 7 November 1868, NNA 2234A-23-469.
33 Martelli to Salvado, 23 April 1868, NNA 2234A-23-178; Maureen O'Neill, 'Sisters of Saint Joseph of the Apparition in Western Australia' (Dissertation, Claremont Teachers College, 1963).
34 Garrido to Martínez, 7 November 1868, NNA 2234A-23-469; Fremantle Asylum Register of patients – female 1858–1873, SRO Acc. 1120/4, folio 110; Bourke to Garrido, 12 January 1869, NNA 2234A-24-5; Martelli to Garrido, 19 November 1868, NNA 2234A-23-481.
35 Martelli to Garrido, 8 November 1868, NNA 2234A-23-471; 27 November 1868, NNA 2234A-23-492.
36 *The Herald*, 5 December 1868, p. 3.
37 *The Herald*, 5 December 1868, p. 3.
38 Martínez to Garrido, 15 November 1868, NNA 2234A-23-476; Matthew Gibney to Garrido, 13 December 1868, NNA 2234A-23-511.

Notes to Chapter Eighteen 'To Convert and Civilise'
1 Federica Verdina and John J. Kinder, 'Selvaggi or Nativi? European and Colonial Perspectives on the Encounter with the Other in the Experience of a Missionary in Nineteenth-Century Western Australia', *New Norcia Studies* 27 (2021), 17–21; Ronald M. Berndt, 'Aborigines of the South-West', in *Aborigines of the West: Their Past and Their Present*, ed. Ronald M. Berndt et al. (Perth: University of Western Australia Press, 1980), 81–89.
2 Policarpo Petrocchi, *Novo dizionario universale della lingua italiana* (Milano: Fratelli Treves, 1884–1890), s.v. selvaggio.
3 Gianfranco Folena, 'Le prime immagini dell'America nel vocabolario italiano', *Bollettino dell'Atlante Linguistico Mediterraneo* 13–15 (1971–1973), 673–692.
4 Michele Morcaldi to Salvado, 29 July 1873, NNA 2234A-28-112.
5 Griver to Salvado, 30 May 1877, NNA 2234A-32-101; Jonathan Richards, *The Secret War: a True History of Queensland's Native Police* (St Lucia: University of Queensland Press, 2008).
6 Kate Fullagar, *The Savage Visit. New World People and Popular Imperial Culture in Britain, 1710–1795* (Berkeley and Los Angeles: University of California Press, 2012), 9–12.
7 Rosendo Salvado, 'Letter to the Colonial Secretary, 19 February 1864', in *Information Respecting the Habits and Customs of the Aboriginal Inhabitants of Western Australia. Presented to the Legislative Council by His Excellency's Command*, ed. Rosendo Salvado et al. (Perth: Government Printer, 1871), 3–7.
8 Salvado to Pigorini, 8 October 1881, MNPE; John J. Kinder, 'Letters and other gifts: on a nineteenth-century Italian-Australian epistolary network', *Life Writing* 12, no. 3 (2015), 325–338.
9 Salvado, Diaries, vol. 17, 54 (March 1867), NNA SD 2234A-17; Luigi Pigorini, *La Paleoetnologia in Roma, in Napoli, nelle Marche e nelle Legazioni. Relazione a*

NOTES

    S.E. il Ministro della Pubblica Istruzione (Parma: Tip. Rossi-Ubaldi, 1867); Lucy Davidson and John J. Kinder, '"A Most Useful Contribution to Science": Salvado's Third Consignment of Noongar Objects and Italian Prehistoric Archaeology', *New Norcia Studies* 23 (2016), 62–74.

10   The lectures were reported in the *Gazzetta di Parma* on 26 and 28 February 1870; Pigorini's lecture notes are kept in APUP.

11   Pietro Regnoli, *Intorno due dipinti di Alfonso Chierici di Reggio: ragionamento* (Roma: Tipografia della Minerva, 1844): this reprints two articles: 'Cristo che caccia i mercanti dal tempio. Dipinto di Alfonso Chierici di Reggio', *Il Saggiatore* 2, no. 3 (1844), 83–91, and 'Dell'altro dipinto di Alfonso Chierici di Reggio. Il S. Baggio', *Il Saggiatore* 2, no. 4 (1844), 114–117; Roberto Macellari, 'Gaetano Chierici, prete e preistorico', in *«Le terramare si scavano per concimare i prati». La nascita dell›archeologia preistorica a Parma nel dibattito culturale della seconda metà dell›Ottocento*, ed. Maria Bernabò Brea et al. (Parma: Silva, 1994), 118–129.

12   Martelli to Salvado, 24 November 1869, NNA 2234A-24-160; Regnoli to Salvado, 11 March 1870, NNA 2234A-25-58; Chierici to Salvado, 21 October 1871, cit. in Bertolini, p. 2 and note 8.

13   Maria Grazia Bulgarelli and Enrico Pellegrini, '1875–1925: i primi cinquant'anni del 'Bullettino di Paletnologia Italiana'', in *«Le terramare si scavano per concimare i prati». La nascita dell'archaeologia preistorica a Parma nel dibattito culturale della seconda metà dell'Ottocento*, ed. Angela Mutti et al. (Parma: Silva Editore, 1994), 235–241; Gaetano Chierici, 'Le selci romboidali', *Bullettino di Paletnologia Italiana* 1, no. 1 (1875), 2–6.

14   Peter Rowley-Conwy, *From Genesis to Prehistory: The Archaeological Three Age System and its Contested Reception in Denmark, Britain, and Ireland* (Oxford: Oxford University Press, 2007).

15   Lerario, 'The National Museum,' 54; Massimo Tarantini, *La nascita della paletnologia in Italia (1860–1877)* (Firenze: Edizioni all'Insegna del Giglio, 2012), 65.

16   Elisabetta Mangani, *Il Museo Nazionale Preistorico Etnografico di Luigi Pigorini* (Rome: Espera, 2015), 231–232; Luigi Pigorini, 'Primo anno del corso di Paletnologia nella R. Università di Roma', *Bullettino di Paletnologia Italiana* 8, no. 7, 8 & 9 (1882), 139–145.

17   Katherine Aigner, 'Aboriginal Australia: Vatican and Italian collections', *reCollections* 10, no. 1 (2015). In her important volume, *Australia: The Vatican Museums Indigenous Collection* (Canberra: Aboriginal Studies Press, 2018), Aigner claims, at p. 42, that a set of objects was sent from New Norcia to the Museo Borgiano and thence to the Vatican Museums in 1862, but this appears to be an erroneous interpretation of Giuseppe Angelo Colini, 'Collezioni etnografiche del Museo Borgiano', *Bollettino della Società Geografica Italiana* 10 (1885), 316–325, 914–932 and *Collezioni Etnografiche del Museo Borgiano* (Rome: Società Geografica Italiana, 1886).

18   Martelli to Gaetano Chierici, 30 October 1874, Reggio Emilia, Biblioteca Panizzi, Fondo Chierici.

19 Gaetano Baluffi, *L'unità della specia umana* (Lucca: Francesco Baroni, 1832).
20 Kay Anderson and Colin Perrin, 'How race became everything: Australia and polygenism', *Ethnic and Racial Studies* 31, 5 (2008), 962–990.
21 Stormon, *Salvado Memoirs*, 109; Massam, 'Spiritual and Material'; Bob Reece, *The Invincibles: New Norcia's Aboriginal Cricketers 1879–1906* (Perth: Histrionics, 2014).
22 Martelli to Salvado, 5 September 1861, NNA 2234A-16-187.
23 Martelli to Salvado, 15 June 1859, Kinder & Brown, letter 83; the census is reproduced in Neville Green and Susan Moon, *Far From Home: Aboriginal Prisoners of Rottnest Island 1838–1932* (Nedlands: UWA Press, 1997); Martelli to Salvado, 5 September 1861, NNA 2234A-16-187.
24 Garrido reported Ferrara's story in a letter to Salvado, 19 May 1865, NNA 2234A-20-101; see also Ferrara's letter in *The West Australian*, 16 November 1892, p. 2.
25 Martelli to Garrido, 19 May 1865, NNA 2234A-20-102; Martelli to Regnoli, 24 May 1861, ASPFM, Fondo Salvado.
26 Bourke to Salvado, 12 August 1869, NNA 2234A-24-124.
27 Larrie Strautmanis, 'Salvado's Faithful Companion, Bigliagoro', *New Norcia Studies* 26 (2019), 91–99; Girola, *Report 1883*, 233.
28 Martelli to Martinez, 25 December 1866, NNA 2234A-21-280.
29 Martelli to Garrido, 26 August 1867, NNA 2234A-22-217.
30 Martelli to Salvado, 23 November 1863, Kinder & Brown, letter 172; Florence Nightingale to Duke of Newcastle, 22 May 1860, cit. in Tiffany Shellam, '"A mystery to the medical world": Florence Nightingale, Rosendo Salvado and the risk of civilisation', *History Australia* 9, no. 1 (2012), 110–135, at p. 119.
31 Larrie Strautmanis, 'A Remarkable Couple: Mary Helen Pangieran and Benedict Cuper', *New Norcia Studies* 25 (2018), 25–44; see also the following letters in NNA: 2234A/17.067, 17.068, 17.073, 18.010, 18.016; Martelli to Salvado, 4 December 1862, Kinder & Brown, letter 156.

Notes to Chapter Nineteen 'My Earthly Paradise'

1 Martelli to Salvado, 2 July 1862, Kinder & Brown, letter 146.
2 Martelli to Salvado, 1 September 1870, ASPFM Fondo Salvado.
3 Elisabetta Patrizi, 'The *Artes moriendi* as source for the history of education in modern history. First research notes', in *Mors Certa, Hora Incerta. Tradiciones, Representacines y Educación ante la Muerte*, ed. S. González Gómes et al. (Salamanca: FahrenHouse, 2016), 195–259.
4 Salvado, Diaries, vol. 10, 56 (5 May 1873), NNA SD 2234A-10; Salvado to Giovanni Simeone, 20 April 1870, ASPF SC Oceania 9, 757–760; Garrido to Salvado, 6 February 1866, NNA 2234A-21-36.
5 Mauro Rignasco to Silvano de Stefano, 13 October 1864, Archivio della Badia della SS. Trinità di Cava de' Tirreni, Sala "Protocolli notarili", Armarium, D, 4.1 (Carte di d. Rudesindo Salvado e del cardinale Schuster); Lawrence Rhoads, 'A flood of reflections: Mauro Rignasco's life through his letters', *New Norcia Studies*

24 (2017), 15–26; 1847: Román Rios, *History of the Benedictine Mission and Abbey Nullius of New Norcia (1943 edition)* (New Norcia: Abbey Press, 2017); 1857: Judith Woodward, 'The diary of Brother Mauro Beleda', *New Norcia Studies* 1 (1993), 45–48; 1857: Martelli to Pescetelli, 25 May 1857, ASPFM, Fondo Salvado; 1883: Girola, *Report 1883*, 90–92.

6   Garrido to Lecaille, 5 January 1869, NNA 2234A-24-1; Larrie Strautmanis, *New Norcia's Buildings and Their Stories* (New Norcia: Benedictine Community of New Norcia, 2019).

7   Garrido to Salvado, 6 May 1867, NNA 2234A-22-101; Venancio Garrido, 'Letter to the Colonial Secretary, 21 December 1867', in *Information Respecting the Habits and Customs of the Aboriginal Inhabitants of Western Australia. Presented to the Legislative Council by His Excellency's Command* (Perth: Government Printer, 1871), 8–20; Salvado to Giovanni Simeone, 20 April 1870, ASPF SC Oceania 9, 757–760.

8   Martelli to Garrido, 10 May 1869, NNA 2234A-24-56.

9   Martínez to Garrido, 8 May 1869, NNA 2234A-24-53; Bourke to Garrido, 9 May 1869, NNA 2234A-24-54; Garrido to Martínez, 12 May 1869, NNA 2234A-24-59.

10 Bourke to Garrido, 12 January 1869, NNA 2234A-24-5.

11 Salvado, Diaries, vol. 8, 30 (21 May 1869), NNA SD 2234A-8.

12 Salvado, Diaries, vol. 8, 34 (31 May 1869), NNA SD 2234A-8.

13 Garrido to Martínez, 19 May 1869, NNA 2234A-24-64; Martelli to Salvado, 6 October 1869, NNA 2234A-24-142.

14 Salvado to Garrido, 17 September 1869, NNA 2234A-24-138.

15 Noel Vose, *Mena: Daughter of Obedience* (Perth: UWA Press, 2013).

16 CCA, Griver papers, no. 355; Garrido to Salvado, 3 January 1870, NNA 2234A-25-4; Martelli to Salvado, 6 October 1869, NNA 2234A-24-142.

17 Garrido to Salvado, 5 November 1869, NNA 2234A-24-150.

18 'The Governor's Tour. Visit to Victoria Plains', *Inquirer and Commercial News*, 17 November 1869, p. 3; Garrido to Martínez, 23 October 1869, NNA 2234A-24-146; Salvado to Garrido, 21 January 1870, NNA 2234A-25-16.

19 Martelli to Martínez, 28 December 1869, NNA 2234A-24-181; Weld to Cardinal Barnabò, 30 January 1870, ASPF, SC Oceania, 9, 478.

20 Martelli to Salvado, 24 November 1869, NNA 2234A-24-160.

21 Griver to Garrido, 22 September 1869, NNA 2234A-24-140.

22 Martelli to Salvado, 25 May 1868, NNA 2234A-23-217; 6 October 1869, NNA 2234A-24-142; Garrido to Salvado, 23 March 1870, NNA 2234A-26-66.

23 Martínez to Garrido, 1 January 1869, NNA 2234A-24b-4.

24 Martelli to Martínez, 22 December 1869, NNA 2234A-24-177.

25 Santos Salvado to Rosendo Salvado, 1 January 1870, NNA 2234A-25-1; Martelli to Martínez, 28 December 1869, NNA 2234A-24-181.

26 Martelli to Salvado, 23 May 1865, NNA 2234A-20-107; Weld to Cardinal Barnabò, 30 January 1870, ASPF, SC Oceania, 9, 478; O'Brien, *Martin Griver*, 194.

27 Griver to Salvado, 2 March 1870, NNA 2234A-25-47.

28 Zovatto, 'La spiritualità dell'Ottocento italiano'; Peter Price, 'Australia's Spanish Bishops at the First Vatican Council', *New Norcia Studies* 23 (2016), 49–61; Martelli to Salvado, 1 September 1870, ASPFM Fondo Salvado.
29 Salvado to Cardinal Simeoni, 20 April 1870, ASPF, SC Oceania 9, 757–760.

Notes to Chapter Twenty 'Et Nihil Coepimus'
1 Garrido, Diaries 1864–1870, 29 January 1866, NNA 2234-28-29; Garrido to Salvado, 6 February 1866, NNA 2234A-21-36.
2 Martelli to Garrido, 27 May 1866, NNA 2234A-21-126; Martelli to Martínez, 27 May 1866, NNA 2234A-21-127.
3 Lecaille to Salvado, 29 March 1864, NNA 2234A-19-74; Lecaille to Barnabò, 1870, ASPF Fondo SC Oceania 9, 1869–72, 877.
4 Garrido to Salvado, 17 June 1870, NNA 2234A-25-129.
5 Martelli, *Per la solenne apertura*, 12–13.
6 Martelli to Salvado, 19 July 1858, NAA 2234A-13-358.
7 Santos Salvado to Rosendo Salvado, 18 June 1870, NNA 2234A-25-130.
8 Martelli to Martínez, 16 June 1870, NNA 2234A-25-127; Martelli to Garrido, 21 June 1870, NNA 2234A-25-131.
9 Martelli to Martínez, 28 June 1870, NNA 2234A-25-137.
10 Martelli to Garrido, 21 June 1870, NNA 2234A-25-131.
11 Lecaille to Martínez, Feast of St Peter & St Paul [29 June 1870], NNA 2234A-25-140.
12 Martelli to Martínez, 28 June 1870, NNA 2234A-25-137.
13 Garrido, Apuntes para el uso de Fr. Venancio, 202, NNA 2234A-24 (G5 1850–1861).
14 Lecaille to Martínez, 12 July 1870, NNA 2234A-25-150; Luke 5:1-9.
15 Martelli to Martínez, Feast of Our Lady of Mount Carmel [16 July] 1870, NNA 2234A-25-252.
16 'P.S.' [Martelli to Martínez, 16 July 1870], NNA 2234A-19-236.
17 Martelli to Martínez, 20 July 1870, NNA 2234A-25-156.
18 Martelli to Martínez, 26 July 1870, NNA 2234A-25-160.
19 Martelli to Martínez, 2 August 1870, NNA 2234A-25-167.
20 Lecaille to Martínez, 4 August 1870, NNA 2234A-24-121.
21 Martelli to Martínez, 13 August 1870, NNA 2234A-25-173; Martelli to Salvado, 1 September 1870, ASPFM Fondo Salvado.
22 Martelli to Martínez, 2 August 1870, NNA 2234A-25-167.
23 Martelli to Salvado, 1 September 1870, ASPFM Fondo Salvado.

Notes to Chapter Twenty-One 'Insignificant Service'
1 Judith McGuinness and Eugenia Schiettino, 'Worlds Apart: The Different Lives of Santos Salvado', *New Norcia Studies* 28 (2022), 1–16; Martelli to Martínez, 13 August 1870, NNA 2234A-25-173.

2   Salvado to Garrido, 20 February 1870, NNA 2234A-25-15; Gibney to Martínez, 27 July 1870, NNA 2234A-25-162.
3   Santos Salvado to Rosendo Salvado, 31 August 1870, ASPFM 14C Salvado Nuova Norcia.
4   Martelli to Martínez, 4 July 1870, NNA 2234A-25-143.
5   Butler, *Benedictine Monachism*, 122–145.
6   Martelli to Martínez, 22 October 1870, NNA 2234A-25-205.
7   Martelli to Martínez, 26 July 1870, NNA 2234A-25-160. Cf. Martelli to Salvado, 26 July 1860, Kinder & Brown, letter 105.
8   Lecaille to Santos Salvado, 23 August 1870, NNA 2234A-37-195; Martelli to Salvado, 1 September 1870, ASPFM Fondo Salvado.
9   Martelli to Martínez, 22 October 1870, NNA 2234A-25-205.
10 Martelli to Salvado, 1 September 1870, ASPFM Fondo Salvado.
11 O'Brien, *Martin Griver*, 193–195; Martelli to Martínez, 26 July 1870, NNA 2234A-25-160; Bolton, *Land of Vision and Mirage*, 36–37; Bob Reece, 'William Monop and his Drawings', *New Norcia Studies* 18 (2010), 48–58; Salvado, Diaries, vol. 9, 28 and 30 (10 and 17 May 1871), NNA SD 2234A-9.
12 Salvado, Diaries, vol. 9, 67 (27 November–2 December 1871), NNA SD 2234A-9.
13 John Butler to Salvado, 1 July 1869, NNA 2234A-24-101.
14 Rica Erickson, *The Victoria Plains* (Perth: Lamb Paterson, 1971), 39–40.
15 Jeremiah Clune, speech, 29 September 1872, NNA 2234A-27a-4; Martínez, speech, 29 September 1872, NNA 2234A-27a-1.
16 'Country Letters', *Inquirer and Commercial News*, 23 October 1872, p. 2.
17 Griver to Salvado, 27 November 1872, NNA 2234A-27-166; Martelli to Martínez, 20 November 1872, NNA 2234A-27-163.
18 Sr Mary Francis Joseph of the Cross to Martelli, 26 February 1872, NNA 2234A-27-29; 'Death of Sister Mary Francis Joseph Goold, Convent of Mercy, Victoria Square', *W.A. Record*, 17 April 1909; Kate Jane Jackson to Martelli, 26 September 1872, NNA 2234A-27-136.
19 The letter to Cardinal Barnabò that accompanied the Address, and another signed by lay people, is at ASPF SC Oceania 9, 1135–1136; Salvado, Diaries, vol. 9, 58 (7 October 1871), NNA SD 2234A-9.
20 Sister Mary Aloysius Kelly to Salvado, 14 December 1870, NNA 2234A-25-184; Salvado, Diaries, vol. 9, 2 (4 January 1871), NNA SD 2234A-9; Gibney to Salvado, 12 July 1871, NNA 2234A-26-99.
21 Gibney to Salvado, 21 February 1872, NNA 2234A-27-24.
22 Griver to Salvado, 17 April 1872, NNA 2234A-27-58 (annotation by Salvado).
23 Griver to Salvado, 1 May 1872, NNA 2234A-27-66 (annotation by Salvado 2 May); Salvado, Diaries, vol. 9, 102 (5 May 1872), NNA SD 2234A-9; Erickson, *Old Toodyay and Newcastle*, 285.
24 'Country News', *Perth Gazette and Western Australian Times*, 21 June 1872, p. 2; 'Western Australia. Sir Frederick Aloysius Weld, K.C.M.G', *The Universe*,

5 September 1891, p. 2; 'Intercolonial. Western Australia', *The Advocate*, 31 October 1891, p. 19.
25 Griver to Martínez, 22 May 1872, NNA 2234A-27-80; Salvado to Bourke, 20 July 1872, NNA 2234A-27-108; Griver to Salvado, 18 September 1872, NNA 2234A-27-133.
26 Griver to Salvado, 11 September 1872, NNA 2234A-27-128.
27 Salvado, Diaries, vol. 9, 131 (8 October 1872), NNA SD 2234A-9.

Notes to Chapter Twenty-Two 'Ripening for Glory'

1 Martelli to Salvado, 18 May 1863, NNA 2234A-18-193; Adam O'Neill, 'A Short History of St. John the Baptist Church Toodyay (former)', 2021, Toodyay Historical Society, Toodyay; Martelli to Salvado, 22 August 1865, NNA 2234A-20-167; Sancta Maria was demolished at the end of the nineteenth century and a memorial plaque now marks the spot, on the corner of Toodyay West Road and Picnic Hill Road.
2 Erickson, *Old Toodyay and Newcastle*, 214; 'Obituary. The Late Canon Martelli', *The Inquirer*, 18 August 1880, p. 2.
3 Martínez to Martelli, 26 October 1872, NNA 2234A-27-152; Salvado, Diaries, vol. 11, 239 (8 June 1878), NNA SD 2234A-11; *The Inquirer and Commercial News*, 3 July 1878, p. 3.
4 *The Inquirer*, 18 August 1880, p. 2.
5 Ascoli, *Raffaele Martelli*, 27.
6 'Cable Clerical Index', http://anglicanhistory.org/aus/cci/, s.v. Pidcock; 'Father Pidcock. Death of a popular priest', *Daily Herald* (Adelaide), 7 February 1919, p. 4; Pidcock to Salvado, 20 December 1879, NNA 2234A-34-239.
7 Girola, *Report 1883*, 175; Salvado, Diaries, vol. 11, 4–5 (6 January 1876), NNA SD 2234A-11.
8 William Hugh Pidcock to Martínez, 23 October 1882, NNA 2234A-37-240.
9 Griver to Salvado, 21 May 1873, NNA 2234A-28-77; Santos Salvado to Rosendo Salvado, 25 July 1873, in Judith McGuinness and Eugenia Schiettino, *The Letters of Santos Salvado (New Norcia, 1869–1879)* (New Norcia: Abbey Press, 2021); McGuinness and Schiettino, *Letters of Santos Salvado*, 149.
10 McGuinness and Schiettino, *Letters of Santos Salvado*, 123; Griver to Salvado, 6 July 1864, NNA 2234A-19-152; Martelli to Salvado, 16 December 1864, NNA 2234A-19-259; 5 January 1866, NNA 2234A-21-5. McGuinness and Schiettino, *Letters of Santos Salvado*, 123; Griver to Salvado, 6 July 1864, NNA 2234A-19-152; Martelli to Salvado, 16 December 1864, NNA 2234A-19-259; 5 January 1866, NNA 2234A-21-5.
11 Martelli to Gaetano Chierici, 30 October 1874, Reggio Emilia, Biblioteca Panizzi, Fondo Chierici.
12 Ann Pheloung, 'James Manning', in *The Dictionary of Australian Artists: painters, sketchers, photographers and engravers to 1870*, ed. Joan Kerr (Melbourne: Oxford

University Press, 1992); *The Western Australian Times*, 1 December 1874 and 12 November 1875.
13   NNA W6.B4.4.383; NNA W10.1.7; Rica Erickson, *The Brand on His Coat: Biographies of Some Western Australian Convicts* (Perth: University of Western Australia Press, 1983), 301–21; Martelli, Certificate, 29 January 1879, CCA Canon Martelli file.
14   *The Inquirer*, 18 August 1880.
15   NNA W6.B4.4.321; Anna Haebich, 'Unpacking Stories from the New Norcia Photographic Collection', *New Norcia Studies* 17 (2009), 55–62; Bob Reece, *The 1867 Photographs of W.W. Thwaites* (New Norcia: Benedictine Community of New Norcia, 2019).
16   Girola, *Report 1883*, 185; Salvado, Diaries, vol. 11, 95 (3 October 1876), NNA SD 2234A-11.
17   Salvado, Diaries, vol. 11, 105 (14 November 1876), NNA SD 2234A-11; the life of Mary Ann Chuberan and Fred Blurton has been told by their great-grandson Gerrard Shaw, 'Vulnerability: an affliction of the powerless. A Nyoongar Story' (PhD thesis, Murdoch University, 2012); Salvado, Diaries, vol. 12, 109–110 (13 April 1880), NNA SD 2234A-12; Neville Green and Lois Tilbrook, *Aborigines of New Norcia 1845–1914* (Nedlands: University of Western Australia Press, 1989).
18   Martelli to Gaetano Chierici, 30 October 1874, Reggio Emilia, Biblioteca Panizzi, Fondo Chierici. Cf. Anna Bertolini, 'Armi e strumenti degli aborigeni australiani nel Museo 'G. Chierici' di Paletnologia. La donazione di Monsignor Rudesindo Salvado della Abbazia di Nuova Norcia (Australia) 1871', *Pagine d'Archeologia* 3 (2000–2002), 1–63.
19   Martelli to Pio Urbani, 1878, letter cit. in Ascoli, *Raffaele Martelli*, 25; Russell McGregor, *Imagined Destinies: Aboriginal Australians and the Doomed Race Theory, 1880–1939* (Melbourne: Melbourne University Press, 1997).
20   Bourke to Martínez, 27 November 1867, NNA 2234A-22-324; Jack Davis, 'The first 150 years', in *Aborigines of the West: Their Past and Their Present*, ed. Ronald M. Berndt et al. (Perth: University of Western Australia Press, 1980), 54–64.
21   'Newcastle', *W.A. Record*, 24 June 1899, p. 11; *The Western Australian Times*, 17 November 1874, p. 3; 'Notes from a Ploughman's Whistle over the Hills', *Inquirer and Commercial News*, 17 January 1877, p. 2; *The Western Australian Times*, 16 November 1877, p. 3.
22   Salvado, Diaries, vol. 12, 88 (14–15 January 1880), NNA SD 2234A-12.
23   Martelli to Salvado, 9 November 1857, Kinder & Brown, letter 65; 24 February 1880, NNA 2234A-35-31; Martelli to Pio Urbani, 1878, letter cit. in Ascoli, *Raffaele Martelli*, 25.
24   Henry Spencer to Salvado, 2 October 1877, NNA 2234A-32-173.

Notes to Chapter Twenty-Three 'Always on the Move'
1   *The Record*, 6 June 1878; Donald S. Garden, *Northam: an Avon Valley History* (Melbourne: Oxford University Press, 1979), 81; Griver to Salvado,

24 March 1875, NNA 2234A-30-38; 'Northam', *The West Australian Catholic Record*, 15 September 1900, p. 6.
2 *The Herald*, 6 October 1877, p. 3.
3 Reilly, *Reminiscences*, 287; 'Grand Fancy Fair', *Northam Advertiser*, 20 January 1900, p. 2; Reminiscences of Evelyn Bartlett Day (née Throssell), SLWA PR4747, p. 3.
4 O'Brien, *Martin Griver*, 81.
5 Pietro Antonio Gugeri to Salvado, May 1871, NNA 2234A-26-62; Hilary Thomas, 'Introduction to the story of the Catholic church at Northam and Particulars of Priests who Served in the Parish', 1998, St Joseph's Parish, Northam; 'Northam', *The West Australian Catholic Record*, 24 April 1879.
6 'New church. Northam', *The West Australian Catholic Record*, 6 October 1876; Adam O'Neill, personal communication, 1 March 2021.
7 *The Inquirer and Commercial News*, 28 March 1877, p. 3.
8 *The Inquirer and Commercial News*, 30 March 1877, p. 3.
9 Martelli, 'Laying the Foundation Stone of the New Church', 2 April 1877, NNA 02129-001; *The Western Australian Times*, 13 April 1877, p. 2.
10 *The Western Australian Times*, 3 May 1878, p. 2.
11 Martelli to Pescetelli, 1 September 1877, ASPFM, Fondo Salvado; Regnoli to Salvado, 9 October 1880, NNA 2234A-35-180; 18 December 1880, NNA 2234A-35-234; *The West Australian Times*, 25 April 1879, p. 2; Regnoli to Salvado, 12 March 1881, NNA 2234A-36-36.
12 'Northam', *The West Australian Catholic Record*, 24 April 1879.
13 Griver to Colonial Secretary, 20 September 1884, SROWA Cons 527 1884/5550; Toodyay Resident Magistrate Burt to L.C. Hogan, 4.11.1884, SROWA Cons. 127/3.
14 *The West Australian Catholic Record*, 11 March 1880.
15 Martelli, Sermons for Easter Sunday and Easter Monday 1880, NNA 02129-005.
16 *The West Australian Catholic Record*, 29 January 1880, p. 5.

Notes to Chapter Twenty-Four 'To Lay My Bones in New Norcia Ground'

1 Luiz Martelli to Salvado, 20 June 1879, NNA 2234A-29-77; Griver to Salvado, 9 December 1879, NNA 2234A-34-232; Griver to Salvado, 2 September 1879, NNA 2234A-34-163.
2 Daisy Bates, *The Passing of the Aborigines: A Lifetime Spent Among the Natives of Australia* (London: John Murray, 1938), 1.
3 Salvado to Fulgencio Domínguez, 14 December 1881, NNA 2234A-36-191; Regnoli to Salvado, 11 February 1882, NNA 2234A-37-287; Comune di Ancona, *Registro generale di popolazione 1861*, ASAn, no. 229.
4 Griver to Salvado, 14 November 1881, NNA 2234A-36-171; 9 December 1879, NNA 2234A-34-232.
5 'Death of Very Rev. Dean Martelli', *The Record*, 3 November 1923.
6 *The Western Australian Times*, 16 May 1879, p. 2; Salvado, Diaries, vol. 10, 336 (28 September 1875), NNA SD 2234A-10; Reynolds to Salvado, 27 January 1879,

NNA 2234A-34-16; Martelli to Louisa Roe, 31 March 1880, CCA Canon Martelli file.
7   Cardinal Simeoni to Griver, 7 February 1880, NNA 2234A-35-130; Regnoli to Salvado, 25 September 1880, NNA 2234A-35-172.
8   Griver to Cardinal Simeoni, 31 March 1880, ASPF SC Oceania, 13, 264.
9   Griver to Salvado, 28 July 1880, NNA 2234A-35-129.
10 Regnoli to Salvado, 25 September 1880, NNA 2234A-35-172; Regnoli to Martelli, 31 July 1880, NNA 2234A-35-136.
11 Santos Salvado to Rosendo Salvado, 6 October 1880, NNA 2234A-35-177.
12 Martelli to Louisa Roe, 2 June 1880, CCA Canon Martelli file.
13 'Old Personalities', *The Northam Advertiser*, 4 May 1929, p. 5.
14 Salvado, Diaries, vol. 12, 124–137 (11 June – 4 August 1880) NNA 2234A-12.
15 Griver to Salvado, 16 June 1880, NNA 2234A-35-104.
16 Regnoli to Martelli, 31 July 1880, NNA 2234A-35-136; Girola, *Report 1883*, 248.
17 Salvado to Pescetelli, 21 August 1880, Rome, ASPFM, Fondo Salvado.
18 Martelli to Salvado, 22 May 1867, NNA-2234A-22-109.
19 Griver to Cardinal Simeoni, 10 July 1880, ASPF, SC Oceania, 13, 350.
20 Girola, *Report 1883*, 249.
21 Salvado to Pescetelli, 21 August 1880, Rome, ASPFM Fondo Salvado.
22 Salvado, Diaries, vol. 12, 137 (3 August 1880) NNA 2234A-12; Salvado, 'Historical Sketch'; Boniface Wimmer, *Album Benedictinum* (La Trobe, PA: St Vincent's Abbey, 1880) [note that Wimmer misinterpreted Salvado's description of Martelli and classified him as *Novitius*]; Salvado, Diaries, vol. 15, 73 (19 November 1890), NNA 2234A-15.
23 Griver to Salvado, 28 July 1880, NNA 2234A-35-129; Regnoli to Salvado, 30 July 1881, NNA 2234A-36-110.
24 Grant: Salvado, Diaries, vol. 14, 22 October 1887, NNA 2234A-14; Consecration: Mauro Rignasco to Dom Silvano de Stefano, 13 September 1864, Archivio della Badia della SS. Trinità di Cava de' Tirreni, Sala 'Protocolli notarili', Armarium D, 4.1 (Carte di d. Rudesindo Salvado e del cardinale Schuster); one depiction showing the cemetery and its crosses is William Ewing, 'Nuova Norcia: Missione Benedettina nell'Australia occidentale', 1864, NNA 73671P; B. Martínez, Eulogy of Fr Venancio Garrido, 12 August 1870, NNA 2234A-25-171.
25 Butler, *Benedictine Monachism*, 258.
26 Katharine Massam, 'Introduction', in *Report of Rosendo Salvado to Propaganda Fide in 1900*, ed. Stefano Girola (Melbourne: Abbey Press, 2016); Mark 3:14; Luke 6:13.
27 Girola, *Report 1883*, 249.
28 Sister Julie Cabagniol to Salvado, 3 August 1880, NNA 2234A-35-140.
29 Regnoli to Salvado, 25 September 1880, NNA 2234A-35-172; 9 October 1880, NNA 2234A-35-180; 18 December 1880, NNA 2234A-35-234.
30 *The West Australian Catholic Record*, 12 August 1880.

31 Regnoli to Salvado, 9 October 1880, NNA 2234A-35-180; 12 March 1881, NNA 2234A-36-36.

Notes to Chapter Twenty-Five 'Conclusion'

1 Anon., *In memoria di Napoleone Ascoli, nel primo anniversario della sua morte 21 novembre 1910* (Ancona: Stab. Tip. Cooperativo, 1910).
2 Regnoli to Salvado, 30 July 1881, NNA 2234A-36-110.
3 Delibera Consiglio n. 261 del 1960, Comune di Ancona.
4 The documentation on the decision to name the square after Martelli cannot be found (letter to author from Comune di Ancona, 7 June 2017). The website had this address: http://www.comune.ancona.it/ankonline/it/uffici/statistica/stradariostorico/Da_Via_Maccari_a_Via_Musone.html
5 Finali, *Le Marche*, 173.
6 Giovanni Battista Montini, 'Roma e il Concilio', *Studi Romani* 10, no. 5 (1962), 502–505.
7 Penco, *Storia della chiesa in Italia. Volume II*, 225–228.
8 Guido Formigoni, *L'Italia dei cattolici* (Bologna: Il Mulino, 2010); Martina, *Pio IX (1846–1850)*, 71; Giorgio Rumi, *Gioberti* (Bologna: Il Mulino, 1999); Benedict XVI, *Last Testament: In His Own Words* (London: Bloomsbury, 2016).
9 NNA W6.B4.4.321 reverse; Reilly, *Reminiscences*, 286–287.

Bibliography

Abbreviations

ACAA	Adelaide Catholic Archdiocesan Archives
ACAn	Archivio Comunale di Ancona
APUP	Archivio Pigorini, Università di Padova (Dipartimento dei Beni Culturali)
ASA	Archivio della Curia Generalizia Sublacense, S. Ambrogio, Rome
ASAn	Archivio di Stato di Ancona
ASDAO	Archivio Storico Diocesano di Ancona-Osimo
ASPF	Archivio Storico di Propaganda Fide, Rome
LDB	*Lettere, Decreti e Biglietti di Monsignor Segretario*
SC	*Scritture Originale riferite nei Congressi*
ASPFM	Archivio del monastero di S. Paolo Fuori le Mura, Rome
ASR	Archivio di Stato di Roma
ASS	Archivio del monastero di S. Scolastica, Subiaco
CCA	Catholic Church Archives, Perth
MNPE	Museo Nazionale Preistorico Etnografico Luigi Pigorini, Rome
NNA	New Norcia Archive
SLWA	State Library of Western Australia
SROWA	State Records Office of Western Australia

à Kempis, Thomas. *The Imitation of Christ*. Translated by Robert Jeffery. London: Penguin, 2013.

——. *Solitude and Silence*. Translated by Robert Nixon OSB. Gastonia NC: TAN books, 2023.

Aigner, Katherine. 'Aboriginal Australia: Vatican and Italian collections'. *reCollections* 10, no. 1 (2015).

——, ed. *Australia: The Vatican Museums Indigenous Collection* Canberra: Aboriginal Studies Press, 2018.

Alessandrini, Alessandro. *Relazione delle Feste Anconitane nella occasione dell'amnistia a' politici conceduta dall'immortale PIO IX gloriosamente regnante*. Ancona: Sartorj Cherubini, 1846.

Anderson, Kay, and Colin Perrin. 'How race became everything: Australia and polygenism'. *Ethnic and Racial Studies* 31, 5 (2008): 962–990.

Anon. *In memoria di Napoleone Ascoli, nel primo anniversario della sua morte 21 novembre 1910*. Ancona: Stab. Tip. Cooperativo, 1910.

——. *Narrazione degli onori funebri resi alla memoria di Carlo Fajani nel giorno XXVIII giugno 1847*. Ancona: Sartori Cherubini, 1847.

——. *Nelle esequie di Carlo Fajani, ai concittadini*. Ancona: Sartorj Cherubini, 1847.

——. *Raccolta dei poetici componimenti già pubblicati in Bologna e di molti degli inediti venuti in luce per l'avventuroso Pontificato di Pio Nono*. Bologna: Marsigli e Rocchi con Giuseppe Tiocchi, 1846.

——. *Regolamento disciplinare per le scuole pubbliche della comunità di Ancona*. Ancona: Sartori, 1822.

——. *Regolamento per l'Istituto di Educazione Gratuita pei figli del povero da fondarsi in Rimini da una Società di Contribuenti*. Rimini: Tipi Orfanelli e Grandi, 1847.

——. 'Settling Migrants. How Thomas Little of Dardanup Fared Years On'. *The Skeleton* March (2003): 2.

——. *Turno Speciale. Anconitana Commissaria Politico-Militare di aggregazioni alla setta Carbonica onde preordinare e promuovere la ribellione. Relazione*. Roma: Nella Stamperia della Rev. Cam. Apost., 1844.

Antonelli, Giuseppe. *Tipologia linguistica del genere epistolare nel primo Ottocento. Sondaggi sulle lettere familiari di mittenti cólti*. Rome: Edizioni dell'Ateneo, 2003.

Aporti, Ferrante. *Elementi di pedagogia ossia della ragionevole educazione de' fanciulli*. Roma: Tipografia della Società Editrice Romana, 1847.

Appleyard, R. T. 'Western Australia: Economic and demographic growth 1850–1914'. In *A New History of Western Australia*, edited by C. T. Stannage, 211–236. Perth: University of Western Australia Press, 1981.

Ascoli, Napoleone. *Raffaele Martelli: discorso*. Ancona: Stab. tip. dell'Ordine di E. Sarzani e Comp., 1881.

Aubert, Roger. 'La Chiesa in Italia fino al 1870'. In *Il pontificato di Pio IX (1846–1878)*, edited by Giacomo Martina, 119–182. Milano: Edizioni Paoline, 1990.

Aubert, Roger, Johannes Beckmann, Patrick J Corish, and Rudolf Lill. *The Church between Revolution and Restoration*. New York: Crossroad, 1989.

Baluffi, Gaetano. *The Charity of the Church, a Proof of her Divinity*. Translated by Denis Gargan. Dublin: Gill and Son, 1885.

———. *L'unità della specia umana*. Lucca: Francesco Baroni, 1832.

———. *La Chiesa Romana riconosciuta alla carità verso il prossimo per la vera chiesa di Gesù Cristo*. Imola: Tipografia Galeati, 1854.

Banti, Alberto Mario. *La nazione del risorgimento: parentela, santità e onore alle origini dell'Italia unita*. Torino: Einaudi, 2000.

Barbadoro, Daniele, and Franco Barbadoro. *A Fonte Avellana e sul Catria. Un monastero e la sua montagna: storia e memorie*. The authors, 2008.

Barreda, Jesús-Angel. 'I rapporti di mons. R. Salvado OSB con san Vincenzo Pallotti'. *Apostolato Universale* 16, no. 34 (2014): 4–13.

Barry, David. 'Shall we walk or ride? Take the spring cart or coach? Perhaps the train? New Norcia-Perth-New Norcia with Dom Rosendo Salvado 1846–1899'. *New Norcia Studies* 22 (2015).

Bates, Daisy. *The Passing of the Aborigines: A Lifetime Spent Among the Natives of Australia*. London: John Murray, 1938.

Battaglini, Celso. *Il prodigio della Madonna del Duomo: Ancona 1796*. Ancona: Arcidiocesi Ancona-Osimo, 1996.

Benedict XVI. *Last Testament: In his own Words*. London: Bloomsbury, 2016.

Benzoni, Riccardo. 'Il culto di San Napoleone. Ricerche erudite nella Milano napoleonica'. *Giornale di Storia* 14 (2014): 1–32.

Berndt, Ronald M. 'Aborigines of the South-West'. In *Aborigines of the West: Their Past and Their Present*, edited by Ronald M. Berndt and Catherine H. Berndt, 81–89. Perth: University of Western Australia Press, 1980.

Bertolini, Anna. 'Armi e strumenti degli aborigeni australiani nel Museo 'G. Chierici' di Paletnologia. La donazione di Monsignor Rudesindo Salvado della Abbazia di Nuova Norcia (Australia) 1871'. *Pagine d'Archeologia* 3 (2000–2002): 1–63.

Bolis, Giuseppe, et al. *Le pietre raccontano. Santa Maria della Piazza*. Castel Bolognese: Itaca, 2011.

Bolton, Geoffrey. *Land of Vision and Mirage: Western Australia since 1826*. Perth: University of Western Australia Press, 2008.

Bonomelli, Lorenzo. 'Il colera del 1836 e il corpo francese d'occupazione di Ancona'. *Il Risorgimento. Rivista di Storia del Risorgimento e di Storia Contemporanea* 68, no. 1 (2021): 34–66.

Borioni, Francesco. *A Dio conservatore che per intercessione di Maria regina di tutti i santi ha liberi gli anconitani da orribile flagello*. Ancona: Sartorj Cherubini, 1836.

Borowitzka, Lesley J. 'The Reverend Dr Louis Giustiniani and Anglican Conflict in the Swan River Colony, Western Australia 1836–1838'. *Journal of Religious History* 35, no. 3 (2011): 352–372.

Bourke, D.F. *The History of the Catholic Church in Western Australia*. Perth: Archdiocese of Perth, 1979.

Braga de Silva, Maria Helena. *Jose Maria Benito Serra: essays on his life*. Madrid Hermanas Oblatas del Santísimo Redentor, 2005.

Brocanelli, Gianfranco. *Seminari e clero nelle Marche nella seconda metà dell'Ottocento*. Roma: Herder, 1978.

Broers, Michael. *The Politics of Religion in Napoleonic Italy: The War against God*. London and New York: Routledge, 2002.

Broeze, F.J.A. 'From the Periphery to the Mainstream: The Challenge of Australia's Maritime History'. *The Great Circle* 11, no. 1 (1989): 1–13.

Bulgarelli, Maria Grazia, and Enrico Pellegrini. '1875–1925: i primi cinquant'anni del 'Bullettino di Paletnologia Italiana''. In *«Le terramare si scavano per concimare i prati». La nascita dell'archeologia preistorica a Parma nel dibattito culturale della seconda metà dell'Ottocento*, edited by Angela Mutti and Maria Bernabò Brea, 235–241. Parma: Silva Editore, 1994.

Burke, Peter. 'Cultures of Translation in Early Modern Europe'. In *Cultural Translation in Early Modern Europe*, edited by P. Burke and R. Po-chia Hsia. Cambridge: Cambridge University Press, 2007.

Butler, Cuthbert. *Benedictine Monachism: Studies in Benedictine Life and Rule*. Second ed. London: Longmans, 1924.

Byrne, Geraldine. *A Basilica in the Making: the centenary of St. Patrick's, Fremantle*. Fremantle: Mazenod Press, 2000.

"Cable Clerical Index." http://anglicanhistory.org/aus/cci/

Carosi, Paolo. 'La provincia sublacense (1851–1867)'. In *Pietro Casaretto e gli inizi della Congregazione Sublacense (1810–1880). Saggio storico nel I Centenario della Congregazione (1871–1972)*, 405–459: Publicacions de l'Abadia de Montserrat, 1972.

Cattaneo, Massimo. 'Maria *versus* Marianne. I 'miracoli' del 1796 ad Ancona'. *Cristianesimo nella Storia* 16 (1995): 45–77.

Chierici, Gaetano. 'Le selci romboidali'. *Bullettino di Paletnologia Italiana* 1, no. 1 (1875): 2–6.

Church, Catholic. *The Catechism of the Council of Trent*. Translated by Rev. J. Donovan. Baltimore: Lucas Brothers, 1829.

Clack, A.M. *Glorious Apostle. A History of the Catholic Church in York*. York: St. Patrick's Roman Catholic Church, 2009.

Colini, Giuseppe Angelo. 'Collezioni etnografiche del Museo Borgiano'. *Bollettino della Società Geografica Italiana* 10 (1885): 316–325, 914–932.

——. *Collezioni Etnografiche del Museo Borgiano*. Rome: Società Geografica Italiana, 1886.

Compton, Sr M. Xavier, Kavenagh, Pullen, Forster, Dyson, and Condon, eds. *The Letters of John Bede Polding OSB* Sydney: Sisters of the Good Samaritan, 1996.

Conati, Marcello. 'Ernani di Verdi: le critiche del tempo. Alcune considerazioni'. In *Ernani ieri e oggi*, 207–272. Parma: Istituto di studi verdiani, 1987.

Condon, Brian, ed. *Letters and Documents Supporting Historical Studies of the Catholic Church in Australia* Adelaide: South Australian College of Advanced Education, 1983.

Cook, John Robert. An account of the lives of James O'Byrne, 1806–1871, soldier, and Nicoletta, nee Salustri, 1814–1892, his wife. State Library of Western Australia, Perth.

Costantini, Enea. *Il decennio di occupazione austriaca in Ancona (1849–1859). Ricordi aneddotici*. Ancona: Stabilimento Tipografico del Commercio, 1916.

Cullity, Olimpia. 'Reform and punishment: Fremantle Prison, 1850 to 1890'. *Studies in Western Australia History* 31 (2016): 63–79.

Da Monterado, Luca. *Mons. Tommaso Gallucci (1813–1897). Prete anconetano, diplomatico, vescovo di Recanati-Loreto*. Loreto: Congregazione universale Santa Casa, 1997.

Da Signa, Boncompagno. *L'assedio di Ancona. Liber de obsidione Ancone*. Roma: Viella, 1999.

Davidson, Lucy, and John J. Kinder. '"A Most Useful Contribution to Science": Salvado's Third Consignment of Noongar Objects and Italian Prehistoric Archaeology'. *New Norcia Studies* 23 (2016): 62–74.

Davis, Jack. 'The first 150 years'. In *Aborigines of the West: Their Past and Their Present*, edited by Ronald M. Berndt and Catherine H. Berndt, 54–64. Perth: University of Western Australia Press, 1980.

De Cesaris, Valerio. *Pro Judeis. Il filogiudaismo cattolico in Italia (1789–1938)*. Milano: Guerini, 2006.

De Imitatione Christi. Translated by Ugo Nicolini. Milano: Edizioni Ares, 1996.

De Laurentiis, Emiliano. 'L'Abate D. Pier Francesco Casaretto e la sua Opera 1832–1839'. *Il Sacro Speco di S. Benedetto* 41, no. 2 (1935): 34–46.

De Mauro, Tullio. *Storia linguistica dell'Italia unita*. Bari: Laterza, 1963.

Dell'Omo, Mariano. 'Ordini monastici II'. In *Dizionario Storico Tematico: La Chiesa in Italia. Vol. II: Dopo l'Unità Nazionale*, edited by Roberto Regoli and Maurizio Tagliaferri. Roma: Associazione italiana dei professori di Storia della Chiesa, 2015.

Desideri, Claudio, ed. *Gualtiero Santini, La Giovane Italia in Ancona* Ancona: Istituto per la Storia del Movimento Democratico e Repubblicano nelle Marche, 2003.

Diamilla-Muller, Demetrio. *Da Roma a Cornuda. Ricordi della Spedizione Romana nel Veneto (Marzo-Giugno 1848)*. Torino: Tipografia Fodratti, 1886.

Dom William OSB. 'Birth of the Catholic Church at Dardanup (Albany, Bunbury and the Vasse), with Topics of Colonial Interest'. *Early Days: Journal of the Royal Western Australian Historical Society* 5, no. 6 (1960): 14–30.

Domenichini, Roberto. 'Il Dipartimento del Metauro nell'età napoleonica (1808–1815)'. *Atti e Memorie della Deputazione di Storia Patria per le Marche* 92 (1987): 463–517.

Donegan, Luke. *Fremantle Prison: Convict Daily Life*. Perth: Government of Western Australia, 2009.

Dowd, Christopher. *Rome and Australia: The Papacy and Conflict in the Australian Catholic Missions 1834–1884*. Leiden: Brill, 2008.

Erickson, Rica. *The Dempsters*. Perth: University of Western Australia Press, 1978.

———. 'Friends and Neighbours: The Irish of Toodyay'. In *The Irish in Western Australia. Studies in Western Australian History Vol. 20*, edited by Bob Reece, 49–58. Nedlands: Centre for Western Australian History, 2000.

———. 'If It Hadn't Been for the Murphys'. *Early Days* 9, 6 (1988): 52–64.

———. *Old Toodyay and Newcastle*. Toodyay: Toodyay Shire Council, 1974.

———. *The Victoria Plains*. Perth: Lamb Paterson, 1971.

Fabbri, Giulio. 'Il monastero di S. Scolastica in Subiaco durante il pontificato di Pio IX'. *Atti e Memorie della Società Tiburtina di Storia e d'Arte* 40 (1967): 58–173.

Finali, Gaspare. *Le Marche: ricordanze*. Pesaro: Istituto per la Storia del Risorgimento italiano, 2010 [1897].

Fioretti, Donatella. 'Persistenze e mutamenti dal periodo giacobino all'Unità'. In *Le Marche*, edited by Sergio Anselmi, 33–119. Torino: Einaudi, 1987.

Flavell, Ambrose. 'Subiaco Congregation missionaries and the British Empire in the nineteenth century'. In *La congregazione sublacense: inizi, ideali e attività missionaria*. Subsidia Monastica, 25, 67–93. Montserrat: Publicacions de l'Abadia de Montserrat, 2012.

Folena, Gianfranco. 'Le prime immagini dell'America nel vocabolario italiano'. *Bollettino dell'Atlante Linguistico Mediterraneo* 13–15 (1971–1973): 673–692.

Formigoni, Guido. *L'Italia dei cattolici*. Bologna: Il Mulino, 2010.

Franceschini, Geltrude. *Gli avvenimenti di Ancona negli anni 1848–49*. Roma: Forzani e C., 1899.

Fullagar, Kate. *The Savage Visit. New World People and Popular Imperial Culture in Britain, 1710–1795*. Berkeley and Los Angeles: University of California Press, 2012.

Garden, Donald S. *Northam: an Avon Valley History*. Melbourne: Oxford University Press, 1979.

Garrido, Venancio. 'Letter to the Colonial Secretary, 21 December 1867'. In *Information Respecting the Habits and Customs of the Aboriginal Inhabitants of Western Australia. Presented to the Legislative Council by His Excellency's Command*, 8–20. Perth: Government Printer, 1871.

Giangiacomi, Palermo. *Ancona: sua storia*. Ancona: Libreria Editrice Giuseppe Fegola, 1923.

———. *Carlo Faiani*. Ancona: Stab. Tip. Cooperativo, 1921.

———. 'Filippo Fiorenzi'. In *Dizionario del Risorgimento Nazionale. Dalle origini a Roma Capitale*, edited by Michele Rosi. Milano: Vallardi, 1931–1937.

———. 'Patriotti anconitani nel Risorgimento.' *L'Ordine*, 24 May 1918, 4.

———. *Tre Patriotti: Faiani, Giannelli, Buglioni*. Ancona: Tipografia Sita, 1938.

Girola, Stefano, ed. *Report of Rosendo Salvado to Propaganda Fide in 1883* Melbourne: Abbey Press, 2015.

Giussani, Luigi. *To Give One's Life for the Work of Another*. Montreal: McGill-Queens University Press, 2022.

Goody, L.J. *Martin Griver. Second Catholic Bishop of Perth (1814–1886)*. Perth: Vanguard Press, 1986.

Green, Neville, and Susan Moon. *Far From Home: Aboriginal Prisoners of Rottnest Island 1838–1932*. Nedlands: UWA Press, 1997.

Green, Neville, and Lois Tilbrook. *Aborigines of New Norcia 1845–1914*. Nedlands: University of Western Australia Press, 1989.

Gretton, Mrs G. *The Englishwoman in Italy. Impressions of life in the Roman States and Sardinia, during a ten years' residence*. London: Hurst and Blackwell, 1860.

Gualterio, F.A. *Gli ultimi rivolgimenti italiani. Memorie storiche*. Firenze: Felice Le Monnier, 1852.

Haebich, Anna. 'Unpacking Stories from the New Norcia Photographic Collection'. *New Norcia Studies* 17 (2009): 55–62.

Hales, E.E.Y. *Pio Nono*. London: Eyre & Spottiswoode, 1954.

Hassam, Andrew. *Sailing to Australia: Shipboard Diaries by Nineteenth-Century British Emigrants*. Melbourne: Melbourne University Press, 1995.

Isabella, Maurizio. 'Freedom of the press, public opinon and liberalism in the Risorgimento'. *Journal of Modern Italian Studies* 17, no. 5 (2012): 551–567.

———. 'Religion, revolution and popular mobilization'. In *Re-Imagining Democracy in the Mediterranean, 1780–1860*, edited by Joanna Innes and Mark Philp, 231–252. Oxford: Oxford University Press, 2018.

———. *Risorgimento in Exile: Italian Émigrés and the Liberal International in the Post-Napoleonic Era*. Oxford: Oxford University Press, 2009.

Kavenagh, Terence. 'Distant echoes: Aboriginal and Islander boys at St Mary's Sydney in the mid-nineteenth century'. *Tjurunga* 76 (2009): 60–96.

Keightley, Ron. 'The Expulsion of Father Venancio Garrido: Causes'. *New Norcia Studies* 12 (2004): 58–73.

Kimbell, David. *Vincenzo Bellini, Norma*. Cambridge: Cambridge University Press, 1998.

Kinder, John J. 'Letters and other gifts: on a nineteenth-century Italian-Australian epistolary network'. *Life Writing* 12, no. 3 (2015): 325–338.

———. 'Rosendo Salvado and Raffaele Martelli: friendship and vocation'. *New Norcia Studies* 22 (2015): 1–11.

Kinder, John J., and Joshua Brown. *Canon Raffaele Martelli in Western Australia, 1853–1864: Life and Letters*. Melbourne: Abbey Press, 2014.

Kinsella, John, and Tracy Ryan, eds. *The Fremantle Press Anthology of Western Australian Poetry* Fremantle: Fremantle Press, 2017.

Kovesi Killerby, Catherine. *Ursula Frayne: a Biography*. Fremantle: The University of Notre Dame Australia, 1996.

Lunardi, Giovanni. 'Giovinezza e formazione di Pietro Casaretto'. *Studia Monastica* 14 (1972): 349–374.

———. *La congregazione sublacense O.S.B.* Noci: Edizioni La Scala, 2003.

———. 'The Missionary Spirit of Abbot Casaretto'. *Tjurunga* 8 (1974): 35–56.

Lupi, Maria. 'Vescovi 1: dal 1848 alla fine del secolo'. In *Cristiani d'Italia. Chiese, società, Stato 1861–2011*, edited by Alberto Melloni, 807–825. Roma: Istituto dell'Enciclopedia italiana, 2011.

Luzzati, Michele. 'Per la storia dei cognomi ebraici di formazione italiana'. In *L'Italia dei cognomi: l'antroponimia italiana nel quadro mediterraneo*, edited by A. Addobbati, *et al.*, 497–509: Pisa University Press, 2012.

Macellari, Roberto. 'Gaetano Chierici, prete e preistorico'. In *«Le terramare si scavano per concimare i prati». La nascita dell›archeologia preistorica a Parma nel dibattito culturale della seconda metà dell›Ottocento*, edited by Maria Bernabò Brea and Angela Mutti, 118–129. Parma: Silva, 1994.

Mangani, Elisabetta. *Il Museo Nazionale Preistorico Etnografico di Luigi Pigorini*. Rome: Espera, 2015.

Maroni, Michele. *L'Arsenale di Ancona. Reminiscenze storiche.* Fano: Società Tipografica Cooperativa, 1901.

Martelli, Raffaele. 'Beneficenza. Azione generosa di un giovane patrizio.' *L'Artigianello*, 6 February 1847 1847, 44–46.

———. 'Epigrafia'. *L'Educatore storico e varietà di scienze, lettere e belle arti (Modena)* III, no. 2 (1846): 97–100.

———. 'Il fanciullo buon cittadino'. *L'Artigianello* 2, no. 49 (5 December 1846) (1846): 385–386.

———. *In morte di Giuseppe conte Ferniani da Faenza milite del Battaglione universitario nella guerra dell'indipendenza italiana morto di sinoco in Bologna di anni 21 il 5 luglio 1848: cenno necrologico letto dal cappellano Raffaele can. Martelli.* Bologna: Tipografia Sassi nelle Spaderie, 1848.

———. *L'eloquenza cristiana: inno.* Ancona: Sartorj Cherubini, 1843.

———. *Necrologie di alcuni giovani crociati militi del battaglione universitario romano nella guerra per l'indipendenza italiana combattuta l'anno 1848 lette nei rispettivi funeri dal cappellano Raffaele professore Martelli.* Loreto: Per le stampe dei fratelli Rossi, 1849.

———. *Nel funere di Francesco Franceschi di S. Arcangelo, milite crociato nel Battaglione universitario romano, mancato in Ferrara il 27 giugno 1848. Parole lette dal cappellano Raffaele can. Martelli.* Bologna: Tipografia governativa alla Volpe, 1848.

———. *Nelle esequie rese all'anima di Luigi Gaudenzi senigagliese studente di legge in Roma, sargente nella prima compagnia del battaglione universitario morto in Ferrara il 27 giugno 1848, d'anni 21, reduce dalla guerra per l'indipendenza italiana. Parole di lode lette dal cappellano Raffaele prof. Martelli.* Publisher unknown, 1848.

———. *Nelle funebri onoranze rese al milite del Battaglione universitario Giuseppe Venturoli di Bologna, studente di matematica morto il di 6 luglio 1848. Parole di lode lette dal cappellano d. Raffaele prof. Martelli.* Bologna: Tip. Sassi nelle Spaderie, 1848.

———. *Parole di funebre encomio lette in morte del milite studente di matematica Carlo Reali di Assisi mancato in Bologna il 3 luglio 1848 dal cappellano del battaglione universitario Raffaele prof. Martelli.* Bologna: Tipografia Tiocchi, 1848.

———. *Per la solenne apertura dell'Istituto Riminese di educazione gratuita pei figli del povero. Discorso letto dal Canonico Don Raffaele Martelli Professore di Rettorica nel Ginnasio di Ancona il 30 Gennaio 1848.* Rimini: Tipi Orfanelli e Grandi, 1848.

———. *Preghiere da recitarsi alla Regina d'ognissanti nella cattedrale di Ancona in un triduo di ringraziamento per l'amnistia accordata dall'immortale Pio 9. scritte dal canonico Raffaele Martelli.* Ancona: Sartorj Cherubini, 1846.

———. *Relazione della sacra cerimonia onde fu inaugurato l'Arsenale anconitano dall'Eminenza Reverendissima del Cardinale Antonio Tosti Pro Tesoriere della*

Reverenda Camera Apostolica il 12 Marzo 1843 fatta pubblicare dalla Camera Primaria di Commercio in Ancona. Ancona: Gustavo Sartori Cherubini, Tipografo Vescovile, 1843.

———. 'Un benefattore dell'umanità. Biografia del P. Nicola Tommasi di Ancona, fondatore di un conservatorio di fanciulle nel 1794'. *L'Artigianello* 2, 19 (9 May 1846), 145–147, and 2, 21 (23 January [sic but May] 1846) (1846): 161–163.

———. 'Un benefattore dell'umanità. Biografia del P. Nicola Tommasi di Ancona, fondatore di un conservatorio di fanciulle nel 1794.' *L'Artigianello*, 23 January 1846, 145–147, 161–163, 333–335.

———. 'Un benefattore dell'umanità. Cenno necrologico intorno a Nicola Rossi, benefattore insigne dell'Ospizio de' Poveri in Ancona'. *L'Artigianello* 1, no. 41 (18 October 1845) (1845): 333–335.

———. *Versi in morte di Antonio Malaccari, studente di rettorica e alunno nel venerabile Seminario S. Carlo di Ancona*. Loreto: Tipografia dei Fratelli Rossi, 1844.

———. *Viaggetto autunnale alla montagna del Catria nell'ottobre del 1842*. Loreto: Tipografia dei Fratelli Rossi, 1844.

Martina, Giacomo. 'Formazione del clero e cultura cattolica verso la metà dell'Ottocento'. In *La Chiesa in Italia dall'unità ai nostri giorni*, edited by Elio Guerriero, 120–206. Cinisello Balsamo: San Paolo, 1996.

———. 'Il clero italiano e la sua azione pastorale verso la metà dell'Ottocento'. In *Il pontificato di Pio IX (1846–1878)*, edited by Roger Aubert, 761–857. Torino: Editrice S.A.I.E., 1969.

———. *Pio IX (1846–1850)*. Rome: Università Gregoriana Editrice, 1974.

Martina, Giacomo, and Wiktor Gramatowski. 'La relazione ufficiale sul conclave del 1846: nel 150° anniversario dell'elezione di Pio IX'. *Archivum Historiae Pontificiae* 34 (1996): 159–212.

Massam, Katharine. 'Introduction'. In *Report of Rosendo Salvado to Propaganda Fide in 1900*, edited by Stefano Girola. Melbourne: Abbey Press, 2016.

———. 'The Spiritual and the Material: Women & Work in the Benedictine Mission of New Norcia 1860–1910'. *New Norcia Studies* 22 (2015): 53–61.

McGregor, Russell. *Imagined Destinies: Aboriginal Australians and the Doomed Race Theory, 1880–1939*. Melbourne: Melbourne University Press, 1997.

McGuinness, Judith, and Eugenia Schiettino. *The Letters of Santos Salvado (New Norcia, 1869–1879)*. New Norcia: Abbey Press, 2021.

———. 'Worlds Apart: The Different Lives of Santos Salvado'. *New Norcia Studies* 28 (2022): 1–16.

Metzler, Josef, ed. *Dalle missioni alle Chiese locali (1846–1965)* Milano: Edizioni Paoline, 1990.

Millozzi, Michele. *Antonio Giannelli. Luoghi, clima, vita di un patriota del Risorgimento*. Ancona: affinità elettive, 2004.

Molony, John N. *The Roman Mould of the Australian Catholic Church*. Melbourne: Melbourne University Press, 1969.

Montanari, Giuseppe Ignazio. *L'arte di scrivere lettere dedotta dall'analisi de' classici scrittori latini ed italiani per opera di Giuseppe Ignazio Montanari*. Firenze: Tipografia Calasanziana, 1840.

Monti, Benedetto, ed. *Componimenti raccolti in occasione delle feste fatte in Ancona ad onore dell'immortale Pio IX Pontefice Massimo*. Ancona: Sartorj Cherubini, 1846.

Montini, Giovanni Battista. 'Roma e il Concilio'. *Studi Romani* 10, no. 5 (1962): 502–505.

Morachioli, Sandro. *L'Italia alla rovescia: ricerche sulla caricatura giornalistica tra il 1848 e l'Unità*. Pisa: Edizioni della Normale, 2013.

Morici, Ottaviano. *I cento anni del Teatro delle Muse di Ancona*. Ancona: Nacci, 1927.

Natalucci, Mario. *Ancon dorica civitas fidei: uomini e monumenti della Chiesa*. Ancona: Cassa di Risparmio di Ancona, 1980.

———. *Ancona attraverso i secoli. III: Dal periodo napoleonico ai nostri giorni*. Città del Castello: Unione Arti Grafiche, 1961.

———. 'Ricordi di Pio IX in Ancona'. *Pio IX. Studi e ricerche sulla vita della Chiesa dal Settcento ad oggi* 8, no. 2 (1979): 245–255.

'Neminem Profecto: Instruction de la Propagande du 23 novembre 1845'. *Mémoire Spiritaine* 3, no. 3 (2019).

O'Brien, Odhran. 'Beyond Melbourne: Nineteenth-Century Cathedral Building in the Diocese of Perth'. *Journal of the Australian Catholic Historical Society* 39 (2018): 45–54.

———. 'Cash, Convicts & Catholicism: Catholic Ministry to Convicts and Church-State Relations in Colonial Western Australia'. *New Norcia Studies* 23 (2016): 75–92.

———. *Martin Griver Unearthed. The Life of a Spanish Missionary Priest Who Became a Bishop in Colonial Western Australia, 1814–1886*. Sydney: St Pauls, 2014.

O'Donoghue, Frances. *The Bishop of Botany Bay: the life of John Bede Polding, Australia's first Catholic Archbishop*. London and Sydney: Angus and Robertson, 1982.

O'Farrell, Patrick. *The Catholic Church and Community in Australia: a History*. Melbourne: Thomas Nelson, 1977.

O'Neill, Adam. 'A Short History of St. John the Baptist Church Toodyay (former)'. 2021. Toodyay Historical Society, Toodyay.

O'Neill, Maureen. 'Sisters of Saint Joseph of the Apparition in Western Australia'. Dissertation, Claremont Teachers College, 1963.

Pagani, Giovanni Battista. *L'anima divota della Ss. Eucaristia*. Vigevano 1835.

Panzini, Mario. *Dizionario del vernacolo anconitano*. Ancona: Controvento, 2008.

Paternoster, Annick, and Francesca Saltamacchia. '(Im)politeness Rules and (Im)politeness Formulae: Metadiscourse and Conventionalisation in 19th century Italian Conduct Books'. In *Studies on Language Norms in Context*, edited by Elena Maria Pandolfi, *et al.*, 263–301. Frankfurt am Main: Peter Lang, 2017.

Patrizi, Elisabetta. 'The *Artes moriendi* as source for the history of education in modern history. First research notes'. In *Mors Certa, Hora Incerta. Tradiciones, Representacines y Educación ante la Muerte*, edited by S. González Gómes et al., 195–259. Salamanca: FahrenHouse, 2016.

Pavia, Rosario, and Ercole Sori. *Ancona*. Roma-Bari: Laterza, 1990.

Penco, Gregorio. *Storia del monachesimo in Italia nell'epoca moderna*. Roma: Edizioni Paoline, 1968.

———. *Storia della chiesa in Italia. Volume II: Dal Concilio di Trento ai nostri giorni*. Milano: Jaca Book, 1978.

Peruzzi, Agostino. *Cenni biografici intorno al sacerdote Don Mariano Bedetti, Arcidiacono della Chiesa Anconitana* Modena: Reale Tipografia Eredi Soliani, 1834.

———. *La Chiesa anconitana, dissertazione. Con note e supplementi di Luigi Pauri e di Sebastiano Petrelli*. Ancona: Gustavo Sartorj Cherubini, 1845.

Petrarch. *Canzoniere*. Translated by J.G. Nichols. Manchester: Carcanet, 2006.

Petrocchi, Policarpo. *Novo dizionario universale della lingua italiana*. Milano: Fratelli Treves, 1884–1890.

Pheloung, Ann. 'James Manning'. In *The Dictionary of Australian Artists: painters, sketchers, photographers and engravers to 1870*, edited by Joan Kerr. Melbourne: Oxford University Press, 1992.

Pigorini, Luigi. *La Paleoetnologia in Roma, in Napoli, nelle Marche e nelle Legazioni. Relazione a S.E. il Ministro della Pubblica Istruzione*. Parma: Tip. Rossi-Ubaldi, 1867.

———. 'Primo anno del corso di Paletnologia nella R. Università di Roma'. *Bullettino di Paletnologia Italiana* 8, no. 7, 8 & 9 (1882): 139–145.

Pirani, Francesco. *Medievalismi nelle Marche*. Fermo: Andrea Livi, 2014.

Press, Margaret. *From Our Broken Toil. South Australian Catholics 1836–1906*. Adelaide, 1986.

Price, Peter. 'Australia's Spanish Bishops at the First Vatican Council'. *New Norcia Studies* 23 (2016): 49–61.

Re, Emilio. 'L'Artigianello'. *Strenna dei Romanisti* 8 (1947): 246–254.

Reece, Bob. *The 1867 Photographs of W.W. Thwaites*. New Norcia: Benedictine Community of New Norcia, 2019.

———. 'Fremantle's first voice: the Herald (1867–1886)'. *Fremantle Studies* 6 (2010).

———. *The Invincibles: New Norcia's Aboriginal Cricketers 1879–1906.* Perth: Histrionics, 2014.

———. 'William Monop and his Drawings'. *New Norcia Studies* 18 (2010): 48–58.

Rees, Daniel. 'The Benedictine Revival in the Nineteenth Century'. In *Benedict's Disciples*, edited by David Hugh Farmer, 324–349. Leominster: Gracewing, 1995.

Regnoli, Pietro. 'Cristo che caccia i mercanti dal tempio. Dipinto di Alfonso Chierici di Reggio'. *Il Saggiatore* 2, no. 3 (1844): 83–91.

———. 'Dell'altro dipinto di Alfonso Chierici di Reggio. Il S. Baggio'. *Il Saggiatore* 2, no. 4 (1844): 114–117.

———. *Intorno due dipinti di Alfonso Chierici di Reggio: ragionamento.* Roma: Tipografia della Minerva, 1844.

———. 'Ultimo episodio dell'assalto di Vicenza, il 10 giugno 1848'. *Il pensiero italiano* 17 (1896): 97–104.

———. 'Ultimo episodio dell'assalto di Vicenza, il 10 giugno 1848'. *La Gioventù italiana* 2, no. 1 (1910): 12–22.

Reilly, Joseph Thomas. *Reminiscences of Fifty Years' Residence in Western Australia.* Perth: Sands & McDougall, 1903.

Rhoads, Lawrence. 'A flood of reflections: Mauro Rignasco's life through his letters'. *New Norcia Studies* 24 (2017): 15–26.

Riall, Lucy. *The Italian Risorgimento: State, Society and National Unification.* London: Routledge, 1994.

Richards, Jonathan. *The Secret War: a True History of Queensland's Native Police.* St Lucia: University of Queensland Press, 2008.

Rikkers, John. *Western Australian Schools 1830–1980. Part One: Schools and Teachers 1830–1871.* Perth: Education Department of Western Australia, 1984.

Rinaldini, Carlo. 'Esequie al benemerito italiano Carlo Fajani di Ancona.' *Il Fanfulla*, 10 July 1847.

Rinaldini, Mario. *Le scuole notturne instituite in Ancona da Carlo Faiani. Noterelle storiche.* Ancona: Venturini, 1897.

Rios, Román. *History of the Benedictine Mission and Abbey Nullius of New Norcia (1943 edition).* New Norcia: Abbey Press, 2017.

Ros, Eladio. *La musica en Nueva Nursia.* Madrid: Ministerio de Asuntos Exteriores, 1992.

Rowley-Conwy, Peter. *From Genesis to Prehistory: The Archaeological Three Age System and its Contested Reception in Denmark, Britain, and Ireland.* Oxford: Oxford University Press, 2007.

Rumi, Giorgio. *Gioberti.* Bologna: Il Mulino, 1999.

Russo, George. *Lord Abbot of the Wilderness: The Life and Times of Bishop Salvado.* Melbourne: Polding Press, 1980.

Salvado, Rosendo. 'Advertisement: To the Editor of the Inquirer.' *Inquirer*, 23 February 1848 1848, 2.

——. 'Historical Sketch of the Monastery and Community of New Norcia'. *Tjurunga* 11 (1976): 30–41.

——. 'Letter to the Colonial Secretary, 19 February 1864'. In *Information Respecting the Habits and Customs of the Aboriginal Inhabitants of Western Australia. Presented to the Legislative Council by His Excellency's Command*, edited by Rosendo Salvado and Venancio Garrido, 3–7. Perth: Government Printer, 1871.

Santini, Gualtiero. *Ancona nel 1848–1849*. Macerata: Tip. P. Colcerasa, 1927.

——. Anconitana gens. Biblioteca Benincasa (Ancona).

——. *Diario dell'assedio e difesa di Ancona nel 1849*. Aquila degli Abruzzi: Officine grafiche Vecchioni, 1925.

——. *Gente anconitana*. Fano: Sangallo, 1969.

——. *Le Marche e il Risorgimento*. Macerata: Tip. P. Colcerasa, 1927.

Sbano, Nicola. *Lorenzo Lesti, patriota, il suo tempo e la processura "anconitana di più delitti"*. Ancona: Il lavoro editoriale, 2016.

Scarabicchi, Francesco. *Una città di scoglio. Breve viaggio ad Ancona*. Ancona: affinità elettive, 2016.

Scataglini, Franco. 'I giorni popolari'. In *So' rimaso la spina*. Ancona: L'astrogallo, 1977.

Shanahan, Mary. *Out of Time, Out of Place. Henry Gregory and the Benedictine Order in Colonial Australia*. Canberra: Australian National University Press, 1966.

Shaw, Gerrard. 'Vulnerability: an affliction of the powerless. A Nyoongar Story'. PhD thesis, Murdoch University, 2012.

Sheetz-Nguyen, Jessica A. 'Catholic Preaching in Victorian England, 1801–1901'. In *A New History of the Sermon: the Nineteenth Century*, edited by Robert Ellison, 207–232: Brill, 2010.

Shellam, Tiffany. '"A mystery to the medical world": Florence Nightingale, Rosendo Salvado and the risk of civilisation'. *History Australia* 9, no. 1 (2012): 110–135.

Sorba, Carlotta. '*Ernani* Hats: Italian Opera as a Repertoire of Political Symbols during the Risorgimento'. In *The Oxford Handbook of the New Cultural History of Music*, edited by Jane F. Fulcher, 428–451. Oxford: Oxford University Press, 2011.

Sori, Ercole. *Ancona 1848–1870. Storia narrativa della città*. Rimini: Bookstones, 2017.

Spadoni, Domenico. 'Morelli, Ercole'. In *Dizionario del Risorgimento nazionale: dalle origini a Roma capitale. Fatti e persone*, 647. Milano: Vallardi, 1930–1937.

Spadoni, Domenico, and Giovanni Spadoni. *Uomini e fatti delle Marche nel Risorgimento italiano*. Macerata: Unione Tipografica Operaia, 1927.

Spadoni, Giovanni. 'Il primo processo politico nelle Marche dopo la restaurazione del 1815.' *Le Marche nel Risorgimento*, January 1925, 1–2.

Sprat, Jack. *Lloyd's Register of British and Foreign Shipping from 1st July 1838 to the 30th June 1839*. London: Cox and Sons, 1838.

Stibi, Frances. 'Profile of an early church architect'. *Australian Catholic Historical Society Newsletter* 19, no. 3 (2009): 4.

Stormon, E.J., ed. *The Salvado Memoirs* Perth: University of Western Australia Press, 1977.

Strautmanis, Larrie. *New Norcia's Buildings and Their Stories*. New Norcia: Benedictine Community of New Norcia, 2019.

———. 'A Remarkable Couple: Mary Helen Pangieran and Benedict Cuper'. *New Norcia Studies* 25 (2018), 25–44.

———. 'Salvado's Faithful Companion, Bigliagoro'. *New Norcia Studies* 26 (2019): 91–99.

Tarantini, Massimo. *La nascita della paletnologia in Italia (1860–1877)*. Firenze: Edizioni all'Insegna del Giglio, 2012.

Tommaseo, Niccolò, and Bernardo Bellini. *Dizionario della lingua italiana*. Torino: Unione Tipografico-Editrice, 1861–1879.

Tonini, Carlo. *Compendio della storia di Rimini. Vol. 2: Dal 1500 al 1861*. Rimini: E. Renzetti, 1895.

Trollope, Thomas. *A Lenten Journey in Umbria and the Marches*. London: Chapman & Hall, 1862.

Veca, Ignazio. *Il mito di Pio IX: storia di un papa liberale e nazionale*. Roma: Viella, 2018.

———. 'Oggetti animati. Materialità, circolazione e usi della figura di Pio IX (1846–1849)'. *Il Risorgimento. Rivista di Storia del Risorgimento e di Storia Contemporanea* 64, no. 1 (2017): 63–97.

Verdina, Federica. 'The correspondence of Rosendo Salvado to Propaganda Fide'. PhD thesis, , University of Western Australia, 2018.

Verdina, Federica, and John J. Kinder. 'Selvaggi or Nativi? European and Colonial Perspectives on the Encounter with the Other in the Experience of a Missionary in Nineteenth-Century Western Australia'. *New Norcia Studies* 27 (2021): 17–21.

Vose, Noel. *Mena: Daughter of Obedience*. Perth: UWA Press, 2013.

Walter, Irma. 'Early Mail Services in the South-West of WA (1829–1901)'. *Harvey History Online* (2019).

Wimmer, Boniface. *Album Benedictinum*. La Trobe, PA: St Vincent's Abbey, 1880.

Woodward, Judith. 'The diary of Brother Mauro Beleda'. *New Norcia Studies* 1 (1993): 45–48.

———. 'Formation of Benedictine Identity and Kinship: Nineteenth Century Preparation of Monks for the Mission of New Norcia'. *New Norcia Studies* 3 (1995): 29–38.

Zamboni, Filippo. *Ricordi del Battaglione Universitario Romano (1848–1849) per cura della vedova Emilia Zamboni*. Trieste: Parnaso, 1926.

Zovatto, Pietro. 'La spiritualità dell'Ottocento italiano'. In *Storia della spiritualità italiana*, edited by Pietro Zovatto, 478–532. Roma: Città Nuova, 2002.

Acknowledgements

My first and deepest debt of gratitude is to Abbot John Herbert and the members of the Benedictine Community of New Norcia, for their generous gift of access to their archive and to the life of the community.

Fr David Barry OSB first introduced me to the presence of Raffaele Martelli in the New Norcia archive. He had done the first work in compiling what was known about Martelli from archives in Subiaco. He was patient and wise in discussing all aspects of my long companionship with the good Canon and I have learned from him more than I can say about the Benedictine life and much more besides.

The New Norcia archivist, Peter Hocking, was unfailingly and extraordinarily generous, patient and encouraging in guiding me through the riches of the archive. He also read a first draft of the book. The book would not have been written without his help at every turn.

Fr Robert Nixon OSB gave advice on musical matters. Staff at the Catholic Church Archives, Perth, provided useful documents.

A linguist setting out to write a biography found himself in the new and unfamiliar world of archives. If I grew to love the hunt and the dust, it was through the generous assistance of many archivists and librarians, custodians of our written history and collaborators in unlocking it. My warm thanks go to them all.

In Ancona: at the Archivio Diocesano, Don Giovanni Carini, Giuseppina Duca and Eleonora Barontini; at the Biblioteca Diocesana, Giovanna Pirani; at the Archivio di Stato, Roberto Domenichini and Carlo Giacomini; at the Biblioteca Benincasa, Simonetta Pirani and Stefano Grilli; at the Deputazione di Storia Patria per le Marche, Gilberto Piccinini; at the Università delle Marche, Prof Luca Andreoni; and the Committee of the Delegazione FAI di Ancona.

Elsewhere in Italy, thanks to Mario Mineo, Museo Etnografico Preistorico Luigi Pigorini, Rome; Monsignor Michal Jagosz, Basilica di Santa Maria Maggiore, Rome; Roberto Regoli, Pontificia Università

ACKNOWLEDGEMENTS

Gregoriana, Rome; Roberto Marcuccio, Biblioteca Panizzi, Reggio Emilia; Natalia Tizi, Biblioteca Civico 'Romolo Spezioli', Fermo; Antonella Imolesi, Biblioteca Comunale 'A. Saffi', Forlì; Michele Cupitò, Laboratorio di Archeologia, Università di Padova; Francesca Valentini, Biblioteca del Monumento Nazionale di Santa Scolastica.

Alessandro Tedesco generously spent time searching in the Central Archive of the History of the Jewish People in Jerusalem; as did Lucy Davidson in the Ancona Diocesan Archive. Stefano Angeletti Rasiej shared his knowledge of *famiglie marchigiane*.

I am indebted, as all teachers are, to the work of my students. Some wrote dissertations on Raffaele Martelli's letters and other aspects of the history of New Norcia: Emily Rourke, Lucia Boerci, Matteo Colombo, Simone Pregnolato, Isabella Binda, Madeline Plester, Lucy Davidson, Lawrence Rhoads, Federica Verdina, Francesco De Toni. Others carried out research work of various kinds: Chiara Brasca, Lucas Calleja, Simon Tebbit, Alexandra Thornton, Thea Lendich, Alice Tickner.

Two former students and now valued colleagues, Josh Brown of UWA and Ashok Collins of ANU, did me the enormous favour of reading the entire manuscript and giving valuable insights. Dr Teresa de Castro read early chapters.

For local historical insights, warm thanks to Margie Eberle, former Museum Curator of the Shire of Toodyay; Adam O'Neill of Toodyay; Daniel Matthys of Northam; Ian and Jackie Phillips of York; Geraldine Byrne in Perth; Judith McGuiness for supplying letters in Spanish.

For information on the literature of Western Australia, thanks to Kieran Dolin; and for expert information on sailing ships, thanks to Michael Gregg, WA Maritime Museum.

On linguistic matters, thanks to Teresa de Castro and Marta Pérez Rey for help with Spanish, Raquel Bra Nuñez with Galician, Hélène Jaccomard with French, and John Melville-Jones and Neil O'Sullivan with Latin.

For help in reading sermons, thanks to Fr John O'Connor (Christchurch), Fr Alex Zenthoefer (Evansville, Indiana), Fr Michael McEntee (Melbourne) and Rev. Campbell Markham (Perth).

Index

Aboriginal children   73, 219–220, 227–238, 253
Aboriginal artefacts   208–211
Aborigines   59–60, 71–73, 93–94, 101–102, 117–118, 122–123, 131, 142, 158, 205–215, 219–220, 227–238, 257–260
Albany   115–119, 152, 194, 282
Ancona
   description and history   1–4, 9, 27–28, 35–42, 49–51, 55–58
   Cathedral   1–2, 10, 11, 35, 36, 51
   dialect   1–2, 5, 163–164
   Jews   4, 14, 36, 38–39
   San Carlo seminary   6–8, 19–20, 22, 49, 59, 64
   Santa Maria della Piazza   4, 10–12, 69, 104, 128, 256, 270, 280
   Teatro delle Muse   37, 56, 62
Antonucci, Antonio Benedetto   67, 198
Aragón, Pietro   96, 142, 166
Ascione, Giuseppe   103, 183
Ascoli, Napoleone   14, 16, 58, 252, 285

Ballomara, Mary Catherine   303
Balsano, Agostino   103
Baluffi, Gaetano   12, 26, 51, 62–63, 155–156, 198, 211
Banti, Alberto   14
Barili, Lorenzo   12, 42, 61, 66
Barlee, Frederick   223

Barnabò, Alessandro   62, 142, 148, 155, 156, 157, 194, 198–199, 223, 225, 229
Barry, Michael   132
Bassi, Ugo   49–51, 55, 58
Bateman, John   235
Bellini, Vincenzo   27, 114
Benedict XVI   288
Benedictine Order   62–64, 69, 73–74, 81, 83, 94–95, 110, 118, 152, 200, 206–207, 218–219, 241
Benedictine Order - Sylvestrines   142
Benson, Walter   166
Bertrán, Ildefonso   106, 159, 192
Bigliagoro   147, 213–214, 249
Bonser, John   132
Bourke, Anselm   189, 192, 203, 221, 248, 259, 268
Brady, John   93, 158
Broderick, Matthew   82
Bunbury   112–113, 118, 133, 143, 228
Butler, Mary   185
Byrne, Frederick   106, 142, 183, 196, 275

Cabané, Agustín   229–237
Cadiz   74, 76, 79–83
Cadolini, Antonio Maria   29, 31, 42–43, 51, 62, 64, 66–67
Cantagoro, Placid   303
Capalti, Annibale   40–41, 155
Caranet, Frederick Mead   257–258
Carbonari   21–24

INDEX

Casaretto, Pietro 9–10, 62–66, 70–78, 83 -86, 94, 142, 153, 156, 169, 192–194, 198, 200
Cassinese Congregation 73–74, 76, 192
Cathedral, Perth 118–119, 179–184, 268, 280
Catholic missions 59–60, 81, 155–156
Cayanga, Thomas 243
Champion Bay 147–148, 157, 228–237, 264
Chierici, Gaetano 208–211, 258–259
Christian Brothers 176, 182, 184
Chuberan, Mary Ann 258
Clarkson, Robert Austin 85–86
Clemina, Mary Louisa 214
Clune family 243–244
Code-switching 163–170, 176, 194–195
Coll, Emilian 171
Conaci, Francis Xavier 303
Convicts 96–97, 99, 105, 108, 113, 122, 136–141, 184, 188, 269
Council of Trent 139, 141, 226
Cuper, Benedict 214, 243
Cuper, Helen Pangieran 214

D'Azeglio, Massimo 16
Dante Alighieri 6, 14–15, 17–19, 47, 56, 77, 84, 166, 195
Dardanup 107–111, 118, 133, 138–139, 144, 152
De Riso, Antonio 74
Dempster, James 124
Diadrini, Costanza 4
Dirimera, John 126, 303
Divine Office 10–12, 69–70, 77, 85, 87, 253, 254, 256–257

Donovan, Timothy 96–97, 102, 105, 133, 138, 147–148
Doyle, Mary Anne 183

English language 138, 147, 162–173, 207, 212, 222, 254, 273, 275

Faiani, Carlo 41–42
Ferrara, Pietro 103, 164, 172, 213
Filomeno, Nicola 103, 172
Finali, Gaspare 14–16, 19–20, 39, 50, 83, 156, 268, 283, 285, 287
Fitzgerald, Charles 96
Fonte Avellana 18
Foscolo, Ugo 16, 19
Fransoni, Giacomo 94
Frayne, Ursula 127
Fremantle
   Lunatic Asylum 136, 202–203
   prison 97, 99, 105, 113, 135–142, 147–149, 153–155, 179, 268–269
   town and parish 26, 96–106, 129, 144–145, 153–154, 176–178, 184–190, 192, 199–204, 221, 245, 248, 265
   St Patricks church 179–181
French language 63, 77, 78, 106, 162, 165, 169, 186, 245, 261, 273

Gabbadah 227
Galician language 125, 165
Gallucci, Tommaso 61–63, 155, 169, 191
Garibaldi, Giuseppe 55
Garrido, Venancio 72–74, 81–83, 87–89, 109, 132–133, 142–146,

346

159, 162, 214, 229, 232, 237, 280–281
   friendship with Raffaele Martelli 105, 123, 129, 153, 169–171, 189, 200–204, 220–225, 232, 238, 239, 289–290
Giacchetti, Giovanni 78
Giangiacomi, Palermo 30, 299
Giannelli, Antonio 42
Gibney, Matthew 182, 204, 225, 239, 241–243, 246
Gibney, Patrick 189, 246
Gigli, Ottavio 43
Giménez, William 257, 292
Gioberti, Vincenzo 24–26, 32, 45, 52, 58, 131, 287–288
Giovine Italia 23–24, 39, 41
Giustiniani, Luigi 128–129
Goicoechea, Francisco 221
Greenough 172, 230–242
Gregory XVI 22, 27, 31, 33, 35, 43, 72, 290
Gregory, Henry 72
Grellet, Henry Robert 82
Griver, Martín 94, 96, 103, 264
   Apostolic Administrator 148–149, 152–153, 157, 159, 173, 181, 188
   Bishop 206–207, 224–226, 243, 264, 267, 268, 274
   relationship with Raffaele Martelli 148–149, 152–153, 155, 157, 159, 164, 176, 179–181, 189, 191–192, 196–197, 199–202, 240, 243, 245–249, 254, 258, 268, 275–276, 277–280, 288
Gugeri, Peter 245, 265
Guilderton 227

Haemorrhoids 125, 138, 147, 175–176, 201, 246–247, 261, 278

Hale, Mathew 148
Hampton, John 149
Harper, Charles 132–133, 253
Homeopathy 83, 138, 279

Il Piceno 44–45, 54, 59–60, 72
Imitation of Christ 19–20, 65, 70, 77, 84, 105, 112, 116, 146, 225, 283
Italian language 5–6, 17, 27, 42, 70, 73, 110, 125, 126, 132, 145, 147, 153, 157, 162–173, 176, 194, 197, 205–207, 212, 213, 229, 236, 273

Jack 101–102
Jackson family (Rottnest island) 214
Jackson, Kate 245, 265
Jimmy 230–232
John Panter 82–91, 93, 96, 97, 145, 229

Keating, Joseph 277–278
Kennedy, Arthur 128, 158, 179
Kirwan, Michael 246

L'Artigianello 43–44
Language *see* Ancona dialect, English, French, Galician, Italian, Latin, Noongar, Portuguese, Spanish, Yamaji
Latin language 5–6, 13–15, 27, 157, 162, 165–166, 206–207, 236, 241, 282
Lecaille, Adolphus 143, 182–183, 228–238, 241
Leopardi, Giacomo 16
Liberalism 21–25, 30–33, 40, 42–47, 52–55, 57–58, 70, 76–77, 111–112, 156, 167, 184, 209, 276, 286–288

Little, Thomas and Eliza and family 109–112, 118, 144
Lodwick, Benjamin 87
Loughlin, Mr and Mrs 108
Ludlow 113
Lynch, Thomas 144, 149, 152, 157, 182, 188–189, 201–203, 224

Malaccari, Antonio 30
Malucci, Gioachino 27, 136
Manning, James jr 255
Manzoni, Alessandro 15–16
Marchetti, Giovanni (Jack) 172
Martelli, Aldemira 7, 57, 58, 173
Martelli, Angelo 4, 7, 58
Martelli, Antonio 22–23, 30, 172, 274
Martelli, Cleofina 7, 173
Martelli, Costanza 4
Martelli, Francesco 5, 22–23, 31
Martelli, Luigi 273–274
Martelli, Raffaele
  as educator 13–20, 30–31, 38, 42–45, 176–178, 229, 242–246, 260
  Benedictines 61, 66, 69–70, 77–78, 81–84, 146, 197–199, 218, 240, 245, 254, 256, 279–281
  bishopric in USA 275–276
  British subject 148–149
  Canon 10–12, 41, 58, 104, 129, 270
  death and burial 217–218, 277–282
  diary 83
  emotions 97–98, 126–129, 138, 146–148, 200, 236, 266
  friendship 10, 43, 61, 65–66, 75–78, 119, 132–133, 169–171, 188, 195, 200, 222, 245, 253, 267, 271, 277, 282, *see* Garrido, Martínez, Salvado and *cf.* Griver, Serra
  letter writing 83, 98, 102, 103–106, 126–127, 131, 136, 143–144, 154, 155–159, 161–173, 189–190, 196–199, 201, 240, 245, 255, 261, 274–275, 291–292
  literary quotations in his writings 104, 154, 165–167, 201
  music 27, 114, 136
  New Norcia, desire to retire there 105, 147–148, 153–154, 161, 172, 175, 192, 194, 196–203, 254–255, 278
  New Norcia, lived there 217–249
  New Norcia, visits 106, 119, 124, 131, 133, 190, 200, 255, 258, 260
  obedience 65–66, 82, 94, 96, 114, 133, 143–146, 154, 176, 240, 289
  orthodoxy 24, 98–100, 156–157, 245, 287–288
  physical appearance 132, 252, 255–257
  prudence 41, 43, 44, 60, 66, 154, 203, 226, 275, 292
  published writings 17–18, 28–29, 30–31, 35–39, 43–45, 127–128, 184–185, 203–204
  sermons 26–27, 109–112, 115–118, 138–142, 177–179, 269–272
  speeches 130–131, 244, 266–267
Martínez, Manuel Bernardo 83, 126, 220, 227, 239–240, 243–245, 253–254
  friendship with Raffaele Martelli 153, 162, 169, 199–200, 204, 220, 227–228, 240, 280
Masotti, Ignazio 276
Matteucci, Antonio 78

INDEX

Mazuyer, Léonce   62, 65
Mazzini, Giuseppe   23–25, 32, 44, 55
McCabe, Patrick   157
McCann, Mary   202
McKay, William   280
Metternich, Klemens von   24, 31, 46
Micalet, Br   142
Missionaries   59–67, 70–71, 114, 205–212, 228, 232–236, 279, 282, 292
Monogenism   210–212
Monop, Benedict and William   229, 243
Montanari, Giuseppe   162
Monte Catria   18
Monti, Vincenzo   16, 47
Moore River   227–228
Morelli, Ercole   33–35, 46–47, 50
Morelli, Teresa   7, 172–173
Mulrooney, Michael   102–103
Murphy, Michael   132
Murra, John David   71, 73
Music   6, 8, 10, 11, 14, 18, 27, 69–70, 83, 84–85, 114, 136, 182, 184, 218–220, 265, 267, 268

Nanonga, Willie   258
Napoleon Bonaparte   4, 5, 21–22, 35, 59, 63, 103
Napoleon, Louis   23, 37, 55
Naudó, Pedro   78
Neo-guelphism   26, 32, 40, 131, 288
New Norcia
    archives   x, 245, 255
    early days   72–74, 94, 114, 142
    Salvado returns 1857   131, 159
    independence from Perth diocese 1859   142–152, 155–159, 192–194
    abbey nullius 1867   192–194, 200

schools   219–220, 227–229, 236–238, 243–245
    horarium   10–12, 18, 69, 218–219
New Subiaco   93–94, 96, 100, 103, 151–153, 158, 179, 192, 194, 254, 256
Newcastle   *see* Toodyay
Nightingale, Florence   214
Noongar artefacts   208–211
Noongar language   73, 108, 132, 205
Noongar people   72–73, 117, 122, 126, 129, 159, 205–215, 228, 229, 258
Northam   113, 119, 124, 133, 157, 252, 258, 260–261, 263–272, 277
Northampton   230–232

O'Neill, Thomas   82, 85, 87, 94, 96, 97, 105, 113
Oltra, Odon   85, 182
Opera   27, 36–38, 56, 62, 144, 154, 166

Pallotti, St Vincenzo   70
Papal States   3, 5, 21, 28, 33, 43, 46, 50
Paul VI   287
Pellico, Silvio   24, 195
Pescetelli, Angelo   76–77, 114, 131, 156, 169, 268, 278–279
Petrarch, Francesco   6, 7, 166, 195
Photography   195, 214, 232, 255–258, 261
Pidcock, Hugh   252–254, 260, 283
Pigorini, Luigi   208–210
Pius IX   31–47, 51, 54–57, 62, 64, 72, 118, 155, 224, 242, 245, 267–268, 287–288
Podesti, Francesco   39, 56–57
Polding, John Bede   12, 59, 70–71, 94, 95, 222
Port Gregory   235–236

349

Portuguese language   273
Prinsep, Charles   109
Propaganda Fide   62–65, 71, 72, 94, 98, 115, 127, 133, 142, 146, 157–158, 173, 192, 194, 197–198, 200, 218, 226, 275–278
Pujades, José   96

Radetzky, Marshall   51
Raphael, Archangel   192
Regnoli, Malvina   208–210
Regnoli, Pietro   50, 52, 60, 83, 155, 156, 169–170, 172–173, 194 -196, 201, 208–210, 213, 252, 267–268, 274, 275–276, 282–283, 286
Reilly, John Boyle   138
Reilly, Joseph Thomas   105, 292
Reynolds, Christopher   106, 142, 183, 192, 196, 275
Ribaya, Salvador   82, 87, 96, 142, 146
Ricci, Matteo   59
Ricci, Achille Maria   51
Rignasco, Mauro   103, 125, 218
Rizzo, Alferio   103, 172
Roe, Louisa   251, 256, 275, 277
Romanticism   14, 18, 25, 37, 154
Rottnest Island   90, 213, 265

Salomone, Alfonso   77
Salustri, Nicoletta   103–104, 172
Salvadó, Francisco   122–123, 129, 145, 157
Salvado, Rosendo
   1845–1849 – founded New Norcia 71–73
   1849–1853 – Europe   72–91
   1853–1855 – Administrator in Perth 94–118
   1857–1864 - New Norcia 131, 138–142, 144, 152–159, 175
   1864–1870 – in Europe   194–201, 225–226, 239–241, 245
   1869–1880 – New Norcia 220–222, 238–239, 243–248, 255, 265, 273–274, 278–282
   travels round WA   107–115, 119, 122
   Aborigines   205–214, 253, 258
   letters to Propaganda   94, 115, 127, 133, 142, 207, 218, 226
   homeopathy   83, 138, 279
   friendship with Raffaele Martelli   x, 76–82, 95, 98, 104, 107–115, 119, 126, 154, 162–172, 192, 194, 196–197, 221–222, 226, 255, 279–280, 289, 291–292
Salvado, Santos   221, 239–240, 254, 257, 278
Serra, José Maria Benito
   founded New Norcia   71–72
   New Subiaco   93–94, 109, 151
   Administrator 1849–1853   90–96, 199
   Toodyay   127–129
   Administrator 1855–1859   106, 118–121, 127, 142–148
   in Rome, resignation 1859–1861 152–159, 192–194
   relationship with Raffaele Martelli 95, 106, 119–121, 126, 127–129, 142–145, 151–159, 168, 195
Sillani, Ilarione   192
Sisters of Mercy   106, 114, 127, 158, 183, 185–186, 202
Sisters of St Joseph of the Apparition 106, 158, 171, 176, 185, 187, 202–203, 268, 282

Spanish language   73, 125, 132, 153, 162, 164–165, 206–207
Spencer, Henry   261
Spinola, Ambrogio   139–140
St Benedict   151, 198, 206
Subiaco, Italy   63, 65–79, 85, 93–94, 106, 256
Subiaco, Western Australia   *see* New Subiaco

Tainan, Eliza   258
Tasso, Torquato   6, 17, 166, 180–181, 195
Terrés, Roman   96
The Herald (Fremantle)   184–185, 204
The Inquirer   184–185, 242
The Vasse   113, 201
Thomas à Kempis *see* Imitation of Christ   21
Throssell, George   264, 267, 277
Tommasi, Eugenio Maria   173
Tommasi, Nicola   298
Toodyay   12, 113, 119, 121–133, 139, 143, 148, 152, 157, 165, 170, 224, 242, 246, 251–263, 272
Tosti, Antonio   27
Tosti, Luigi   16
Trollope, Thomas   2
Turi, Costabile   103, 172
Tuzi, Aristide   57–58, 173

Ultramontanism   29, 225
Upumera, Benedict   303
Urbani, Pio   259, 261
Urbani, Urbano   169

Vatican Council, First   222, 225–226, 241
Verdi, Giuseppe   36–38, 56, 62
Voltaire   206

Wadjemup *see* Rottnest Island
Webbe, Samuel   182, 268
Weld, Filumena   222–223, 245
Weld, Frederick   222–223, 225, 242, 247–248
Willyway, Willie   258
Wonnerup   113

Yamaji language   228–229
Yarawindah School   243–245
York   113, 119, 122, 124, 126, 129–130, 133, 152, 157, 192, 203, 246, 259, 261, 267–268, 272

Zamboni, Filippo   52

www.ingramcontent.com/pod-product-compliance
Lightning Source LLC
Chambersburg PA
CBHW051535230426
43669CB00015B/2609